William Sharp McKechnie

The State and the Individual

An Introduction to political Science, with special Reference to socialistic and

individualistic Theories

William Sharp McKechnie

The State and the Individual
An Introduction to political Science, with special Reference to socialistic and individualistic Theories

ISBN/EAN: 9783337132569

Printed in Europe, USA, Canada, Australia, Japan

Cover: Foto ©ninafisch / pixelio.de

More available books at **www.hansebooks.com**

THE STATE AND THE INDIVIDUAL

PUBLISHED BY

JAMES MACLEHOSE AND SONS, GLASGOW

Publishers to the University.

———

MACMILLAN AND CO., LTD., LONDON.

New York, · ·   The Macmillan Co.
London, · · ·   Simpkin, Hamilton and Co.
Cambridge, · ·   Macmillan and Bowes.
Edinburgh, · ·   Douglas and Foulis.

———

MDCCCXCVI.

The
State & the Individual

An Introduction to Political Science, with
special reference to Socialistic and
Individualistic Theories

By

William Sharp M'Kechnie, M.A., LL.B.

Lecturer on Constitutional Law and History in the
University of Glasgow

Glasgow
James MacLehose and Sons
Publishers to the University
1896

PREFACE.

THE practical object of this Essay is twofold: first, to state impartially the points at issue between Socialism and Individualism, and to mediate between their claims as rival schemes for the regeneration of society; and, secondly, to offer a contribution towards the solution of some of the problems to which both systems address themselves. A preliminary investigation is, however, necessary; since it is futile either to estimate the value of current opinions or to devise remedies for social evils, apart from the fundamental principles underlying all political phenomena alike. The volume has thus assumed the character of an introduction to the Theory of the State with special reference to one of its divisions—the methods and limits of government interference.

In spite of a steadily increasing interest in social and political questions there is, perhaps, no topic upon which popular thought remains so lax and uninformed, no inquiry which has received so few attempts at systematic and unbiassed treatment as the legitimate province of law and government. The copious literature on the subject is polemical rather than constructive; negative rather than positive. Its destructive and unsystematic nature, however, is not the only characteristic calling for supplement if not for correction. Most existing treatises either confine their investigations to the economic features of the inquiry, to the neglect of those broader aspects which confront statesmen and legislators; or else they are the work of ardent partisans of one or other of the competing theories in its most uncompromising attitude.

The following Essay is primarily an attempt to supply in an elementary form a systematic introduction to the study of the problem, subordinating its economic to its political aspects, and endeavouring to discard all *a priori* presumptions either for or against individual liberty and initiative, on the one hand, and government intervention, on the other. At the same time an effort has been made to give unity to the various speculations by viewing them all steadily in the light of one philosophical conception.

Any claim it may have to originality must be based upon the re-arrangement and combination of old theories rather than upon the invention of new ones. The distinction between direct government management and indirect government control cannot assuredly be claimed as a discovery : but it is perhaps new to make this the keystone of a system of practical politics ; and to show how, by its aid, some at least of the aims of the more moderate Socialists may be achieved in safety from the pitfalls dreaded by even the more moderate Individualists.

The double character of the Essay as, on the one hand, an introduction to political science in general, and, on the other, a detailed investigation of Socialism and Individualism from a stand-point which identifies itself with neither, may, it is hoped, render it of some use to students of social philosophy, of constitutional history, or of systematic politics, by bringing within a reasonable compass information otherwise accessible only in the many bulky volumes of a somewhat scattered literature.

The various authorities placed under contribution are too numerous to be specified here ; but the sources of borrowed ideas have been, as far as possible, indicated in the text or in footnotes. I am indebted to my friends, Mr. W. R. J. Gray and Mr. R. A. Moody, for their kindness in reading the proof-sheets and for many valuable suggestions.

GLASGOW, 21*st September*, 1896.

CONTENTS.

INTRODUCTION.

PART I.

THE STATE: ITS NATURE, ORIGIN, AND END; ITS MEMBERS AND ORGANIZATION.

PART II.

THE PROVINCE OF LAW AND GOVERNMENT.

PART III.

THE APPLICATION OF THEORY TO PRACTICAL POLITICS.

INTRODUCTION.

student of humanity must accept the individual specimen
finds him—one man associated with his fellow-men in a
or less highly organized community. To separate arbi-
ily in thought things essentially related in reality, would
to vitiate at the start the premiss to be founded on. A
onal being can no more free himself from the ideas and
ts of the nation that has produced and still encircles him,
he can shake off his own shadow. Every individual is
ndent on society for his origin and up-bringing, and he
ains an integral part of it, in a sense, even in the solitude
desert isle or the isolation of a convict's cell. Every man
member of a community, and every community needs
nization of some sort, and is therefore potentially, if not
ally, a body politic. All human beings, then, are necessarily
ens of a State.

his assertion by no means implies that every group of men,
lized or savage, is necessarily part of a vast organized
on like one of the great powers of modern Europe. These
ers are States indeed, and in common speech monopolize
exclusive right to be so named. The word State, however,
ere employed with a much wider connotation, embracing as
oes every independent group of men, whether large or small,
ng whom the most embryonic rudiments even of organiza-
can be, however indistinctly, traced. In this wide meaning
he term, every individual is born, lives, and dies the member
a State. Apart from the community of his fellows, the

A

human unit could never have come into existence or atta
maturity. The State, on the other hand, is equally depen
for its very being, if not on any one individual, yet on
viduals as a class. No body politic can exist apart from
citizens of whom it is composed. All its institutions
organizations fade from the world of realities and become
logical abstractions when taken away from the lives,
interests, the aspirations, and the pleasures of the men
women whom they control. The form and structure of
national institutions and the moral characteristics of
citizens are necessarily related to one another in the co
sition of a commonwealth, like the outside and the insi
a vessel, or like the body and mind of a man.

The State cannot exist without the individuals nor
individuals without the State. To analyze and examine
relations which unite them constitutes the entire scop
political science. Two results seem to follow from the n
sary connection between men and States. On the one ha
is impossible to form even a vague estimate of the true n
of the State, or of the ends of its existence, without kno
something of the nature and aims of individuals; and, or
other hand, it is equally impossible to trace the origi
prophesy the destiny of the latter without knowing the hi
and the tendencies of the former. Man is a spirit.
Socrates to Pope, and from Bacon to Robert Brow
thinkers of every school have agreed that his chief intelle
duty and his greatest privilege lie in the endeavour to
his own spiritual nature intelligible to himself. "Know thy
is as imperative a duty to-day as it was two thousand
ago. "The proper study of mankind is man" is an a
which new men and changing manners cannot shake.
universal and familiar truth has been re-affirmed only yest
in a new dress by Robert Browning, who declares that ou
of the "incidents in the development of a soul, little e
worth study."[1]

If man is "by nature a social and political animal"—
no lover of paradoxes has dared openly to deny this
truth since Aristotle gave it utterance—then it is absu

[1] Vide Dedication to Sordello in the collected edition of 186

endeavour to fulfil the mandate "Know thyself" without striving at the same time to know that community of selves in which the nature of each is inextricably involved. "The development of a soul" must indeed be determined from within, but it cannot find the environment it needs for its growth in a vacuum, or in the prison of its own subjective individuality. Society and the State (which is only another name for society considered as politically organized) mould the individual after their own image, and furnish him with the nutriment necessary for making his latent potentialities real.

The welfare of the individual is bound up in the welfare of the State, and whatever affects the one affects the other.[1] Thus there is no part of the subject-matter of social and political science which is not of vital interest to the student of mankind. Every question which may be raised as to the form of the national institutions, or the duties of government, or the position and rights of the subject, has important bearings on the spiritual development of the individual man. Broadly speaking, these questions may be divided into two classes: (1) The first group treats of the structure of the machinery of government. Its chief question (of which the others are merely phases) is: Under what form of constitution can the State best fulfil its destiny or attain the ends for which it exists? Or more briefly: What ought the form of the State to be? (2) The second group deals with the duties of the State and the limits of the province of government. It examines the extent to which the common welfare of the whole and the highest interests of each separate part can be furthered by the active intervention of the State in the affairs of its citizens, and how far these ends are best achieved by a policy of *laissez faire*. In its shortest form the question becomes: What ought the State, acting through its government, to *do*?

These two questions, simple as they seem, are an abstract of all the possible problems of practical and theoretical politics. They are constantly presenting themselves under endlessly

[1] Cf. Sheldon Amos, *Science of Politics*, p. 456. "So far as our knowledge extends, it is in the life of the State, and only there, that human life, in all its ramifications, can obtain the nourishment it needs for its appropriate expansion and development."

varying forms. Full answers to them would involve a complete political science, and perhaps a complete philosophy of the universe as well. The following essay aims at setting forth some of their chief aspects, and at indicating the general lines upon which any attempt at solution must proceed. Before trying to discover, however, either the most perfect form of the constitution, or the proper province of the agents of the State, it is necessary to fix on some criterion or principle of judgment, some aim or ideal the furtherance or hindrance of which is the test of the excellence or failure of all institutions and methods of government. Thus, before a systematic attempt to answer either group of questions can be made, a preliminary investigation is necessary into the nature, origin, sphere, aims, and destiny of the individual, of society, and of the State.

Starting from the fact that the State is necessarily composed of individuals whose nature is moulded by the whole community, it seems plain that a perfect comprehension of the State would involve a knowledge not only of its own aims and destiny, but also of the essential characteristics of all its members, and the nature of the relations between the two. Now, the solution of all these problems lies in the analysis of the relations between the State and its individual citizens. In making this analysis the natural method is to begin with the whole whose essence is the centre of the system, and work outwards and downwards towards the members, considering each in the light of the whole.

Three propositions may be laid down at the outset, not as self-evident axioms upon which a system is to be built, but rather as hypotheses whose truth must be verified or disproved in the course of the subsequent inquiry. These propositions are:

(1) The relations which are observed to exist between the individual and the community are essential and not merely accidental. (2) Every community attaining to any permanent existence—every society which is not merely a mob—implies political organization or government of some sort, forming the rudiments, at any rate, of a State. (3) The nature of the relations binding the individual to the State (or organized

society) may be better classed as "organic" than under any lower category.

Each of these hypotheses requires a word of explanation; and in especial, it is necessary to guard against certain misconceptions which are frequently made as to what is meant by describing the structure of society as "organic." (1) The first proposition is most readily understood in relation to a rival theory of man's nature which exercised for more than one century a complete sway over modern Europe. It has been a common practice with men in all ages, when feeling themselves out of harmony with the existing social order and methods of government, to look upon the evils of life as in great measure due to the restraints placed upon the individual man by the community of which he is a member, and to picture the imaginary perfection to which he would attain if he lived in a golden age and a state of nature where his inherent excellencies had free scope to blossom forth in their full beauty unblighted by the breath of a corrupt civilization. To such men—and such have existed in all countries and ages—the true nature of the individual man is to be discovered by isolating him from his fellows, and studying the problematical course of his development on the assumption of its being as little as possible influenced from without. To attain to maturity he only needs to be left alone. Social influences merely cramp and deform him. To such philosophers the State with its laws and rulers is an evil, necessary, mayhap, but if so, only because each man cannot have a whole world to himself in which to develop. In the absence of these necessary evils, constant collisions would occur between man and man. The golden age and the state of nature are thus unfortunately found to involve a "state of war," and men must associate together for mutual protection. Thus the State has sometimes been described as "an association for the protection of life and property." On this ground it has been argued that its sphere of activity and powers should be extended no further than is absolutely necessary for fulfilling these purposes for which alone its baleful and mischievous influence is tolerated. That this picture is hardly a caricature of the extreme form in which the theory of the merely accidental relations of men to the State is sometimes seriously put forward will be apparent on a comparison with the words of John Locke. "Men," says Locke, "being by nature all free, equal, and independent, no one can be put out of this estate and subjected to the political power of another without his own consent. The only way whereby any one divests himself of his natural liberty, and puts on the bonds of civil society, is by agreeing with other men to join and unite into a community."[1] This belief, that the relations binding each member to the society are merely accidental, will by force of contrast explain the opposite theory which is here maintained, that man is by his nature *essentially* a social animal. If it were not for such expressions of a contrary opinion as that just quoted, it would seem almost unnecessary seriously to postulate that one individual could never exist apart from others. He cannot attain to manhood without the help and protection of his fellow men. The child is born less able to obtain the nutriment and warmth which the body needs than the young of any of the lower animals. If it were possible for society and the family (which forms a part of society) to minister to the material needs of the child until able to help himself without contributing anything to the development of his mind, his "state of nature" would be a state of idiotcy or imbecility. The individual mind has no content apart from what is received from direct or indirect educative influences of society. Man attains to his true nature not in proportion as he retires into a hermit's cell and shuts out all contact with the world; but in proportion to the closeness of the sympathy he attains with every current of thought and feeling pervading the society of his own age and country, and in proportion as he reduces all discordant elements into a harmonious whole at one with each other and with the rational principle which forms his distinctive right to the name of man. The individual can never shake himself free from the conditions of society; but he may try to do so, if he is so foolish as to rebel against the inevitable.

[1] *Treatise of Civil Government*, II., § 95.

If he make the effort he will only succeed in stunting himself in the process. He will fall behind his fellows in seeking to outstrip them. If he wishes to rise in the scale of humanity he should rather learn that this is possible just in proportion as he realizes more intimately his connection with all the factors of the community of mankind. The full height of his mature development as a rational man can be reached only in and through society. This then is what is meant by saying that his relations to the State are necessary and not accidental.[1]

(2) Society cannot exist without a principle of organization or order of some sort. Only extreme anarchists imagine that it could. Lawlessness is merely another name for violence, robbery, and bloodshed. The existence of an efficient law implies some sanction to enforce it and some executive authority constituting at least the rudiments of a government, and therefore the beginnings of a State. A strong executive, however, while restraining disorder in others is too apt to use its power to make good its own arbitrary desires—a lesson which may be read in the history of all nations—Republics as well as Monarchies. Thus complicated and elaborate constitutions arise, partly to supply the needed checks upon the prerogatives of a too-powerful executive, and partly to meet the growing needs of the community for increasing governmental control, legislative, judicial, and administrative. More and not less guidance is needed by a society as it increases in civilization, and as its individuals progress upwards in the scale of humanity, and in the attainment of knowledge and culture. The further the stage of development reached by the individuals, the greater is the progress of society as a whole and the higher the degree of organization that is needed.

---

[1] Cf. Professor D. G. Ritchie's *State Interference*, p. 11. "The individual, apart from his surroundings, is a mere abstraction—a logical ghost, a metaphysical spectre, which haunts the habitations of those who have derided metaphysics. The individual, apart from all relations to a community, is a negation. You can say nothing about. him, or rather it, except that it is not any other individual." See also F. C. Montague's *Limits of Individual Liberty*, p. 55.

Thus, as the State is only another name for society properly organized under an orderly government on a permanent political basis, it develops as the society itself develops, both keeping pace with the approximation of individuals towards that ideal of fully realized manhood which is for rational beings the true "state of nature." If the perfect State, however, can only come with the perfection of humanity, its undeveloped potentialities are necessarily bound up with the individual savages in their wildest stage of primeval barbarism. Man—even barbarous man—is essentially a member of society, and society is necessarily a State/*community*

(3) It is not enough to say that the relations which bind the individual to the State are necessary and essential to the existence of both. A further field for inquiry remains in the exact *nature* of these relations—as to the precise position with regard to the whole occupied by each part. Now in using the word "organic" as the best description of this relationship, it is necessary to make some attempt at explaining and defending the exact position which is thus taken up.

It may be best at the outset to confess that the word is adopted not because it is fitted with absolute accuracy and freedom from ambiguity to express the truth which it is intended to convey; but simply from want of a better. The student of natural history divides the world into the "organic" and the "inorganic"; and by the former, he means, broadly speaking, all forms of animal and plant life.

The word "organism" thus took its rise as a scientific term, and was in use in a specific and somewhat limited acceptation long before it was adopted by philosophers and political students as a convenient formula for conveying a comparatively new conception of the nature of society. It has now passed from the scientific world to the street, and the words "organism" and "organic" have long been familiar to the comparatively illiterate as applied to the class of objects in connection with which they were originally used. Thus it is not surprising to find that in popular thought these words are closely associated with the ideas of animal or vegetable life, especially the former; nor is it astonishing that naturalists or biologists, **finding a** word which **they** have long been accustomed to **regard** as their **exclusive** property applied **in what** seems to them an altogether new and unwarrantable manner, should be inclined to laugh at or to misunderstand the new **departure.** It is astonishing, however, to find that the greatest of living " scientific " philosophers—who has himself done more than any other living author to popularize in current English thought the application of the "organic" conception to social subjects— should support his doctrine upon a series of minute and accidental parallels instead of the broad universal principles underlying all such minutiae. In his *Principles of Sociology*, Mr. Herbert Spencer draws a series of detailed analogies between the growth, functions, and structures of animals on the one hand, **and** of societies on the other.[1]

It is equally surprising to find how far a crude method **of** applying this idea of an organism to the manifestations **of** social and political life vitiates much of the reasoning **of** Bluntschli—the father of modern political science—whose chief **fault seems** to lie not **so much** where the compilers of the authorized translation have placed it (in too thorough-going and extreme an application of his "organic or psycho-logical conception of the State "), as in using that conception in a one-sided and inadequate way. Indeed, the chief defects in Bluntschli's theory of the State seem to result from his failing to apply the organic conception in a sufficiently thorough and systematic way; minor faults spring from his tendency to neglect the broader aspects of the category employed and to trace misleading parallels between the nature of the State and the physiological structure of existing animals. His conception of the political organism is contorted by his failure to throw off the influence of con-fusing analogies from the animal world, whence the idea was originally **borrowed.** Thus, while Mr. Spencer warns us that society is to **be** compared only with low forms of animal life, Bluntschli insists, in more places than one, that **the** State is

[1] See *Principles of Sociology*, Part II., chapters ii. to xi. See also the criticism of **Mr.** Spencer contained in Prof. D. **G.** Ritchie's *State Interference*, p. 15, **note.**

essentially a *male* organism, while the Church, in his opinion, is also an organism, but of the opposite sex.[1]

When such expressions as these are found in two so great exponents of the organic theory of society as Bluntschli and Mr. Spencer, it is hardly to be wondered if the enemies of that theory have little difficulty in caricaturing it in many ways. These hostile critics demand to be told what species of animal society is, if it is really an organism at all ; or they triumphantly pronounce against it because they cannot obtain satisfaction as to the exact position of its " sensorium," or, mayhap, of its back-bone. Thus, Count Leo Tolstoï[2] sums up against the claims of humanity to rank as organic, because it lacks what he considers an essential characteristic of every organism, viz. a centre of sensation or consciousness. " We call an elephant as well as a bacterium," he goes on to say, " organisms, only because we suppose by analogy in these beings unification of sensations or consciousness. As for human societies and mankind, they lack this essential ; and therefore, however many other general character-signs we may find out in mankind and in an organism, without this the acknowledgment of mankind to be an organism is incorrect." Several points in this argument are open to criticism. To emphasize or even to indicate these would, however, only lead to confusion by distracting attention from the object with which these words are here quoted ; which is to point out the mode of attack usually adopted against the organic conception of society and to illustrate its special vulnerability unless duly fenced from misconception by a clear definition of its meaning.

The truth is that society may be, and is, an organism without resembling any animal organisms whatever : it is not only neither like a lion nor an elephant, nor a bacterium, nor a mass of protoplasm ; but has characteristics which all forms of animal life—and of plant life too for that matter—utterly lack, and it wants characteristics which they one and all possess. For all that, it remains emphatically an organism in the sense in which that word is used in this essay and

[1] Cf. D. G. Ritchie's *State Interference*, p. 15, note.
[2] *What must we Do then*, English translation, p. 116.

by all writers on social science **who are** favourable **to the** theory here **upheld.**

Plant and animal forms of life **are thus** merely two **species** of organisms, and **by no** means exhaust **the** genus. **It is as** absurd to **reject** the claims of society to **rank as** an organism **by showing** its essential difference **from all known** forms of animal **life as** it would be to argue that a mollusc is not an animal because it is confessedly not part of the sub-kingdom **mammal.** Animals are **only one** kind of **organism,** and **assuredly** not the highest **in** the list.

The organic school have themselves to blame in **great** measure for opening their lines of defence to the enemy ; for undoubtedly they **have** often indulged in that most dangerous **of** all forms of argument—reasoning from analogy. This process has **its uses,** like many other aids, which have first to be used **and then** thrown aside to enable the user to advance **beyond them.** It must, **however, always be employed** with **caution, and never taken as the final stage in the search** for truth. Undoubtedly the analogies between society and **that** particular **class of organisms called animals** have **afforded** many clues **or hypotheses invaluable** as suggesting methods **of advance to a** clearer knowledge of the nature of social **and political** phenomena. It is apt, however, **to** be forgotten **by** friends as well as foes that these are mere analogies, and **must** never be accepted by themselves as proofs.

The device of illustrating theories **of the** constitution of the commonwealth **by tracing** analogies between the body politic and the material frame of animals is **as** old at least as **the** days of Menenius Agrippa,[1] who **used it** to prove the danger of dissensions and the necessary subordination of the plebs **to** the patricians who formed by nature (as interpreted by the speaker) the **head or government** of the whole. The healing effect **of this** reasoning is well known, and illustrates the political **value of the** analogy where **used** in a broad and popular **way.** It is equally clear, however, that had Menenius Agrippa proceeded to make his hypothesis the basis of a system of philosophy he would **have** been drawn **into** serious **error** by allowing those details **of the** analogy (so useful for

[1] Suggestions of it are **to be found in both** Plato and Aristotle.

oratorical effect) to prevent his seeing that the nature of a commonwealth of men transcends in many ways the nature of a merely physical organism, and has many phenomena which cannot be so explained.

In applying the idea of a developing organism to social and political problems it is necessary to be more than usually careful not to be misled by false analogies. Society is an organism not because it resembles any particular type of animal, nor even because it presents analogies to the elements which are common to all animals, but because it possesses the essential characteristics to be found in all organic life of which animal and plant life are merely lower phases. In drawing any comparison, attention must be fixed on the essential elements involved, not on the mere accidental features of structure or functions. In fact, when once the analogy has played its part by furnishing a clue to direct our thoughts to the true nature of society, it is safer to throw it away entirely, as a whole man throws away the crutch he leaned on in his convalescence. Otherwise what has been a help in the past may become a hindrance for the future. Language—the most useful of man's servants—often ends by enslaving its master, if constant care is not exerted to define the phrases that are employed.

It is necessary then to explain carefully the meaning of the word "organic" as here applied to States or political communities. It is best to begin negatively by pointing out what it does not mean. Indeed, the first inducement towards calling the relationships existing between communities and their members "organic" seems to have been that social relations were *less unlike* those of animal bodies than any lower form of existence. It is well, then, to begin by explaining the total inadequacy of these lower relationships to afford even partial analogies to social phenomena. There are at least five ways in which the parts of any object whatever may be related to the whole. These may be described in general terms as Monadistic, Monistic, Mechanical, Chemical, and Organic.[1]

[1] Cf. J. S. Mackenzie's *Social Philosophy*, p. 128 *seq.*, where the various forms of unity are clearly explained and the nature of the social organism analyzed.

(1) It is possible to imagine a system of social philosophy founded on the assumption that society is an aggregate made up of isolated individuals independent of one another. On this theory every man would be an atom or monad, and the theory of society might be described as monadistic. It is true that the logical consequence of this view is not so much to give a special interpretation to the relations between the part and the whole as to deny the existence of any relations at all; for if each individual is complete within himself, he can evidently with difficulty be considered as part of a wider whole. The State would thus cease to be an entity or reality; and society would be not a thing but a mere word—a convenient collective name for the sum of a number of separate human beings. This nominalistic view in its extreme form (which is, however, the only one logically self-consistent) carries its refutation so clearly on the face of it that it is always in practice subjected to modification of some sort. No individual can be either complete in himself or independent of others, unless he has absolutely absorbed the whole universe into his own personality; and this even an Alexander with a thirst for world-empire cannot do. Each human atom is only one among other atoms in a society, and only one among other objects in the consciousness of the observer. Society is, in this view, an extremely loose aggregate of monads, like a cairn of stones or a heap of cannon balls. This is only one application of the nominalistic view, which regards the particulars as the only realities and all universals as empty names. When this theory is used to explain the nature of society, the State, along with the Church and the Family, become meaningless abstractions, and the individual citizen alone is real.

(2) The extreme view on the opposite side is even more clearly inadequate as a correct and full account of social phenomena. Only approximations to it—if even these—are likely seriously to affect speculative thought or practical politics. As the monadistic view seems to negative or minimize the relations between whole and part by denying the existence of the whole, the monistic theory tends to the same result by denying the separate existence of the parts.

It is difficult to ignore so thoroughly all the personal aspirations and sufferings, strivings and despairs that make up human life as to consider the existence of the individual merely as a manifestation of the universal spirit of the society in which he moves. The old Greek States in some aspects seemed to be unconsciously influenced by such an idea as this. The individual life was counted valuable only in so far as it contributed to the common life of the commonwealth. In this view, if the individual is not so completely absorbed in the whole as to cease to be, he becomes at best merely like a wave of the ocean—a mood or aspect of a 'reality which exists apart from him. This is merely an application to the structure of society of the extreme Realist doctrine, which looked on the universal alone as real, while the individual counted for nothing. It receives illustration from the expression used by Auguste Comte that "man is a mere abstraction, and there is nothing real but Humanity."[1]

(3) The third conception of this relationship is the mechanical one. The State, it is sometimes said, is like a machine or engine—the resultant of a number of separate pieces put together artfully, and connected by rivets and joints and bolts. A little reflection is sufficient to show that while many of the functions of government may receive explanation from such an analogy as this, it is utterly incapable of furnishing a complete explanation of social phenomena. Indeed, according to modern ideas, the more closely the constitution and government of any country approximate to this conception, the worse they become. A despotic government is a mechanical one, where the power of the ruler is something alien to the life of the subject, presses down upon him from above, and interrupts the free current of his life instead of aiding it. Even the lowest and worst forms of political organization cannot be fully explained by this analogy, but the higher the stage of civilization, the less adequate the idea becomes.

(4) Chemistry affords illustrations of a closer form of relationship between whole and part. Two or more atoms are joined together into one whole called a molecule, and their individual

---

[1] Cited by the Master of Balliol, *Comte's Social Philosophy*, p. 76.

natures are so transformed in the process that they lose completely their original attributes. Professor Huxley found in this an analogy of the position of men in society. " The process of social organization," he asserts in his famous *Essay on Administrative Nihilism*,[1] " appears to be comparable not so much to the process of organic development as to the synthesis of the chemist, by which independent elements are gradually built up into complex aggregations—in which each element retains an independent individuality, though held in subordination to the whole. . . . Each atom has given up something, in order that the atomic society, or molecule, may subsist. And as soon as any one or more of the atoms thus associated resumes the freedom which it has renounced, and follows some external attraction, the molecule is broken up, and all the peculiar properties which depended upon its constitution vanish."

The inadequacy of this conception becomes apparent when we reflect that it is impossible to remove the atom man from the so-called molecule society; for the individual has no pro-perties and no existence apart from society. He does not find his true nature by withdrawing from the State. As will be more clearly apparent in the sequel, the individual does not lose his true self in the compound, but rather finds it. This chemical analogy stands to the monistic view very much in the same relation as the mechanical stands to the monadistic. An advance in each case has been made towards qualifying the extreme one-sidedness of the original crude conception by some admixture of the other; but the mechanical theory still under-estimates the closeness of the tie, and so leaves elements of dualism or plurality; while the chemical theory underestimates the independent existence of the parts, and so fails to preserve the individuality of the separate citizens.

(5) The fifth and last conception contains in a sense the various elements of truth conveyed by all the others, but con-tains also incalculably more. The organic theory of society seeks to combine the liberty and semi-independent existence of the part with the authority of the whole, and to explain their intimate and essential connection. Men are "members one of another." The social atoms are to the State like the

---

[1] *Vide Method and Results*, p. 274.

branches to the vine, like the cells of which a plant is made
to the structure of the whole.   Injure one and you injure all.
The life of the whole pulses through all the parts, which in
turn contribute something needful to the welfare of the whole.

When it is said that society is organic, it is not meant
that it is exactly like a plant or like an animal, but simply
that the forms under which plants or animals live suggest a
less incomplete analogy than those afforded by such words
as " chemical " or " mechanical."   This is what is meant by
writers such as the late Sheldon Amos; who, in referring to
the British constitution " as an organic whole and not as a
mere aggregate of distinct institutions and laws," uses these ex-
planatory words:[1] " If any metaphorical language were to be
adopted (which is a very dangerous experiment in the case
of politics—a study crowning all other studies, and therefore
eminently *sui generis*) the parts of the English constitution
might be said to be connected together physiologically rather
than chemically, and least of all mechanically."

To have progressed beyond mechanical and chemical to
physiological categories is then much ; but after all it is only
an advance from the more to the less inadequate.   If organic
is to be used—for want of a better word—to include society
and the State, it must be extended to cover a wider connotation and to embrace many objects besides animal
organisms.   Society ought perhaps to be described in Mr.
Spencer's phrase as super-organic, or hyper-organic, rather
than as simply organic.

Thus it is possible that within the realm of the organic
taken in its widest sense, there may be several subdivisions,
and it would be not unnatural to expect that these should
bear some resemblance to the distinction already met with
in dealing with lower categories.   Thus, as the mechanical
conception bore a certain relation to the monadistic, and
the chemical to the monistic, it is not surprising to find
two classes of organisms reproducing in a still less extreme
form the characteristics of mechanical and chemical unities—
the one laying stress on the part, and the other on the
whole.

[1] *Fifty Years of the English Constitution*, p. 11.

Thus (*a*) the individual man, considered as a combination of mind and body, may be called an organic union of two factors—one material and the other spiritual. Here we have, at least in appearance, a remnant of that dualism which was seen to be one characteristic of mechanism. Mind and body are mysteriously welded into one; but they are not inseparable, for the former may embody itself, or part of itself, anew in a manuscript or printed volume, and so live on after the brain which gave it birth is decomposed, while the body exists as a lifeless mass after death has given wing to the soul. The two factors cannot be identified, and are indeed, in popular thought, considered the very opposites of one another in the familiar antithesis of "body and soul." The relation between the two, in the life of one human being, forms an excellent type of the first class of organic unity, where, though elements of union and separation are both found, the latter seem to outweigh the former. But (*b*) there is a second kind of organic unity, where just the reverse holds true—where the tendencies towards a complete union seem to overbalance those towards separation. Of this latter class, animal organisms afford the best types. These are made up of cells which are alive only as they share the life of the whole; but which might yet in other circumstances have formed the germs each of an independent organism of its own. The relationship is still organic, but the parts have no separate consciousness nor even separate lives. They have been absorbed entirely in the whole. Here is a reproduction on a higher plane of some of the characteristics of a chemical union. (*c*) A third class combines and transcends the characteristics of each of these. It is possible to imagine other and still more perfect forms of organic or super-organic life embodying what is best in all the more partial or one-sided phases—preserving the unity more completely than the first, and giving greater scope for liberty and individual life than the second. The individual mind is a type of this. The self-consciousness, or unity of apperception, or principle of identity, which is the centre of the system, cannot exist without the moods of volition, feeling, and cognition through which it manifests itself; while

B

these are inconceivable apart from the unity of the conscious mind.

Various other examples of organic unities might be mentioned, some of which it is difficult to classify. Every work of art, for example, is an organic whole, and so is the system of positive laws and customs which regulate the life of every nation. It is needless to multiply examples. The main point to observe is, that many forms of organisms exist, widely different from one another and from the animal and plant systems to which the term was first applied. Different writers on social science have pictured humanity under one or other of these varied forms.

(a) Thus Mr. Herbert Spencer holds that[1] "the parts of an animal form a concrete whole; but the parts of a society form one, which is discrete." A few pages further on,[2] he points out "a cardinal difference in the two kinds of organisms. In the one, consciousness is concentrated in a small part of the aggregate. In the other, it is diffused throughout the aggregate; all the units possess the capacity for happiness and misery, if not in equal degrees, still in degrees that approximate. As, then, there is no social sensorium, the welfare of the aggregate, considered apart from that of the units, is not an end to be sought. The society exists for the benefit of its members, not its members for the benefit of the society." It is thus by making society what he calls a "discrete" organism—and what from the point of view of this essay might be called an organism of a somewhat mechanical type—that Mr. Spencer reconciles his organic conception of the State with a theory of thorough-going individualism in politics, such as he has expounded in his famous work, *The Man versus the State*.

(b) Quite an opposite conception of the social organism is, however, possible—one approximating rather to the chemical than the mechanical type. By straining the analogy between the body politic and the animal body, the organic conception is often pressed into the service of socialism. The relations of the individual citizen to the State are compared to the position of the cells which make up the tissue of a tree or

---

[1] *Principles of Sociology*, 2nd edition, p. 445.   [2] P. 449.

animal, the life and independence of each being sapped and "exploited" for the benefit of the whole. The cells of an animal have neither separate consciousness nor separate aims and interests from those of the whole. Similarly, a few extreme socialists would prevent the individual from being an end to himself, and make him the bond-slave of the needs of the community. It is as a reaction against such a one-sided interpretation as this that many moderate-minded men are led to condemn the idea of a social organism altogether. Thus Professor Laurie[1] "maintains that the organic conception, if accepted in any unqualified sense, would reduce all individuals to slavery, and personal ethics to slavish obedience to existing law." Obviously this criticism, however applicable to the organic conception in the hands of socialists, has no force against such an interpretation as that of Mr. Spencer.

(c) Thus it is possible to use the same idea in support both of the excessive authority of the State and of the unbridled license of individual liberty, according as we emphasize one or another of the two leading moments which it contains. A third course is, however, open. Just as it was possible to combine the mechanical and chemical conceptions of society, and at the same time to transcend them both in the idea of organic union, so it is possible to rise above both inadequate ideas of such an organic union to one which is neither concrete nor discrete, but a truly "organic" organism in which neither the whole is sacrificed to the part nor the part to the whole, but each finds its complement, or *alter ego*, in the other, and so realizes its full life and perfect well-being.

The true and full interpretation of the organic conception of society is opposed to both of the caricatures used to support one-sided socialistic or individualistic theories. It is, unfortunately, impossible to obtain a perfect analogy of such a conception of the highest form of unity in difference and difference in unity with which to compare the State. The body politic, indeed, in its highest development is essentially *sui generis*, and the imperfection of all other organisms must be judged by their shortcomings when compared with the standard which its perfection sets up.

[1] S. S. Laurie, *Ethica*, p. 212.

Every nation has a life of its own, and every citizen has a life of *his* own.

Thus every man is both an end and a means—an end as regards his own realization, and a means as regards that of the State; and these two realizations in their ultimate form must coincide. To understand this fully, two truths must be borne in mind. In the first place, when mankind as a whole is called an organic unity, it is a unity of minds and not of bodies that is meant. The State has undoubtedly power over men's physical frames and material goods, but it is primarily a union of spirits—of beings capable of understanding and following the universal as embodied in the form of the laws and institutions of the State. Thus the ultimate conception of society is assuredly not of a number of animal existences, or even of an aggregate of beings capable of feelings or passions, but of a union of persons endowed with reason who attain to true maturity in proportion as their rational nature triumphs over their lower instincts, and who, by the very same process by which they attain self-realization, come closer into sympathy and unity with others of like nature with themselves. In the second place—and this is merely another aspect of the same truth—the organic unity of society is rather an ideal to be aimed at than a goal already reached. The solidarity of the race holds good of humanity at every stage of its development, but among savage tribes it is potential rather than actual. Centuries of slow progress have been needed before the brotherhood of men of all races and colours has become consciously realized, even to a partial extent. The practical results, which ought to flow from the discovery of the truth that all men are brothers, can as yet hardly be said to have begun. If modern evolutionists are right, the whole vegetable and animal kingdoms, including man with his power of speech and thought, his moral and rational nature, his political and social organizations, are present in embryo in the uniform mass of " protoplasm *plus* chlorophyll," out of which all living forms have come.[1] Similarly it may be said that the universal brotherhood of man exists in spite of the criminal and even

[1] Cf Edward Clodd, *Primer of Evolution, passim.*

cannibal instincts of the rudest race of barbarians. **All these**
theories may be **true, but they contain** only one aspect of
truth as seen from **a philosophic standpoint.** No simple thing
can progress towards a complex **ideal,** unless that ideal **is**
already existent. The acorn contains **the** oak only to the
mind already familiar with **the** idea of the full-grown tree.
Similarly, the organic conception of the State, though always
involved potentially in the rudest beginnings of political life,
is an ideal to which civilization approximates more and more,
and **not** the point from which **it** starts. While **it forms** the
clue **in** guiding us towards a true conception of society **as**
it ought to be in its perfection, we must **not suffer** ourselves
to be disappointed, nor yet regard the idea as untenable,
because it has never yet been adequately realized. On the
contrary, the **whole** of history shows a struggle towards **this**
idea through **lower** categories. Governments have gradually
been emancipating themselves from mechanical theories of
their duties, and approaching to **a nobler** understanding of
the intimate organic connection **between** rulers and their
subjects.

It is impossible, as has been already said, **to find** any
exact **analogy of** the constitution of society thus conceived;
but **a** clearer general idea of what is meant **may perhaps**
be obtained by comparison with the unity **of thought and**
sound which presents itself to the ear and **mind of the lover**
of music when he listens to the rendering **of a** symphony
by an orchestra of a hundred performers, each drawing the
appropriate sounds from his own instrument **in** obedience **to**
the law of the conductor's baton. **Clearly the** performance
of the symphony—if a **satisfactory one**—is a unity of a
very **perfect,** intimate, and organic kind. Yet if attention
were directed chiefly to the hundred bodies of the performers
or to the hundred different instruments—string and brass and
wood—the verdict **would** be, like Mr. Spencer's on society,
that the **unity was a** very "discrete" one indeed. **It** is
somewhat different **when** the unity of action is chiefly thought
of—how each man subordinates his own impulses and im-
pressions of time and emphasis **not** only to the composer's
thought, but to **the** interpretation put on it by the conductor;

and thus the individuals cease to be a law to themselves, because they work in obedience to an external law. Thus a conception of a higher kind of unity is attained. The highest and truly organic level is only reached when all idea of a mechanical obedience is thrown away, and when each individual, while voluntarily obeying an apparently external law, is really thereby making it his own, and finding he thus gives the most perfect rendering of which he as an individual is capable, and at the same time contributes to the harmony of the whole in proportion as both conductor and performers rise to the full height of their rational nature in giving the most perfect rendering of which their powers are capable. This imperfect comparison is only the faintest image of the way in which a truly organic view of society may be obtained by gradually rising above the consideration of the mere bodily peculiarities of the various members with their antagonistic animal needs, and petty individual feelings and desires, and by fixing our minds on the highest eternal welfare realized by each in attaining to true self-development along the lines of those universal principles of reason and morality, the consciousness of which really makes them men, and which alone can lead them towards the ultimate destiny of mankind.

While it is apparent that it is by no means a simple task to state exactly what kind of organism society is, every illustration makes it clearer that it is possible to use the term without implying any ridiculous comparisons between its members and the limbs of any particular animal. When the ideas meant to be conveyed by the application of the term "organic" to such entities have been fully grasped, it is of no consequence though the word itself be discarded. The analogy has served its day as a half truth, by which the searcher has been led to a whole truth, which is at last seen more clearly apart from the avenue of original approach.

The full significance of the application of this idea to society has probably not yet been exhausted, and it would be vain to hope to sum up in a few sentences all the consequences involved, but a few of the chief amongst them may be briefly indicated.

(1) In the first place, when the relations between the State and its citizens are spoken of as organic, this necessarily implies that the parts are essentially and intrinsically—not merely accidentally—related to the whole. Indeed, it is these relations to the whole that make the individual what he is. Again, the whole is not merely an aggregate of its parts. Its characteristics are not to be found by simply enumerating those of its various parts. "We must not ignore the truth," says Professor Ritchie,[1] "which to abstract logic appears absurd, that an organic whole is not merely the sum of its parts. The body corporate is mysterious, like the personality of the individual." Indeed, the sum of its parts considered away from the whole is not only less than that whole; it is nothing and less than nothing. Each part is like the 0, which when added to a sum multiplies it tenfold, but is by itself nothing at all. The mutual relations make up the essence of both whole and parts.'

(2) As the State is a true and intimate unity, the parts must be subject to the authority of the whole. This is the philosophical basis of the doctrine of "sovereignty." The rational will of the community must prevail.

(3) Each part, however, retains its independent existence. The man is not the slave of the State, but enjoys freedom and the full participation in the common life. This is the basis of the doctrine of the rights of the subject—rights within the State, and not against it.

(4) The sovereignty of the State and the liberty of the individual are not really opposed to one another. It is within the State, and in obedience to its laws, that positive freedom is found for man to develop his rational nature, while the authority of the State is founded on the will of the people. The whole recognizes the rights of the parts, and the parts acknowledge the authority of the whole. In this light the fatal antithesis so often absolutely drawn between the authority of the State and the freedom of the subject is overcome. It is seen that to increase the former is not necessarily to subtract something from the latter, as though they were the positive and negative sides of an algebraic

---

[1] *Limits of State Interference*, p. 69.

equation. Authority when guided by rational principles in preserving order is the friend of all freedom that is not mere anarchy.

(5) The State develops from within, and is an end to itself This is the basis of the doctrine of the independence of each nation from foreign intervention.

(6) No *abstract* description of this end or ideal can be adequate. It consists in nothing short of the full and harmonious development of all the latent capacities contained in it and in all its members. This self-realization of the State as a rational embodiment of man's spirit or will involves the attainment of all the highest interests of mankind and the true *summum bonum* of every individual citizen.

(7) Thus the end of the whole is one with the end of every part; still, the individual, before fully realizing this truth, must have risen to the highest level of which he is capable— must have caused his rational nature to triumph over his mere animal nature, and so reached a standpoint of duty. He must allow no private selfish interest to outweigh his sense of what is due to other individuals and to the State as a whole.[1] These characteristics might be elaborated still further and subdivided under many heads; but enough has probably been already said to indicate the sense in which the State is here described as organic. The propositions above laid down are given as hypotheses, not as axioms. They are intended to suggest the main lines upon which a philosophical justification of the practical conclusions arrived at in

---

[1] **Professor J. S.** Mackenzie in his *Introduction to Social Philosophy,* approaching the same problem from a somewhat different side and with different objects in view, arrives at conclusions not materially different from those of the present writer. In his third chapter (on the *Social Organism*), he gives three features wherein society realizes the essentials of an organism. These are (*a*) that it is a "whole whose parts are intrinsically related to it"; (*b*) that "it develops from within"; and (*c*) that "it has reference to an end which is involved in its own nature." See too the opening pages of the fifth chapter, pp. 238-9; and also (for the bearings of the idea of organic unity on theories of government) the Master of Balliol's *Social Philosophy of Comte,* p. 246.

this essay may be based, if such is asked for or expected. The conclusions themselves, however, are the results of an investigation of existing facts, and are not deductions from any *a priori* theory They must accordingly stand or fall on their own intrinsic merits, and quite apart from the truth or falsity of the philosophical basis on which it has been sought to reconcile them with one of the chief conceptions of modern speculation.

Many more or less minute analogies might be traced between the growth, structures, functions, and organs of various societies or parts of societies on the one hand, and those of different species of animal life on the other. Mr. Spencer, indeed, has chronicled many of these in rich variety in his *Induction of Sociology*. Of these the development from simple to complex, the differentiation of organs and the division of labour may be quoted as notable examples. All such points of similarity are, however, merely analogies—mere coincidences, mayhap—any or all of which might be absent without endangering the truth of the main proposition which is here urged—that society is "organic." It is important that attention should be fixed not upon mere accidental resemblances, but upon those essential characteristics possessed by all States and societies which render the application of the term organic to them not only admissible but necessary. These features may be resolved into one, and may after all be best expressed in the negative form—in the assertion that no community and no body politic can be adequately described in terms of any lower category. No conceptions that are merely quantitative, or mechanical, or the like, can ever afford a satisfactory foundation upon which to build a theory of the State.

The features of a purely "natural" or physical organism we have seen to be also inadequate. The essential characteristics in which the body politic differs from these may be reduced to two. In the first place, the end, or destiny, or ideal it exists for is one capable of appealing to the rational nature of the members of the community, and tending to come to clearer self-consciousness with the advance of civilization. In the second place, this end is one that the direct efforts of the citizens, as men capable of willing and doing, may help to realize. They may, by their joint or independent action, help forward its fulfilment. A purely natural organism, on the other hand, has no knowledge of the type towards which it tends, and is powerless to accelerate or retard its own progress.

(2) THE SCOPE AND PRACTICAL BEARING OF POLITICAL SCIENCE, OR THE THEORY OF THE STATE.

THE systematic study of political institutions as they are, and as they ought to be, is sometimes called the Theory of the State, and sometimes the Science of Politics or Political Philosophy. The former name is perhaps the best, for three reasons. In the first place, it gives a clear indication of the wide nature of the inquiry involved. When the full significance of all that is included within the term "State" is firmly grasped, there is no danger of forming an inadequate conception of the importance or scope of the branch of philosophy that professes to plumb its mysteries. In the second place, the expression "Theory of the State" avoids the necessity of a delicate and intricate discussion as to whether "philosophy" or "science" is the right word to apply. The relations of science to philosophy on the one hand, and to the political arts on the other, cannot be here discussed; and without some such inquiry it is impossible to say how far the investigation now entered upon partakes of the nature of each.[1] In the third place, the word "political" has become somewhat belittled by its application to the special needs of party warfare,

---

[1] This discussion really resolves itself into one of method. The whole question as to how far the methods of philosophy and science are applicable to social and political phenomena is approached from different points of view in Mackenzie's *Introduction to Social Philosophy*, pp. 10-45, and in Sheldon Amos' *Science of Politics*, chapter i.

and ought perhaps to be avoided **lest** it should suggest a wrong idea of **the** objects to which it **is** applied.

The expression **Political** Science or Science of **Politics, in** spite of all **these drawbacks, has** already taken its place in the English **language as the most** usual name for the inquiry **into the** nature **of the State** with its institutions, **government,** and laws. The name is of course of little **importance so** long as it suggests no associations **likely to raise** prejudices or misconceptions. It must then **be clearly understood** that "the State" in the widest **meaning of the word** is the object of this inquiry; and **it is equally** necessary to gain a clear idea of all that this term **includes.**

Political science, in **the proper sense, is, in the words of** Bluntschli,[1] "the **science which is concerned** with the State, which endeavours **to** understand and comprehend the State in its conditions, **in** its essential nature, its various forms **or** manifestations, **its** development." It has thus, in spite **of the** vast extent of the subject, both its beginning and **its end** within **the State. When the science of politics** is **thus** understood **to be merely another name for** the theory **of** the **State, an important step is already** made towards **answering the** question **sometimes** asked as to the **possibility of the existence** of such a science **at all. If any rational** principles can be found to regulate the formation of constitutions, the making of laws, the laying **down** of the foundations **of** national institutions on an enduring **basis, or** the limits within which the **State** is justified in interfering **with** the liberties and rights of individuals—and **no one** seriously doubts that such exist, if **we can only discover** them—these principles **of** themselves form a **theory of the** State progressing from rude beginnings **to a** complete and systematized branch of knowledge in proportion as such rules are clearly formulated **and** understood in the full complexity of their mutual **relations.**

The phrase **"Science of Politics"** is indeed doubly **unfortunate, for** science is generally associated with **rigorous and** unbending methods of **investigation and experiment** applied to **those** tangible **material** objects to which alone

[1] *Theory of the State.* Introduction, chapter i.

they are **strictly adapted**; while the word politics **is associated** with **all that is changeable** and contingent **in the** affairs of a **nation rather than with** principles of **absolute and** universal truth ; as the **two** words are ordinarily understood, " science " **and** " **politics** " seem opposites and mutually irreconcilable.

It would be out of place here **to** discuss how far **the adjective** " scientific " is justly applicable **to** any particular methods of investigation for fathoming the nature of social, economic, educational, or political phenomena, or whether "philosophic" might not be the better **word to** employ ; but **some** explanation seems to be called **for as to** what is **meant by** " politics." To men whose acquaintance with the questions of statecraft and **the** nature of laws **and** constitutions **is** chiefly confined **to** their experiences **as** candidates for parliamentary **honours, or in** supporting or opposing **the** claims **of those who are, the** word " politics " will **naturally** suggest **all that is unstable in** the commonwealth. **If that word is to** be narrowed **down to the art of** electioneering, **to the platform** oratory which the **constituencies expect, and** the making of party **programmes fitted to attract votes, or** arouse the enthusiasm **of partizans, it is** doubtful if any science of politics could **exist at all, and** certain that it could not claim a place among academic pursuits.

To most men, indeed, who interest themselves actively **in** politics, it seems something nobler than this, and **they are** not without a glimmering of the high issues at stake **and the** deep foundation on which **a** nation's institutions **must be built.** Yet, even to such men the idea of politics **as the** pursuit of ever varying ends by means equally changing and not always disinterested or even honest, **is** difficult to discard, and **when** they talk of the impossibility **of** a science **of** politics, they are really **influenced by a** sordid **and ignoble** conception of what that **phrase means.** "Politics" **to them is** the unstable or dynamic element **in a State—an attempt to** overthrow its institutions **or** to defend **them from attack—not** an investigation of the eternal **principles** upon which all constitutions rest. It **means a** conflict of different forces, the effects of which cannot be calculated beforehand—blind powers that cannot be reduced to any principle of order—producing an **unforeseen** resultant related often in an apparently accidental **manner** to all its antecedents.

Another unfortunate impression **conveyed by the name** "political science" is that it is merely a study to be entered on as **a** means to party ends, not as a resolute endeavour to find truth for its own sake—a pursuit subservient to the **art of** politics, not primarily one in which the acquisition **of** knowledge is its own reward. Nothing **can be** farther **from** the truth. Political science is not a manual of practical maxims intended to teach statecraft as a profession, **any** more than political economy aims directly at showing merchants and manufacturers how they may best conduct their private enterprises or secure in trade or commerce **a** larger share **of business** than their neighbours.

It is impossible that these ignoble views of the true scope of "politics" **should** obscure the vision of scholars trained in the study **of** antiquity, who **can trace** the origin of the word **from** the Greek city-state, through the writings of **Plato and** Aristotle, down to the present day. Indeed, **the ideas instinctively** suggested to the scholar when a science **of** politics is mentioned, are so essentially different from those **of** the practical politician with no **tincture of academic culture,** that it is difficult for the former to **understand the source** of error of the latter; and without comprehension **and sympathy** it is impossible **to** dispel the difficulties of those who move in a different plane **of thought.**

Political science rightly understood deals with the stable elements of the State as well as with the unstable—with the foundations of order as well as the principles of change. In fact, it is the former elements with which it chiefly concerns itself. It treats of the national institutions and the laws, government, and constitution, which may be called the skeleton of a State, **since** they give to **it** a definite form and **permanent** structural characteristics. The momentary variations and currents of "political" life, using the word in its **narrower** signification, are treated as only of secondary importance, and valuable chiefly with reference to their bearing on the more permanent **parts.** The theory of politics, law, **and national** institutions **would** better express its scope, though **even that** is somewhat **too** narrow, and **no** word satisfies the requirements of the **case equally with** the simple phrase, " the theory of the State."

The objections sometimes raised to **the** possibility of a science of politics, however, are by no means entirely based on a misconception of its nature. Very serious arguments, founded **upon** the wide scope **of** the field which **it** covers and the consequent complexity **of** its investigations, have to be considered and answered. These objections, however, while they prove **that** the attempt at a systematic analysis of the principles and **the** phenomena of the State **is** subject to serious difficulties, are far from proving that it **is** impossible.[1] If it is true that the higher nature of mankind **in** all its grandeur **and** complexity can only be realized through **the** medium **of the** State, of which **all** men are willingly **or unwillingly members, it** follows that to know that **State** thoroughly it is **necessary to examine the nature of the** individual men, their connection with material **objects, and** also their mutual relations—moral, **intellectual,** aesthetic, political, legal, and hygienic. It **would seem, then,** that a complete theory of the State is impossible until all the more restricted sciences and arts **are** complete too. Finite creatures must, however, **be** content with limited knowledge, and must not despise the broken rays of light **that** penetrate to them, because they cannot get at once the **full** effulgence of the truth, which indeed their immature **powers** of vision are unable to sustain. A complete political science is as yet impossible, and, perhaps, will remain for ever an ideal whereto knowledge approximates rather than an end that has been reached. This, fortunately, does not preclude the possibility of making a beginning, or even of attaining to a considerable degree of proficiency and discovering many **rays of that eternal truth which** cannot change.

The opponents of political science are at this point ready with another line of attack. Although results of a " specu-

---

[1] Cf. Sheldon Amos, *The Science of Politics,* pp. 1-20, for a detailed examination of some of these difficulties.

lative interest and abstract value" may be obtained, **they** allege that these are useless for all every-day **purposes.** Practical politics **are** so far removed from such academic discussions that whatever conclusions **the** so-called **science of** politics may arrive at, the art of politics **will** go on its way unheeding and unaffected by the barren discoveries of unpractical men. Unfortunately this estimate **is** not without its element of truth. There *is* a gulf between theory and practice, and the blame is chargeable to both sides. Party leaders, **in** the press and din of battle, in the urgent necessity **of** obtaining popular support by the most obvious and **rapid** methods, often spare too little time for approaching **the** problems that engage them in a broad and academic spirit. On the other **hand,** philosophers, whether of the synthetic or analytic sort, are too prone to despise and ignore the actual **results of** what they consider a muddy and ignoble warfare. **They all** admit the need of testing their hypotheses **by experience;** but they too often lay undue stress **on the** *a priori* element, basing their theories on an induction from too narrow an observation of phenomena, or upon facts drawn **from a** different and alien province.

Current speculation and current practical politics might be mutual gainers by a closer connection with one another; but the partial estrangement of the two only proves that practical men neglect the services of a useful ally. It does not follow that that ally is necessarily useless to them. **If** political science can make good **its claim to** rank as a branch of systematic knowledge in reality as in name, no statesman, legislator, or politician can wisely neglect its guidance any more than the shipbuilder **can ignore** the results of applied mechanics or naval architecture. **He** must assuredly struggle to keep himself **from** falling under the dominion of any theories at all, and especially of crude and half-digested **ones.** Otherwise he will be branded with the fatal adjective *doctrinaire,* and his **place in** the esteem **of his** constituents **or** party leaders will sink inestimably. **This by** no means involves that his attitude to all theories of **the State ought** to be a **purely** negative one. Indeed, there is only one **way** to make sure that theories do not master **you,** and that is, to master them. It is not more impossible to live in any district without breathing its air and being affected by its climate than to live in any section of society while preserving a strictly neutral attitude to the theories which pervade it. Consciously or unconsciously men's actions are moulded in conformity with, or in opposition to, the current opinions of the day. The power of erroneous theories cannot be shaken off by simply ignoring them. Ignorance merely increases their power of doing harm. It is the soil in which dangerous half-truths most easily take root. If false theories either of a popular or profoundly scientific character are in the air, they will find adherents among those practical men who are unacquainted with the true principles of the science they caricature.

To refuse to know the nearest approximation to the truth available in the present state of science is not to shake off the influence of theory, but to be a ready prey to the first erroneous opinion that happens to drift that way. The most casual student of history knows the potent influence of the theories, both false and true, of "mere philosophers" on the destiny of nations. Who can estimate the effects of Rousseau's writings on the course of the French Revolution, and, indeed, of European politics generally, or the results of the academic labours of men like Adam Smith and Bentham on the direction taken by legislative change in Britain? No statesman can be worthy of the name who has not mastered the principles of political science. He cannot counteract the hurtful influence of false theories upon his conduct by simple indifference or even by ridicule; for they will hamper him until he is able clearly to refute them. A true political science would be necessary if its only conclusion was this—that all other conclusions are false. "Political science," says Sir Frederick Pollock, "must and does exist, if it were only for the refutation of absurd political theories and projects."[1]

This practical dependence of the art of politics upon its kindred science is the best vindication of the claim of the latter to usefulness. There is, however, a wider aspect of the subject which must be glanced at. The theory of the

[1] *History of the Science of Politics*, p. 4.

State is not primarily intended as a weapon of party warfare. In so far as it is a true branch of philosophy or of science, its primary object is truth, not utility. There is little danger of forgetting this when several of the most emphatic forms of its expression have taken rank among the trite commonplaces of literature—when we have the dictum of Bacon on philosophy, that " like a virgin consecrated to God she bears no fruit"; and the advice of Hegel, that philosophy must guard itself against seeking to be edifying, and confine itself to a search for truth. The necessary complement of these axioms, however, must be equally borne in mind, that though the search for information is a delusive pursuit, if undertaken directly for selfish or ulterior ends; yet truth, once discovered, cannot help being useful in every practical aim of life. This wide aspect of the subject is not special to the study of politics, but is rather the general problem of the relations of the practical arts to science and philosophy as a whole,—too wide a field to be here embraced.

The specially intimate connection between the art of politics and the theory of the State is best brought out by an examination of the way in which general principles are necessarily involved in every isolated act of statesmanship and in every legislative measure. The series of questions seem, however, to emerge in practice in a rotation exactly the reverse of their logical order. The politician is confronted with the concrete individual problem, and it is only in seeking its solution that he is confronted with deeper and deeper groups of questions gradually unfolding themselves. Bold and rapid action is often the one thing needed from the statesman, leaving him little or no time for mature reflection; yet in every act of statecraft, however hurriedly performed, and though unaccompanied by a single word, a complete theory of government, of society, and of the State—an entire system of philosophy—is implicitly involved, and tacitly, if not expressly, approved. The detailed examination of the grounds of this assertion is worth entering upon, as it will not only show the relations of political science to the arts of legislation and statecraft, but will also explain the extensive scope and the various divisions of the science.

Problems usually come up for the decision of the cabinet or the legislature in a simple concrete form. A thousand practical matters present themselves every session,—whether Britain ought to interfere for the protection of the Armenians ; whether to hold the Chinese Government responsible for the massacre of Christian missionaries ; whether to grant a guarantee to some new railway enterprise, and if so, how to raise the necessary funds ; whether to give legislative recognition to the principle of " local veto," or to enforce some compulsory scheme of old-age insurance. These are the apparently isolated individual questions as they arise. It is not difficult to show that not a step can be taken towards answering any one of them without assuming the existence of the fundamental principles of a science of politics. The affairs of a great nation cannot be carried on in a haphazard way. General rules must be formulated and lines of conduct laid down by a government for its own guidance to secure some continuity of policy. Definite methods of administrative action must be devised. It is still the province of politics as an art rather than as a science to deal with these methods as well as with the individual cases. Yet, to formulate a scientific basis for such rules involves an examination of the machinery through which it is lawful for the executive and legislative authorities to act ; and this is clearly one of the chief duties of political science. The theory of the State must determine under what sort of national institutions the work of government may best be carried on. To examine the rules which regulate the internal workings and mutual relations of such institutions is to theorize upon the best form of constitution ; and this has been, from the time of Plato and Aristotle to the present day, one of the chief objects of the science of politics.

It soon becomes evident that the inquiry cannot rest here. Before forming an opinion as to how the work of government may be best performed, it is necessary to know what that work is. This raises the question, What is the proper sphere or province of government ? Only in the present day is it beginning to be more clearly understood that the former question must be answered before the latter, that we must know clearly the work the government has to do before we can determine under what form of constitution and laws it is best able to do it. Neither a democratic, nor an aristocratic, nor a monarchic form of constitution—neither an entirely representative government, nor a hereditary second chamber, nor a royal veto—is a good thing in itself, but merely in so far as it enables government to perform justly and efficiently its proper functions in furthering the highest interests of the whole community.

This consideration has again widened the scope of the inquiry, and brought it to another and deeper issue. In determining what is the proper work or the true sphere of government, it is necessary to ascertain its nature and the ends for which it exists. If it is true that governments exist for the benefit of the nations governed rather than *vice versa*, it follows that their work is to further the well-being of the whole community politically organized into a State. It thus becomes a necessary preliminary to inquire into the origin, nature, and composition of society and the State—to discover the final and ultimate good for which these exist at all. Arrived at this point in the inquiry, it appears that the true well-being and ultimate ideal of the State cannot be determined apart from the examination of the well-being of the individuals of whom it consists, and the destiny of humanity as a whole. Thus there is involved the old and never-ending question of the *summum bonum*, or "chief end of man," which in turn cannot be determined without an exhaustive analysis of all ethics and metaphysics —in fact of every department of human knowledge, art, history, science, and philosophy.

The theory of the State, unless it would stretch itself out to be identical with the whole sum of human knowledge, must be satisfied to accept the conclusions of philosophy and of the various more limited sciences, contenting itself with examining them anew in the light of the special aspect in which they are now viewed.

To attempt to start with absolutely no assumptions, and

to treat the inquiry from the beginning logically and with absolute thoroughness, it would be necessary to examine man's past history on earth and his future destiny. If to any one " man's chief end is to glorify God and to enjoy Him for ever," that individual will form totally different conclusions on each successive question of political science from those of the man who takes as his creed that " we must eat, drink, and be merry, for to-morrow we die."

However unwilling to admit the influence of theological considerations he may be, no man can shake himself free of them in any branch of speculation. In spite of all his efforts, they colour his whole range of thought and enter into his estimate of the value of every object of human pursuit.[1] Suppose then a positive conclusion of some sort is arrived at as to the ultimate goal of humanity, it must still be asked how far the governments of the various States ought to make it their conscious object to help forward humanity towards that goal. Men, it is observed, are banded together into societies, and a series of intricate relations exist between the individual and the State. Each human unit receives certain benefits from his connection with the whole, and also suffers certain restrictions on his liberties. It is understood that some of the interests of the various units are held in common, and are best looked after by the government (or recognized common agents) of the whole community, while other interests are best left for each individual man or woman to push forward on his own account. Thus arises the problem how to determine which of these interests may be safely entrusted to the government, and which ought to be withdrawn from its control. It is necessary to investigate the reasons of the State's existence, and what limits (if any) are to be placed to the sphere of the activity of its authorized agents. If the government of a nation ought to look to its highest and noblest interests, and to aim at the fullest development of man as man, then it would seem as though statesmen were under the necessity of judging in what that fullest development consists. If that is found to include a high standard of moral and spiritual enlightenment, then it

[1] Cf. Stephen's *Liberty, Equality, and Fraternity*, p. 319.

would seem to be the duty of government directly to enforce such systems of morality and religion as meet with its approval. This would make every cabinet minister not only a professor of theology and moral philosophy, but also an evangelist and a censor of morals.

A contrary answer may be given, however. It may be said that the State *as* a State has nothing to do with such things—that these are matters for the individual conscience. A wide sphere is left even then for government action. Many problems would face our rulers, though their province were confined to matters affecting the material prosperity of the nation. Neglecting for the moment the fact of the impossibility of separating the temporal and spiritual, there is still to determine in what a nation's highest material good consists. It is necessary to judge between the conflicting systems of rival political economists.

It is possible, of course, to deny that government should concern itself even with the material progress of a nation. The State, it may be said, should stand aside and allow the economic influences—the laws of supply and demand and the haggling of the market—free play to settle the material prosperity of individuals and of the nation as best they may. This would involve a negative solution to the problem of how far the State should interfere with trade. The conclusion would be, "Do not interfere at all." That may be quite a logical answer, but still it is *an answer* all the same, before giving which the problem must be faced.

Having satisfied ourselves in some way then (either by thinking out the matter for ourselves, or by jumping at a ready-made conclusion) as to what the true ends and aims of government should be, it is possible now (but not before) to descend another step in the scale of problems, and consider the *methods* by which these aims can best be furthered. The preliminary inquiry is a necessary one, because methods must vary with the ends which are sought. To one man the end of government may be foreign conquest and universal dominion over neighbouring States, to another "peace at any price." The holders of these opposite theories of the State will not agree as to either the proper work of government or the best **methods** of procedure. **As soon, however, as a** clear idea is formulated as to **what work** ought to be done, a more or less elaborate series **of rules** may be laid down for its accomplishment, and a determination arrived at under what form of institutions this work may be most efficiently **performed.**

If the enforcement of order and the dispensation of justice **are** among the legitimate objects for **which** States exist, **we can** then (but not sooner) discuss the **best** form of organization for the suppression of violence, and **the best** means of settling disputes between man and man ; that is to say, we can settle **what** form the executive and judicial institutions respectively ought to assume.

Many **new** questions now suggest themselves. Granted that the State should make laws binding on the whole nation, **to whom ought this duty to be** entrusted ? What **powers should be given to this** legislative authority? What **restraints ought to be placed upon** their hasty or selfish **use ? Again,** granted **that the** State should interest itself **in** the moral welfare of **its** citizens, ought it to proceed towards effecting this directly or indirectly ? Should it try to make men good by Act of Parliament, **or** by enforced education, or how ? Granted that the State should foster and encourage the arts and sciences, ought it to found a Royal Academy and museums, and support them out of the public funds as is done in England ? Ought it to endow theatres and opera **houses, as is** done in Germany ? Finally, to take just one **more** instance from among many, what attitude ought government **ment** to observe towards religion and the question of an Established Church ? These are a few specimens of **the** practical questions upon which the science of politics may be expected to throw some light.

In thus tracing the connection of the theory of the State with philosophy on **the one hand,** and practical politics on the other, some insight **has** been gained into the various classes of questions with which it deals. These may be grouped broadly under four heads in the order of their logical priority.

(1) Its first work is the investigation of the true nature and essence of the State, of the society of individuals who compose it, and of its government, laws, and constitution ; its historical origin and its ultimate destiny ; its end or final cause. (2) In the second place, it has to determine the proper sphere or province of the authorized agents of a State ; to decide what government ought to do. (3) In the third place, it has to examine the various forms of national institutions under which that work may be most efficiently performed ; to decide what the constitution ought to be. (4) In the fourth place, although the detailed application of its theoretical results to actual cases is not properly within the scope of the science, it is open for it to lay down general rules for the guidance of practical men in attempting to make such an application.

It is the third of these inquiries which has usually occupied the greater portion of most treatises on political science; while the second, or the inquiry into the proper sphere of government, has been comparatively neglected.[1] It is proposed in this essay to reverse this, and to devote the greater portion of its pages to a consideration of the latter question, while the former, which may be found discussed at great length in many volumes, is entirely omitted. The object is to ascertain what the ideal government ought *to do*, and not what the ideal constitution ought *to be*. The analysis of the State as a whole is of course as necessary a preliminary of the one inquiry as of the other, while both yield results which may be applied to practical problems.

Accordingly, this essay falls naturally into three divisions : Part I. investigates the nature, origin, and end of the State,

[1] Almost all systematic writers on Political Science, following the lead of Plato and Aristotle, confine their attention to the *Structure*, as opposed to the *Functions* of Government. Professor Sidgwick, however, recognizes the equal importance of both inquiries, and divides Political Science accordingly into two main branches. "The study of Politics," he says (*Elements of Politics*, p. 12), "has two main divisions, (1) one relating to the Functions of Government, and (2) the other to its Structure or Constitution ; but it also includes—as an important though less extensive division—an inquiry into the relations that ought to exist between government and governed, besides such relations as are already defined in the determination of governmental functions."

with its laws, government, and constitution. Part II. treats of the sphere of government, and is thus led to attempt to adjudicate upon the respective claims of socialism and individualism as rival schemes seeking the political regeneration of society. Part III. suggests the lines on which some of the theoretical conclusions previously arrived at may be applied in practice, and thus comes near the boundary line separating the science from the art of politics.

PART I.

THE STATE: *ITS NATURE, ORIGIN, AND END;
ITS MEMBERS AND ORGANIZATION.*

CHAPTER I.

THE DEFINITION OF THE STATE.

A PERFECT definition of the State forms the last and crowning achievement of political science rather than its starting point. **Every** proposition, as it is established in the following **pages**, will throw more light on the nature of **the** body politic. Meantime, a State may **be** defined provisionally **as** an *independent organized society*. Brief and easily understood as this statement is, it will be found to contain an accurate description of every essential characteristic. Each of its three words, rightly understood, involves a number of intricate considerations. Thus "independence" is hard to define; and it is not easy to determine what measure of freedom from foreign control is indispensable to the realization of a State. Absolute independence is impossible. The difficulty increases in proportion as we push our inquiries back into the mysteries that enshroud early institutions and the customs of primitive man. Some considerable amount of self-sufficiency is clearly necessary, else the community would cease to form a State by itself, and become the province or dependency of another. The word "organized" has also intricacies of its **own.** A high degree of organization is neither necessary nor to be expected in every commonwealth. The merest rudiments only are traceable in some primitive communities; while in a fully-developed political society there are always involved a complete system of national institutions performing all the recognized functions of government, an elaborate code of **laws** and conventions, and a definite form of established constitution. Complete organization involves the embodiment of the idea of sovereignty in a definite and recognized legal form, and the distinction between government and governed. However widely organizations may vary in degree and in kind, we cannot imagine a community that has absolutely none.

A society may indeed become comparatively disorganized without ceasing to be a State; but total absence of organization means anarchy and the disintegration of the whole into its constituent atoms. Sometimes the State is spoken of as though it included merely the "political" organization; but this is to introduce an untenable restriction. It includes all ties of whatever nature that bind men together and define their mutual positions.

Sometimes it is allowed to embrace all the organizations, while it is made to exclude the individuals who are organized. "The State," it has been said,[1] "seems to indicate that external form which society assumes in consequence of its organization; it is the body of society, the political manifestation of its growth." This is true, so far as it goes; but the State, in its widest and truest sense, includes the society itself as well as its outward form—the mind as well as the body.

Lastly, the conception of "society" thus embraced in the provisional definition of a State involves a union more or less intimate of a number of individual men and women, with all their interests and attributes, and the relations that bind them together. Everything that pertains to the nature of its citizens, or of any of their associations and institutions, forms part also of the body politic.

At this point several possible roads of divergency are seen to open up for those who are desirous of framing a more elaborate definition of the State, but who differ as to the essential nature of the individual men who enter into its composition, or the reasons of their forming associations at all.

Various ideas may be entertained of what constitutes the essential characteristic of the human beings who are the units of a community; or, again, different views may be expressed as

[1] W. A. Watt, *Outline of Legal Philosophy*, p. 56.

to the presumed purposes for which society is supposed to
exist. It is probably a mistake to **try** to crowd into **a** short
definition of the State any special philosophic theories of man's
nature and **destiny, or to cast suspicion on** the statement of
its more essential features by hazarding **an** opinion as to the
aims, conscious or unconscious, that have caused men to band
themselves together. It is to attempts in one or other of
these directions, however, that we must attribute **the** extremely
complicated and highly controversial nature of most definitions
of the body politic contained in treatises of philosophy and
political science.

Thus Kant holds "that the civil constitution is a **relation**
of *free* men who live under coercive laws, without prejudicing
their liberty otherwise in the whole of their connection with
others,"[1] and in this way he incorporates with the idea of
the State his **peculiar** theory of Right as an equality of all
men in **as complete** a freedom as is compatible with the like
freedom **of others.**

Hegel, again, viewing reason as the essential feature in man,
and looking on the will **as** the practical side of that reason
acting as a self-determining principle from within, and **so**
realizing freedom in an external world of other men, has
described the State at once as a "manifestation of will" and
as "objective freedom."[2] It is evident that such metaphysical
subtleties, however valuable as throwing light on the mysteries
of human nature, are wanting in the certitude and accuracy
so necessary in a technical scientific definition. Writers with
an individualistic bias, again, such as John Locke and
Rousseau, or, in our own days, Mr. Herbert Spencer **and** Mr.
Auberon Herbert, laying stress not so **much on** their pet
theories **of** the nature of men as on their assumption of the
purposes for which individuals **band** themselves together into
communities, **define the State as** "an association for the
protection **of life and** property."

It is safer **and fairer** in every way, in framing at anyrate
a preliminary **definition** of the body politic, to throw aside all

[1] Kant's *Principles of Politics* (translated by Prof. Hastie), p. 35.
[2] Cf. T. H. Green's *Works*, Vol. II., p. 312, and G. S. Morris, *Hegel's
Philosophy of the State*, pp. 79 to 82.

theories of every kind as to the nature of men and the presumed purposes of their association, and to keep to established facts. All *a priori* doctrines seem to be avoided by defining it as "an independent organized society." This formula can be used as a *schema* into which the various schools of philosophers and politicians may afterwards insert their own favourite dogmas whenever they are so disposed.

Whatever theory is advanced, however, of the nature of the individual men composing society, it is clear that these must not be primarily looked upon as mere animals with bodily capacities and needs, but as spiritual beings endowed with wills and reasons, and knowing good from evil.

A subsidiary question may indeed arise as to whether the State necessarily includes the property or possessions of its subjects or the territory they inhabit; but this need not here detain us, since such things are in any case *accidentalia* not *essentialia* of a commonwealth.

It ought to be clearly realized how wide the definition here given really is; for it makes the State comprise not only all its citizens (without annihilating or absorbing their individuality), but also the infinite series of relations of every kind that unite them to one another and to the central organization.

It is hard, at first, to grasp all that is involved in this; but the full extent of its bearings will gradually emerge throughout the sequel. Meantime, the wide conception here entertained of the State may be contrasted with the view only too current in some quarters at the present day, which would reduce it in theory to a mere abstraction, and in practice to a great power hostile to the welfare of the individual, needing to be jealously watched as an evil tolerated only because of its necessity.

"It seems indeed," says Dr. Hutchison Stirling,[1] "to be the creed of the highest enlightenment nowadays, that what is called a State is but an expensive superfluity; that society, civilization, is nothing but the raising of commodities and the exchange of them, and that no control is required there but that of the policeman to keep the workmen quiet."

[1] *Lectures on the Philosophy of Law*, p. 40.

It will be the chief object of the following chapters to evolve the whole **theory** of the State, from its definition **as** "a society organized and independent," simple as that description at **first seems**. Before proceeding to this analysis, however, it **is** necessary to examine **some** of the more limited theories of the nature of the body politic which would give it a narrower application and a more circumscribed "sphere of influence."

An unfortunate ambiguity lies on the threshold **of this** inquiry. The word "State," as commonly employed, **has two** clearly distinct meanings. On the one hand, it is often loosely **used** indiscriminately with the term "nation." On the other **hand,** it is often employed as a useful synonym for "government." It has thus a wider and a narrower signification. The former, it is here contended, is the legitimate meaning of the word, and must be uniformly kept in view throughout this essay. In laying it down as an **axiom** that the State is something inestimably wider than its government, there **is** no need to enunciate any philological theory as to the primary or derivative meaning of the word, or even as to the signification which **in** general **literature** it ought to bear. All that is required is to make clear beyond a doubt what subject is here dealt with under the name "State." The province of political science then is co-extensive with the body politic, and comprises the people of a nation, with **all** their characteristics, mutual relations, and tangible possessions, as **well** as the administrative and legislative machinery constituting its government. The fundamental difference between a State on the one hand, and its authorized agents and institutions on the other, must be grasped at the **very** outset, and every step which is taken will only emphasize its importance.

Sir William Anson[1] has clearly enunciated this ambiguity. "When we talk of **the State**," he says, "its rights, or its structure, **we are** necessarily led to **the** inquiry, What do

---

[1] *The Law and Custom of the Constitution*, **Vol.** I., p. 3. See also for further explanation of **this** ambiguity Sheldon Amos' *Science of Politics*, p. 64 ; Professor D. G. Ritchie's *State Interference*, p. 23 (note) ; and Professor **A. C.** Bradley's *Essay on Aristotle's Conception of the State* in *Hellenica*, **p. 190** (note).

we mean by the State? The expression is sometimes used as equivalent to an entire community or independent political society; sometimes it is limited to the sovereign body in that society. When we say that a man has deserved well of the State, we generally mean that all persons in the community ought to be grateful to him. When we say that such and such things should be provided or attended to by the State, we mean that the law-making force of the community, or its administrative force, should require the observance of a certain course of conduct in certain matters."

Here then we have a tolerably clear statement of both significations.[1] The State sometimes means the whole community, and sometimes merely its rulers; but throughout this essay it is exclusively applied to the former, while the word "government" is reserved for the latter. Political science, it must be clearly understood, is a wider thing than constitutional law, and treats of all the individuals and all the currents of life and action which make up the State—not merely of its government and laws.

The habitual application of one substantive, however, to two things of widely different connotations is, to say the least of it, unfortunate. The confusion of language has given occasion to considerable confusion of thought. It has often led hazy theorists to identify the mere machinery of government with the complex mass of common interests, history, and destiny of that community which includes its government as only one of its factors. As a general rule the word has been used in its wider sense by those who have approached the subject from its speculative or philosophic side, while the narrower signification has found favour with investigators of a practical turn of mind. This has occasioned several bad results. In the first place, when disputes arise, each side misunderstands the other. In the second place, many investigators have been hampered by this confusion of ideas. They have been afraid to rise to a sufficiently broad and

[1] The use of the equivalents in German of these two words helps to emphasize the difference between the two things denoted. Vide the translator's preface to the authorized edition of Bluntschli's *Theory of the State*, p. 7.

noble conception of the nature and destinies of the State, from an unfounded dread that in so doing they were opening the door for a more extended and mischievous action of a meddle-some and "grandmotherly" government. In the third place, if this confusion of nomenclature has an unfortunate effect in belittling our ideas of the State, it has also an equally regrettable tendency towards exaggerating the importance of the government. The conclusions arrived at by theorists as deductions from the nature of the State in its wider and truer signification have been smuggled into practical politics as applicable to the government. Thus, executive officials may be led to meddle in matters beyond their proper sphere from confusing that sphere with the province of the State itself.

It is probably to a desire to counteract such tendencies as these that we must attribute Mr. Goldwin Smith's disappointing answer to the question, "What is the State?" "People seem to suppose," he says, "that there is something outside and above the members of the community which answers to this name, and which has duties and a wisdom of its own. But duties can attach only to persons, wisdom can reside only in brains. The State, when you leave abstractions and come to facts, is nothing but the government, which can have no duties but those which the constitution assigns it, nor any wisdom but that which is infused into it by the mode of appointment or election."[1] Here we have the conception of the State belittled to an identity with its own officials, to prevent the individual, in an undue reliance upon it as a *deus ex machinâ*, from slackening his own exertions after success. Such an attitude towards the theory of the State is, how-ever, quite unnecessary. The body politic is one thing, and the government another; and the more distinct these ideas are kept in thought, the less likelihood there is of errors either in theory or practice.

It must then, in the meantime, be accepted as an axiom that the State, as the term is here employed, is something considerably more than the government, even when the latter is stretched to its widest extent so as to include the legislative,

[1] Goldwin Smith, *Questions of the Day*, p. 9.

executive, and judicial authorities of a country all taken together.

The significance of all that is embraced in the term will emerge more clearly in the sequel. As the inquiry proceeds, the full extent and variety of its contents will be more apparent. At present it need only be said in justification of this wide use of the word, that it is not at variance with the accepted usage of the English language, and does not run counter to ordinary popular conceptions ; while it is strictly in accord with the technical employment of the term in the department of legal speculation which treats of the relations of States to one another—the important science of International Law.

Thus the " State of Great Britain and Ireland " means something more than Parliament, the Cabinet, the Law Courts, and the Queen all taken together. It embraces the whole nation or nations, " Teutonic or Celt, or whatever we be," who inhabit the British Isles, to say nothing of the Colonies, along with the entire territory and possessions over which the Queen holds sway. It is a great organized community of millions of men with a common history behind them, a prestige and tradition " handed on from generation to generation," and a great future in front of them. To take another instance, the State of France is more than the present government, more indeed than any or every of the many governments and forms of national institutions it has had within the last century. It is a something which retains its identity though constitution after constitution is swept away, and remains one with itself whatever form it assumes of Monarchy, Republic, or Empire.

Even in the confused popular use of words, then, the State means something more than its rulers or its constitution. This conclusion is, as will be shown immediately, amply borne out by the accepted usage of the term in Public Law.

The extent and variety of the factors that together make up a State constitute only one reason why its definition must be a wide one. The same result follows from the fact that particular States differ from one another radically in their size and importance, in the degree of their internal cohesion, in the form of their constitutions, in the methods of their organization, and in the progress they have made from rude beginnings towards maturity.

The definition must be comprehensive, since the thing itself *grows*. It must include the embryo and the perfectly matured specimen along with all partially developed types at every possible stage of the intervening process. It must include all the species and varieties that have been differentiated within the genus.

It is difficult to frame one formula sufficiently precise for scientific purposes and yet wide enough to include all the forms at present in existence or known to history though now extinct. Without attempting an exhaustive list of these, the following classes of States may be enumerated: (*a*) The germs and undeveloped beginnings, or, at anyrate, the precursors of the State, existing in the family and tribe before any wider organizations of society have been formed;[1] (*b*) Asiatic despotic empires, such as the Persian or the Babylonian; (*c*) the Jewish theocratic state; (*d*) Athens, Sparta, and the other Greek city-states; (*e*) the Roman Republic; (*f*) The Holy Roman Empire; (*g*) the medieval feudal state; (*h*) simple "unitarian" modern states such as Belgium or Greece; (*i*) states like Great Britain, which include as integral portions subject empires such as India, and colonial dependencies with or without their own laws and institutions in every corner of the globe; and, lastly, (*j*) federal states such as Switzerland or the United States of America, where each member of the whole is, in a sense, an *imperium in imperio*, or rather a semi-independent polity within a larger polity.[2]

All of these are within the proper province of political science, and, therefore, none of them can be excluded from the definition which it adopts of the body politic.

[1] Cf. Prof. Huxley, *Natural and Political Rights*, reprinted in *Method and Results*, p. 352, where he speaks of "this most rudimentary of polities, *the family*."

[2] Sir J. R. Seeley gives a classification of the various types of State from a different but not inconsistent point of view in his *Introduction to Political Science*, p. 100.

It is convenient, however, to begin with the examples which are most familiar—the modern fully developed States —"the great powers" of modern diplomacy and the chief units dealt with by Public Law.

The conclusions of International Law, scrappy and incomplete as they often may be, are still the result of an honest induction from experience. An attempt is made to find the essential characteristics of a State as these are observed to exist from an analysis and comparison of the features common to all examples of actual States. This method of research has its dangers, it is true. It is apt to proceed on too narrow a basis of induction. It is prone, too, to be one-sided in neglecting such features in the composition of a State as have a less direct bearing on the limited class of phenomena of which it treats. It looks too exclusively to the external and material sides of a community, for these are, of course, the chief factors in the international relations of peace or war. But one great merit partly balances these defects. International Law escapes the dangers of a too abstract philosophy, with its proneness to trim its definition of such a term as "the State" into harmony with a general theory of the universe. The conclusions of International Law profess to cling closely to experience, whatever other faults they may have. It is well, therefore, to begin with the findings of this branch of law. The units of International Law include every community or society which is able to point to certain "necessary marks."[1] "The marks," says Professor Hall, "of an independent State are, that the community constituting it is permanently established for a political end, that it possesses a defined territory, and that it is independent of external control."[2]

Evidently "States," as defined by International Law, include whole communities with their territories, and are by no means confined to their constitutions and governments. The word would seem, then, to cover the whole of an organized and independent society, its territory, and every individual under its jurisdiction. If the idea thus obtained of a State in its international or external relations

[1] See Hall's *International Law*, p. 20. [2] *Ibid.*, p. 1.

be a true one, it is clear that it must be equally correct as applied to the same State in its internal affairs—in its relations with its own subjects. International Law and Constitutional Law are both branches of Public Law, and their results ought to be in harmony. For several reasons, however, the definitions used in the former are more reliable on this point than those of the latter. The former concerns itself exclusively with modern States, and so steers clear of the mists of antiquity, and avoids such historical theories as tend to involve the origin of States, with their laws and governments, in mystery. International Law, further, is not entangled in the disputes of party politics, and thus rises more easily above the influences of prejudice. In Constitutional Law, on the other hand, there is unfortunately much danger of definitions being contorted by zealous partizans on one side or the other to support some special theory of internal politics. As a matter of history, too, the struggles of the constitution take place not between the whole State and any part of it, but between the rulers and the subjects, or between one part of the government and another—between king and people or between Crown and Parliament. Thus the word "State" has rarely been called into use in historical literature in the same wider and more accurate sense in which it is used in the science that deals with international affairs. From all these causes Constitutional Law has thrown a less clear light on the distinction under discussion. The same difference exists, however, in that sphere as in the other. It is evident to the student of the growth of constitutions that the State is something greater than the mere governing authority. When William III. displaced James II. from the throne, the government for the time being fell, but the State of England remained as before.[1]

Public Law, then, lays down certain definite characteristics

---

[1] In Aristotle's *Politics*, III., 3, 9, a doctrine inconsistent with such an assertion is maintained: " It is evident that the sameness of the State consists chiefly in the sameness of the constitution." In Aristotle's day, however, neither International Law nor international politics in the modern sense existed. *Vide* Prof. Jowett's Introduction, p. 56.

as possessed by every State recognized as such by the other powers and by enlightened public opinion.

In enumerating these "marks" or characteristics, that greatest of authorities on political science, Bluntschli, bases his results on an exhaustive analysis of the features found in all known States. Those which are common to all he regards as *essential* to the conception of State in general.

His conclusions are summed up in seven propositions. Some of these will require a word of criticism, but it may be well first simply to repeat them in the order he has chosen, and under, as far as possible, his own forms of expression. The following are, then, in Bluntschli's view, the essentials of a "State":[1]

(1) A considerable number of men—more at least than a mere family.

(2) A permanent relation of the people to the soil—*i.e.* a definite territory.

(3) "The unity of the whole, the cohesion of the nation."

(4) "In all States we find the distinction between governors and governed."

(5) The State has an *organic nature* in being (*a*) a union of body and soul—of material elements and vital forces, (*b*) a whole with members, and (*c*) an existence which develops from within, and has an external growth.

(6) It has a moral and spiritual nature—a personality.

(7) "The State is masculine in form as opposed to the Church, which is feminine."

Uniting all these together he arrives at a final definition, that "the State is a combination or association of men, in the form of government and governed, on a definite territory, united together into a moral organized masculine personality," or more shortly, it is "the politically organized national person of a definite territory."

Now, while admitting the substantial accuracy of these definitions, there are several points that call for comment.

The first question, as to the minimum number of individuals who can form a State, is more of theoretic than practical importance. Even here there is room for dispute. Certainly

[1] *Theory of the State*, p. 15.

no one being, however great and however isolated from his
fellow-men, can ever form a State, but it is sometimes argued
that *two* human beings might together form "a State" if
thrown together on a desert island, or otherwise made
independent of all control by their fellow-men. This view
is becoming more widely received, and has been expressed
by writers of widely differing schools.   Mr. Wordsworth
Donisthorpe, one of the most prominent of modern individualists, has given it voice. "I will venture to say that
the very first State which ever existed was a human family,
consisting of a mother and her offspring. With all deference
to sociologists, the family is a State and the earliest form of
State."[1] The point, however, need not detain us here. Its
bearing is important on the theory of origin, but has no direct
connection with the nature of a well-developed State like
Great Britain or France at the present day.

The second of the marks mentioned by Bluntschli is a
settled territory. Every State whose existence is politically
recognized has a territory of some sort ; and, though the *logical*
necessity of this may be open to question, such abstract speculations may be meantime dismissed. The third and fourth
features may be taken together. They are really both aspects
of the same characteristic.

It is, of course, true that no State can exist without
cohesion and unity ; but this principle of fusion can only
be found in the subjection of all to one government or
constitution. It is just the difference between government
and governed which welds the society into a State, in forming
the basis of the voluntary or enforced acquiescence of the
individual in the sovereignty of the whole. The union of
Austria and Hungary, for example, into one State, so far as
it may be said to have been accomplished at all, consists in
their mutual dependence on a common government. For a
perfect cohesion in an ideal State much more is required,
but the common central authority making itself obeyed is
the one essential bond without which the actual State would
fly into fragments. Thus *the sovereignty of the whole* may

---

[1] *Individualism: A System of Politics*, p. 2. Compare also the passage
from Professor Huxley already cited.

be taken as the one great feature, implying both the third
and the fourth of Bluntschli's characteristics. This involves,
on the one hand, the unity of everything subject to its sway,
and, on the other hand, the existence of organized and
established machinery for making that sway effective—it
implies, that is to say, a government that rules and a governed
people that obeys.   Both requirements are covered by one
word—"organization."

So far Bluntschli's conclusions—under the modifications
already hinted at—are unimpeachable, and agree substantially
with the accepted results of Public Law; but, in discussing
the next three of his selected characteristics, he passes to more
dangerous ground. So far he has kept on the surface of
things, but when he goes on to assert that the State has
an organic nature of some sort, a statement is made which
many will refuse to accept. That this theory is not only
correct, but contains the germ of the whole truth of political
philosophy, is one of the chief objects of this essay to prove;
but, however true, it is not a conclusion which can be regarded
as a self-evident postulate bearing on its face an irrefutable
answer to all objections.

By thrusting the organic conception of society into his
definition of the State, Bluntschli strays from the world of
facts into that of theories, and so challenges criticism. The
danger of thus mixing theories with facts becomes more
apparent when he goes on to endow the State with certain
fanciful characteristics founded on an erroneous or inadequate
view of what the social organism means.

The organic and personal nature of the State is the root
idea of all Bluntschli's reasoning on political science; but,
instead of carrying it out exhaustively to its logical conclusion
in every possible direction, he is apt at times unconsciously
to caricature its application to social and political phenomena
by forcing analogies with these animal organisms of which
biology treats.[1] It is this tendency that leads him to add
a seventh characteristic—"the masculine character of the
modern state."[2]

---

[1] Cf. *Theory of the State*, Translator's Preface, p. 5.
[2] *Theory of the State*, p. 22.

Dismissing this seventh mark then as a fanciful analogy, we may complete the examination of Bluntschli by taking his fifth and sixth propositions together, noting that by them the State is made not only an organism, but a moral and spiritual organism—a person capable of thought and action, meriting praise or blame. " History," he says, " ascribes to the State a personality which, having spirit and body, possesses and manifests a will of its own."

These two characteristics are the only part of his definition not borne out by the authority of almost all practical writers on International Law. The others may be reduced to three simple features, viz.: a number of individuals or community, some extent of territory, and an effective sovereignty or established government or constitution. These three are included in the definition of Hall (already quoted [1]) under words very nearly the same, viz.: " a community or society," " a defined territory," and the fact that the whole " is permanently established for a political end." Hall, as we would expect from so practical a writer, makes no attempt to enter the arena of philosophic speculation by either affirming or denying the organic nature of the State; but he adds one characteristic, as important perhaps as any—" independence of external control." The secret of the strange omission of this important factor from Bluntschli's list is probably to be found in his theory that independence is an integral part of sovereignty.[2] However this may be, it is more convenient to emphasize so important a factor and to give it a place to itself. It is evident that for a State to take its place among the recognized nations of the world, it must be able to set at defiance the interference of foreign nations. Independence of the dictation of powers outside its territory is as essential to its existence as is its sovereignty to enforce its will within its own confines. Thus the necessary elements which go to form a fully matured modern State may be shortly given as (1) a group of individuals, (2) a specific territory, (3) an efficient organization giving effect to its sovereignty, and (4) independence. Each of these might be analyzed into two parts. The citizenship of

[1] *Supra*, p. 52.   [2] *Theory of the State*, p. 64.

each individual in the State implies a recognition by him of his obedience to its laws and his allegiance to its authority. The possession of the territory involves rights over it for all purposes of use and enjoyment. Independence implies recognition by foreign nations. Sovereignty may be likewise divided into two elements—power and the consciousness of power.

Some German theorists have attempted to create an absolute separation between society and the State. Now, while it is possible to separate the two in thought according to the aspect in which the same units composing both are viewed, it should be clearly understood that there can be no absolute separation in fact. No society can exist which is not a State or part of one, and every State is necessarily a society or group of societies. Gneist, in the opinion of Bluntschli,[1] "has done a service to political science by accentuating the difference between 'State' and 'society,' and calling attention to the friction between them." Now, the antithesis is only a relative one. The State, rightly understood, is nothing more than organized society, and, on the other hand, no society can exist without the organization which binds it into a State.[2] "Society," says Bluntschli,[3] in enforcing its contrast with the State, "is an unorganized mass of individuals"; but an utterly disorganized society can only exist in imagination. Even a mob must have some rudiments of order among its members. Society then, despite the high authority of Gneist and Bluntschli, is merely the State considered without special reference to its organization ; while the State, on the other hand, is society viewed with special reference to that feature.

To adopt an algebraic form of definition, the State is equal to society *plus* a constitution, a body of positive laws, and a regular government. In these three its system of

[1] *Theory of the State*, p. 104.

[2] Compare the Master of Balliol, commenting on Comte (*Comte's Social Philosophy*, p. 41): "There can be no society without a government, any more than there can be a government or effective power among men without society."

[3] *Theory of the State*, p. 103.

organization consists.[1]   Law, government, and constitution
are distinct, although there are points where they seem to
fuse imperceptibly into one another.

This conception of the State as organized society affords
some guidance to the determination of how far it is safe
to apply the term to independent groups of utter savages,
or of men whose civilization is of a primitive type.   The
want of proper organization of every sort is the chief
characteristic of barbarians.   Custom is the early substitute
for law—the idea of a constitution could not be understood by savages—while their government consists of the
application by each individual of such force as he can
command.

The boundaries of a State are fixed by the limits within
which its laws and institutions have sway; that is, it extends
as far as its organization has no rival system to interfere
with it.   Where there are only the undefined and unformu-
lated rudiments of an organization, these boundaries must
necessarily be extremely vague.   The most primitive State
is very narrow and its limits indeterminate.   It is merely a
family or tribe, whose "sphere of influence" cannot be laid
down with scientific precision.   In its full maturity, on the
other hand, the body politic is necessarily very distinct in
its boundaries.   It then becomes clear how far its jurisdiction extends and what individuals owe allegiance to it.   The
modern commonwealth is usually very wide both in extent
and content.

Whether in its simple or developed form the State may
be defined as a system of political organization, together with
all the men and all the material things which are subject
to its influence—the organization *plus* everything to which
its sovereignty extends.   There is no difficulty in applying
this definition to the great powers of Europe, because
everything is therein defined and accurate.   It is only in an
advanced stage of society, where law is understood and obeyed,
and where a government and constitution of some kind exist,
that the limits of the several systems become disentangled and
each State stands clear of its neighbours.   The powers of

[1] Cf. Professor Ritchie's *State Interference*, p. 23 (note).

modern Europe **arose from the break-up of the Roman** Empire, and gained **independence and distinct** individual existence as they gradually **shook off the influence of the Church** of Rome.

If all the nations of the globe formed a federal **or** a still closer union with one another, bringing the whole of humanity **under** the sway of one system **of law,** backed by an executive authority as efficient as that which enforces municipal law, political science would require **to stretch** its definition of **a** State so as to include the world with all its inhabitants, **and all** its continents and seas.

Each State is co-extensive with the **sphere** throughout which its will is **law** and its government **can** enforce obedience. All the individuals within this radius, with all their interests, pursuits, **and** possessions, are parts of **the** body politic. Various **ties unite these men** to one another **and to** their **governors.   These relations are** of many kinds—legal, **social,** political, ethical, economical, aesthetic, physical, and **hygienic.** The **State includes all these,** and therefore political **science can afford** to ignore none of **them.**   Auguste Comte has, according to Sheldon Amos, **the merit of** being the first to express clearly its full scope **and breadth.**   He taught "that political science was a composite study, and presupposed the complete apprehension of every branch of science, beginning with the physical, such as astronomy, **and** ending with the moral, such as **ethics** and sociology."[1]

The science **of** politics is thus composite because of the complex nature of its object.   It **is** necessary at the outset **to** guard against too narrow an interpretation of the elements **that are** involved.   "The State," to quote again from Amos, "**in** the modern acceptation of the term, carries with it the **ideas of** territorial limitation ; of population, past, present, **and to come; and of organization for** purposes of government."[2]

---

[1] *Science of Politics,* p. 52.

[2] *Ibid.,* p. 65.   **Compare the** well-known passage from Burke's *Reflections on the Revolution in France,* where he compares the State to a "partnership not only **between** those who are living, but btween those who are living, **those who are** dead, and those who are to be born."   Compare also William Cunningham's *Politics and Economics,* p. 119, as to

All this is expressed in the **simplest and** briefest formula possible in the definition **already** suggested—the State **is** an "independent organized **society.**" [1]

the right of **posterity to** be **included in the** conception of the commonwealth.

[1] An excellent definition of the State and a discussion of its leading **features** are contained in **Professor Henry** Sidgwick's *Elements of Politics* (p. 211). "I **shall** mean by **a** State what I **have** also called a Political **Society;** *i.e.* **a** body of human beings deriving its corporate unity from **the fact that** its members acknowledge permanent obedience to the same government, which represents **the** society in its collective capacity, and ought to **aim in** all its **actions at** the promotion of their **common** interests."

CHAPTER II.

THE ORIGIN AND NATURE OF THE STATE.

THE inquiry into the origin of the State is primarily one of speculative interest, though dangerous political tenets and policies have frequently been based upon the conclusions to which false theories have given rise. The simplest form of the question is, " Why or how does the State exist ? " Now this query, innocent as it looks, conceals an ambiguity. It asks at least two, perhaps four, distinct questions; and the theoretical answer given to one is often smuggled into practical politics as though it were an answer to the other. We must realize clearly in which of the four senses following we ask the question :

(1) What is the process through which any particular State—Great Britain, for example—has come into existence ? History must furnish a reply. The process which gives rise to any State—the record, for example, of the unification of Italy—is simply one branch of ordinary history.

(2) What is the process through which *the* State (that is to say, the institution of the State in general) has come into existence ? Here again we must look to history for an answer—to universal history proceeding upon a generalization from experience. The only difficulty involved lies in the impossibility of obtaining correct information of the prehistoric times in which *the* State took its origin. Aristotle derives it from the family and the tribe.

(3) The inquiry as to the origin of the State may, however, bear a third and entirely different meaning. What, it

may be meant, is the *justification* for the existence of any particular State? What right had Germany or Greece to come into being? What right has Turkey to continue to exist at all? This third question, while it must look to philosophy rather than to history for an answer, is yet a perfectly legitimate one; because the formation of special kingdoms or commonwealths, and the forms that their constitutions assume, are subject (partially at least) to human conscious control; and, therefore, motives come into play which may be condemned or approved.

(4) Lastly, it may be asked, What is the justification of the existence of *the* State? This, unless very carefully guarded from misconception, is not a legitimate question; for it involves an unproved assumption. It assumes that the State is a creation of man. The object of the inquiry, then, is to put the State on its trial and to determine if men did wisely in *making* an institution which they might have done very well without.

The utterly unfounded assumption is made that it is optional for men either to have or to want a State. Now, it is true that they may change the form of the government under which they live, or federate two or more communities into one, or emigrate from one body politic to another; but no individual can live except as a member of some State—of a society of some sort. It would be as absurd to ask for the justification of the existence of *the* individual as of *the* State. Both exist "by nature," just as the universe itself exists. The origin of both is an integral part of the mystery of the universe that has baffled the endeavours of uninspired finite reason to solve.

A particular individual, just like a particular State, comes into existence, and maintains his life in accordance with definite laws of nature; and he ought, perhaps, to be able to justify his own existence on ethical or other grounds. It is not unfair to ask the slothful or vicious man who lives on the labour of others and gives nothing in return to prove his right to exist; just as a corrupt State like Turkey, which abuses all its powers and acts as a standing menace to the peace of Europe, may be put upon its trial at the bar of public opinion. But it is a different thing to ask the reason why either *the* State or *the* individual exists. To ask a justification of the existence of individuals as a class would be treated as an idle metaphysical quibble, but the same inquiry as to States has frequently been taken seriously, and has led to grievous practical consequences. In the latter case, the assumption is made that the State came into being some-time subsequent to the creation or evolution of individual men, and by means of their conscious or unconscious action; and fallacious answers are then given either that the mutual fear of men led to a social compact, or that the strong hand established its authority over the weak by violence, and then justified its assumption of power as best it could.

The student of political science must eschew all such pre-liminary prejudgments. His only allowable assumption is that involved in the postulate (founded on experience) that "the State *is*," just as the botanist, for example, assumes that plant life exists without asking its origin or justification. He may then proceed to classify the various species, and trace the process of their development; or he may analyze them into their constituent factors, and explain the origin of particular States, though not of the State in general.

It is well, however, to glance at the various theories of the origin and nature of the State, if only to free ourselves from misconceptions involved in false theories that have obtained currency.

The problem may be stated very briefly. As a matter of experience, the individual man, willing or unwilling, must obey the laws imposed on him by the community to which he belongs; and, go where he will, he can never escape the necessity of being a member of some community. In a word, the individual is forced to obey the State. The problem is to find the ultimate reason for this obedience— the origin and nature (for the two go together) of the existing relation between the man and the State. As Professor Green puts the question, "What are the grounds of political obligation?"[1] If you explain the bond con-

---

[1] T. H. Green's *Works*, Vol. II.

necting individuals into one whole, you explain the very essence of the State. Two contradictory sets of answers have been given by theorists who are yet agreed in viewing a community as a mere aggregate of unconnected units. Starting from the unconscious assumption that these atoms were originally quite isolated, an attempt is made to explain the origin of the connecting links. One school finds the solution in the idea of a "social contract," the other in the principle of "authority," or force applied from above. The laws, and the State which enforces laws, are in both theories looked on as something thrust upon the mass of individuals from without. According to Hobbes, the individual man, in his isolated independence, is a product of nature; while the State is an article of human manufacture, alien to him and added as an afterthought. "By art," he says, "is created that great leviathan called a commonwealth, or State, in Latin *civitas*, which is but an artificial man, though of greater stature and strength than the natural, for whose protection and defence it was intended." Again, "the pacts and covenants by which the parts of this body politic were at first made, set together and united, resemble that *fiat*, or the *Let us make man*, pronounced by God in the creation."[1]

Thus it would seem that God made the individual and man made the State. The latter is then a sort of unnecessary addition tagged on by the invention of men to the work of providence. Its formation is due to pact or contract. How this idea of a "social compact," expressed or implied, influenced the course of philosophic thought for a century or more, is too well known to require to be dwelt on here. Even in the nineteenth century it unconsciously, and in a modified form, tinges the theories of those who would be the first to laugh at the crude attire in which its earliest adherents dressed it. That the State is based on contract is the basis of the theories of Locke, Rousseau, and Puffendorf, while even Kant[2] is influenced by it.

To quote only one example: "That which makes the community and brings men out of the low estate of nature

---

[1] *Leviathan* (Molesworth's edition, Vol. III.), Introduction, p. 9.
[2] Kant's *Principles of Politics*, p. 33, and again p. 46.

E

into one politic society, is the agreement to incorporate, and act as one body, and so be one distinct commonwealth."[1] The theory stated in this crude form has been refuted over and over again so thoroughly that it would be merely waste of time to criticise it further. It has been condemned after a searching criticism by writers of such different types as Hume, Burke, and Bentham, and more recently by Sir Henry Maine and other exponents of the historical method. Sir Frederick Pollock has stigmatized it as one of the most successful and "fatal of political impostures." It is more profitable, perhaps, to extract from it the residuum of truth it contains when properly sifted from its chaff. It is quite true that in an ideal State each man ought to have some influence upon the government—that he should have a voice equally with his fellow-men in passing laws and in moulding the constitution. If this were all that was meant by the theory, no one would object. But it is absurd to maintain that it is open to the individual to decide whether he shall submit to any law at all. This is the root error of the school of "contract"—to imagine that man is by nature free, and assumes the yoke of his own accord. Every man, on the contrary, who comes into the world is born into bondage in one form or another. The restraints which limit the free-play of the evil passions of the savage are different in kind, but perhaps greater in degree, than those that bind the subject of a civilized State. Man is born a member of a community that has a right to place some limits to the exuberance of his individuality, as surely as he is born into dependence on the control of the laws of nature and subject to the restraints imposed on him through the mere necessities of his animal existence. The individualist, in his extremest form, first makes an insoluble difficulty for himself by treating each man as an isolated unit, and then proceeds laboriously to bridge over the gulf which he has thus gratuitously made. Every man is by nature a member of a society. The "State" of the savage is a rude undeveloped one, but still is there in embryo; and its despotism is not likely to be less objectionable because it rests upon no organized basis. The forces

[1] Locke, *Treatise of Civil Government*, II., § 211.

that control civilized peoples are in essence the same—only focussed to a centre, and arranged in proper order by means of positive laws enforced by an established government. To maintain that all men *ought* to have a share in moulding the form of the constitution of a State is a logical and intelligible position ; but to hold that the individual atoms vote the State itself into existence as the result of a unanimous plebiscite is absurd. It is to ignore the great truth established for all time by Aristotle, that man is *by nature* a social and political animal, and therefore necessarily the member of some State, however crude.

As this school of philosophy chooses *contract* as the basis of society, its opponents select in manner equally arbitrary the idea of *force*. This theory, in its crudest form, has not come so prominently before the world, because it has lacked exponents as able as those whom its rival found in Locke and Rousseau. All constitutions and systems founded on the idea of *authority* are really modifications of the theory of force; and under this guise it has played an important enough *rôle* in the history of nations. "The divine right of kings," the great foundation of unconstitutional rule in the seventeenth century, in its blind dependence on the powers that be, was simply a deification of established power or force. The king, it is said, is actually seated on his throne and holds the reins of the executive government in his hands. He *has* power ; therefore that power is derived from God ; therefore he cannot be deprived of it. Many systems of authority have existed, but at bottom they are all based on the actual possession of effective force on the part of the rulers.

Bluntschli quotes, without citing its source, the following exposition of the theory of force in its crudest form : "The State is the work of violent domination, it is based on the right of the stronger." [1]

Spinoza is perhaps the greatest exponent of the theory that would base the State on force. In his *Tractatus Politici* he identifies power (*potentia*) with right (*jus*), and thence arrives at the result that the "right" of the community

---

[1] *Theory of the State*, p. 274.

against its individual members is only limited by its
"might." Sheer force would thus be at once the origin
and the justification of the State. This attempted solution
of the problem by the thing called *force* seems at first sight
diametrically opposed to the solution by the thing called
contract, involving voluntary *consent*; but a deeper insight
shows how much they have in common. Each stands on
an individualistic basis, isolates each man from his fellows,
and so makes the same wide and unwarrantable assumption.
Each theory next proceeds to explain how units thus separate
by nature have come to be bound so tightly together by art.
Each looks for an explanation of the bond to something
outside of man's essential nature; but while one fixes on
free and arbitrary contract as the principle of cohesion,
the other looks to the compulsion of an external force
or authority which keeps men together by sheer brute
strength, whether they will or no. The first line of argument carried to extremes would make it impossible for a
just State to impose any obligation whatever on an unwilling individual; the latter would justify any brutal and
arbitrary violence powerful enough to ensure its own success.
Force, indeed, like contract, has its place—and an important
place it is—in the fabric of the State. Indeed, in Bluntschli's
phrase: "Force shows itself more often in the formation of
States than contract."[1] It must never be forgotten that
force has always existed, and always will exist, and that
the progress of the world has not been towards eliminating
might altogether, but towards regulating and refining it. In
a highly civilized State force is indeed present, but it may
better be described as the force of righteousness than the
force of might. Neither contract nor force, however, can
afford a full explanation of the problem. The truth is, that
both schools of theorists make the solution impossible for
themselves by the common postulate with which they unconsciously start, in assuming that the individuality of man
is inconsistent with the solidarity of the race. It would
be not more false, though more palpably absurd, to begin
by assuming the existence of States without citizens, and

[1] *Theory of the State*, p. 274.

then go on to discuss how they afterwards became differentiated into individuals. The true solution is only to be found in a union of force and contract—of freedom and constraint—and in a recognition that the forces which surround and hinder and support each man are in truth a very part of his own nature—that the factors which make the individual make also the State.

The basis of the State, indeed, is neither contract nor force; but an element which is involved in both of these—Will. Contract itself is based on Will; for its essence is the free and intelligent consent of a personality come to maturity and subject to neither constraint nor fraud. Authority again, even such as was founded originally on brute force, depends on Will. It is the Will of the conqueror that has proved itself more efficient than that of the subject; and it is the Will of the latter that has preferred subjection to death on finding itself unable to shake the conqueror off. It is Will, then, that is the basis of the State. Arrived at this view, we have passed far beyond a merely individualistic standard; for it is the common will—the *volonté générale* of Rousseau, and not the mere sum of individual wills—that rules. It is the universal Will or practical reason, which is the same in all men while they are true to the principles of the rational nature that makes them men. Neither the social compact, whereby the governed hand over the whole or part of their natural rights to a sovereign, nor the successful force used by the ruler to coerce his subjects, can form a satisfactory theory of the binding force of law. Only in the universal Will acting on righteous moral principles can a sure foundation be found for it.[1] This principle of Will affords the stable foundation of the body politic that neither force nor contract can give. Force is a dangerous argument even for the tyrant,

---

[1] This theory of the rational Will or practical reason as the basis of the State is the doctrine of the German idealists, and Hegel is, perhaps, its best known and most systematic exponent. English students of politics of a practical turn of mind, who are not unnaturally repelled by the difficulty and uncouth diction of "the unreadable Germans," will find an easily understood and invaluable exposition of the doctrine in the 2nd volume of Professor Green's *Works*.

for the same reasoning that justifies his usurpation will justify also his overthrow by a successful rebellion. On the other hand, if the ruler holds his sceptre only because his people have consented, then the consent being withdrawn, the sceptre would go with it.

It is, however, as unnecessary to account for the origin of the State as for that of the individual man. Man is composed of elements derived partly from heredity and partly from environment, and each of these is part of society. The origin of the State and the origin of man, then, must be sought together, and the problem must wait for its answer till all science and all philosophy are complete. The primeval state, like the primeval man, is lawless and arbitrary. It is a chaos from which an ordered world will some day grow. The progress of the State and of the individual go on hand in hand. As man becomes more civilized, society becomes better ordered and developed; and the ideal State will be possible only when the subjects who compose it have reached perfection too.

The origin of the State, then, as a separate inquiry from the origin of man, need occupy us no longer. It has always existed since the world was inhabited by men endowed with reason. Its genesis is coeval with the genesis of human intelligence. "The germ of the State must, of course, be looked for and found in that phase of social development known as complete savagery,"[1] but this is merely the germ, and the full manifestation of the State as "an organic brotherhood of ·man" has never yet been attained.

The Greek City, the Roman Empire, and the modern European State have alike fallen short of this idea in different respects. The first of these failed by curtailing the initiative powers of its citizens and sacrificing individual freedom; the last, by emphasizing these elements unduly by the prominence given to competition; while the Romans never rose above a mechanical theory of the relations of the rulers to the people.

The works of Hegel contain many criticisms of the imperfections of both Greek and Roman ideals, and many suggestions for a more perfect State formed from the union of what was

[1] Wordsworth Donisthorpe, *Individualism*, p. 2.

best in both. **In his** conception the Greek State was "a unity of individuals who regarded themselves not as isolated **persons,** but simply as citizens whose life **was in** the State, and **who** had no personality apart **from it."** [1]

The high attainments **of Athens in every** art and pursuit were founded on the absorption of **the life** of every citizen **in the** life of the State. By this insufficient recognition of **the** individuality of its members, it fell below the organic **ideal.**

It would not be quite accurate to say **that Sparta** and Athens deliberately and consciously crushed **out the in-**dividuality of the citizens in order to aggrandize the common-wealth. It would be truer to say **that** the two conceptions were not yet properly differentiated from one another. The individual, in the modern sense, strange as it may sound, did not exist. **Only at a later date in the** history of specula-tion was he **disintegrated** from the State as the subject **of** specific rights. **He became a distinct** object of consciousness **as** a legal **entity through the labours** of the Roman jurists in applying the conclusions of the Stoic philosophy to the elucida-tion of jural relations. **The** elaboration of the **doctrine of the** *persona,* implying a legal *status* and a capacity for rights, **was** the chief work of the founders of the Civil Law; **and thus, for the** first time, the individual as such was given a **recognized** position within the commonwealth.

The shortcomings of **the Roman State were** different **altogether from those of the Greek cities, and** due to different **causes. In its** theories of administration there was necessarily **involved,** from the smallness **of the ruling** city and the vastness **of** the empire, a hard line of demarcation **between govern-ment** and governed, and thus the fulness of the organic unity was interfered with by **the intrusion of** purely mechanical factors. "Rome," **it** has **been** said, "turned **the** State from **an** organic unity **of** life, which took up into **itself** the whole **being** of its citizens, into a dead mechanism **of government,** externally applied to a powerless mass of sub-jects." [2] **In another** way, however, it gave, as we have seen,

[1] *Vide* the Master **of** Balliol's *Hegel,* p. **36.**
[2] *Ibid.,* p. 32.

more emphasis to the personality of the individual citizen, by developing an elaborate legal system defining his rights.

The modern State, while escaping some at least of the imperfections conspicuous in the ancient one, has dangers and weaknesses peculiarly its own. The chief among these has been the tendency to belittle the body politic in the mistaken hope of thereby glorifying the individual. Every philosophy that has had an appreciable direct influence on modern English politics has been framed on a purely individualistic basis. Not to speak of the way in which the theories of Locke and Rousseau have permeated society, the doctrines of utilitarians like Bentham and Mill, and the exertions of *laissez faire* politicians like Bright and Cobden, have all helped in this direction. These doctrines and these exertions alike have done good service in their day, and they have thus proved themselves to have a *relative* value when used for the redress of abuses. Consciousness of this relative truth unfortunately blinds men to the fact that, now that the pernicious restraints on liberty have been removed, the same principles that did good before may now do evil, if treated as an absolute and final truth and used to break up the wholesome restraints of society. Reformers must build up as well as pull down, turning their attention to the integration of the whole as well as to the enfranchisement of the parts. " The reconstruction of society, not the liberties of individuals, is now their most pressing task."[1]

The burning need, then, of the present day is not to render the individual independent of the State, nor to enable the latter to crush out his separate existence, nor even to balance one against the other like two antagonistic forces. The real problem is to combine both principles, and so to develop the State to its fullest perfection without annihilating individuality, and, at the same time, to make the most of the citizen without undermining the sovereignty of the whole. Each principle, rightly understood, is the complement of the other, and the two must be united into a perfect and harmonious structure.

To help on the realization of such a union in practical

[1] F. C. Montague's *Limits of Individual Liberty*, p. 16.

politics ought to be the aim of every statesman. To find
a speculative solution of the problem was one of the chief
objects of Hegel's philosophy. He tried to find a clue
to reconcile the sovereignty of the whole with the free
existence of every part—to emphasize fully the requirements
of both individual and State. To effect this he rejected
utterly the mechanical theories of the system of administration of Imperial Rome.

"Hegel's ideal," it has been well said, "is not that of a
machine moved by one string, which communicates motion
to all the rest of the endlessly complicated works, but of
a social organism in which life is continually streaming from
the centre to the extremities, and back again from there
to the centre."[1]

The democratic enthusiast may be pardoned for thinking
that this ideal will be best realized under a full system of
popular or representative government, where no arbitrary
line is drawn between the governing class and the governed;
where each man has his right recognized to bring all his
influence to bear in a legitimate way on the counsels of
the nation. The same enthusiast will do well to remember
that the individual is fit to have such high confidence
reposed in him in proportion only as he is able to lay
aside prejudice and self-interest, to absorb into his own
being the fulness of the national existence in all its variety
and vigour, and so to find his own interests and life again
in a nobler form by merging them in the life and interests
of the State.

[1] The Master of Balliol's *Hegel*, p. 85.

CHAPTER III.

THE END OF THE STATE.

THE theory that the State is an organic unity developing from a lower to a higher form, forced upon us by the investigation of its nature and origin, helps also to explain its final end or goal. If the very existence of mankind involves the presence of the State in some form, actual or potential, it is equally true that the ideal polity is that in which men can fully realize the perfection of their individual lives. The individual and the State include one another in every stage of their common development, and so have a common origin and a common destiny.

No theory of the State can be complete which does not make its aim sufficiently wide to include the perfect development of all its citizens in the highest, noblest, and fullest form of social, political, and individual life. This is no new truth. It is implied in the well-known saying of Aristotle, that "the State comes into existence, originating in the bare needs of life and continuing in existence for the sake of a good life."[1] Apart from the State, the mere physical existence of man as man is impossible; but this is its beginning, not its end. It must develop the life it originally makes possible. Its end is only reached with the perfecting of every individual's latent capacities, and this implies the perfecting of its own. The end, then, we are in search of must be a very wide one. It is nothing short of the highest welfare of the individual and of humanity.

[1] *Politics*, 1., 2, 8, Jowett's translation.

It is, in other words, to carry forward towards fulfilment the eternal purpose of the universe.

More than two centuries ago, John Locke emphatically wrote,[1] "the end of government is the good of mankind"; and only a few years ago Professor Huxley[2] declared this "the noblest and at the same time briefest statement of the purpose of government known to me."

Whether this is really the end of *government* will be discussed in a later chapter. Here it is merely maintained to be the end of *the State*. The necessity for so wide a definition will be apparent after a rapid survey of the various inadequate substitutes that have been proposed.

There are five different directions in which the end of the State's existence has been sought:[3] (1) As something outside and independent of both the commonwealth and its individual members. (2) In the good of a section of the community—of a privileged or ruling class. (3) In the good of all the members considered only as an aggregate of isolated units. (4) In the good of the whole as something entirely distinct from the welfare of the parts. (5) In the union of the two last-mentioned theories, where the State is both an end and a means.

(1) It is sometimes held that all States, with their various peoples, exist for certain purposes, natural or divine, in which their own realization has no share. In this view the State is merely a means for the furtherance of something foreign to it. It is the plaything or the tool of some outside power for the benefit of which it exists. This power may be, on the one hand, a blind impersonal process of evolution sweeping

---

[1] *Treatise of Civil Government*, II., § 229.

[2] *Method and Results*, p. 278 (" Administrative Nihilism "). It must, however, be remembered that this was merely an *obiter dictum*, as it were, of Locke. He has in the same treatise declared (§ 3) that "government has no other end than the preservation of property," and it is in the light of the latter definition that he has endeavoured consistently to develop his system.

[3] This chapter may be read in connection with book v. of Bluntschli's *Theory of the State* and with chapter IV. of Mackenzie's *Social Philosophy*, from each of which suggestions have been taken.

onwards on a course that man's exertions may modify or delay, but cannot essentially alter ; or it may be, on the other hand, the will of God, as that is sometimes conceived as something apart altogether from the nature of man. The first alternative is accepted by those who would explain the apparent evidences of a general or special providence, and also of man's free-will, as the resultants of the combination of various forms of material energy. The second alternative is the theocratic theory, that the end of the State is the realization of God's will on earth, on the basis that that will is something altogether external to the world it has created. The Jewish State was a direct embodiment of this last idea. It existed merely to support the Church. More or less extreme forms of the same theory have been frequently put forward in comparatively recent times among European nations. Thus in England in the seventeenth century, according to the late J. R. Green,[1] " under the Commonwealth the State was regarded primarily as an instrument for securing through its political and social influences the moral and religious ends of the Church." In this view the civil government would almost cease to have any ends of its own, and exist merely as an instrument to further those of the Church. All the highest objects of human attainment would be withdrawn from its control.

No theory of the State, however, can be adequate which makes it either the plaything of the blind forces of nature or the handmaid of the Church, without ends and aims of its own.

(2) It is needless to speculate whether any nation has actually been formed on the basis of a deliberate assertion that it existed for the sake of a privileged minority ; but there is no doubt that, whatever the theory, rulers, in the absence of practical constitutional checks, have always been prone to act as though this were the case. Aristotle's three corrupt forms of constitution are those that exist for the benefit of the governors, and his three good ones those that aim at the well-being of the whole. The opposite theory does not need special refutation, as it is not likely to be

[1] *Shorter History of the English People*, p. 588.

seriously advanced in the nineteenth century. The only difficulty is to prevent its being put into practice under the hypocritical cloak of some more respectable doctrine. Any deliberate expressions of this theory that exist are not meant to be taken seriously. Such is the saying attributed to Voltaire, that "the art of government is to make two-thirds of a nation pay all they possibly can pay for the benefit of the other third"; or the cynical *bon mot* of Colbert, that "the art of taxation consists in so plucking the goose as to procure the largest quantity of feathers with the least possible amount of hissing." Such opinions are more likely to be put in practice surreptitiously than to be avowed as the basis of a theory of administration.

(3) While the good of all classes and individuals is admitted to be necessarily implied in every adequate theory of government, it is possible to emphasize too much the separation between the units, and so treat the good of the parts as distinct from that of the whole. Lord Macaulay[1] enunciates what he calls "the great principle that societies and laws exist only for the purpose of increasing the sum of private happiness." In this view, the State has, properly speaking, no end at all. It is a means, not an end—an instrument for forwarding an aggregate of distinct ends, comprising all those of the various isolated individuals. Such a theory is the outcome of an exaggerated individualistic view of society; such, for example, as is expressed by John Stuart Mill[2] in the dictum, that "human beings in society have no properties but those which are derived from, and may be resolved into, the laws of nature of individual men."

(4) The opposite view has not been without its adherents—that the life of the State is the true end, and the individual's life, with its joys and sorrows, only a means. The nations of antiquity, looking on the State as an end in itself, unhesitatingly sacrificed the rights and interests of individuals for the good of the community. The expedient of ostracism, by which Athens cut adrift her foremost citizens on grounds of unproved suspicion, seems unwarranted and unjust to modern

[1] "Essay on Machiavelli," *Essays*, Vol. I., p. 47.
[2] Mill's *System of Logic*, 2nd edition, II., p. 543.

minds.   Undue emphasis was evidently placed on the whole, and the life of each citizen counted for next to nothing.

(5) These two last-mentioned theories must be combined. The State is both a means and an end, and the same is true of the individuals. Equal emphasis must be laid on both factors. The highest end of the one must also be the highest end of the other. "The best life" is the same both for the State and the individual.[1] Some form of the organic idea is the only philosophic foundation for such a reconciliation of these two theories.

The conclusion thus arrived at, that the good of the society and that of its citizens are one and the same, while it affords a valuable clue, by no means closes the discussion. The whole of philosophy is an attempt to find the *summum bonum*, or "man's chief end," and for every theory of ethics we may expect a counterpart in political science. To examine all these in detail is impossible, and a bare enumeration of those that have most directly influenced the subject under discussion is all that can be attempted.

Of these the following are the chief: (1) Order; (2) progress; (3) constitutional forms by themselves, for example the maintenance of democracy, or aristocracy, or monarchy; (4) liberty; (5) equality; (6) fraternity; (7) a combination of two or more of these ends; (8) happiness; (9) abstract justice; (10) "utility."

(1) The maintenance of security or order is often postulated as the sole end of government. It is possible, however, to take a broader or a narrower view of what is implied in "security," according as we define the objects to be secured. Thus, according to Locke,[2] "the great and chief end of men's uniting into commonwealths and putting themselves under government is the preservation of their property." Von Humboldt[3] lays down the principle, "that the maintenance of security, as well with regard to the attacks of foreign armies as to the danger of internal discord, constitutes

[1] Cf. Aristotle's *Politics*, VII., 1, 13.
[2] *Treatise of Civil Government*, II., § 124.
[3] *Sphere and Duties of Government*, English translation, p. 53.

the true end of the State, and must especially occupy it actively."

This conception is found in the minds of those who approach the subject from very different sides. It is the watchword of many a politician of strong conservative instincts, who sees in the retention of the *status quo*, if not perfection, at least the best to be hoped for in an imperfect world. It is consistent alike with an optimistic belief in the present and a pessimistic dread of the future. An opposite school of politicians comes very near the same conclusion, from the other side, in holding that social welfare is to be best furthered by the government simply standing aside and allowing individual energies free play. The State is asked to preserve order and to leave the rest alone. The latter phase of the opinion is dependent to some extent on the confusion between the ideas of "State" and "government." The former phase is inconsistent with the healthy life of a community at all. To stand still is impossible. To continue to develop is the only means of resisting decay. Cease to grow and decay will immediately set in. Progress is the law of life. The bare maintenance of order, then, is too narrow a goal to absorb the whole energy of the State.

(2) John Stuart Mill saw this, and made *progress* the great end of government and State; and progress, in his view, included the maintenance of order as a necessary factor. "The requisites of progress," he tells us,[1] "are but the requisites of order in a greater degree." "Conduciveness to progress thus understood includes the whole excellence of a government." This aim, however, is by no means wide enough. Even order and progress together do not suffice. We must know to what we are to move. To say "progress" is to indicate a race to be run, but to say nothing of the direction or the goal.

(3) A number of other defective theories arise from a confusion of thought between means and end. Practical

---

[1] *Vide Representative Government*, p. 24. It would be interesting to test how far the abstract idea of "progress," upon which Mill's *Representative Government* is based (*vide* pp. 30-33), could be reconciled with the doctrines of the *Essay on Liberty*, where the abstract idea of "freedom" is accepted as the only criterion.

politicians often speak as if the form of a constitution was
an end in itself, instead of a "means to an end." Thus, to
hold democracy as the ultimate perfection of the State is as
misleading as to hold out monarchy as such.   It may be true
that the national welfare is best gained by democracy, or by
monarchy, or by what is called a "mixed constitution"; but
that does not make any of these things in itself the ultimate
end to be striven for.

(4) The idea of the individual *liberty* of each man, considered as an isolated and self-sufficing being, is sometimes
set up as an absolute end.   This thought underlies every
page of J. S. Mill's well-known *Essay on Liberty*.   It finds
expression in a somewhat different form in the dictum borrowed from Kant by Mr. Spencer, that "it is the duty and
eventual tendency of society to allow the widest liberty to
each of its component individual members compatible with the
equal liberty of all."   The same idea is to be found in the
mind of a writer of so widely different a school of thought as
Professor Hearn of Melbourne,[1] who says, "The unimpeded
exercise of all the faculties of each individual is the true end
of government."   Now liberty and individuality, however
good things in themselves, must not be exaggerated into the
sole ends of humanity.   We may not be prepared to go as
far as the late Mr. Justice Stephen and maintain,[2] "To me
the question whether liberty is a good or a bad thing appears
as irrational as the question, whether fire is a good or a bad
thing.   It is both good and bad according to time, place, and
circumstance."   We may not be prepared to deny that liberty
is an end in itself at all, while we repudiate its claim to
be the sole end of the national life.

(5) As "liberty" is sometimes made the sole end of the
State's existence by individualists, "equality" is often elevated
into that position by socialists.   In subsequent chapters an
attempt is made to determine in what sense equality is
attainable, and how far efforts in that direction are expedient
or equitable.   It is hardly necessary to prove that although

[1] *Government of England*, p. 571.

[2] *Liberty, Equality, Fraternity*, p. 48.

it may be *one* of the ends of government, it is not the only one, or that to which all others are subordinate.

(6) "Fraternity" is too vague a term to influence practical politics in any definite direction. It points, however, to another aspect of the social ideal, in which society is to be like one great family, where all the "brothers" are regulated by the constant interference of a paternal government.

(7) An attempt is sometimes made to combine two or more of these ideas in formulating a supreme political aim. The phrase "Liberty, Equality, and Fraternity" has played an important *rôle* in its day, and has been sufficiently disposed of by Sir James F. Stephen. The ideas of liberty and order have sometimes been bracketed together in a somewhat similar manner. "The ideal of a State," it has been said, "is reached in proportion to the individual liberty attained, and the order which is maintained in the commonwealth of a free people."[1] By combining two conceptions a resultant is sometimes reached containing more than a mere aggregate of its constituents; but, making all allowances, such conclusions are too narrow to exhaust the problem.

(8) None of these theories, perhaps, has formed a nucleus for so much speculation, or has had so great an influence on the aims and methods of legislation as that which postulates happiness as the ultimate end of all well-spent efforts. A separate volume would be required either to examine the arguments that are urged for and against it or to trace the history of its practical results. Indeed, whether right or wrong in theory, there are few ideas that have done better service in the cause of humanity than "the greatest happiness of the greatest number." There can be no doubt that the influence of this idea on English legislation has been both extensive and beneficial. It afforded an object for legislative effort easily understood and apparently definite. When carried to extremes, however, it becomes a theory fruitful of more evil than good. Beneath the surface, its apparent definiteness disappears, and it is found both deceptive and inadequate. The greatest happiness of the greatest number as a practical

---

[1] *Vide* George Howell's "Liberty for Labour" (published in a *Plea for Liberty*), p. 110.

F

goal for a community to aim at has been criticised, and indeed pulverized, so often that it would be useless to do more than recapitulate its imperfections very briefly here. Its first fault is its individualistic assumption. It separates society into its constituent atoms, and looks to the sum of the enjoyments of each separate man instead of the welfare of the whole. Then it fails to see the impossibility of judging what constitutes the happiness of different men, and the absurdity of balancing the feelings of one against those of another, as so many tons of feathers may be weighed against so many pounds of gold. It further would justify the infliction of terrible suffering on one individual (however arbitrarily and unjustly imposed) if outweighed by the sum of the pleasurable sensations enjoyed by the rest of the community. Its individualistic bias and its impracticability, however, are not its only faults; for happiness itself is a misleading term, and not synonymous with "welfare." It is one ingredient in the national prosperity, but not the whole. Pleasure is not synonymous either with the individual welfare or the public weal. It is only a test or symptom of well-being, and not the only one. It is not a value, but only "a sense of value."[1] It is merely a sensation that leads to the inference (which is often a mistaken one after all) that all is well with the subject experiencing the pleasure.

(9) The dispensation of abstract justice is sometimes spoken of as the sole legitimate aim for which the State exists. Its claims may be dismissed on two grounds—that it is at once too narrow and too inexact. Apart from the consideration that justice must be tempered with mercy, no conception of the duties of government can be adequate which leaves out of account the feelings and pleasures of the governed. Again, this criterion of abstract righteousness will come too late to be of practical benefit, if we wait till mankind is agreed as to wherein justice consists, and how it may be applied to the actual cases that arise.

(10) The idea of "utility" may be dismissed in a word—to maintain that utility is the only end of the State is to

---

[1] *Vide* Mackenzie's *Social Philosophy*, pp. 202-227, where an admirable and detailed refutation is given of Hedonism.

assert that it must be useful for some purpose without giving
the least indication of what that purpose is. It is merely
to hold that the State must have an end of some sort without
giving the slightest clue where that end is to be sought. The
utilitarian theory, properly so called, never gets beyond the
conception of "means," from which it starts. Everything good
must be of use, but the great question is, "What use?" Is
all legislation to be useful for maintaining order, for dispensing
justice, for establishing a democracy, for making an equal
distribution of property, or for advancing the happiness of
individuals? It is usually with the last of these ideas that
utilitarianism is associated. The theory—meaningless by
itself—acquires some content from its alliance with another
idea less empty than itself.

Every theory thus breaks down if it makes the end sought
narrower than the highest welfare of the whole group of
citizens as inseparable members "one of another," and as
an integral part of the wider fraternity of mankind as a
whole. The good of humanity is the end of the State, and
this must include *all* the elements already enumerated in
their due sequence and proportion—order, progress, liberty, and
the rest. Two of these deserve somewhat further consideration,
since by expanding and combining them a wider end may be
arrived at indistinguishable from the "good" we are in search of.
"Abstract justice" by itself is a conception too empty of content to afford the criterion we need. "The happiness of the
citizens" fails on the other side, because it is void of form
and indeterminate. By combining the two, a concrete whole
is formed fit to answer our purpose. "Right" is the principle
of Kant, "Happiness" that of Bentham and his followers.
Each school has laid hold of one half of the truth.

The complete elaboration of this thought would involve
too comprehensive an inquiry. A whole philosophy indeed
seems to lie in it. A word or two of explanation may not
be out of place. "The welfare of the State as its own highest
good," says Kant,[1] "signifies that condition in which the
greatest harmony is attained between its constitution and
the principles of right—a condition of the State which reason

[1] *Philosophy of Law* (Professor Hastie's translation), p. 173.

by a categorical imperative makes it obligatory upon us to strive after." It is difficult to express in a few words what this principle of right is, but it may be practically identified with an abstract justice which forbids that any one human being should have his liberty interfered with in any way, except in so far as this is necessary to secure an equal freedom to all his fellows. "Right, therefore," he says,[1] "comprehends the whole of the conditions under which the voluntary actions of any one person can be harmonized in reality with the voluntary actions of every other person, according to a universal law of freedom." The welfare of the State would therefore come to mean simply, that every individual should be let alone as much as possible. It would be easy to show that this negative idea of social welfare is already implied in the essentially individualistic basis from which Kant starts. It is more important for our present purpose to notice that it takes the form of an absolutely empty universal—absolutely void of content. As one pure universal is identical with every other, Kant easily deduces from his principle of a negative abstract "right," first an equally negative and abstract "freedom," and then an "equality" of the same meaningless kind. It is only by confusing these negative conceptions with the concrete positive things bearing the same names that he gets anywhere at all. Otherwise he would remain for ever in a vacuum encircled by the abstract universals from which he started.

Kant, then, begins by declaring that "a State (*civitas*) is the union of a number of men under juridical laws,"[2] and reduces its functions to the dispensation of justice according to the somewhat attenuated formula already quoted. The body politic would thus represent an embodiment of a sort of negative version of the golden rule—"Do *not* unto others what you would *not* have others do unto you." In the language of modern politics, its only duty would be to enforce a universal regime of *laissez faire*. The State, in Kant's opinion, must confine itself to its own business—the promulgation and enforcement of laws on a basis of right—and

[1] *Philosophy of Law* (Professor Hastie's translation), p. 45.
[2] *Ibid.*, p. 165.

leave individuals free to pursue their own business—the
attainment of happiness or virtue, each after the rule of his
own being. The English utilitarians take exactly the opposite
view, holding that the direct end of legislation is the happiness
of the citizens. The criterion of good laws to the Benthamites
is not right as an abstract universal, but the sum of millions
of particulars involved in the happiness of all men, "each
counting for one and no person for more than one." The
defects of such a criterion (or rather of such an infinite sum
of criteria) have already been in part exposed.

This theory has been subjected to a trenchant criticism, and
its opposition to the doctrine of "right" has been well brought
out by Professor Hastie in his preface to the translation of
Kant's *Principles of Politics*.[1] The whole passage is well
worth quoting :

"The traditional political doctrine, that conventional utilitarianism, which has been the natural child of individual
selfishness and the step-mother of socialistic discontent, is no
longer capable of satisfying the growing political needs, or
of solving the more drastic political problems of the time.
As a political theory its formula of 'the greatest happiness
of the greatest number' furnishes neither a rational doctrine of
government, nor a principle of equal right, nor a criterion
of just administration. At the best, happiness is a particular
and variable element in individuals, which cannot be secured
in a universally satisfying degree by any form of public
legislation, or by any political wet-nursing of majorities ; and
the utmost that a government can really do for the people
is to enable every individual to realize his liberty and to
seek his happiness in his own way through the actualization
of his own rights."

While rejecting with Professor Hastie the Hedonistic
principle as a complete solution of the problem, it is not
necessary to acquiesce in the adequacy of the rival formula
of Kant. The doctrine of right and the doctrine of happiness
are alike incomplete as an explanation of the supreme good
of humanity. The two must be combined. How a union
is possible between them cannot be here discussed, but it

[1] P. 37.

is confidently asserted that such a combination actually exists. It is a union of a universal with a mass of particulars, of form with matter, of a principle of abstract right with the infinitely varied pleasures and interests of individuals. Thus a concrete whole is formed, and constitutes the *summum bonum*—the mark at which all laws and governments should aim—the purpose for which the State exists. This is not abstract but concrete right—not the happiness of isolated units, but the welfare of humanity as an organic whole. The conceptions of right and happiness thus understood are not irreconcilably opposed, but the necessary counterparts of each other. The conflicting claims of individuals in the struggle for enjoyment and existence can only be reconciled by the universal laws of right or justice ; and these laws must manifest themselves in relation to the happiness of the citizens. The citizens, it must be remembered, are rational beings endowed with a knowledge of good and evil, and capable of acting upon moral and immoral motives. Finally, these individuals, and the societies and states they compose, are all undergoing a process of development. Thus, the conception of the good as a union of what is right and what is useful for the welfare of men implies also the idea of progress. The final end of the State thus conceived is no empty abstraction, but something tangible and capable of approximate realization. It is not limited to one factor in human life, such as the production of wealth, or the distribution of justice, or the enforcement of contracts, or the protection of property. It includes everything that makes the citizens of the State men and their life worth the living.

The end of the State is thus seen to be the present welfare and future perfection of all the citizens considered as an integral portion of humanity. This great truth is admitted in principle by many writers who yet refuse to carry out in detail the results logically involved in it. Passages may be cited from authors of all schools in support of it. Even individualists are found among its zealous advocates. Thus, Mr. Wordsworth Donisthorpe, perhaps the most profound, certainly the most bright and suggestive, among the modern adherents of individualism, in trying to find a more definite and correct test of actions than that given by Bentham, writes as follows of the ultimate criterion of good government: "What, then, is the test of which we are in search? To any one who has grasped the conception of the group as an organism—as a whole not to be expressed in terms of its component parts, any more than a man can be expressed in terms of the cells of which he is composed—the answer is clear enough: the welfare of the group."[1] Here we have, under the name of the "group-welfare," the same idea as is expressed in the phrase, "the perfection of the whole community"; and if, as we must, we consider the community again as an organic part of humanity, we reach the same conclusion as is contained in the criterion proposed by the late Professor Lorimer, "the realization of the idea of humanity."[2] Professor F. S. Hoffman expresses this conception with great power and distinctness. After describing the State "as an organism, as a brotherhood of man," he proceeds as follows: "The chief and ultimate end of the State, to which all other ends must be subordinate, is evidently the perfection of the brotherhood, the bringing of man here upon the earth to the highest degree of civilization of which he is capable. . . . The other ends of the State may properly be regarded as the means for the attainment of this ultimate end."[3]

There is one way of expressing this truth which, though supported by the great name of Bluntschli, seems open to objection. This may be called the purely nationalist theory. In Bluntschli's own words, the true end of the State is "the development of the national capacities, the perfecting of the national life, and finally its completion."[4] He goes on to add as a proviso or after-thought words which really involve an absolute departure from the exclusive principle of nationality which they are used to qualify, "provided of course that the process of moral and political development shall not be opposed to the destiny of humanity."[5] On another page he says: "The life task of every individual is to develop his capacities and to manifest his essence. So,

[1] *Individualism*, p. 276. [2] *Institutes, passim.*
[3] *The Sphere of the State*, p. 16.
[4] *Theory of the State*, p. 300. [5] *Ibid.*, p. 301.

too, the duty of the State-person is to develop the latent powers of the nation, and to manifest its capabilities." Now, this theory of individual development—maintained in this country with his usual vehemence by Carlyle—if carried to excess would produce two evil tendencies—selfishness and eccentricity. It is not the duty of each man to bring to maturity all the traits of natural depravity or bearishness of manners he may have latent in him. Similarly, in every nation there are traits of nationality that are best suppressed, such, for example, as the insular prejudices inherent in most Englishmen, and the intense jealousy and liability to periodic attacks of ungovernable fury of the French. If national tendencies, which are truly rational, require development, those that are selfish and depraved often need suppression. The idea of nationality is defective if carried too far, and Bluntschli's rider contains, perhaps, a safer principle than his main proposition.

The end of the State ought to be the development of the group, not so much as a selfish and self-sufficing nation, with all the narrowness and prejudice of merely national aims, but rather as a branch of the wider whole of humanity—a part "of the brotherhood of man." It can, of course, best fulfil the purpose of its being by moving in the line of its natural characteristics; but this is not the whole truth. A great people must not be selfish as a nation, but be ready to interfere on behalf of humanity even at the sacrifice of its more immediate exclusive interests. There would seem, then, to be no objection to making the full development of the national "self" the ultimate end of the State's existence, *provided* that a true, full, and sufficiently noble conception is formed of what that self includes. The truth must be clearly grasped, that in its nature are included intimate relations both to the other States and to its own individual subjects. The national "self" is an organic member of the wider whole of humanity, and is itself the smaller organism of which each citizen is part. In this view, "self-realization" may be taken as comprising the whole duty of a State, just as it is that of an individual. In moving towards this goal it is fulfilling its destiny. It is the rational and not the animal or material self, **however,** that must be so developed. Thus understood, the highest well-being of the community and **its** self-realization are seen to be only different names **for** the same thing.[1]

It is not difficult to trace the intimate connection between **the** principle **here** enunciated as the end of **the State** and the account previously given of its origin. The **good** of the community must be determined with reference **to** the nature of the individuals who compose it as beings endowed with reason **and** power of will. **On the** other hand, **that** will which, acting partly consciously and partly unconsciously, is the foundation of all societies, is bound by the necessities **of its** nature as practical reason to aim at realizing itself in such a form as will most conduce to the common good.

It may be urged that the ideal here sketched is too vague and indefinite to afford any practical rule of guidance. The criticism **is just,** as far as it **goes.** But it is set up not so much **for a** practical end **to** be consciously aimed at as for a philosophic solution of a problem. The **statesman and** legislator will find **in** their own commonsense and **that of** the community, which they partly lead and **partly** follow, **a far** safer guide than any speculations of philosophers. The theoretical value of " self-realization " as **an ultimate end lies** in its very breadth. The welfare of **the** nation **as** a developing organism forms an ultimate aim wide enough **to** include within it all those minor and **subordinate** aims of which it is composed. It includes the material prosperity of the nation as well as its intellectual interests; the bodily health, and happiness, and wealth of its individuals **as well** as their education and moral worth. The practical statesman must confine himself to practical ends. He will sometimes have one of these in view and sometimes another. He should never press any one of them,

---

[1] **Cf.** Prof. Ritchie's *Natural Rights,* p. **89** : " The conception of evolution, or, more **precisely,** the theory of natural selection, has at once corrected the errors **and** vindicated the truth of utilitarian ethics and politics. That **is 'good'** for any particular society which furthers **its success in the** struggle for existence with nature and **with other societies; that** is 'evil' which hinders such success."

however, so far as to interfere with the unity of the whole, as seen in the light of that one final aim which it is the duty of philosophy to emphasize and explain. This is the welfare of the nation as a natural unity and as part of the greater unity of humanity, including the highest development of the humblest individual.

In truth, the very vagueness of the definition of the end suggested is its greatest merit.[1] The highest philosophy must be concrete, not abstract. It can accept as final no conclusion which is emptied of all content except one abstract and unreal entity, such as "progress," or "justice," or "equality," meaningless except in its relations to other entities. The problem is not to fix upon one competing end among many, but rather to find one which includes all the others as subordinate and auxiliary.

It is always dangerous to attempt in this world of change to lay down a simple definite formula professing to be good for all times and countries. It may be that the true end of the State is only slowly and partially disclosed as the gradual evolution of the universe reveals the ultimate destiny of mankind. The ideas that men have of the ideal State develop as does the State itself. What satisfies one age may fail to meet the requirements of the next. If self-realization is taken as the general formula of progress and the goal of all social and political aims, room is left for future readjustment in accordance with any new light that may be thrown upon the true nature of that self which is to be so realized. Meantime, a sufficiently definite criterion is obtained as a partial clue to a permanent solution. It is well at least to occupy the ground that would otherwise be cumbered with inadequate conceptions exerting a hurtful influence.

The righteous community is under the imperative necessity of endeavouring to fulfil the end here indicated. Some writers would deny the very name of State to any polity which did

---

[1] Cf. Prof. Ritchie's *Natural Rights*, p. 98: "Professor Sidgwick complains that writers, such as Bluntschli, to whom he specially refers, give no definite conception of the 'good of the State' beyond what a utilitarian can give. But how if the end of human life, individual and social, does not admit of a *definite* conception?"

not consciously **or** unconsciously tend **to** realize the common good. Thus, in **the** words of Professor Green:[1] "**We** only count Russia a State by a sort of courtesy on the supposition that the power **of** the Czar, though subject to no constitutional **control,** is so **far** exercised **in** accordance with a recognized tradition of **what** the public **good** requires **as to be on the** whole a **sustainer** of rights." **It is** better, however, to incorporate as few theories as possible in our definitions, and to say that the *righteous* State must aim at realizing the common good, without denying **the** title State to any community the policy of whose government **does not directly** tend in that direction.

[1] **T.** H. Green's "Principles of Political **Obligation,"** *Works,* ii., p. 443.

CHAPTER IV.

THE SPHERE OF THE STATE.

IF the purpose for which the State exists is no less than the perfecting of the whole community, it follows that nothing can be excluded from its proper sphere which advances it towards that goal. Thus, by implication, the description of the sphere of the State is contained in the definition of its nature and end. Its province is necessarily a very wide one. If the life of the members is only another aspect of the life of the whole, no factor that enters into the composition of the one can fall outside the other.

The same conclusion flows logically from that conception of sovereignty which is involved in the efficient organization of every proper State.

As everything within the territory of a State is subject to its control, it follows that its proper sphere is co-extensive with the range of its dominions. Its province of action includes the sphere of every individual citizen, and this gives it wide powers and wide responsibilities.

It is impossible, then, to place any limit to the sphere of the State within its own dominions. Wherever its will prevails, that is its normal sphere. This view—though the only one consistent either with the doctrine of sovereignty or with the philosophical theory of organic unity—will probably be regarded as extreme by theorists who fail to bear in mind the distinction between government and State. Even those writers, however, who have fully appreciated this distinction, have shrunk from extending the theoretical sphere of the

State to so extreme a length, and have sought to fence off, more or less absolutely, certain sanctuaries from its interference. It may be instructive to examine a few of these attempts.

The chief exemptions claimed from the jurisdiction or sphere of the State may be reduced under four heads: (1) the sphere of the individual; (2) family relations and domestic life; (3) ecclesiastical institutions and the religious life of the citizens; (4) morality, and indeed all relations of whatever sort other than those of an exclusively legal nature.

(1) It is a favourite device to separate the sphere of the individual from the sphere of the State. Under the name of the "Rights of Man" (a doctrine more fully examined in a later chapter) it is held that each rational creature has certain inherent, inalienable, and absolute rights which no society or authority can in any way infringe. This theory assumes that the nature of each man is something essentially apart from that of society as a whole. When the artificial barrier thus created is broken down, there falls with it the possibility of carving out of the wide sphere filled by the State a number of smaller spheres from which its influence is excluded. There exists in reality no hard and fast line between the two. Waves of the same life pass from one to the other. The sphere of the State includes the spheres of all its members.

(2) Failure equally awaits any attempt to exclude the sphere of the family from that of the State. It is thought proper—in all societies except those of an extreme socialistic type—that the law should refrain in certain ways from interference with the domestic relations of its members, leaving the internal administration of each home to be regulated, as far as possible, by itself. But the law will interfere within even this sacred precinct in all States to prevent and punish crime, in most to regulate the succession to property, and in some to enforce the education of the children; while the State's abstention from interference in other matters is not a confession of its inability or want of right to act if so disposed. The sphere of the family is one part of the sphere of the State.

(3) The attempt to exclude religion is illustrated by the old medieval conception of the relations between the See of Rome and the Holy Roman Empire. It was held that the world might be split as by the stroke of a knife into two compartments—the spiritual and temporal—over which Pope and Emperor should respectively rule. The course of history, with its constant internecine warfare between Guelphs and Ghibellines, is sufficient of itself to prove the fallacy on which this division rested. Philosophy gives an equally clear denial to the possibility of any such absolute dualism.[1]   Man is a spirit whose religious aspirations are bound up intimately with his temporal necessities. His personality develops through his rights, and these again are dependent on material circumstances, such as the possession of property. Who can say where his spiritual nature ends and his temporal nature begins? His attitude towards the State is determined even more by his higher than his lower necessities, and the same is true of its attitude to him. Mr. Justice Stephen, in this connection, has well said: " The whole management and direction of human life depends upon the question whether or not there is a God and a further state of human existence." [2]   The sphere of the State includes the sphere of the Church and all the spiritual, as well as the temporal, needs of the citizens.

(4) It may still be asked whether the State's proper sphere includes morality. It is sometimes said that it does not, but several reasons show that it is impossible for the legislative and administrative authorities utterly to banish all moral considerations from their ken. In the first place, each State must act among other States, and is forced to deal with matters involving questions of morality whether it like it or no. It may, at its peril, consistently ignore the ethical aspects of what it does, or boldly declare its defiance of them, but this refusal to see the light does not evade penal responsibility or avoid the consequences of a violated moral law. In the second place,

---

[1] Cf. Sir J. F. Stephen's *Liberty, Equality, Fraternity*, chapter iii., for an exhaustive analysis of the distinction.

[2] *Ibid.*, p. 319.

it is composed of individual men endowed with will-power
and a rational nature. Thus it is impossible to disavow its
responsibilities as a moral agent, nor can it remain in organic
relation to its members without partaking of the essential
factor that makes them capable of citizenship. It is by his
knowledge of right and wrong that man is distinguished from
the brute creation, and the commonwealth as a union of men
cannot ignore this basis on which it rests. So far, however,
from endeavouring to escape their ethical responsibilities,
most highly civilized States are, as a matter of experience,
recognizing and acting upon them more consistently every
year. Dr. H. D. Traill, speaking of the tendencies that are
actually observed to guide the action of the central government
of Great Britain,[1] says: "We appear in all our legislation to
be more and more unreservedly accepting the principle that
the physical well-being and the mental and moral training
of the community are matters within the special care of
the State." The sphere of the State, it would thus seem, is
an essentially moral sphere.

To this doctrine is directly opposed one which asserts the
exclusively *legal* character of the State. The genesis of the
theory of the "legal State" is associated with the name of
Kant. It owed its origin to a desire to limit the meddlesome
action of existing governments. Kant's definition of the State
as "the union of a number of men under juridical law" has
been already quoted.[2] Kant excludes from the sphere of the
State all bonds but such as are juridical. The body politic
is allowed its own province—a somewhat narrow one—and
each citizen has *his* independent province. The sphere of
influence of each is exclusive of that of the other. The
State would thus be reduced to an equality with the sum
of the strictly legal relations that bind the citizens together,
while individuals would be left free to work out their own
moral natures without let or hindrance. The State's sphere,
it is maintained, is that of law, while each individual regulates
his own morality. The State is thus identified with its own
laws, as previously we found it identified with its government.[3]

[1] Traill, *Central Government,* p. 160.
[2] *Supra*, p. 84.   [3] *Supra*, p. 47.

Now, while it is true that the individual ought not to have his moral spontaneity crushed out and his conscience intentionally violated by the government, this does not imply that his moral nature can possibly find a sphere for its realization outside of the nation. Morality lies without the constitution but within the State. This exclusively legal sphere, so far as it is realizable at all, is to be found in the constitution which is only one part of the State. The constitution, however, is a mere logical abstraction depending for its actuality upon its vital connection with the reality called the State, and its citizens with their moral and spiritual energies. Thus the constitution is dependent on the moral worth of the men who supply its vital force. Institutions are dead without the living force of character to move them. Constitutional forms of liberty exist in vain without their counterpart in men trained to turn them to account. Parliamentary forms existed under the Tudors quite uselessly, until backed by the real power which came with the moral force of the Puritans and their religion. The State of England is a greater and more complicated thing than the mere mass of laws and rules which form its constitution.

The whole fabric of the State, indeed, rests on moral considerations. All laws depend upon enforcement. Legal rights are useless unless practically enforceable in a court of law. Thus the pivot of the individual's rights, which are secured to him by the most legal of States, depends upon the integrity of the judges. This uprightness is the hinge upon which the whole constitution really hangs, and this rests in turn upon the moral sense of the whole community.

Every community, and particularly every democracy, depends for its stability upon the education and moral training of the body of the people. If these fall behind, the nation will become corrupt and rotten. Thus, if it is the business of the State to preserve itself from dissolution, the supervision of the morals and intelligence of its people lies, undoubtedly, within its normal sphere. It may, of course, resolve that the best service it can do to morality is simply to secure that the government should let it alone; but even that is a different thing from ignoring it as a factor in the national life, and, therefore, a part of the legitimate sphere of the State.

The argument for the exclusion of morality has perhaps never been more powerfully formulated than in the words of Bluntschli.[1] "The two powers which determine and condition the moral life, viz. the Spirit of God and the spirit of the individual man, are both outside the control of the State. The domain of morality is far more comprehensive than the domain of politics, and if the State attempts its control it oversteps its proper limits, and exerts a harmful influence upon morality."

Now, in the first place, the opening portion of the quotation is not consistent with its close. Morality, if entirely free from the control of the State, can hardly be influenced by such control either for evil or for good. In the second place, the independence of the spirit of the individual man is inconsistent with Bluntschli's own theory of the organic nature of the State as a moral and spiritual personality. In the third place, every State which takes any interest in the training of its youth must attempt some control over their moral nature. Lastly, try as hard as it may to leave individuals alone, the community cannot fail to have a powerful influence on the moral development of every member. It is impossible for it to leave morality alone, even if it wished.

In spite of all its defects, however, the theory of the strictly "legal State" has taken root in many places. This is due partly to the influence of Kant, and partly to the school of political economists who sought a basis for their free-trade doctrines in the general principle of *laissez faire*.

In this respect, however, there is a marked difference between the practice of modern States and the prevalent theories.[2] Governments are every day more fully accepting their moral responsibilities both to their own subjects and to foreign nations. The "legal State" may figure prominently in the schools, but it is the "moral State" which takes its place among the great powers of the world.

While this restricted view of the State's sphere has never

---

[1] *Theory of the State*, p. 299.
[2] Cf. Professor A. C. Bradley, *Hellenica*, p. 201.

G

been consistently applied in practice, signs are not wanting that its influence is on the wane even as a speculative tenet.

"I hold the principle of *laissez faire*," says Mr. Goschen,[1] "to have lost favour, chiefly owing to moral considerations, to the assertion of the claims of other than material interests, and to a growing feeling that it is right deliberately to risk commercial and industrial advantages for the sake of reforming social abuses, and securing social benefits."

"There is no serious thinker at the present day," says Sheldon Amos,[2] "who, if pointedly questioned, would deny the applicability of the terms Right, Wrong, Duty, Conscience, Morality, and Immorality to the conduct of States and governments as well as to that of individual men and women."

Lastly, there may be cited the opinion of Hegel, who has not only corrected the one-sided theory of the legal State, but has gone to an extreme in an opposite direction by emphasizing the moral nature of the State as its chief feature. "The Idea," he says,[3] "is the inner spring of action; the State is the actually existing, realized moral life. For it is the unity of the universal essential Will with that of the individual; and this is 'Morality.' The individual living in this unity has a moral life—possesses a value that consists in this substantiality alone." These words contain a refutation of two false doctrines—the individualistic nature of man and the exclusively legal nature of the State.

The State, indeed, is nothing if not moral. This does not, of course, imply that the State should directly inculcate moral codes or precepts by thrusting the opinions of the rulers or of a majority of the citizens upon the rest. Its control ought to be only indirect. In a sense, the spirit of man *is* independent of the State—he can die rather than obey coercion—but it is the community generally which affords him a sphere of development, and furnishes him with the particular nourishment that his spirit needs. Thus there is no part of the life of man that can claim to lie outside of the sphere of the State. To prevent the possibility of

---

[1] Address on "*Laissez faire* and State Interference."
[2] *Science of Politics*, p. 447.
[3] *Philosophy of History* (Sibree's translation), p. 40.

misconception it is well here to repeat that this does not imply that no part of his life lies outside of the legitimate sphere of the interference of executive officials. The subject under discussion is after all only a theoretical one. The practical question will have to be fully treated in connection with the functions of government. If the State is not the same as the government, it follows that the two spheres do not necessarily coincide. At present no opinion of any kind is expressed as to how far the work of the government should extend; the object at present being to insist on a sufficiently wide conception of the nature of the State. All ignoble notions must be abandoned of " the State shrunken into a Police Office straitened to get its pay,"[1] as they form a quite inadequate basis of any satisfactory science of politics.

[1] The phrase is Carlyle's, *Sartor Resartus*, p. 161.

CHAPTER V.

THE CONSTITUTION OF THE STATE.

THE conception of the State as an unity embracing every individual citizen, with every branch of his spiritual, moral, scientific, artistic, and economic spheres of action, is a very wide one; and it may be urged that it is of such a nature as to furnish a perfectly unworkable foundation for any conclusions of practical utility.

Indeed, as so defined, the State is something rather for philosophers to discuss than for lawyers to explain or politicians to quarrel about. The composition of every State, however, must include solid as well as fluid elements. If it embraces embraces also a stable system of laws and a constitution. all the fluctuations of public opinion within its sphere, it Modern States are so vast, both in the extent of territory they cover and in the range of interests they embrace, that their existence is rendered possible only through a most complex organization under a recognized system of rules or laws. The more highly developed forms of animal organism require a proper system of organs, a series of nerves and muscles, and a skeleton. It is the same with highly developed States. They require a skeleton to keep the various members together. That skeleton is called a constitution. Much confusion of thought has resulted from the failure clearly to differentiate the State from that part of it called its constitution. Indeed, much of the argument in favour of a purely legal State is based on a confusion between the two. The constitution is a legal entity—a thing whose whole existence is defined and limited by law—by the positive law of the particular country. * The State includes this legal entity along with much more; for example, the whole province of ethics. It is the duty of the expert in public law to expound the rules that go to make up the constitution, and in doing so to avoid entangling himself in ethical discussions. The whole field is one that a lawyer may explain without going beyond his own proper sphere; but it is different with the State which includes a thousand elements as well as law.

" It is only by a constitution," says Hegel,[1] "that the *abstraction*—the State—attains life and reality." Now, it is true that no independent community could exist without a constitution of some sort; but to phrase it as Hegel does is to place the emphasis on the wrong factor.[2] The State is the complete reality, and the constitution, the abstraction. The State is a living thing, but the constitution is merely one aspect of it, and incapable of separation except in thought. It is useful to make the distinction as a relative one for the purpose of analysis, but it must always be remembered that the idea of a constitution is merely an abstraction becoming real through union with the vital forces of the commonwealth.

The constitution, then, is a rounded whole or sphere within the wider sphere of the State. Yet it is not self-sufficing or complete in itself. It can never assert an independence of its own. Within it, indeed, everything is theoretically complete and regulated by law. Its legal nature is its very essence, and it forms the centre of the judicial system of the nation. Its whole being is wrapt up in law. It is like a point in which all laws are brought to a focus. Everything works within it by legal deduction. In a complete constitution everything is provided for. The relations between the general body of law and every part of it are therein

---

[1] *Philosophy of History*, p. 45.

[2] It must be remembered, however, that "abstract" is to Hegel an essentially relative term. He regards any conception as abstract when it is used without explicit reference to the rest of the universe as a whole, or to any part of it, however insignificant.

expressed. The whole law of the country, whether of the nature of private law or public law, depends upon it; while it in turn depends upon that law. The constitution, then, is the concentrated essence of the legal system of a nation. It defines the judicial rights and duties of each part of the government to every other part and to the subjects governed. It determines who is to make the law, to enforce the law, and to interpret the law. It defines the bounds of the power of kings and lawgivers and judges. It cannot be said to have attained to theoretic completeness until it has obviated every possibility of ambiguity in any such matter.

While in theory the constitution may thus be made absolutely complete within itself, this is accomplished only by abstracting it from its surroundings. In practice, this small world of law is dependent on the great forces of life that rage around it. From these it draws its vitality, and it may be invaded and overthrown by violence from without. The law-ordered universe rests on rude forces which it cannot always chain. At any moment these may break through the forms of the law, and violently alter the structure of the constitution. Any such forcible invasion of the sphere of law constitutes a revolution. When the reign of positive law is thus disturbed by the eruption of other forces from without, the State is not overthrown with the constitution: it survives all changes of form. Revolution takes place within the State without overthrowing the political sovereignty of the general will, although its particular manifestation in the legal sovereign is annihilated. To rebel against the State is a different thing from rebelling against the constitution. Only the habitual criminal is a rebel against the former.

"No men or body of men," says Professor Hoffman,[1] "can ever have the right of revolution against the State. . . . But the people may easily have the right of revolution against the government."

Every change of the constitution is not necessarily a revolution, for there may be provided within itself perfectly legal methods for its own alteration. England is not a dead unprogressive country like China. Its constitution provides

[1] Hoffman, Sphere of the State, p. 24.

a lawful method **whereby** it can change itself. Indeed, it is
a terribly simple process. An ordinary Act of Parliament
will suffice. But this is the only legal method possible.
Any other mode **is** unlawful, and involves an invasion of
the rounded **legal** sphere called the constitution by forces
of an alien **nature.** Even apart from actual revolution, however, the **legal** constitution of a country **can never** be independent of the other factors in the State. **There is** always
the fear of revolution which influences the use made of the
powers confided to individuals, though they **still act** in a
perfectly legal way. Thus every element in the **national**
life has a bearing more or less direct upon the constitution.
It is girt about with various lawless powers that act upon it.
The world of law is exposed to raging oceans that may **break**
down the dykes and overwhelm it—waves of throbbing
human passion that are never still. The blind rage of an
angry mob, a victorious army at a general's command, a band
of mercenaries hired by the treason of those in power, the
hand of the **assassin, or the bomb of** the dynamitard; all
or any **of these, or the mere fear of** them, may subject the
constitution to the influence **of forces** outside the realm of
law. Thus its legal framework is bound up inseparably with
the whole sum of the forces which form the nation.

We must not therefore make *absolute* the division between
constitutional and other forces. Yet the process by which
these legal forces separated themselves from **the** surrounding
disorder and made themselves obeyed, forms the whole history
of England. This **process** took centuries to bring itself to
completion, and even its outline cannot **here** be sketched.
A group of constitutional rules and usages, however, gradually
formed **themselves** around the strong **central** authority of the
king, and still more gradually reduced **every** part of the
life of the State beneath the sway **of one** universal **all-**
pervading law—the last principle **conquered** being that very
authority of the kings from **which the** reign **of** law originally
took its rise. Thus the constitution gradually formed itself
into a rounded **sphere, much as the** world is **sometimes**
pictured to have formed **itself out** of chaos. The nation
took centuries of growth before **it** organized itself into a

fully-matured **State, and that organization upon its** purely
legal **side is** just another word **for its** constitution, which
is thus the skeleton or backbone **of the** nation.   **Sir** Wm.
Anson has described it as "the working machinery of the
State."[1]   It is rather the series of rules defining what that
machinery shall be.   The government does the work—*it* is
the active agent, while the constitution lays down the rules
for its regulation.   Thus, while **on one** hand the constitution
is the source and essence of all law **in** the State, on **the
other** hand it **is** in an especial **sense the body** of laws that
regulate the government.

The relations between the constitution and the govern-
ment are intricate and interesting. **The one represents
theory—the** other practice. The former **is** therefore above
the latter **in so** far as it lays down the **law** which the
government cannot break ; but beneath it practically, because
(in Great Britain at least) one part of the government—the
legislature—can change the law and the constitution.   While
the constitution has its end as well as its beginning within
the sphere of law, the executive government must take **its**
place in the world of action, and has to assume some attitude
towards every element in the life of the nation.

If then the "legal State" has any existence in reality at
all, it is only when used as a synonym for "constitution,"
and is thus only one phase or aspect of the real State which
embraces the whole nation, with its people and institutions,
its spiritual **needs** and material possessions, as well as its
legal **machinery** or skeleton.

[1] *Law and Custom of the Constitution*, Vol. I., p. 2.

CHAPTER VI.

THE GOVERNMENT AND OTHER AGENTS OF THE STATE.

THE first requisite of cohesion in any group of individuals is some central and directing agency. If a community has common aims and interests, some mutual representative must have power to look after them. This central authority or agent in a State is called the government, and must have somewhere within it the supreme legal power in the community for the time being. If no one were authorized to act for the nation, concord and unity of aim would be impossible. Any class or locality might claim to act for the whole. There would be no principle of cohesion. The body politic would fly asunder and resolve itself into its constituent elements. A strong guiding hand is needed to keep the whole together. Adherence to a common government is thus an indispensable factor in the existence of a State. It is important then to understand exactly what this government is. We have already seen that it is often confused with the State itself. Even when this fatal confusion of thought is surmounted, another difficulty remains. Two restricted connotations of the word are common in every-day conversation, and are both inaccurate. In the first place there are such phrases as "a change of government"; "Her Majesty's government"; "the Queen reigns but does not govern," all pointing clearly to administrative or executive functions. Then we find such statements as the following: "England is governed by Queen, Lords, and Commons." Here "the government" is used synonymously with the legislature or the "Queen in Parliament." In neither case is the use of the term absolutely incorrect; but yet it is in both instances incomplete and misleading. Throughout this essay the word is used in its widest meaning to include both of its phases, and to cover in addition the judicial functions of the higher courts of law.

"Government" then (unless a qualifying adjective is joined to it) is here used to include all the branches of the central organization—legislative, executive, and judicial.

The central government, thus understood, is the active political principle of cohesion in the State. Subjection to it, or allegiance to its head, marks the right to the claim of citizenship. Every man or thing not subject to its control is "alien."

This government is, or contains as an integral part of itself, the chief official recognized agent of the State. All negotiations conducted with foreign nations proceed through its agency. When a criminal rebels against the laws it is the government that acts as the agent of the nation in avenging its outraged majesty. Again, the government is the arm of the community in all important national affairs. If the laws binding on the whole community must be changed, it is the central government that acts through its legislative organ. Lastly, the government through the civil and criminal courts interprets the law, and applies its provisions to individual cases.

Although the State appoints these various organs of its central government to act as its chief official agents, it is not thereby precluded from nominating other agents—even other official agents. The latter must be more or less under the control of the government or of some part of it, else the seat of the legal sovereignty would be taken from the central authority. Thus the army and navy are agencies of the State, and may involve their principal in serious responsibilities. In Great Britain these are placed under the immediate control of the War Office and the Admiralty; while the ultimate responsibility is shared with the Cabinet collectively. In like manner established church or churches in a nation are undeniably State agencies. Again, all universities empowered to grant degrees, **all of** Her Majesty's inspectors of schools or of factories, **and** all royal commissions, are national institutions and recognized agents of the State, though they cannot be called parts of the central **government**. Nor **is this all**, for every **town or county** council to which **Parliament** has delegated rights of **taxation** and local control, however limited to circumscribed areas, is still a recognized agent of the nation in the exercise of those powers which the laws have given it. **Every** justice of the peace or notary public acts for the State in **every** official function he performs. Every policeman and custom-house officer, every government employee, every **doctor,** druggist, or dentist who is "licensed" **to** practise under regulations sanctioned by **the** legislature,—all these are agents of **the State.** [1] Indeed, every private individual in his most intimate act is an agent, though an unrecognized one, of the nation. The body politic is an organic existence, and **therefore whatever is** done by one member is done by **the** whole. **If it wishes to** free **itself from all** responsibility for **the acts of a subject, it must either cut** him adrift by making **him** an alien or an outlaw, **or** else prevent him from performing the acts complained **of.** Thus each member of a community is an **agent** in some measure of the commonwealth, and the consequences of his act **must** be borne by the whole of which he **is a** part. This may seem an extreme doctrine, but it **is** amply supported by facts; and the actual rules and usage of International Law have given it authoritative recognition. One well-known instance will prove this. On 29th **July,** 1862, the "Alabama" left Liverpool wholly unarmed. **At** Terceira she received guns and ammunition which had been previously brought from England in two separate ships. When these were safely on board she became a fully equipped man-of-war,

---

[1] *E.g.* any doctor giving a certificate in terms of the Lunacy **Act, 1890, if** acting *bona fide* and with reasonable care is, under section **330, free from** responsibility The **load thus** lifted from his **shoulders must be borne** by his principal, **the State, whose** will authorized **the provisions of** the statute that shield him.

and as such inflicted damage upon merchant ships sailing
under the flag of the United States of America. The recognized authorities of Great Britain had no knowledge of the
matter. The "Alabama" was not built, nor were her guns and
ammunition manufactured or supplied, by the government,
which had indeed no knowledge that anything of the kind
was in contemplation. It was entirely the work of private
individuals having no official connection with the nation or
authority to involve the community in responsibility for their
actions. Yet the Tribunal of Arbitration at Geneva found
the State of Great Britain liable for the whole damage that
had been caused. This is, of course, an extreme example
of the principle that a State is liable for every act committed within its jurisdiction which it has failed to prevent
being performed. It may be modified by future decisions;
but the general doctrine that neutral States are liable for
every act performed by private individuals within their
boundaries in breach of neutrality is not likely to be changed.
The whole doctrine is a striking illustration of the position
here maintained that every individual subject is to some
extent an agent of the State, however much that State disapproves and disclaims his misdeeds.

The State, then, must accept responsibility for every
influence at work within it which it does not suppress. The
official expression of its opinions comes from legislative
enactments, from the decrees of its judges, and from the
mouths of its recognized diplomatic representatives. The
civil and criminal law of the land, and the lines of foreign
and domestic policy pursued by the Ministry of the day
are the chief organs of the country, but it is also responsible,
though in a diminishing degree, for the views expressed by
either House of Parliament, for the sentiments of the press,
for the resolutions of public meetings, and even for the
stray words of private citizens, all of which go to make up
the great whole called public opinion.

CHAPTER VII.

NATURE AND OBJECTS OF GOVERNMENT.

IF the government is the chief agent or servant of the State, its *raison d'être* is easily deducible. It exists solely to fulfil as well as possible whatever duties are entrusted to it by its principal—the State. The doctrine that governments exist for the good of the governed—or rather of the whole community, including both rulers and ruled—is as old as Aristotle, who based upon it his famous classification of the various forms of constitution. Monarchy, aristocracy, and polity are, according to him, the three normal or beneficent types, because they look to the good of the whole; while the three contrasted forms of tyranny, oligarchy, and extreme democracy are respectively their perversions, because they seek exclusively the good of the rulers. Governments are now held to exist "for the public good," and not for that of the persons in power, and the chief end of all administrative action would seem to be, simply to forward the ends of the State, according to instructions received.

It is sometimes said that the sole object of the government is to make the State possible. Now this is indeed one object though not that ultimate end to which all others are subservient. It is true, of course, that no State could exist as such without a central government to hold it together against all disintegrating tendencies. To make the State possible is, however, rather the beginning than the final goal of government. Such an achievement is perhaps its lowest use, rather than its highest—its minimum of attainment, not its maximum. It remains to be asked whether it ought not to broaden out its aims as the State itself expands, and go on to make perfect what it has first made possible, or at least, so arrange things that the individual members may attain perfection for themselves.

This question is for the State itself to decide; but, however limited may be the powers entrusted to a government, and however restricted by tacit understanding, or express enactment, may be the ends for which these powers are to be employed, these must include the duty of enforcing such law and order as are necessary for the continued existence of the whole. The commonwealth cannot refrain from endowing the government with powers for the task of preserving the existence of the State; because to bestow less would be to vote its own annihilation. Organized communities *always*, either directly or indirectly, authorize their rulers as a minimum of business to make their continued existence possible, however little additional authority they may be disposed to bestow.

In any case it is for the will of the society to decide the extent and nature of all authority exercised over its members. This will must be expressed by means of the constitutional machinery prescribed by the laws of each State. When we have satisfied ourselves that the end of the government is just to do what it is told to do, we have not exhausted the inquiry. We have still to ask what instructions that master ought to give. This question again divides itself chiefly into two. What extent of authority ought the legislature to have ? and what ought the executive to have ? The general answer seems to flow from the fact that the State exists for the perfecting of its "brotherhood of man," and ought therefore to entrust to its rulers whatever extent of power seems most likely to further that end. The wisdom of the community may conclude that its highest interests will be served by making its rulers absolute despots, and then leaving them with an unobstructed hand to do what they choose in the interest of all. If, on the other hand, the community judges that it will prosper best by restricting the powers of its rulers within the narrowest bounds consistent with its continued existence, then it should make its government a mere machine for preserving order. It is all a question of expediency. "Granted," a community should say, "that our final goal is so and so, we have to determine how far government can help us to get there, and how far it can hinder. Let us extend or limit its functions accordingly."

It is simply a matter of judgment in which each nation must think for itself, and about which many different conclusions may be reached—about which, indeed, perfect wisdom would reach different conclusions concerning even the same State at different stages of its development. On this point no philosopher need thrust his views upon the world. Thus when Mr. Herbert Spencer insists that the restraining of wrong-doers is the only just object of government, he is passing from the sphere of the philosopher to that of the statesman. It is for the latter to determine how far the welfare of the State can, consistently with the present state of society, be furthered by extending or limiting the objects entrusted to the care of government. No abstract theorist ought to attempt to dictate one course of conduct as suitable for every possible situation and emergency.

While the end of the *State* would be held by a religious man to depend on the will of God, and by a scientific man on the laws of nature; the end of *government*, both would agree, is a thing dependent on the will of man. The question, how far the will and conscious efforts of men can mould the constitution, has received much attention from speculative writers. The same inquiry may be expressed in several forms. It may be asked, for example, whether the constitution is a product or a growth; whether it is natural or artificial; or how far men can alter it at pleasure.

There is a danger that such discussions may end in mere verbalism, and, indeed, in one sense the distinction is entirely meaningless. Man himself is a product of nature, and therefore whatever is made by man is made by nature. Yet there is another sense in which the question is not only a legitimate one but has an important and direct bearing upon practical politics. Everything in the world is indeed "natural" as being subject to physical, economical, and social laws ; yet all objects fall into two clearly differentiated classes, to one of which "artificial" as opposed to natural may be appropriately applied.

A mountain, a tree, or the fruits of the earth, all fall within the latter; while a house, a railway, or the clothes a man wears are familiar instances of the former.   The labour of man may, indeed, play a certain subordinate part in the production of some of the fruits of the earth, while no process of manufacture is entirely independent of the forces of nature. Nevertheless a clear distinction exists, one class being on the whole the product of nature, and the other of the conscious action of man.   In this light the question of the naturalness or artificiality of the State and its government acquires a new and real significance.   It may be quite legitimate to ask, Do these entities belong to the former or the latter class ? Does the constitution of England, for example, participate more in the nature of a house that has been built, or in that of a cave hollowed by the action of the waves ?   It may well be said that it belongs exclusively to neither class ; but it cannot be maintained any longer that the saying, when thus expressed, is meaningless or absurd.   John Stuart Mill in a well-known and often-quoted passage has fairly stated the points at issue, though his answer is somewhat one-sided and unsatisfactory. He explains the two conflicting theories under their most extreme aspects as follows :

(*a*) Forms of government are "regarded as wholly an affair of invention and contrivance.   Being made by man it is assumed that man has the choice either to make them or not, and how and on what pattern they shall be made. Government, according to this conception, is a problem to be worked like any other question of business.   The first step is to define the purposes which governments are required to promote. The next is to inquire what form of government is best fitted to fulfil these purposes."[1] This theory makes government a machine.   (*b*) "To these stand opposed another kind of political reasoners who are so far from assimilating a form of government to a machine that they regard it as

[1] *Representative Government*, p. 3.

a spontaneous product, and the science of government as a branch (so to speak) of natural history. According to them, forms of government are not a matter of choice. We must take them in the main as we find them. Governments cannot be constructed by premeditated design. They 'are not made but grow.' The fundamental political institutions of a people are considered by this school as a sort of organic growth from the *nature* and life of the people."

Both doctrines, according to Mill, are equally absurd when pushed to these extremes; yet he ends by virtually siding with the former almost without qualification. Within certain limits, he concludes, "institutions and forms of government *are* a matter of choice." He thus gives the full weight of his authority to the first theory (though not absolutely in its most crude form) that constitutions are rather artificial products than natural growths—more like machines than trees.

In an often quoted passage he ridicules the thought that political institutions "resemble trees, which, once planted, are 'aye growing,' while men 'are sleeping.' In every stage of their existence they are made what they are by human voluntary agency."[1]

This is, of course, true; but is it not possible that this "human voluntary agency" is itself included in the whole which grows? The commonwealth is, in some respects, like "a tree," but yet each of its members has free-will and an independent rational existence of its own. The idea of "growth," if applied to society, must be modified in much the same way as was seen to be necessary in applying the organic idea itself.

It is true that to declare that the government has nothing of the nature of a "growth" about it, does not absolutely contradict the organic theory of society. It might quite well be that while the State was itself an organism, its agent, the government, was merely a machine, having no intimate connection with the life of the community. Thus it is not absolutely necessary for the vindication of the organic theory, to refute the doctrine maintained in the *Essay on*

[1] *Representative Government*, p. 4.

H

Representative Government.   Still, there undoubtedly is a connection between the two, and it is not difficult to show that Mill's position is based on a misconception.   When he asserts that our national institutions are rather machines that can be easily adjusted at pleasure, than growths rooted in the national life, he is influenced in forming this opinion chiefly by his wish to remove the possibility of a spirit of fatalism in politics that would make men content to shelter themselves from the trouble of remedying existing evils under the mistaken idea that these were due to the action of laws of nature, over which men have no control.   There are few who will not share to the full with Mill the desire to free men's minds from so degrading and so benumbing a superstition.   Free-will, and not fatalism, is the rule of guidance in all modern politics outside of Turkey.   In denying strenuously that the constitution is an organism, Mill is simply desirous of asserting that it is more or less amenable to the action of men directed towards altering its form nearer to an ideal perfection.   It is not only quite possible, however, but absolutely necessary, to maintain this very truth in conjunction with the organic theory of the State's existence, and Mill's hostility to the latter theory proceeds chiefly from a misconception.   Its supporters have no desire (as Mill assumes that they have, in his statement of the views he supposes them to hold) to narrow down the organic nature of the State, so as to *exclude* man's free-will and conscious action from its range.   On the contrary, the true view incorporates the individual men with all their thoughts and actions, and the objects of their endeavours in the organism called the State.   To make the constitution, then, a necessary part of the life of a people, by no means withdraws it from the influence of that people's actions.   On the contrary, it is only to show more clearly how intimate, subtle, and innumerable are the ways in which the individual, through every channel of his daily life, influences, consciously and unconsciously, the forms under which he is ruled.

The organic theory is thus the best friend, so far from being the enemy of Mill's contention, that by conscious effort men can mould their institutions to keep pace with their changing needs. In comparing national institutions to machinery he makes two mistakes. In the first place, he creates an absolute distinction between governors and governed, which does not hold in modern States, or in such of them, at any rate, as are under popular institutions. The government is not a machine coercing from without. Great Britain appoints its own real rulers, or acquiesces, at least, in their right to rule. In the action of the government the people recognize the expression of their own will through the legitimate channels they have themselves authorized. It is not a machine which rules them, but bone of their bone and flesh of their flesh. In the second place, whether a machine or no, it is a factor without which no society can exist. In a rude state of nature men may have very little government, and that of a shifty, arbitrary, and bad quality; but some rudiments must always exist. It is thus wrong to speak of all government as the product of human energy consciously shaping itself towards a goal. Government of some sort is bound up in man's nature as a social being. He cannot escape from it. It is true, however, that the structure of that government is moulded during the course of its development, partly, at least, by "human voluntary agency." In other words, while government itself (like the State which it makes possible) comes by nature, and cannot be shaken off by man; the *form* of that government and much of its development are the products of man's energy and will.

A people, then, can never develop themselves out of the necessity of all government whatever, but they may help to mould the particular form of constitution under which they live; and in this limited sense it is correct to say that governments are artificial and subject to human control. Even here, however, there are natural limits through which man's energy cannot break. Even Mill allows that this is so. His limits are given under three heads—the people for whom the institutions are intended must be willing (1) to accept them; (2) to do or suffer whatever is necessary to keep them going; and (3) to make whatever exertion or sacrifice is needed to enable them to fulfil their purposes.

The admission of these three conditions, by which man is chained to the existing elements of the national life at its given stage of development, goes far to prove that the institutions of a State are part of the wider organic whole; but it does not go far enough. A survey of English history tends to show how small a share the conscious efforts of men have had in shaping our time-honoured constitution into its present mould. A good illustration is furnished by the genesis of the Cabinet system of government—that central pivot on which the whole modern constitution turns; that mysterious hinge connecting legislature and executive together. The advent of the Cabinet finally set at rest the problem which the whole seventeenth century had failed to solve. Yet who could lay claim to its discovery or invention? What man or group of men could say that it was the product of their brain or will, or that their conscious action had helped it towards fulfilment in ever so small a degree? The truth is, that every man who brought deliberate action to bear on the matter tried strenuously to oppose the development of the modern Cabinet. Sir William Temple's scheme for the reorganization of the Privy Council took its origin in an attempt to crush the rising power of the Cabinet. Two clauses in the Act of Settlement itself were consciously directed against it. Even now—at the close of the nineteenth century—though the Cabinet has struggled into the most prominent place in our polity, it has never obtained proper legislative recognition. So far, indeed, from having been consciously created by man, it seems to have come into being and into power to meet a natural want, and under pressure of what we can with difficulty discriminate from a blind, unconscious law of necessity realizing itself, not because of, but in spite of all the recognized legal and political agencies of the day. The influence of human will was felt upon it undoubtedly; but it was the unconscious rather than the conscious actions of men that produced it.

Other instances might be given, all tending to show that Mill seems altogether to exaggerate the ability of men to determine the forms of their institutions. Government is, however, although not a product exclusively of the

conscious efforts of men, still a product of the sum of all such
efforts, whether conscious or unconscious, working in harmony
with the other manifestations of the common organic life of
the whole, and under close dependence on the laws of nature.
The political institutions reflect the national characteristics,
and in turn react on the national life. British institutions
are influenced more—inestimably more—by the unreasoning
feelings, prejudices, and hereditary predispositions of the mass
of ordinary John Bull Englishmen, and by the modes of life
and feeling into which such men unthinkingly *drift*, than by
the ratiocinations and conscious efforts of brilliant theorists
like John Stuart Mill and Mr. Herbert Spencer, or even of
commanding practical statesmen like Mr. Gladstone and the
late Lord Beaconsfield. Doctrines of government have, of
course, a very important bearing upon current politics, but
only such among them as the masses are ripe for, produce
far-reaching effects. Those theories are most influential which
explain existing prejudices by the light of reason, making the
hitherto unspoken tendencies of the national life articulate
in the mouth of its spokesman. Constitutions cannot be
built from architects' plans like houses. Unless a scheme of
government is suited to the national life and needs—and even
faults and prejudices—it will remain a mere dead letter, and
no amount of arguing will make it work. France has had
a long and humiliating experience in constitution-building.
America, it might be said, has fared better; but the framers
of the constitution of the United States were fortunate in
having merely to adapt the existing types of Anglo-Saxon
institutions to meet the needs of a new Anglo-Saxon nation.
They succeeded because they merely made explicit what was
already implicit in the people. Nor must it be forgotten
that their success was but partial after all. The way in
which the constitutional provisions for the formation of an
Electoral College to appoint the President work in practice
shows that national tendencies are too strong for legal forms
when the two come into conflict.

 While remembering, however, that there are barriers through
which the will of man can never penetrate—that "there's a
Divinity that shapes our ends, rough hew them how we

may "—it must not be forgotten, on the other hand, that the conscious endeavours of men form one element (and an important one) in the process whereby the world-spirit works towards its goal.

Human will *is* one factor in shaping the constitution—and therefore in moulding society and the State. Thus, to return to Mill's illustrations, systems of government are essentially different from both " trees " on the one hand, and " machines " on the other. They do not " grow " like the former, nor are they " made " like the latter. In Professor Ritchie's phrase they have " the remarkable property of making themselves."[1] Society is an organism of a very special type, to which such a verb as " grow " can be applied only in a special sense. M. Alfred Fouillé has described it as a " contractual organism," and again as " an organism which realizes itself in conceiving and willing itself."[2] The government may indeed be the product of man's energy on the one hand, and yet a mere manifestation of a developing organism on the other. Thus understood, it is both the creation of the State and an integral part of it. Constitutions make themselves; they are not made, and they do not grow.

Whatever its origin and history may have been, most politicians will agree that government must be the servant, not the master of the community. It exists to carry into execution the commands of the State.

There only remains to ask, In what way are these orders to be conveyed ? What marks do they possess of authenticity ? The answer which a properly organized commonwealth makes to this question must be contained in its constitution. If the laws do not speak clearly on this head, there is a serious danger to the public peace.

The government must not obey the behests of the mob or the merely numerical majority. Its duty is not to attend

---

[1] *State Interference*, p. 49.

[2] *La Science Sociale Contemporaine*, pp. 114, 115, quoted by Professor Ritchie, *State Interference*, p. 49. Cf. S. R. Gardiner's *History of the Great Civil War*, Vol. I., p. 9. " The laws by which the progress of human society is governed work not irrespective of human agency, but by the influence of surrounding conditions upon human wills, whereby the activity of these wills is roused to react upon the conditions."

to those voices of selfishness and greed that cry most loudly for what they need. It is not what the words of a modern statesman would make it, "an organization to carry out the wishes, interests, and desires of every class and section of the community,"[1] but only to carry out the rational will of the whole. The administration of the day must obey the will of the people only when that will is legally expressed in accordance with the terms of the constitution.

These terms, of course, differ with peoples and times. It is the business of the constitutional lawyers of the various nations to give an answer according to the positive law actually existing at the time the question is asked.

[1] These words are attributed to Mr. Asquith, and are cited in Prof. Hastie's *Introduction to Kant's Principles of Politics*, p. 39.

CHAPTER VIII.

CLASSIFICATION OF THE VARIOUS FUNCTIONS OF GOVERNMENT.

THE functions which every central government performs for the good of the whole community are usually arranged under three heads—the executive or administrative, the legislative, and the judicial. Although all three are so closely related that they frequently in practice encroach on one another, yet in most modern States not only is the theoretical distinction between them well established, but an effort is made to prevent the three sets of powers falling into the same hands. In rude nations this differentiation is not found except in a very incomplete form; and the three main functions of government, in so far as they exist at all, are vested in one ruler. In half-savage communities, indeed, the necessity, or even the possibility of changing the laws or the customs (and the latter have all the binding force of laws) is not realized, and such judicial decisions as are pronounced proceed upon the circumstances peculiar to each case. The executive power is the only authority that is absolutely indispensable. It is impossible to discover any tribe or people without an executive of some sort. No nation can exist as a State without some principle able to make itself obeyed, and forming the cohesive force which keeps the atoms from flying apart.

Physical power in varying degrees is bound up in every living creature. If each individual is allowed to regulate the use he makes of this power at his own caprice, anarchy results. **A** primary function of government is to allow no force except its own **to be** used with impunity against its members. It acts as the ultimate director and applier of the **force** of the community, and is thus the sole executive. **If this power of** coercion is taken away or **set** at defiance, **all** government **is for the time being** at an end, till the old order is re-established, or a new one is strong enough to take its place and make good its claim to the ultimate right of coercion.

Upon coercion, and therefore upon the executive authority, all **the** functions of government ultimately depend. The legislature would be no better than a debating society in the absence of an executive power to enforce its laws; and the judges' decrees would have only a speculative value if **not** backed by force.

This truth will become clearer after an examination of the various duties actually discharged by the governments of civilized communities. These may be arranged as follows, viz.:

(1) When the necessity **for** action of any kind arises, some authority must be entrusted with the duty of deciding what **should** be done. Some one must have a right to determine **the** policy to be pursued by the nation. Otherwise nothing will be done at all, or else conflicting schemes will struggle **for** the mastery. To avoid a deadlock, there must **always** be **a** supreme authority somewhere. Whoever **has vested** in him this right or duty (for it **is both)** performs the deliberative function. It may well be **that** in different provinces this power is placed in different hands; but on every case that can possibly occur there ought to be some authority vested with the right to say the last word. In England the seat of this power is **not** always easy to explain in theory, though no serious practical difficulty is likely to arise. Omitting, for the sake of simplicity, all reference to the wide measure of initiative power (subject, **of** course, to an ultimate control) allowed to local authorities, the deliberative **function** in Great Britain may be said to **be** vested by **the constitution** in the hands of the members of the Cabinet as ministers of the Crown. It is their duty to determine (within **the** limits prescribed **by law)** what

steps are necessary to maintain order at home, and to protect the nation's interests abroad.

The Ministry of the day is responsible for all the nation's official dealings with foreign States. It has to look after the interests of its subjects who happen to be abroad; to decide when to act, and when to let alone; whether to declare war or maintain peace; what steps to take to prevent the possibility of invasion—in fine, to deliberate and resolve on all matters of home and foreign policy.

(2) To enforce, or see enforced, the results of these deliberations, is a separate function of government. When a certain course has been resolved on by those who have a right to decide—that is, by the supreme deliberative authority of which we have just been speaking—it must be the duty of some one to see it carried into effect. No interests of any disaffected individual or class must be allowed to stand in its way. All opposition must be borne down by sheer force if required. The necessary coercive powers must be vested somewhere. The constitution must determine the depositary of this great trust—the function of carrying out its deliberations by brute force if need be.

(3) The legislative function in modern progressive States is the most important of all. In stationary countries, such as China, everything is regulated by unvarying custom. What has been must still be. In nations like the great powers of Europe at the present day, the necessity for altering the old laws to meet rapidly changing circumstances is constantly felt. The constitutions of such nations must define the depositaries of this power to change the laws. This legislative function (as it is called) has two chief branches—the regulation of criminal and of civil law. In any alterations in either of these departments of law the rights of individuals are necessarily modified or interfered with. To make an action criminal which was not so before, is to restrict the freedom of individuals. To alter the laws that define the civil rights of citizens, is either to contract or to extend these rights.

(4) Next comes for consideration the duty of enforcing these laws when once they have been made. It is not the

province of the power that makes **them** to see them **carried** into effect. Yet, **if a** new law is to take effect, some one must be responsible for its enforcement, and be armed with power to strike down all who resist. It is necessary, too, to make provision that every convicted criminal be duly punished. All laws, in fine, must be executed, and this again implies coercion if need be.

(5) The fifth function of government (according to our present classification) lies in expounding and applying the laws (whether common law or statute) and **in** settling, **when** appealed to, the rights in dispute between two individuals thus defined. Such duties are performed **by the** law courts. Hardly any theorist would be bold enough to deny that it is the duty of the State to provide **proper** tribunals for the settlement of such disputes instead of leaving them to be determined by voluntary arbitration. Judicial procedure differs from arbitration in this, that either party **may be coerced by the** whole might of the State **to** submit his rights to the jurisdiction of the proper tribunal even against **his will.**

(6) The sixth function of the **government is** to enforce (if necessary) those decrees delivered by its judges. **If** the individual does not, of his own accord, fulfil the finding of the court, diligence will be used against him. His goods will be distrained and **sold to** meet the sum decerned for; **and** if he forcibly resist he will he imprisoned. Here, again, is the principle of coercion in its most emphatic form.

(7) The government, however, does more than enforce the results of its own deliberations, the provisions of its laws, and the decisions of its judges. It undertakes to enforce every private contract between two or more of its subjects, which is not illegal. When an agreement has been once entered into with such formalities (if any) as may be required by law, neither party is at liberty to resile from his bargain. If he tries to do so **the** State, through the agency of **the** government, brings its whole weight to bear upon him, and crushes him till he comply. Here, again, is coercion. **The** enforcement of the decrees of arbiters against parties **who** have voluntarily agreed to submit their claims to such decision

is also undertaken by the State, but is only one phase of its general readiness to enforce all private contracts. The doctrine of contract has been extended to include what are called quasi-contracts or agreements which an individual is assumed to have tacitly made by acting in a certain way.

These are, then, the seven normal functions of government. The first is the deliberative—the duty of determining what should be done in name of the State as a whole. The third is legislation—the duty of changing the laws. The fifth is the judicial duty of applying laws and settling disputes. The second, fourth, sixth, and seventh may all be classed together as executive duties—the enforcement of the results of deliberations upon foreign or domestic affairs, of the provisions of laws, civil and criminal, of the judges' decrees, and the terms of private compacts. Thus all functions of government depend ultimately upon the executive, and therefore upon coercion.

It need only be added that in most States, and Great Britain is among the number, the supreme deliberative power and the supreme executive power are placed in the same hands. Under the law of England the Queen in Council (or the Queen acting through and by advice of her responsible ministers) possesses both the deliberative and executive authorities combined; while the Queen in Parliament is the supreme legislature, and the law courts discharge the judicial function. It is perhaps more correct to talk of the administrative function of government when the executive and the supreme deliberative powers are combined.

(8) We have not yet, however, exhausted the list of the various duties actually performed by governments. A number of miscellaneous duties remain for consideration, and may best be grouped together under an eighth and final head. There is, on the whole, unanimity of opinion as to the functions already discussed. All schools (except Nihilists or Anarchists) agree that it is the clear duty of every State to see that its institutions perform all the normal duties of government, including legislation, administration, and the dispensation of justice, together with the enforcement of such measure of coercion as all these necessarily involve.

There are, however, many subsidiary duties which some States are in the habit of performing for their subjects, and about which very grave differences of opinion exist. These are both numerous and varied, and will be discussed more in detail in a later chapter. Here a few well-known instances must suffice. Thus, for example, in England the government acts as a builder of ships of war, and as a manufacturer of ammunition. Among some foreign nations—Switzerland is a well-known instance—the government is an owner and regulator of railways. In most countries, including our own, the post office and telegraph systems are under State management, while there are innumerable duties of a miscellaneous nature which the central government undertakes for the benefit of its subjects, such as the coining of money, the fixing of standards for weights and measures, and the collection of statistics relating to trade. These are merely instances taken at random from among many. Differences are to be found in regard to these between every two nations. Thus, while in Great Britain the post office regulates the telegraph service in addition to the carrying of letters, in the United States of America the former duty is left to private enterprise.

There is one point of similarity among all these examples of State action. No necessary logical connection exists between them and the *essential* work of government, nor is there any practical reason to make it impossible for all or any of them to be left to private enterprise. It may be expedient that an administrative department should carry letters and build ships, but no one can say that no government could possibly exist without directly performing such duties. They are all abnormal functions of government, things undertaken by it in addition to its more pressing duties, in order to facilitate the work of the administrative departments, or to benefit individual subjects. There is another respect in which they are all similar. They all fall within the sphere of the executive. Some administrative department is charged with the additional labour of superintending each new burden that the government has taken upon its shoulders. Thus, when it was decided that the government should carry at fixed rates every parcel under a certain size and weight entrusted to it, new duties were laid upon the post office, and upon the administrative officer, called the Post-Master General, with whom the final responsibility rests.   **Every new duty, then, performed by the** State adds to the work of the **executive.**

It is necessary to form a clear conception of the distinctions between these various functions performed by existing governments, in order to be able to **judge,** when the question **is** afterwards raised, which among them are legitimate and which **are spurious,** and so to avoid misconceptions arising from want **of a proper** discrimination between things essentially different. **It is not sufficient** to say that a certain matter lies beyond the proper province of " government."   **It is** necessary to specify whether its legislative, its executive, its judicial, or **its** deliberative function is specially referred to.

CHAPTER IX.

THE CONCEPTION OF SOVEREIGNTY.

"Sovereignty" is one of the essential characteristics of every independent State which has attained to a complete and permanent organization. No term used in political science has given rise to more discussion, or is indeed of such intrinsic difficulty, for there are at least three meanings of the word "sovereign." (1) In the phrase, "our gracious sovereign Queen Victoria," the formal or nominal sovereign of Great Britain is referred to. It is here implied that the Queen is the head of the constitution. It is *not* meant that Her Majesty is "sovereign" or supreme in the sense that she can by herself make such laws and legally do such acts as please her, nor that from her personal decisions there is no appeal. It is equally clear that the phrase does not mean that the entire effective force of the State—or even the commanding majority of it—is centred in the person who, for the time being, occupies the throne. All that is meant is that Great Britain is a kingdom, and that the Queen is formal or titular sovereign—that all actions of government and laws proceed in Her Majesty's name.

(2) "The sovereignty of Parliament" is a well-known expression, which illustrates a second meaning of the word under discussion. "Parliament" (or rather the "Queen in Parliament," for with lawyers the two are synonymous) is the "legal sovereign." As the supreme legislative power it can change all laws, and is therefore above all laws. Its formal decisions embodied in statutes are legally irre-

sponsible, irresistible, and irreversible—except by Parliament itself.

(3) Those who talk of "the sovereign people" generally use the expression loosely. Yet there is a sense in which, subject to certain modifications, it is strictly accurate. The supreme power in the State is obviously the resultant of the forces of all its parts multiplied into one another. The effective force of a nation remains with the whole body of its members, whatever forms of expression or outlet it may find, and whatever agents may be legally empowered to act or think for it. The real or "political" sovereignty lies in the will of the people. The sanction that enforces this third species of sovereignty is not legal, but partly physical and partly moral.[1]

Endless wrangling and misconception have arisen from the failure to preserve clearly enough the distinction between these three uses of the same word. Serious confusion between the first and second of these is not indeed likely to occur in future. There was a time in English history when the monarch was legal as well as titular sovereign; or at any rate grasped the lion's share of the former.

When the two Houses of Parliament had shaken off their complete dependence on the Crown, under the shadow of which they had been once only too glad to find shelter, they began to lay claim first to a share, and then to the whole of the legal sovereignty. The House of Commons and the King set up rival claims to represent the nation. Each refused to recognize the sovereignty of the other. When the Long Parliament met in 1640, where, it may be asked, was the legal sovereignty in England? The only answer is, that it was equally or unequally divided between two conflicting powers. After 1689, the supremacy clearly rested with the legislature, and not with the King as head of the executive, though accuracy requires us to add that the monarch was still included as an integral portion of the legislative body.

Long after the facts had changed, the old theory lingered,

[1] Cf. Dicey, *Law of the Constitution*, p. 69 and p. 352; and Ritchie, *State Interference*, Appendix B.

though no longer applicable. Conservative instincts and loyalty to the occupants of the throne kept up the old tradition, no longer borne out by facts, that the legal and titular sovereigns were still the same. This is the fallacy of an "ambiguous middle," that vitiates much of the reasoning of both Kant and Bluntschli,—not to mention less important names,—in treating of British institutions.

Within recent years many lucid expositions of the distinction have been given, and the honour of dealing the death-blow to so dangerous a confusion of ideas is probably due to Professor Dicey and his luminous exposition of the seat of the legal sovereignty in Great Britain.

There is, perhaps, more danger for the future of mistakes arising from want of a clear differentiation between the conceptions of "legal" and "political" supremacy. The difference between these is of so great importance that it is necessary to explain it with some fulness.

The nature of the political sovereignty must first be analyzed. It forms the very essence and prerequisite of a State, and its conception was involved in the definition with which this Essay started. It is negatively implied in the independence of a State, for where there is effective foreign intervention the sovereignty lies *outside* the community. It is implied positively in its efficient organization; for the laws and government are useless if the citizens professedly subject to them are able with impunity to set them at defiance. It is true that when the institutions are rudimentary and imperfect, it is difficult to see where this idea of sovereignty finds a place.[1] Yet the embryo must be there, however hard to discover. In civilized communities the connection is more obvious.

Sovereignty implies the right to command and the power to enforce obedience. If it is to be a reality it must be able to crush rebellion. On its practical side it represents the power of the whole over every part—of the State over

---

[1] Sir H. S. Maine in his *Early History of Institutions* (p. 349), and Professor T. H. Green, in his *Principles of Political Obligation* (*Works* II., p. 399), have shown the difficulties of applying Austin's conception of sovereignty to primitive communities.

the individual with all his associations, institutions, and relations. The effective political sovereignty would thus involve the aggregate of the forces of every kind that really coerce or persuade the people into obedience. It is, however, not so much the sum as the resultant (or, better still, the organic compound) which includes the forces of every man and of every agency made or directed by human skill and intelligence within the society. Viewed in this light it is difficult to distinguish it from the State itself. Further, if it is the resultant of all, evidently none of the included forces can escape its sway. "It follows," says Professor Huxley, "that no limit is, or can be, theoretically set to State interference."[1] This kind of supremacy—unlike the legal sovereignty—cannot be lost unless the State itself is annihilated. The political sovereignty is the concentrated essence of the national life, majesty, and power focussed to a point, and so rendered most intense and irresistible. Now, the men and women whose united powers it thus includes are rational beings, and therefore the ultimate nature of all their forces must be sought in that same practical reason or will, which we already saw to be the true source of the State itself. Sovereignty is thus built up of the wills or moral forces of the citizens, and must always, in a sense, reside with "the people." It rests, however, with the community considered not as an aggregate of equal units, but as a composite organism gathered round an established constitution. It is the outcome of the common will—not the sum of the isolated wills of individuals—the volonté générale, not the volonté de tous—and is thus (though democratic in a sense) by no means the creature of the mob, or

[1] It is necessary to remember, however, that this sovereignty is not omnipotent. While Professor Huxley is right in denying that any limit can be placed upon it by anything within the State, it is still subject to two important restrictions. In the first place, it may be controlled not only by its own incapacity to subject the forces of nature to its will, but by the alien influence of other States. In the second place, it is subject to the mandates laid upon it by its own rational nature. It must obey what may, in the phraseology of Kant, be termed the "categorical imperative" inherent in itself, commanding it to act only for the common good.

the instrument of a bare **numerical** majority of **votes**. In a word, it is organic and not mechanical. " This sovereignty **of** the **people**," says Professor Ritchie, "this general will, **is only** an idea, **it** will be said. It *is* an idea; **but not** therefore unreal. **It is real as the human spirit is real,** because **it is** this very spirit **striving for objective** manifestation. **It** lives and grows **and becomes conscious of** itself. It realizes itself in different **forms, in the family,** the clan, the city, the nation, perhaps some **day in the** federation of the world."[1] To determine all about this political **sovereignty is the** province of philosophers. They may differ, **but truth** cannot vary. There is one truth which **all aim after.**

Now that we have ascertained the nature of the political sovereignty, we are **in** a position to examine the legal sovereignty which forms its expression or embodiment. **The** supreme political power popularly alluded to as "the people," and **here** described as the will of the community, is evidently **too** vague a thing for practical purposes. It is a useful philosophical conception; **but the** practical sovereignty must **be** embodied **in** some determinate person or institution available for the ordinary purposes of government and patent to all who are called on to obey. **In** other words, **the** common will or supreme political power in the State **must find some** recognized constitutional method of expressing itself. **This** embodiment or manifestation is the legal **sovereign or the** principal part of the government. It is **the chief business of the constitution** to define the seat **of this legal** power.

The legal sovereign is, then, the authorized embodiment **of** the political one. The whole constitutional history of a nation is a record of **the** efforts made by the general will, which is the source of law, to realize itself **in** an external form. The will of the people **is blindly** and instinctively groping about to find adequate expression **in** a suitable ruler **or** organization. The simplest **plan** adopted in the early **history** of most, **if not all, States, is** the election of a king, **who is at once the titular and** the legal sovereign. **The** difference between **the two,** indeed, has not **yet** been **evolved. The** imperfections of such **an** arrangement soon suggest them-

[1] *State Interference*, p. 69.

selves.   Checks are placed on the royal power, and complex
constitutions arise, resulting generally in the gradual transference of the legal sovereignty to national assemblies more
or less independent of the king's control.   The theoretical
title of all rulers, whether monarchic, aristocratic, or democratic, is derived, in the view of philosophy, from the fact
that they represent the general will, and act for the common
welfare.

To quote again from Professor Ritchie,[1] "The Czar of all
the Russias rules by the will of the people as much as does
the executive of the Swiss Federation.   The belief in the
Czar's divine right is the source of his power and the ground
of their obedience.   The difference between two such cases
is, that the general will has found a more adequate way of
expressing itself in the one instance than in the other.   The
general will expresses itself by opinion in speaking and
writing, as well as by electing representatives.   When prevented from such means of utterance it expresses itself by
prostration before a God upon earth, or by assassination,
both of which are very inadequate ways."

While the political sovereign, then, is the intangible source
of all government, the legal sovereign is simply that part
of the actual machinery of government which is superior to
the other parts, having legal control over the rest, and being
itself subject to none.   The latter is only a particular and
perhaps temporary embodiment of the former which is
perpetual and inalienable.

The legal sovereign may be changed without interrupting
the continuity of the national life.   It varies with the
changes in the laws and customs of the land, and the
currents of opinion that act and react upon them; but,
however it alters its form or its seat, it must exist somewhere within the government.   This truth was fully grasped
as far back as the middle of the fifteenth century by Jean
Bodin, and clearly enunciated in his treatise *De Republica*.
He arrived at his conclusion as a result of an actual analysis
of the observed phenomena of existing governments.   He
satisfied himself that in every form of constitution, if you

[1] *State Interference*, p. 68.

go deep enough, you arrive at some ultimate part of the government which is supreme within it, and therefore so long as it lasts, supreme within the whole State. The seat of this power must, in Bodin's view, be above the law itself—must be the source of law, giving actuality to all positive enactments, and enforcing their execution.[1] This is the seat of legal sovereignty within each State, and the first problem for the student of each constitution is to find it. Although it is the invariable rule that this sovereignty lies somewhere inside the organs of the central government, it is not always easy to lay a finger exactly on the spot. To determine *where*, is the province of the constitutional lawyer, not of the philosopher. The legal sovereign is different in every State. The problem is to discover in what person or organ the laws of a country place the right to say the last word in event of a dispute between the other parts. All doubt as to where the sovereignty rests in regard to practical matters must be removed. Where there is no legally appointed sovereign, different men or powers will fight for the supremacy. The constitution ought to provide means whereby all battles of contending interests may be fought out bloodlessly within itself in open debate in the national assembly or at the council table by vote or otherwise. If it does not do so, the battle will be fought outside of the constitution with deadlier weapons. Sometimes an originally good constitution suffers change through sympathy with the altered political condition of the nation, and so ceases to provide such a safety valve. Sometimes two parts of it break asunder, and each claims the supremacy. Such a contingency might happen any day in England in consequence of a serious divergence of opinion between Lords and Commons, if it were not for the existence of a series of mysterious rules that are not exactly laws, but are called "conventions of the constitution," which make pro-

---

[1] Cf. S. R. Gardiner, *History of England*, Vol. III., p. 22. " In every constitution there must be some fundamental power the authority of which is received as binding without dispute. In our days that authority is lodged in the constituencies. In the beginning of the seventeenth century it was lodged in the king."

vision for reconciling such conflicts. A more important and more fatal divergence showed itself in the seventeenth century, when the old constitutional organ, called the *Concilium ordinarium*, had ceased to act as a reconciling medium between king and Parliament; because it had lost its independence and been absorbed within the sphere of the personal prerogative of the Crown. King and Parliament each set up a title to embody the will of the nation. Each claimed to be sovereign. There was no proper machinery provided by the constitution for determining this dispute; and so when the sentimental bonds of sympathy that had kept Elizabeth and her Parliaments at one, in spite of lovers' quarrels, had been broken by the Stuarts' pride and insincerity on one side, and by the stubborn spirit of the Puritans on the other, the possession of the sovereignty was made the occasion of an actual civil war. Both parties fought for legal supremacy, since the laws had proved insufficient to determine where this really lay.

Thus every perfect, even every tolerable constitution must place the legal sovereignty somewhere beyond the reach of dispute.

One important question still remains, and is by no means free from difficulty.

Must we maintain, with John Austin, that the sovereign is necessarily a "*determinate*" person or persons? Must we further agree with him that these are always at all times and in all circumstances *the same* individuals?

"The notions of sovereignty and independent political society," says Austin, in a well-known passage, "may be expressed concisely thus. If a *determinate* human superior, *not* in a habit of obedience to a like superior, receive *habitual* obedience from the bulk of a given society, that determinate superior is sovereign in that society, and the society (including the superior) is a society political and independent. . . . In order that a given society may form a society political and independent, the two distinguishing marks which I have mentioned above must unite. The *generality* of the given society must be in a *habit* of obedience to a determinate and common superior; whilst the determinate person or determinate body of persons must *not* be habitually obedient to a determinate person or body."[1]

A detailed criticism of this exposition of the theory of sovereignty is unnecessary. The subject, indeed, is a somewhat hackneyed one, exhaustively treated in many easily accessible volumes.[2] One or two observations, however, on some of its more conspicuous features may help to elucidate the real nature of the legal sovereignty and its relations to the political one. At the outset, it must be noticed that Austin introduces a gratuitous element of difficulty into the whole investigation by failing to preserve clearly enough the crucial distinction between the two kinds of supremacy. When he substitutes the electors for the House of Commons among those determinate persons who share the sovereignty, he is clearly going beyond the conception of legal to that of political sovereignty.[3] This confusion of thought sufficiently explains, perhaps, the defect of Austin's theory as applied to the government of Great Britain. More serious difficulties occur when an attempt is made to reconcile it with the phenomena of the constitution of the United States of America. Considered as an explanation of the working of the machinery of government in Federal States, the theory breaks down. The error, however, does not lie in declaring that the seat of the legal sovereignty is necessarily a "determinate person or persons," but rather in the corollary that these must always be the same for all classes of acts. The latter proposition is difficult to reconcile with the doctrine of the division of powers, which is the basis of all the public institutions of America. The object of those who framed the constitution of the United States was precisely to prevent any one set of "determinate persons" from usurping the legal sovereignty. Their desire was to make each organ of government act as a check on the other, and so produce an exactly balanced whole, in which no part had an absolute supremacy over the rest. They perhaps failed in this effort;

[1] *Lectures on Jurisprudence*, Vol. I., p. 227.

[2] *E.g.* in T. H. Green's *Principles of Political Obligation* and Professor Sidgwick's *Elements of Politics*, p. 15 *seq.*

[3] Cf. A. V. Dicey, *Law of the Constitution*, pp. 67-70.

but, at any rate, they seem to have so far disguised the whereabouts of the ultimate "monarch" as effectually to puzzle the analytic genius of Austin. Professor Green's weighty opinion may be here quoted: "In the United States, with a written constitution, it required all Austin's subtilty to detect where sovereignty lay, and he places it where probably no ordinary citizen of the United States had ever thought of it as residing, viz. 'In the States' Governments as forming one aggregate body: meaning by a State's government, not its ordinary legislature, but the body of citizens which appoints its ordinary legislature, and which, the union apart, is properly sovereign therein.' He bases this view on the provisions in the constitution, according to which amendments to it are only valid 'when ratified by the legislature in three-fourths of the several States, or by convention in three-fourths thereof.' But no ordinary citizen of the United States probably ever thought of sovereignty except as residing either in the government of his State or in the Federal Government consisting of congress and president, or sometimes in one way, sometimes in the other."[1]

To find the definite seat of the supreme legal power, at any given moment, in a federal nation like the United States is, indeed, a difficult task; and it becomes, perhaps, an impossible one when it is maintained that for all the acts and functions of government, and in all times and circumstances, this seat of power is necessarily the same.

A brief glance at the complicated provisions of the American constitution explains the difficulty of the problem that Austin set himself to solve in looking for one uniform and permanent depositary of the legal sovereignty.

The two Houses of Congress share the right to initiate all laws, but the executive head of the nation has rights of veto. The President appoints public officials and makes treaties, but the concurrence of a two-thirds majority of the

[1] T. H. Green's *Works*, II., p. 410. The remarks of A. V. Dicey (*Law of the Constitution*, p. 139) on the seat of the sovereignty in the United States may be profitably compared with the passage here quoted.

upper of the two legislative chambers is here required. The President, again, may declare war; but Congress is entitled to refuse the necessary supplies. The legislature is able to enact only such laws as the constitution allows, and the judges are bound to refuse to enforce those that are forbidden in their opinion by its fundamental principles. Finally, elaborate provisions are framed for the purpose of altering the constitution when necessary. Where, then, within the various organs of the government of the United States, is the sovereignty to be found? Does it lie with the President, who can command neither money nor legislative support? Or with Congress, whose laws may be blocked by the President or disallowed by the Federal Courts? Does it lie with the Federal Courts, which, to some extent, act as umpires between President and Congress, and have power to set aside as "unconstitutional," laws in which the Senate, the House of Representatives and the Executive Government have all warmly concurred? Lastly, does the legal sovereignty lie with that dead body of rules called the constitution itself, or with the living piece of machinery endowed with the rights of a constituent assembly, to alter this code when necessary? It is the duty of the expounders of American constitutional law to solve this difficult problem. The present purpose is served, without answering it, by merely showing how difficult it is to find an answer at all.

Whether the determinate group of persons in whom the legal sovereignty is vested is always the same, or varies with the act in question, three propositions seem beyond the reach of doubt. (1) The legal sovereignty must always exist somewhere within the "government," using that word in its most extended sense. (2) The legal sovereign, whether in the form of a monarchy, or aristocracy, or democracy, while forming the ultimate source of law and government beyond which the lawyer *quâ* lawyer cannot go, must justify its position of supremacy in the eyes of the philosopher by its success in affording *a true manifestation* of the will of the people, the true political sovereign. (3) This will of the people must never be identified with the blind passions of the mob or the mere mechanical majority of unenlightened voters.   Only a rational will acting disinterestedly for the common good **can** claim the right to appoint the magistrates and national assemblies in whom legal powers are vested, and so **to** regulate the destinies of the commonwealth. " That which generalizes the **will**," **to** quote from Rousseau,[1] " **is** not so much the **number** of voices **as the common interest** which **unites them.**"

[1] *Contrat Social,* II. iv.

CHAPTER X.

THE SEAT OF THE LEGAL SOVEREIGNTY IN GREAT BRITAIN.

NATIONAL characteristics vary as do those of individuals. No two nations are alike. The customs and habits by which one people is distinguished from another, result from differences of soil and climate, of race, of past history and traditions, and of a thousand influences sometimes too subtle to admit of exact analysis. It follows that the constitutions and governments of the various groups of men must change with all alterations in the common life of which they form the outward manifestations. Just as the mind and body of the individual act and react on one another—as the developing character and the past deeds of a man write their tale on his face and frame, while in turn the physical changes and sufferings he has undergone sharpen or deaden his mental faculties and readjust their mutual relations— so it is with nations.

Everything that affects the circumstances of a people— increase of material prosperity, extension of territory, changes of climate, alteration in religious or moral sentiments or in the mode of living—all these ultimately influence in some degree the form of the national institutions—the skeleton of the State. We are thus prepared, on a *priori* grounds, to find no two constitutions alike. This is simply another way of stating that the national will, or common conscious- ness of a community of rational beings, embodies itself in different forms—that though the political sovereignty is always the same, the seat of the legal sovereignty is distinct for each community. Great Britain in particular possesses outstanding characteristics which distinguish it from all others. It would be out of place to attempt here an exhaustive analysis of the British constitution ; but it is necessary to indicate the seat of the legal sovereignty, since this is the leading feature which stamps the character of the whole. The great first principle of the British constitution is what Professor Dicey calls " the legislative sovereignty of Parliament." [1] It is often more graphically though less accurately termed the Omnipotence of Parliament. The true sovereignty of Great Britain is vested in the legislature, and not in the Queen as the head of the executive. Whatever may be true of the constitution of other nations, in England the legislature has made good its supremacy over the executive. It is Parliament that controls the Cabinet, and not *vice versa*. The legislative sovereignty of Parliament is the one great truth which cannot be overthrown.[2] Parliament is the sole legislative organ of the central government. This is not a theory. "Its existence is a legal fact, fully recognized by the law of England." "The sovereignty of Parliament is (from a legal point of view) the dominant characteristic of our political institutions." [3]

One important explanation (already hinted at) must here be made, and made emphatically. When the word " Parliament " is used synonymously with the legislature as a whole, it invariably means not only the Upper and Lower Houses, but also the Monarch who summons them to deliberate together, who dissolves them when their duties are done, and without whose assent formally expressed no bill can become a law. The sovereignty of Parliament means then that the Queen in Parliament is supreme in Great Britain, and can alter any part of the law of the land.

This truth has been insisted on by every theoretical writer since De Lolme, and by every practical lawyer since Blackstone. It is now recognized as the very keystone of the whole fabric. Every opposing principle must give way before

---

[1] A. V. Dicey, *Law of the Constitution*, p. 34.
[2] Ibid., Part I.   [3] Ibid., p. 37.

the supremacy of an Act of Parliament. There are no "fundamental laws" it cannot change, no "inalienable" or "guaranteed" rights of individuals it may not invade. The entire constitution—indeed the State itself—and every individual citizen, are legally at the mercy of the enactments of the legislature. There is no privileged class, principle, or power within these islands so exalted, and no place so sacred or so secluded, as to claim or make good exemption from its sway. No other legislative body can compete with the exclusive right of Parliament, and no executive or judicial power can ignore or set aside a law which has once been made. In the well-known words of De Lolme, quoted perhaps by every man who has since written on the powers of Parliament: "It is a fundamental principle with English lawyers that Parliament can do everything but make a woman a man, and a man a woman."

This is what is meant then by the "omnipotence" of Parliament—not an absolute omnipotence, of course, but perhaps approaching as near to it as any human institution can. The sphere of the State itself has already been seen to be in theory extremely wide, and it now appears that practical lawyers in expounding the actual law of England find that that wide political sovereignty of the State has been embodied in a correspondingly wide legal sovereignty, and conferred unreservedly upon Parliament.

It seems, then, that a simple and complete answer can be made to the question: In what part of the government of Great Britain does the supreme legal power rest? It is found in Parliament. This is definite and satisfactory. A little deeper thought, however, shows that this "Parliament" is a complex body, and therefore that the solution of the problem is not so simple in a limited monarchy like England as under a despotism where sovereignty is absolutely vested in one individual. To say that the man who holds a sceptre in his hand and sits on a throne is a supreme monarch, whose will is above all restraints of law, is to end the discussion. Not so when a body like Parliament is found to be the supreme source of law. The former is a single individual; the latter is an extremely complex body. Parliament consists of the Queen, the House of Lords, and the House of Commons, acting all conjointly and under recognized rules as to the relations that exist among them. The more closely this seat of the ultimate sovereignty is analyzed, the more intricate it becomes. Thus the House of Commons consists of 670 members elected by the constituencies, which thus have a share in the composition of an integral part of the supreme power. Immediately before a general election there is no lower Chamber in existence at all. The share of sovereignty to be exercised by the House of Commons after election must therefore immediately before that event be held to be diffused throughout the constituencies, since it can flow only into such individuals as they choose to appoint. The House of Lords is another integral part, and hence arise new complications, for it is made up of princes of the blood royal, of archbishops, dukes, marquesses, earls, viscounts, bishops, and barons of England, the representative peers of Ireland and Scotland, and certain Lords of Appeal. Here we have, in the first place, the hereditary principle pure and simple, and again modifications of it by the principle of election. In the second place, we have the admission of the dignitaries of the Church; in the third place, the professional element is represented by the law lords; while in the fourth place, the right of the Crown to elect new members introduces still another element of complexity. The place held by the Queen in the sovereign legislature is still more difficult to estimate, for Her Majesty's legal rights are in practice hedged round with a whole mass of rules which are not " laws " in the strict sense, but only " conventions of the constitution." Some of these rules practically forbid the monarch ever to reject any bill passed by both Houses; while others regulate the rights of the Crown in the summoning and dissolving of Parliament, requiring that such steps should only be taken on the advice of responsible Ministers. This results in giving the Cabinet Council and the Privy Council an indirect share in the control of the legislature, and therefore of that sovereignty which is embodied in it. Lastly, there exist also other " conventions " or constitutional rules, which require, under certain circumstances, that the Upper House of Parliament should lay aside its own share of legislative rights, and act more or less at the dictation of the House of Commons. Thus all these conventions or rules, which define the relations existing between the various component parts of Parliament, must be considered almost as parts of Parliament, and so included within the sovereign legislature.

The supreme Parliament, then, may be said to admit within itself, in one way or another, almost every holder of any share, however small, of political power in the realm. It cannot act without collecting these scattered fractions of power together into one focus in their due proportions, and subject to the laws and other rules as to their relative weight and influence. Without these powers being reduced to a unity and acting in harmony, no law can be passed at all. If the chief constituent parts of the legislature (in especial the Upper and the Lower Houses) fail to agree, no Act of Parliament can be passed, and the existing body of laws would thus remain unchanged for ever. In other words, as the sovereign power is composite, an absolute legislative deadlock might in practice ensue, unless a concord of opinion were willingly arrived at or forced upon the various factors. A simple example occurs when either House refuses to pass a bill approved by the other. The peculiarity of our constitution is that positive law makes no provision at all for reconciling the conflicts that may arise within this composite sovereign Parliament. It is unnecessary to show here in detail how the possibility of such a deadlock is practically prevented by the existence of that mysterious body of rules, before alluded to, called "conventions," which share to some extent the binding force of laws, and yet are not laws in the ordinary sense in which the practical lawyer uses the word.[1] The first important point to be borne in mind is that, whenever unanimity is arrived at (however this may be effected) nothing can resist the resulting act of joint sovereignty. An enactment of Parliament sweeps everything before it. The second important point is that the constitution does provide within itself practical expedients for securing harmony. Within the

---

[1] The reader who wishes fuller information on this important subject is referred to the works of Dicey, Anson, Hearn, and Walter Bagehot.

supreme legislature it is thus necessary to search for a still more intimate supreme principle. There are various ways of explaining this ultimate principle of harmony. It may be said, on the one hand, that the supreme constitutional power lies with a newly-elected House of Commons, or, on the other hand, that the supreme political power lies with the constituencies when an election is pending.

This is the sphere of the constitutional theorist, and need not detain us here. It is sufficient for the general purposes of this Essay to accept the sovereignty of Parliament as absolute and final in the domain of law without attempting any further analysis.

The legal supremacy of the Queen, when acting along with a duly constituted Parliament, over every other part of the government, executive or judicial, over every individual and class, and over the State as a whole, is the first axiom which both the theorist and the practical man must learn in treating of the constitution of Great Britain.

There is no *legal* means of avoiding the effects of an Act of Parliament except by a subsequent Act. It may be unjust or inexpedient, or both, but it must be lawful, and is indeed the essence of positive law. There is no avenue of escape short of revolution.

CHAPTER XI.

THE IDEAL STATE AND THE STATE UNIVERSAL.

An ideal State would be one which had already attained the end of its existence by realizing to the full the common good, in accordance with universal principles of right, and so securing to all its members their highest well-being, and such measure of happiness as is possible for men. To discover all that is involved in this Utopia, and, if possible, the direction in which the world must travel to get there, it is necessary to return to the definition already given of a State, as "a society organized and independent." A perfect State would, on this basis, be a perfect society, perfectly organized and perfectly independent. This implies (*a*) the perfection of all its members as rational beings possessed of an essentially moral nature, and the perfection of the union between them ; (*b*) the perfection of all the institutions, laws, and systems of government regarded as the external expression of the moral progress of mankind, and as supplying the material through which the inner morality of the citizens must be realized ; and (*c*) perfect freedom from all foreign or external interference.

The last of these conditions in particular demands our close attention. No single nation, considered as one power among others which have equal rights, has ever attained to such independence, or ever can. Thus no State, as that word is most commonly used at present—France or England, for example—can ever become "perfect," if that implies the absence of all foreign control. In some respects, indeed, States are more independent of one another now-a-days than they

K

were in the Middle Ages; but in other respects—and these
undoubtedly the most important—they are less so. In the
future, in all probability, the various nations of the globe
will become still more vitally connected with one another.
The only hope of a perfectly independent State, then, must
be sought in the conception of a world-empire where all are
absorbed into one.

The same conclusion seems to be reached when the problem is approached from the side of the individual. The
wider man's sphere becomes, the higher the stage of development he attains. To shun society is to narrow that sphere,
and so to starve or mutilate the mind. No individual can
shake off his nature as a social and political being; but he
may thwart and contort and stunt it, if he will, by depriv-
ing it of nutriment and a fitting environment. Man cannot
become his true self or develop the end of his destiny apart
from his fellow-men. There has been implanted in him an
impulse leading him in the direction of association with
others. This instinctive and vague prompting of nature is
a guide from heaven not to be lightly thwarted, but to be
made conscious and determinate. If the family is the highest
form of community which, at a given stage in the history
of civilization, has attained to organization and a recognized
existence, then the family for that epoch contains the whole
life of man. Other and higher interests lie beyond the
domestic circle, however, and to take advantage of these and
make them part of himself, the individual must grow beyond
the family in forming ties with the wider world outside. This
greater whole, forming a tribe or village community, gradually
takes definite shape as the family had previously done. A
fitting organization is evolved to give it a definite and permanent existence.

The aims and pursuits of the individual man are now
circumscribed by the life of the tribe in place of that of
the family. The old domestic life is not left behind, however, but included in a wider whole. Soon the needs of his
expanding nature swell beyond what the tribe can supply,
and the City-state is founded. With many forward and
backward movements the process of evolution sweeps slowly

onwards. Highly complex modern States are at last evolved, giving within their confines room for full and varied manifestations of character and life. The exclusively national State has, for many centuries, marked the extreme limit hitherto attained by individual men in their efforts to make explicit and embody in suitable institutions and laws that solidarity of mankind which is vaguely implied in the rudest consciousness even of savage man.

To one who has marked that the progress of individual men in science, art, and ethics, has kept pace with the growth in size of the organized community from the tribe to the modern national State, two questions can hardly fail to present themselves. First, is the State as it at present exists the highest unity capable of attaining recognized existence in a permanent political form ? Secondly, is the nature of the individual man fully matured before he becomes in reality "a citizen of the world"? No dream of world-empire has yet realized itself, but experience cannot be taken in an unmodified form from a lower stage of evolution and applied to a higher. No new civilization can hope to thrive if it is not built upon the results of those which it is destined to supersede. The higher form of life must include the lower. No "federation of the world" is possible which is not founded on a desire to strengthen rather than to weaken the lower forms of organization. True cosmopolitanism can only be achieved by the man who combines it with true patriotism. The former is too often assumed as a watchword by those who wish to exchange the strict code of conduct and the definite duties they owe to their country for the looser morality and the vaguer obligations of a wider whole. Similarly, any attempt to bind mankind together under one constitution, set of laws, and government, thus realizing a universal State or world-empire, must not seek to proceed by loosening the obligations, and undermining the foundations of the governments that exist in localities and nations. It must proceed gradually by building itself upon the solid foundations of the past.

This idea of a universal State may never be realized , but, undoubtedly, it is the ultimate ideal short of which perfec-

tion cannot be attained. **Plato** and Aristotle placed the
limits of the perfect State **at** some 4000 inhabitants. The
modern **European** nations **have** out-distanced that conception,
and the great republic of America has realized on democratic
principles a vast extent of empire—such as even a few centuries ago would have been held impossible; while the cry
for Imperial federation, if far from being realized, seems at
last within measurable distance of the sphere of practical
politics.

There are elements of imperfection, however, in every State
which does not embrace the **whole territories of** the world
and include all races of mankind. The modern Utopia may
long—indeed for ever—remain unrealized, but it cannot afford
to stop short of " the Parliament of man, the federation of
the world," **and even** federation ought in time to give way
to **a closer** form **of** constitutional bond.[1]

There **are numerous** aspects in which the modern State is
dependent upon its neighbours. A few of the most prominent
of these may be briefly noticed.

(1) International **law may not possess the** full characteristics of ordinary **law, but so far as** it has force at all,
its requirements place limits **on** every nation from without.

(2) Then brute force may **be brought to** bear by other
powers upon any so-called **independent State.** Even the
fear of war is **a form** of dependence.

(3) No State is self-sufficing, but depends for its food
supplies, **or at** least for many articles of daily use in its
ordinary life, upon foreign lands and peoples.

(4) There **are** many miscellaneous forms of outside
influences that practically demonstrate to each State its
close connection with its neighbours. Thus the spread of
cholera or of any other infectious disease may make one
nation suffer **for** the want **of** proper sanitary precautions
within the confines of another.

---

[1] Cf. Bluntschli, *Theory of the State*, p. 25. "The perfect State is, as
it were, the visible body of humanity. . . . Merely national States
have only a relative truth." In another part of his first volume (p. 77),
he laments that "mankind has not yet found a collective organization
in a world-empire."

(5) New ideas, systems of philosophy or spiritual forces, having their seat in one country, may benefit or hurt all the peoples of the world. England was for centuries subject, in many ways, to the influence of Rome, while the effects of Luther's opinions and course of policy in Germany shook many of the constitutions of other European powers to their foundations.

(6) The binding force of international *moral* obligations is being more and more clearly recognized. The ethical isolation of each State from its neighbours, so prominent a feature of all ancient civilizations, whether Jewish, or Grecian, or Asiatic, has been replaced by the recognition of the solidarity of all branches of humanity. The moral sense of one nation is brought directly to bear upon foreign States. On this subject no writer has expressed himself with more point than Sheldon Amos.[1] "The difference lately brought about is that, owing to the closer approximation in thought, speech, habits of life, and, above all, in forms of government, of the populations of different States, coupled with the increased influence of these populations on their several governments, the relations of States to each other are found to be much more numerous and important than was at any previous time imagined. It is disclosed that not only are the large sections of humanity, personated by the different States, morally bound to concern themselves actively in each other's welfare and progress, but that, economically, the advance of each is the advance of all; and, politically, disorder or retrogression, existing anywhere, tends to diffuse itself everywhere. It is being found less and less possible for a State, however signal its geographical advantages in separation from its neighbours, to venture to ask whether it is its brother's keeper. . . . Thus the notion of the independence of a State no longer means exemption from moral responsibility to other States any more than it has meant, since the days of Grotius, the exemption from legal responsibility. The conception of moral relationship of a distinct and positive kind, reaching far beyond the rights and duties alone recognized by international law, has been much fortified of late

[1] *Science of Politics*, p. 348.

years—and will probably be still **more so in the** future—by the **inducements to** commercial **and** industrial co-operation which increasingly prevail."

For many **reasons, therefore, no State can reach** perfect independence until **all** are joined **in one. Before the** goal of humanity is attained all nations must unite in the bonds of love. Hitherto, the force inspiring alliances has rather been hate than charity—common enmity to a common foe.

Many schools of philosophy declare **this** conception **of** a World-state **owning** obedience **to one** government and substituting **the decision of the law courts** for the horrors **of war to be an** impossible ideal; and, indeed, it seems **one not** likely **soon** to be realized. Still, no ideal is impossible merely **because** it is extremely difficult to attain. Bluntschli [1] brings forward several arguments in opposition **to the views of Vinet, Laurent,** and others who deny the possibility of a **universal State**; but the chief **argument he omits** to give. **It is** simply this, that such **a** State actually **exists** already, though in an imperfect and unsatisfactory **form.** A State is **a society of human** beings *plus* a political organization including common institutions, constitution, laws, **and** government. Now, the **world** considered as a whole **has** not yet any one of these **four elements of** organization fully developed, but it has the germs of each. Let us take them in succession. It is the province of jurisprudence to determine the exact nature of international law. This body of rules and maxims has partly grown up as a generalization made by theorists, from the observed practice of nations **in** their mutual relations of peace and war, and is partly **the result of** conferences **and** treaties between the Great Powers, **and** embraces likewise the decisions of arbiters **or of** the **national** courts of individual States. Many people **are** in-**clined** to deny the name **of** law to this code observed by the comity of nations, **alleging various reasons,** but **in** especial, that it does **not possess** a binding force. Indeed, the chief defect in **its title to rank as** law seems to lie **in** the want of **an** adequate and constitutional *sanction* to en-force its decrees. The vagueness of many of its provisions,

[1] *Theory of the State*, p. 32.

and the refusal of certain nations over which it professes to hold sway to admit its decisions, are also among its short-comings. There is no doubt that these defects are sufficient to differentiate international law from the positive law which prevails within the confines of any highly developed and properly organized State; but the difficulty disappears in great part when we apply the idea of evolution to the history of law. The difference is then seen to be one rather of degree than of kind, marking merely a stage in development, not an insuperable barrier to advance. International law has not reached maturity, and therefore cannot claim the full dignity of the title; but it is fast developing towards it. Further, we can see that the stage it has already reached is part of the life-progress of all law—whether municipal or constitutional. All early law was defective in those very respects that mark the shortcomings of the international law of to-day. Among primitive peoples we find want of precision in the details of law, a tendency to deny its authority, and, above all, the absence of a proper sanction to enforce it. It is only as a nation becomes organized that swift retribution follows on the breach of law. The condition of English constitutional law, amid the feudal anarchy of the reign of Rufus or the reign of Stephen, is no bad analogy of the condition of international law to-day. The rules protecting the rights of individuals and regulating the powers of government possessed few of the characteristics of proper law as we now understand that term, but yet contained the germs from which the constitution of to-day has grown. Most of the objections that are urged against the provisions of the treaty of Paris, or of Berlin being ranked as laws, might with equal justice have been used against the articles of Magna Carta. So far as these stipula-tions were meant to bind the king they could only be en-forced by armed resistance—by what has been called " a limited right of rebellion"; just as the sanction of inter-national laws depends to-day upon the right to declare war where they are infringed. Even in the Great Britain of the nineteenth century we cannot say that law has obtained a complete triumph until it is impossible that any law should ever be broken, or at least that such breach should ever go unpunished. Now, England many centuries ago obtained a proper government and constitution for the guaranteeing and enforcing of her law within her own territories; while the rules of international law have still to seek such an organization, without which they can never be complete. International law can never attain maturity apart from the realization of its necessary complements, an international government, international institutions, and a body of rules for their regulation, forming an international constitution, and defining the legal seat of the international sovereignty.

The rudiments of such a government already exist. Thus when two powers appoint arbitrators to decide a disputed point, the tribunal thus constituted performs in a sense the judicial functions of an international government. Unfortunately, however, it forms *merely the rudiments* of a court of law, and that for the following among other reasons: (1) The tribunal does not sit permanently. (2) It has jurisdiction only where and so far as both parties are agreed. The plaintiff State cannot force an unwilling defendant to appear in court. Its jurisdiction depends on contract. (3) It has no executive arm at its back to enforce its decrees if the unsuccessful party should repudiate them.

With all their defects, however, such courts of arbitration form the germs of an international judicatory. The rudiments of a central legislative body again are met with in such meetings of Plenipotentiaries as those that led to the treaties of Paris or Berlin; and the provisions of these treaties bear a close analogy to statutes effecting a change in existing customary law. This legislative chamber for the world (or for Europe at all events) has not only no fixed times of meeting, but no recognized rules exist to determine the method of its summons, its composition, and procedure. Lastly, the only rudiments of an international executive lie in the armies and navies of the separate nations which own, of course, no directing voice of the assembled powers as a whole. Each military agency is at the disposal only of its own home government. Brute force has been shown to be an essential factor in all executive functions, and therefore in all governments; but if anarchy is to be successfully opposed, this brute force must obey the voice of the central authority. Indeed, government within a State comes to mean that whenever an appeal to force is necessary, the coercion of the whole must prevail over the coercion of the part.

Here, then, it is possible to lay a finger on the very essence of the difference between the loose ties that bind together independent States, and the close ties that subject the citizens of one nation to its common will. There is no central authority in international politics authorized to direct the ultimate application of brute force. Before the nations of Europe or of the world can form one organized whole, the first essential is a central executive government. The first step towards the making of a united English nation was taken when William the Conqueror established an almost despotic central government, able by sheer force to curb the anarchy of the barons' misrule, and the chaotic powers of feudalism. The shortest road to the organization of humanity into one universal State would seem to demand a world-conqueror whose iron rule would crush out all absolute dualisms and all rebellions against his sovereign power. It may be that the dream of a universal empire under some new Caesar Augustus or Napoleon must be realized before the nations are welded into one, and that a universal despotism of one man is a necessary precursor of the ideal democratic State whose citizens number all races, colours, and classes of humanity.

The process of the growth of a World-state may, however, take quite a different direction. Everything leads us to suppose, indeed, that if an organized polity for the whole earth is ever accomplished, men must look for a precedent to the consolidation of the States of America into a united nation, though starting as a loose confederation or aggregate of almost isolated powers. Whatever the process, no material progress can be made without the establishment of a central government with a common executive organ, which will take its directions from a deliberative or legislative sovereign, ready to use its powers in a recognized and legal way. The place filled by physical force in the universe must never be ignored, and every law or government or constitution will be a sham unless it has behind it or within it a supply of actual coercive power to enable it successfully to contend with the un-systematized forces opposing it.

The necessity of actual force must never be forgotten in any scheme of world-organization. But this involves no stigma; it merely means the triumph of a systematic, orderly, and legitimate coercion over the unruly, tyrannic, and anarchic one which would otherwise prevail.

Coercion is necessary to keep effectively together any State or federation already formed; and it may be both expedient and just to compel outside powers to join the confederacy. As within the territory of Britain it is at present considered the duty of the government to compel every body of evil-doers to join the community of law-abiding citizens, or to punish them if they refuse, so it would be the duty of an international federation to compel the obedience of any barbarous nation which defied the provisions of inter-national law, or of the common code of humanity embodied in the admitted private law of all civilized States.

The great powers of Europe do not yet form a federation in name, but they all own adherence to the same general rules of international law, and to the same elementary code of morality. It is their duty to compel such nations as Turkey to join them in adhering to the laws of humanity and of international usage, and to punish them if they refuse. Turkey ought to be coerced to join the federation of mankind, or to be swept out of existence as a State.

To those, then, who maintain that it is impossible that all the races of humanity should be joined into one empire, under one government and constitution, we may answer that this has been already done, but that the cohesion of the parts is still imperfect because of the imperfection of the machinery that connects them. The World-state is there already, but it is just emerging from a condition of anarchy, and struggling slowly and painfully towards a more highly developed life. It lacks proper organization.

There is no absolute bar to the realization of this dream in the fact that the various nations of the world are at different stages of civilization, though this undoubtedly is a great and serious difficulty, which may retard its consummation for many ages. Yet, in the first place, all nations seem progressing towards the same ideal, and in time the more backward may make up to some extent on the more advanced. In the second place, the increase of facilities for travel and the growth of international commerce help to diffuse ideas more equally over the globe. Lastly, in a World-state, it does not seem necessary that all nations and races (at first, at least) should stand upon a level. The more backward may be coerced by the more civilized for the common good. Coercion, of course, in which the conquered cannot ultimately be brought willingly to acquiesce, must never be a final ideal, only a necessary preliminary that will lead to better things.

The ultimate ideal union must be a very close one—must be, in fact, organic in its nature. The "federation of the world," or the federation of civilized nations, and the subjugation of barbarous ones, would thus be only a beginning. A perfect union would involve a constitution which gradually bound the originally separate States more and more together until they became one nation, one commonwealth, one State.[1]

It is impossible to forecast the exact way in which this organized commonwealth of mankind will be brought to pass, or even to prophesy that it will ever be a reality. It seems, however, quite within the province of the political theorist to maintain that there are no insuperable difficulties which render it impossible.

This world-empire of love cannot become perfect until every part is perfect too. Every division must be, both in

---

[1] Cf. Kant's *Principles of Politics* (Hastie's translation), p. 24, where he declares that the States of our Continent "are beginning to arrange for a great future political body, such as the world has never yet seen. Although this political body may as yet exist only in a rough outline, nevertheless a feeling begins, as it were, to stir in all its members, each of which has a common interest in the maintenance of the whole. And this may well inspire the hope that after many political revolutions and transformations, the highest purpose of Nature will be at last realized in the establishment of a universal Cosmopolitical Institution, in the bosom of which all the original capacities and endowments of the human species will be unfolded and developed."

legal constitution and in its heart and life, **in touch** with
every other, and each individual must have his political rights
assigned to him in the constitution of the whole, and must
freely share in the common interests and life.   Thus the ideal
would involve a perfect adjustment of that nice balance
between individual freedom and the sovereignty of the whole,
which is the essence of the organic conception as applied to any
State.   The life of the part and the life of the whole would re-
quire to pass into one another, and so find their fullest and most
perfect realization in this organized community of humanity.

PART II.

THE PROVINCE OF LAW AND GOVERNMENT.

CHAPTER XII.

THE PROBLEM OF THE PROVINCE OF GOVERNMENT.

POLITICAL speculation of former centuries centred round
the problem of the ideal form of constitution, to the neglect
of the equally important inquiry as to the limits that
should be placed to government interference. Plato and
Aristotle laid the foundations of the science which attempts
the study of constitutions in comparison with one another.
It is only within the present century, on the contrary, that
serious attempts have been made towards a systematic solution of the other great question of political science : What
is the proper sphere of the government's activity ? Indeed,
until comparatively recent years, no one seems to have been
conscious of the difficulty which the inquiry involves.
Particular governments went on doing whatever happened
to lie to their hand, without stopping to ask whether they
were going beyond their legitimate province. Not only did
the question of the best form of constitution divert all
attention from that of the proper work of government, but
it is on the answers given to the former that every acknowledged system of party politics has been based. It is the
only ground for the division of politicians into two great
opposing camps of Liberals and Conservatives. It has thus
made possible in Great Britain that " standing wonder " of
the English Constitution, described by Walter Bagehot [1] as
" government by a *public meeting*—by a club "—for so he
characterizes the predominance of the House of Commons

[1] *The English Constitution*, p. 139.

within the sovereignty of Parliament. There is only one way in which such a government can work at all, and that is by having the cumbrous assembly of 670 individuals organized on party lines.

Hitherto in the history of party government the principle of classification has always been mainly the *form* of the constitution—whether the present institutions should be maintained intact, or, if not, what extent of change should be effected upon them, and in what direction. This is the basis of the separation between Petitioners and Abhorrers, between Whigs and Tories, between Conservatives and Radicals, and even between Unionists and Home Rulers.

With the advent of practical democracy, however (in the sense that the influence of the people as a whole is now the chief factor in moulding the nation's destinies, whatever be the nominal form of government), the line of demarcation between party and party is less clearly defined than formerly; and there are those who prognosticate that the old basis of division is almost played out and a new one needed to take its place.

Now, behind the question of what is the best form of constitution lies the problem of determining the proper sphere of the work of government. The latter inquiry indeed lies deeper than the former, and ought in strict logical sequence to be answered first. It is becoming clear to many minds that it is necessary to determine what the government ought to perform before deciding what shape it should assume in order to perform it.

It is possible and even probable, then, that the line of cleavage in party politics in the future will be determined by the answers which men give to the question: "What ought the State *to do*?" According as they hold that more ought to be done or less than at present, politicians may come to range themselves into two great classes adopting the watchwords of Socialism and Individualism respectively, using these words in their broadest meanings. Here, then, is a new possible line on which distinctions of party in the future may be based. The politicians of the past have confined their conscious exertions to moulding the

structure of the government. Those of the future will look
more to its *province* or sphere of action.

Without prophesying for the future, however, it becomes
increasingly apparent in the present century that, underlying
the division of Liberal and Conservative, or of Home Ruler
and Unionist, another principle of classification is showing
itself. In addition to openly avowed Socialists holding opinions more or less extreme, there are many statesmen of even
cabinet rank in both camps whose policy involves principles
essentially socialistic, if carried out to their legitimate logical
conclusions, though many of them would indignantly repudiate the name. This fact has been insisted on by Mr.
Herbert Spencer with his accustomed vigour—not to say
violence—in his well-known Essays on *The New Toryism*
and *The Coming Slavery.*[1] He assumes rather than proves
the principle that increased interference by the State means
necessarily a proportionate decrease in the liberty of the
individual; and then goes on to show that Liberals of the
new school, in joining with Tories to extend the province
of government interference, are pushing the nation headlong towards a system of State Socialism, which is for him
synonymous with slavery. "The coming slavery" is thus
Socialism; while "the new Toryism" denounced by Mr. Spencer
is simply the supposed anti-individualistic tendency of the
modern school of Liberals. Thus the foes as well as the
friends of Socialism recognize the important place its doctrines
hold in present politics, and the likelihood that this will
increase in the future. A clear idea of the issues at stake
is as yet confined to theorists; but the opposition between
practical politicians exists although not yet clearly defined.

One party holds consciously or unconsciously that the
State ought through its government directly to interfere in
the affairs of its subjects, with the view of ameliorating the
material lot, and advancing the spiritual interests of the
people. It is urged, for example, that the government should
undertake the management of the railways, and go further
in the direction of providing free education, literature, and
art, along with increased material comfort in the form of

[1] Vide *The Man* versus *the State.*

L

poor-law relief or compulsory insurance. Others hold that the subjects, in their private capacity, are the best judges of what they want, and best able to obtain it when least troubled by the meddlesome legislation of a government whose sole duty ought to be the protection of society from crime and from foreign interference.

On every hand evidence is forthcoming that, both in the world of speculation and in that of practical politics, the question of the limits of government interference is pushing rapidly to the front.

"Now for the first time," says Sheldon Amos,[1] "government is put upon its trial, and required to justify its retention of a hold upon any part of human activity—and to justify it on exactly such grounds as would supply a logical test of the justice of any other usurpation on human liberty."

Two strong currents of feeling are running in opposite directions; and their frequent collisions seem to call for a systematic attempt to find some principle by which they may be reconciled, or at least some criterion in the light of which they may be judged. On the one hand is the tendency to question the right of the State to interfere with vested interests or individual rights or inclinations. On the other is the tendency of every distressed class or industry to cry, not "*Can* you help us?" or "*Ought* you to help us?" but "*What* help are you bringing us?"—assuming that government must and will do something. "The extension of State-action," says Mr. Goschen,[2] "to new and vast fields of business is not the most striking feature. What is of far deeper import is its growing interference with the relations between classes, its increased control over vast categories of transactions between individuals, and the substitution in many of the dealings of trade and manufacture, of the aggregate conscience and moral sense of the nation for the conscience and moral sense of men as units. The parent in dealing with his child, the employer in dealing with his workmen, the shipbuilder in the construction of his ships, the shipowner in the treatment of his sailors, the houseowner

---

[1] *Science of Politics*, p. 380.
[2] Address on *Laissez faire and State Interference.*

in the management of his house property, the landowner in
his contracts with his tenants, have been notified by public
opinion or by actual law that the time has gone by
when the cry of *Laissez-nous faire* would be answered in the
affirmative."

Each of these comparatively new departures in the intervention of government thus indicated by Mr. Goschen is
subjected to the closest scrutiny and criticism. Some urge
that it has gone too far. Others that it has not gone
nearly far enough. Most agree, however, that the line
should be drawn somewhere ; and the difficult problem for
all such is to show *where.*

Thus John Stuart Mill[1] thought that the great problem
was to discover exactly where to place the boundary "between
individual independence and social control." This is substantially the same ground which Wilhelm von Humboldt
had previously taken up in his great work on the sphere
of government, in which the problem is viewed as one
of balancing security against freedom, like two forces that
tend to act in opposite directions.

The answer to this question as to the proper province of
government must obviously depend to some extent upon the
view taken of the nature of the State. If the latter, for
example, is held to have no connection whatever with the
morality of its subjects, the government could not consistently
claim to act with the object of regulating their ethical
relations to one another. The converse, however, does not
necessarily hold ; for the State may include much within
its own sphere which it does not deem expedient or just
to confide to the care of government. The sphere of the
State is fixed and unchangeable ; but the province of
government is alterable, and may be changed as expediency
requires, and that even in an arbitrary or capricious fashion.
It is for the State itself, by its sovereign legislature, to
map out the respective provinces of its various institutions.
It is quite possible—and indeed probable—that what is a
proper subject of interference in one nation or race is improper in another, and even that what is suited for any

[1] *Essay on Liberty*, p. 18.

community at one stage of its development may be unsuitable for the same community at another. The determination of the province of government, then, is eminently a practical matter, and is usually settled on grounds of expediency.

Modern theories of both sorts—those which would restrict the limits of government action and those which would extend them—usually spring from the purest motives. The most obstinate optimist cannot shut his eyes to the existence of evils which are at least relatively and temporarily real, even if capable of absorption in an ultimate and eternal good. Suffering and discomfort, unhappiness and want, are seen on every hand. Some of these are undoubtedly inseparable from the imperfections of human nature as it exists in its present fallen or undeveloped phase. Yet conscious action of individuals may do much to increase or lessen particular evils. If such action cannot be proved to alter their sum materially, it does often move part of the burden from one shoulder to another. The government, acting in the name and with the united power of the whole community, has a hundredfold more ability to grapple with such evils than the simple citizen ever can have. It is difficult to resist the conclusion that the conduct of governments, whether in acting or in letting alone, is largely responsible for the existence, or at any rate, the distribution, of most of the suffering that exists in the world. If this is so, the great problem of the statesman ought to be to frame rules of action, by adherence to which the government may be enabled to do the utmost that is possible to alleviate existing evils; or, at lowest (if State-action is found in the last analysis to be not a source of direct good, but merely a necessary evil), to do the least possible amount of harm.

It is thus a genuine desire to benefit humanity which leads most men consciously to enter upon this discussion. They ask, What attitude must the government adopt towards the suffering and sorrow, the distress and poverty that everywhere abound? Many different answers are given to this question; but all of them may be reduced under five heads.

(1) The first answer is that government, in the discharge of both its legislative and its administrative duties, ought simply

to go on as it is doing at present. Evils should be dealt with piecemeal as they arise. In this view all *systems* are misleading. The only guide is common-sense. There is no use of making generalizations at all, for each evil has its own special causes, and must be considered by itself. Government is working well enough on the whole on its present basis. It cannot cure everything, and does its best when any social distress becomes unbearable. This is the attitude of the " practical politician," who is nothing more than practical. He waits till evils show themselves and then tinkers them one by one as they arise. This attitude has its dangers, however, apart altogether from its want of a scientific basis. To wait till the various troubles raise themselves to the surface, and then give them just sufficient treatment to cause them to hide themselves in their ordinary lurking-places again, is both heartless and absurd. It is the policy of a superficial doctor who attacks the symptoms instead of the root of the disease ; and is more likely to throw the illness inwards to a vital part than to effect a cure. The " practical politician "— that object of Mr. Spencer's scorn—is apt to alter the seat of a social evil rather than to root it out. He is apt to cause ten new evils to come into existence, each worse than the one he sought to cure. His theory, or rather lack of a theory, may be called the opportunist solution of the problem.

(2) The second answer to the question is that of the Socialist—let the government step in boldly and undertake far more than it does at present—let it, in fact (say extreme votaries of this doctrine), regulate *everything*. The evils complained of are due in great measure to the free play of the unrestrained evil passions of individuals. Government ought, by force, if necessary, to hold these in check, and it would then become a kind of terrestrial Providence, whose duty would be to remedy every ill that flesh is heir to. It would in particular supersede the evils of competition and the unequal distribution of wealth, by regulating all trade and industry by a central system of control. It would own all land, railways, machinery, and, in short, all property of every kind—leaving only the rights of use to the private citizen.

(3) A third opinion is the direct opposite of this. Existing evils which are by their nature remedial, so far from being curable by government intervention, are directly caused by it. Government has no business to meddle with things outside its proper province, and that is at best a very narrow one. In whatever direction the State carries its well-meant but fussy interference with private interests, it does harm. So far from seeking to extend its province, its only wise policy is to recede as quickly as possible from the abnormal functions it has already undertaken, and so allow nature and the free play of individual interests to restore a healthy tone to the community disordered by the intrusion of artificial restraints. Few advocates of this doctrine have the courage to carry it to an extreme equal to that of the Socialists on the opposite side. Few of them hold—as, to be consistent, they ought to hold—that government should never interfere by force at all; for this would be practically to reject government altogether. Many of them think that it should do nothing further than what is, in their opinion, absolutely necessary for the preservation of an organized society in which men's rights are safe from violent invasion. This is the individualistic solution.

(4) The fourth view tries to distinguish between the provinces of the individual and of the State. The latter lies (as it were) round the centre of the circle, while each social atom has his individual sphere somewhere near the circumference. Thus the respective fields of State-action and of individual-action are mutually exclusive. To say that anything is a matter for the individual to decide, is (in this view) equivalent to saying that the government has no right or (at any rate) no business to interfere. A hard and fast boundary line exists somewhere, and the problem is to discover it. Government may therefore sin either by excess or by defect. It approaches perfection according as it correctly estimates the whereabouts of this boundary and acts accordingly.

When men attempt to draw this line even in theory, however, a thousand disagreements spring up. No two authors of any note agree as to its exact position. The practical difficulty is even greater than the theoretical one. This doctrine of compromise acquires **more** importance from the fact **that** it is adopted in practice by almost all of those who are professed Individualists **in** theory. Few **of them** are ready to **abolish** government **interference** altogether, however they **may narrow** it **down.** They usually allow some small province in **which it is** both right **and** expedient **that the** will **of the** State should **overrule that** of the particular **citizen.** Mill would **fix** the **limit at** "self-protection," and Mr. Spencer at "negative **as** opposed **to** positive coercion." Each of these so-called Individualists makes some concession to socialistic tendencies, and so falls short of absolute Individualism pure **and simple. Each** attempts to draw his line somewhere, **so as to** bind **up** government's right of action within **a** limited circle. **All** practical Individualists have thus something in common with this fourth **school,** which may be called the school of compromise. **Unfortunately, however,** no such line exists by nature. **It is artificial and** arbitrary in every case; and this is proved alike by the logical impossibility of any such absolute dualism existing in **nature, and by the practical** failure of any two theorists to **agree** as to its actual **where-abouts.**

(5) There is yet another solution which rejects all **these views** equally. It may be held that, while extreme Socialism and extreme Individualism are equally impossible in practice and unsound in theory, because each ignores **the essential** factor in human nature exaggerated by the other, all compromise between them is also impossible and unsound, in starting from a false antithesis between the individual and the State. A fifth theory, then, asserts that no province **can be** found which is absolutely that of the State, in the sense of excluding individual action, while equally there is no province of the isolated subject which absolutely excludes the government. **The** individual finds his sphere to be no narrower than **the State** itself, while the sphere of the government **may be logically extended** to embrace all the interests and actions **of every** man and woman. This is the theory of organic unity, **which** holds it absurd to **draw a line** between two

things whose essential nature lies in their connection with each other.

This may seem merely a theoretical answer to the problem, but it prepares the way for the only solution that will work in practice. No absolute barrier of any kind can be set up anywhere to the action of the government, which has both a right and a duty to do everything the State entrusts it with; and the State must insist on government undertaking everything which will further its ultimate end, or any of its more immediate aims legitimate in themselves and consistent with the final goal. The actual province of any government, then, is just whatever is entrusted to it by the sovereign legislature as the source of positive law. The ideal province is that which is best fitted to fulfil the final destiny (or, what is the same thing, to realize the highest welfare) of the nation as a branch of the family of mankind. Its limits may thus shift from time to time, and from country to country. No absolute boundaries or rules can be laid down a priori. Granted the final goal of humanity and end of the State, the province of government must be mapped out on the ordinary lines of justice and expediency. It must advance or retire with the changing requirements of circumstances and affairs. The justification of interference is in each case a matter of degree. The government ought to interfere in any place to which the sovereignty of the State extends, if the good it thus effects outweighs on the whole the evil. But in estimating such evil and good, reference must be made to remote contingencies, as well as near ones— a broad statesmanlike view must be taken, founded on a wide experience of affairs and on the principles of human nature as laid down by the most advanced science of the day.

This fifth solution of the problem, which is here taken to be the only sound one, differs from all the others. It differs from the first in condemning the policy of mere drifting with the current, without formulating principles of guidance and without listening to the voice of science. It condemns the treatment of each case as an isolated problem, and the see-saw inconsistent policy that results—one thing straggling in one direction, while its fellow drifts in the other. Every act of policy must be ultimately judged by the final end of the State itself, and by those approved minor ends which political science has declared to be for the time consistent with and conducive to that higher goal. Thus a principle of order is introduced.

It differs also from the socialistic plan. For, though it concedes that the government *may* be lawfully and justly endowed with powers to do everything, it admits no absolute presumption in favour of community of property or of government interference as opposed to private initiative.

It differs from Individualism in refusing to admit the truth of any philosophy which would find man's highest good apart from his fellow-men, and because it refuses to admit any absolute limits to the action of the central authority acting for the good of the whole.

It differs from those who would effect a compromise between the last two theories, because it cannot admit any distinct province of the man apart from the State. It does not look on the government and the subject as two unconnected principles which approach each other from opposite sides, and it does not try to allocate the sum of human interests between them, settling by a contract or compromise that everything on this side of an imaginary line goes to the one party and everything on that side to the other.

It vindicates the claims of science over the haphazard policy and caprice of opportunist politicians ; the claims of individual liberty against the cramping bondage of a State-regulated Socialism ; the claims of the sovereignty of the community against the pretentions to an absolute independence of any class or person within it ; the claims of the final goal of humanity to prevail over every more restricted good ; the claims of the subject to share the full free life of the commonwealth ; and the claims of practical expediency not to be set aside by any " doctrinaire " theory made up of hard and fast rules, which it cannot bend to its own will.

Dangers attend all extreme theories, and without some knowledge of their nature and some rule of guidance it is impossible to steer a clear course in their midst. Sheldon Amos well expresses the evils on either hand : " The advocate of over-government only succeeds in his ends by sacrificing personal freedom, by weakening private and public energy, and by substituting machinery for life. The advocate of doctrines which would restrict government to the mere functions of defending property and order, must account it a success when the convenience, the health, the morality, and the prosperity of the innumerable weak and poor are placed under the irresponsible control of the limited number of strong and rich." [1]

According as men lean to one side or the other they may be classed as Socialists or Individualists, and their respective solutions of our problem call for detailed examination.

[1] *Science of Politics*, p. 125.

CHAPTER XIII.

THE SOCIALISTIC SOLUTION.

THE word Socialism covers almost as many systems of thought as the word philosophy itself. There are theorists of a hundred different shades of opinion, and politicians belonging to every party and country, who yet agree in being proud to call themselves Socialists. Further, there are men of all complexions, from Radicals to Tory Reactionaries, who would equally unite in an indignant repudiation of any connection with Socialism, while all the time their whole practical influence as voters and as legislators, or even as Cabinet Ministers, is unconsciously exerted towards giving an impetus to the existing tendencies that make for Collectivism. Thus Socialists differ among themselves widely in kind, as well as infinitely in degree. There are thorough-going Communists who consciously hold the principles of the sect, and would boldly and consistently apply them to every phase of human life. Others own the name with equal pride, but would put limitations more or less wide on the range of topics to which it may safely be applied. Others, again, are only unconsciously Socialists, stumbling, as it were, blindly in its direction in their efforts to remove specific economic or political evils, or in trying generally to advance mankind. In practice and theory, then, Socialism assumes a thousand forms.

From this very wealth of material comes the chief difficulty of the student. He is baffled in trying to grasp its essential characteristics, to describe what it really is, and

to estimate its merits and defects.   It is hard to find what
is really common or necessary to every one of its phases.
It is harder to state a criticism that applies to all.   To one
who praises the methods or raises objections to the tendencies
of any known form of Communism or Collectivism, the
rejoinder is simple—that the criticism does not apply to
Socialism generally, but merely to that warped manifestation
of it which has been arbitrarily selected for eulogy or
attack.

The difficulties of stating the essentials of Socialism, so as to
satisfy all its votaries, are increased from the variety of motives
which lead different individuals to adopt its tenets.   Some seek
it as the only remedy for the wide-spread misery caused by the
excessive inequality of the distribution of wealth.   They cry
to the State to step in and prevent this inequality (by force
if need be).   Such people again are of many classes.   Some
are merely the idle refuse of the population, who wish a
share of the prosperity which their own laziness or vice has
prevented them from gaining honestly for themselves.   Others
are rich men, acting from motives of the highest and most
disinterested philanthropy.   Between these two extremes are
many varying shades of men and principles, agreeing yet
in this, that the primary object of their aspirations is a
more equal distribution of property.   Socialism is, by many
of its adherents, looked upon chiefly as a system of
joint-ownership.   Other consequences may be logically and
practically involved, but its primary object is to attack the
institution of private property.   All possessions should, in
this view, be merged in the community.   Socialism thus to
many comes to mean State ownership of property.[1]   Even
here, however, there are minor differences of motive and
degree.   Some content themselves with the State-ownership
of land ; others think that all mills, factories, and machinery
should also be held in common by the State.   Some would

[1] Cf. the late Mr. Bradlaugh's definition cited by Professor Flint,
Socialism, p. 16 : "Socialism denies individual private property, and
affirms that society organized as the State should own all wealth,
direct all labour, and compel the equal distribution of all produce."

simply confiscate,[1] while others would allow compensation.
To annex to the use of the State all incomes above a certain
amount; to limit the rights of bequest and succession, are all
phases of Socialism, or at least of theories that would set
bounds to unrestricted Individualism. Some would have a
yearly or weekly redivision, while others would boldly abolish
all rights of individual property at once and for ever. Other
types of men, again, are led to Socialism by quite different
roads. By the doctrine of original sin all men are naturally
wicked. Indeed apart from all theological dogmas, it is easy
to see how evil passions run wild if left to themselves. Tendencies to all forms of depravity are rooted in man's nature,
and need only fit occasion to ripen and bear bad fruit.
Individual men, if left to themselves, will work for their
own selfish interests. Thence will follow their own moral
degradation on the one hand, and injury to the temporal
and eternal welfare of their neighbours on the other. The
strong arm of the civil law, or the intervention of the
spiritual power equipped with book and bell, is needed to
restrain these evil passions. Man needs guidance. Both
the State and the Church ought therefore, it is said, to
interfere to protect him from himself as well as from others.
Such an attitude of mind leads men to regard liberty
almost as something evil in itself, because likely to be
abused. Authority is thus invoked; and so those who
call for it are led consciously or unconsciously in the
direction of Socialism. Under this aspect, Communism may
be organized under the wing of the Church as well as of
the State. Traces of it indeed may be found in the claims
constantly put forth by the Roman Catholic Church. Many
tendencies of a similar nature are found in civil institutions
both ancient and modern, and in the programmes of each of
the rival political parties of the present day. Thus Local
Option would authorize the community to step in and
save the individual in spite of himself from the tempta-
tion which his moral nature is unable to resist, while
compulsory insurance against old age makes the State
the forcible guardian of each man against the effects of his

[1] See Mr. Henry George's *Progress and Poverty.*

own improvidence.   It is from this point of view that
Mr. Hyndman,[1] in his historic debate with Mr. Bradlaugh,
defined Socialism as "an endeavour to substitute for the
anarchical struggle or fight for existence an organized co-
operation for existence."

Amid so much diversity of motive, form, and degree,
where are we to look for the constant and essential features of Socialism, most comprehensively considered ?   What
is the one test which may be applied to all systems alike
as a sure criterion ?   Such a test is to be found in the
undue subordination of individuality to the community, in
the triumph more or less complete of the State over the
man.

In determining the relations between the State and the
Individual, all systems of Socialism, however they may differ
in methods or aims, place the chief emphasis on the former
to the detriment of the latter.[2]

The trouble experienced by some writers in deciding
whether Socialism is primarily a social or a political scheme,
is only one phase of the initial difficulty of definition.   The
truth is that it is necessarily both ; but the place where
the emphasis is laid varies with the point of view.   Those
who look primarily to the end to be obtained, picture
Socialism as a reorganization of society, especially in its
economic aspects, while those who concern themselves more
with the means of realization—on a universal scale and a
compulsory basis, at any rate—regard it as a political system.

Thus men whose kind hearts sicken at the misery and
poverty of the proletariat and who expect some alleviation
from a more equal distribution of material wealth and of
the enjoyment it brings, desire a new organization of society,
and to this they give the name of Socialism.   When they

---

[1] Cited in Professor Flint's *Socialism*, p. 15.

[2] Cf. Professor Flint, *Socialism*, p. 17.   "Socialism, as I understand it,
is any theory of social organization which sacrifices the legitimate liberties of individuals to the will and interests of the community."   The word
"legitimate" indicates an individualistic bias ; but if such an adjective as
"selfish" or "aggressive" were substituted, the definition would probably
be accepted by Socialists.

seek a practical means of realizing their dream, they **find**
that, apart from small select communities founded **on a
voluntary** basis, **the** only effective agency is the coercive
power of the State. The name comes then to be transferred
from the aim to the machinery which effects the **aim. It**
becomes now **a system of** regulation by **the government, or**
what Professor Huxley calls " regimentation."

Thus Socialism in its ends is a social scheme, **and** in its
means a political system.

Socialism is usually divided into **two** branches—Communism and Collectivism. The main difference is that the
former tries to attain its ends on a voluntary or contractual
basis, and is consequently only possible upon a limited
scale; while the latter[1] seeks to make its principles universal
and compulsory through the legislative and executive powers
of the State.

The idea of political organization is naturally more closely
associated with the **latter**; but even in a small community
voluntarily practising socialistic principles, some system of
"government" is essential. **The element of** "control" is
present, though willingly submitted **to. All** socialistic aims
require a regime of regimentation **to** enforce them; while all
regimentation tends in the direction of Socialism. **They are
always closely** combined in practice, though logically distinct.

The essential characteristics of Socialism may then be
roughly given as two—one social or economic and the other
political. "In the first place," says M. Ed. de Laveleye,[2]
"every Socialistic doctrine aims at introducing greater equality
into social conditions; and secondly, it tries to realize these
reforms **by the** action of the law or the State."

The essence of all such schemes is the absorption **of the**
individual **in** the community—of his rights **in the** rights

---

[1] **Cf.** Professor Flint's definition **of** Collectivism (*Socialism*, p. 63) as
"Society organized as the State intervening in all the industrial and
economic arrangements of life, possessing almost everything, and so
controlling and directing its members that private and personal enter-
prises and interests are absorbed **in** those which are public and
collective."

[2] *Socialism of To-day*, p. 15.

of all, of his property in the property of the State.   The
more logically and thoroughly the doctrines of the sect
are held, the more readily this is perceived, and the more
complete the disappearance of the unit in the mass becomes.
Its opponents say that its ultimate goal is slavery.   This
annihilation of the individual is, however, the feature most
strenuously denied by most of its advocates.   While it is
usually admitted that some sacrifice of liberty, or perhaps
rather of caprice, is involved, it is at the same time maintained that so small an offering should be willingly made
to gain so much happiness for oneself and for humanity.
In some systems this feature is less prominent than in
others, but that is only because less of the essence of
Socialism is there realized.   Look on it as we may,
Collectivism always means the triumph of coercion over
freedom, of authority over rights of private men, of the
condition of *status* over that of contract.   It is not to be
assumed that therefore Socialism stands condemned, or that
coercion is always an evil.   Proof is required before this is
taken for granted.   There is no benefit to be gained, however,
by denying the necessary connection between Socialism and a
severe regime of government control.[1]   This control may be
of various kinds.   It may be such as the individual gladly
welcomes, or an aggressive authority thrust on him from
without.   His acquiescence or resistance will naturally make
a difference in the extent to which he feels the weight of
the yoke.   His attitude will be influenced further by the
nature of the sanction or penalty by which this control is
enforced, and also by the nature of the authority wielding
the coercive powers, which may be either an irresponsible
monarch or a representative assembly.   While all such
systems absorb the rights of the individual in the community at large, the form called Collectivism or State
Socialism—Government Socialism would be a better word
—seeks to place everything under the direct management
of the ordinary civil authorities.   It is a sacrifice of each
individual self to the exigencies of the government.   It

[1] *Infra*, p. 198, the question is discussed how far the benefits of
Socialism can be obtained under voluntary association.

is true that on the organic theory of society each man must lose himself in the State; but that State becomes for him an outer or second self. He finds there his own life "writ large." ' It is a losing of a lower self to find a higher one—"a dying to live." To be dragged into the mechanism of a bureaucratic administrative system is a very different matter. Such a government is a cold dead thing, and if the separate lives of the citizens are swallowed up in it, this means the end of life altogether. Man's life is only realizable in the society of other men; but it becomes unbearable and impossible if absorbed absolutely in the government.

Thus the old distinction between State and government comes to the surface again. To say that the individual life ought to be absorbed in the former, may be termed philosophic Socialism, and is quite true in a sense of every community, though only one half of the truth, but to absorb it in the latter is a practical Socialism, as untenable in theory as it would be deplorable in practice. The union between the whole and its members, between the Sovereign and the subjects, must be organic and not mechanical. Socialism, like Individualism, is a relative truth. Both must be taken together. No travesty of a healthy State is more deplorable than a practical Socialism in the form of an absolute government directing with inquisitorial and irresistible sway every detail of human life.

Socialism has been described[1] as "a political organization in which the individual is sacrificed to society." In a sense this is true of every society. The individual's selfish interests must give way to those of the community when a conflict of interests arises; but on the other hand he is a member of that society to which he subordinates his own petty aims, and the true good of the whole must include what is best for him. Extreme forms of Socialism might perhaps better be described as a sacrifice of the good of the individual to the exigencies of *government*; while the organic theory requires merely a subordination of what is evil in the citizens to the welfare of the *State*.

[1] By M. Lerouse, cited by Professor Flint, *Socialism*, p. 17.

M

For reasons already stated, it is difficult to select any one writer as a type of the whole school. For the purpose of obtaining a rough and ready statement of the aims and uses of Socialism from the point of view of its average warm advocate, no better choice can perhaps be made than the exposition contained in *Merrie England*. The great popularity which has greeted this book, particularly among the working classes, testifies to the degree of accuracy with which it has caught the special aspects of Socialism floating in the air and likely to appeal to the mind of the British voter of average education and intelligence. Mr. Blatchford's book aims at being practical, and avoids to a great extent extremes of all kinds both in style and matter. It is right to state, however, that it is specially referred to here by no means because it is the best or strongest exposition of the case for Socialism —though it is by no means the worst—but because from its very mediocrity it represents accurately enough the common ground occupied by all. Mr. Blatchford begins by dividing Socialism into practical and ideal.

"Practical Socialism," he says,[1] "is so simple that a child may understand it. It is a kind of national scheme of co-operation managed by the State. Its programme consists essentially of one demand, that the land and other instruments of production shall be the property of the people, and shall be used and governed by the people for the people. Make the land and all the instruments of production State property; put all farms, mines, mills, ships, railways, and shops under State control, as you have already put the postal and telegraphic services under State control, and Practical Socialism is accomplished. . . . Socialists point out that if all the industries of the nation were put under State control, all the profit, which now goes into the hands of a few idle men, would go into the coffers of the State—which means that the people would enjoy the benefits of all the wealth they create. This then is the basis of Socialism, that England should be owned by the English and managed for the benefit of the English instead of being owned by a few rich idlers and mismanaged by them for

[1] *Merrie England*, p. 100.

the benefit of themselves. But Socialism means more than
the mere transference of the wealth of the nation to the
nation. Socialism would not endure competition. Where
it found two factories engaged in under-cutting each other
at the price of long hours and low wages to the workers,
it would step in and fuse the two concerns into one, save
an immense sum in cost of working, and finally produce
more goods and better goods at a lower figure than were
produced before. . . . But Practical Socialism would do
more than that, it would educate the people. It would
provide cheap and pure food. It would extend and elevate
the means of study and amusement. It would foster
literature and science and art. It would encourage and
reward genius and industry. It would abolish sweating and
jerry work. It would demolish the slums and would erect
good and handsome dwellings. It would compel all men to
do some kind of useful work. It would recreate and
nourish the craftsman's pride in his craft. It would protect women and children. It would raise health and
morality; and it would take the sting out of pauperism
by paying pensions to honest workers no longer able to
work. . . .

"Under Ideal Socialism there would be no money at all,
and no wages. The industry of the country would be
organized and managed by the State much as the Post
Office now is; goods of all kinds would be produced and
distributed for use, and not for sale, in such quantities as
were needed; hours of labour would be fixed; and every
citizen would take what he or she desired from the common
stock. Food, clothing, lodging, fuel, transit, amusements, and
all other things, would be absolutely free, and the only
difference between a prime minister and a collier would be
the difference of rank and occupation.

"I have now given you," Mr. Blatchford concludes, "a
clear idea of what Socialism is. If I wrote another
hundred pages I could tell you no more."

Much of this description is vague and unsatisfactory, but
it gives on the whole a clear enough conception both of the
scheme of reform of the ordinary practical Socialist and

also of his motives for desiring the change. A formal analysis of so informal an exposition of the doctrine would be out of place; but the following elements among others seem to be involved in the system of government here proposed: (1) Co-operation upon a gigantic and national scale. (2) State ownership of all land and of all instruments of production. (3) Enforced labour for those who do not wish to starve. (4) No competition, and therefore no private enterprise in trade or commerce. (5) Prosperity and plenty for every one. (6) A complete system of government control over every form of industry. (7) Social and economic equality.

Without attempting to show how far some of these elements are mere unattainable ideals, it is sufficient for the present to emphasize the fact that they all (so far as realizable at all) may be reduced under two heads: the attempt to effect an approximation, at any rate, to material equality by the abolition or limitation of private property; and an increase of government intervention.

The first of these is insisted on in every socialistic pamphlet that one can open. Thus Dr. Schäffle[1] declares that "the alpha and omega of socialism is the transformation of private and competing capitals into a united collective capital." Similar terms are used in the joint official manifesto issued by the representatives of three of the leading communistic societies of England, viz. the Fabian Society, the Social Democratic Federation, and the Hammersmith Socialistic Society. "On these points," runs the document,[2] "all Socialists agree. Our aim, one and all, is to obtain for the whole community complete ownership and control of the means of transport, and the means of manufacture, the mines, and the land. Thus we look to put an end for ever to the wage system, to sweep away all distinction of class, and eventually to establish national and international communism on a sound basis."

The other essential—the agency by which all this is brought about—is usually kept more out of sight. A system

---

[1] *Quintessence of Socialism*, p. 20.
[2] Cited by Professor Flint, *Socialism*, p. 93.

of grinding coercion under the heel of an all-powerful government with its graded hierarchy of officials is (its opponents
say) the only means of crushing out competition and enforcing
universal co-operation in a common organization of industry
embracing every individual in the nation.

In each of these leading characteristics it is directly opposed
to Individualism as ordinarily understood,[1] the aims of which
are (first) to reduce to a minimum the interference of the
government and of the community with the free play of
individual wills, and (secondly) thus to allow each man to
heap up for himself such wealth and social distinctions and
pleasures as he may, regardless of the unequal lot of his
poorer brethren, except in respect of such charities as he may
voluntarily bestow. Collectivism is best understood as directly
the reverse of the system of *laissez faire*.

Such then is Socialism, and such are its general aims and
methods. It remains to be seen what elements of truth or
falsehood its ideals contain, how far they are logically self-
consistent, and how far they are capable of realization, and,
lastly, whether they can be justified on a scientific or philosophical basis.

Its ideals are lofty; and if it could realize them, only an
ignoble few would be content to remain its opponents. The
accomplishment of all its high aims, granting for a moment
that these could be made consistent with one another and
with the world of reality, would supersede any need for a
detailed statement of its merits. It professes (1) to remove
the inequality of men's lots and all the misery and injustice
therein involved, and (2) by the aid of mutual help and forbearance to abolish free competition and the struggle for
existence, with the material waste and moral degradation
they bring in their train. These are high aims with which
every right-minded man is ready to sympathize. Who would
not, if he could, abolish the misery of grinding poverty and
the need for overtaxing muscles and brain to gain a bare

---

[1] One phase of Individualism, however, by emphasizing the equality of
individuals rather than their liberty, seems in practice to pass over into
that very Socialism which is theoretically its opposite. Cf. Prof. J. S.
Mackenzie's *Social Philosophy*, p. 250, and authorities there cited.

subsistence ?   The evils of unbridled and unscrupulous competition are hardly less obvious : " Enormous power spent in securing mean objects, energy cancelled by conflicting energy, weakness trampled under the feet of strength, and strength dissolved in the triumph of its own victory : all these things are of the very essence of unqualified competition, and these are the very things which must revolt the lover of the ideal, so that in his eyes much of our vaunted progress seems altogether futile." [1]

If Socialism can remove these evils, then God speed its advent ! Before embracing this creed, however, the prudent man will ask two questions : Is it ·really able to remove these evils, or does it promise what it cannot fulfil ? In the second place, what price must be paid for its benefits ? Has the picture no dark side at all ? Its opponents have, at least, a right to a dispassionate hearing.

The arguments against it may be ranged under five heads : (1) The whole system, it is said, is based on bad philosophy, and ignores the fundamental principles of human nature and society. The State and the Individual—government action and self action—are two things inseparable. You cannot hurt one so that the other remains unaffected. Socialism, its enemies say, ignores and degrades and blots almost out of existence the principle of individuality, and in doing so it cripples the State as well. It is founded on a one-sided philosophy that exaggerates one factor at the expense of another, whereas the two can only live and thrive together. Their true health lies in the maintenance of a proper and free interchange of life between them, and it is false to hold that what one loses the other gains. If the hand or foot is hurt, the whole body suffers. A true theory of the State must be socialistic and individualistic at once ; and it is a false science which finds place for only one of these.

This is the central argument from philosophy, with which the various special lines of attack are more or less clearly connected. Thus Socialists are said to run counter to the laws of nature. Man may use the forces of the material universe for his own ends, it is true, by directing their course,

[1] F. C. Montague, *Limits of Individual Liberty*, p. 6.

but he cannot run counter to their unalterable laws. **If** he attempts this, nature will sooner **or** later avenge itself bitterly **for** the indignity. It is maintained, then, that all **schemes** of an essentially socialistic origin **run** in the teeth of many of these laws. If this is not actual **sin, nature, at** any rate, will punish its outraged **majesty as if** it were. You may keep back the rising tide **by mud walls for a** while, but ultimately it will break through **all such** insignificant restraints. The longer you hold out and the more apparent success you meet with, the greater is the force **arrayed** against you when the catastrophe occurs, and the more utter will be your overthrow. The operation of the old English system of Poor Law is always pointed to in **this** connection. All systems for the relief of paupers by State aid are socialistic in their bearings, and the old system in vogue prior to 1832 was especially so. Yet this only carried, it is urged, the principles underlying all poor relief to their legitimate logical conclusions, though in doing so it accentuated the evils inherent in all such systems to such an extent that the most casual observer could no longer refuse to see them. · **It** proceeded on an entire ignorance or wilful neglect of the **laws** of supply and demand that regulated and still regulate labour, like every other marketable commodity. This deliberate defiance of nature continued for a long period, and being intensified as it progressed, plunged the whole country into penury, and brought Great Britain to the verge of national bankruptcy. Nature took in the long run a terrible revenge for the apparent success with which **for a time** its laws seemed to have been resisted. No candid investigator can deny the deplorable condition to which all commerce, trade, and finance were reduced prior to 1832, nor the existence of **the** relation **of** cause and effect between the system of poor **relief** then discarded and the universally prevalent distress. Socialists, however, have one line of defence **open to** them. They may admit that the **old** system **was** opposed **to** nature, and therefore productive **of** bad results, but deny that the opposition arose from **its socialistic** basis. They **may** argue that it failed because **it was** an ill-considered system. Wise Socialism is not responsible for the misdeeds of stupid Socialism, and increased knowledge may enable its votaries in the future to avoid the errors of its pioneers. Mr. Herbert Spencer and other thinkers of his school would, however, refuse to accept this vindication, holding that all socialistic schemes for poor relief are intrinsically hurtful. Here the argument must be left in the meantime at a point where the two sides directly disagree. The sequel may throw light on the points in dispute. Meantime the two facts certain are that the system of relief administered under the old Poor Laws utterly broke down, and that that system was more or less based on socialistic principles.

This is only one instance, however, of many such specific accusations made against Socialists of running in the teeth of nature. It is urged that all schemes that aim at the abolition of private property, or at its more extended distribution, are founded on mistaken doctrines of equality. This idea is at the root of all communistic theories; whereas *inequality* is the fundamental basis of human nature and therefore of society. Again, it is sometimes maintained that in society, as at present constituted, all progress is affected by the strivings of men actuated by motives of personal aggrandisement. "Take away," it is said, "the right of the individual to accumulate the produce of his labour for his own use, and you make an end of all progress in destroying the incentive of gain." "The aspirant for a newly wrought material and artificial equality," says Sheldon Amos,[1] "annihilates the sources of production by withdrawing the stimulus to accumulate capital, and only substitutes general poverty for unevenly but widely distributed wealth." *If* this incentive is an essential factor in human progress, the Socialism which abolished all property would undoubtedly run counter to a

---

[1] *Science of Politics*, p. 125. **See also W. H.** Mallock, *Labour and Popular Welfare*, p. 291: "Socialism, regarded as a reasoned body of doctrine, rests altogether on a peculiar theory of production, . . . according to which the faculties of men are so equal that one man produces as much wealth as another ; or if any man produces more, he is so entirely indifferent as to whether he enjoys what he produces or no that he would go on producing it just the same, if he knew that the largest part would at once be taken away from him."

law of nature; but then most Socialists deny the **truth of
the assumption.** It is useless to blink the fact, however,
that as society **is** at present constituted, and until human
nature has **attained** a higher **level than** at present, self-
interest is not only one, but perhaps **the** chief factor in
human progress. A few noble **souls may,** from absolutely
disinterested motives, devote **themselves to the** cause of
humanity in general; but the **great** majority **are** ready to
exert to the utmost their powers of brain and **muscle to**
benefit themselves and those dear to them, **when they would**
be **too lazy,** careless, **or** indifferent to **do more than what**
necessity compelled, from a vague enthusiasm **of humanity,**
and in furtherance of an aim so remote **as to be completely**
out of sight.

~ The Socialist **must find a** place, however circumscribed,
within his system **for** individual interests, and even for
individual selfishness, **if he wishes to** realize his dreams on
earth. Every philosophic system is false and incapable of
being put in practice, if it magnifies "that great leviathan
called **a** commonwealth," and **crushes out** the spontaneous
energy of the individual man. ·

(2) The second line of argument adopted by the opponents
of Socialism is that which is well known—perhaps **too** well
known—in **all** branches of politics, "as the thin end of the
wedge." The fact that this controversial weapon has been
frequently used unfairly in debate has so discredited it in
public estimation that it is usually dismissed summarily with
a sneer **which is often** undeserved, **since no** argument is more
valid or **more** potent where it is applicable. Unfortunately
it is only too easy to employ it with oratorical effect where
its use is manifestly unfair. It **may, indeed, be** brought
forward as **an** objection to every reform **that can** possibly be
proposed, and it is too often the last resort when all other
pleas have failed. **Hence** come the disrepute and ridicule
with which it **often meets.** The frequent abuse of a par-
ticular line of **argument, however,** while it may justly excite
an attitude of more searching criticism, by no means vitiates
the argument in itself. Whether conclusive or not, the use
made of it by Mr. Herbert Spencer against Socialism in

The Coming Slavery is certainly not irrelevant. It forms, indeed, the chief part of his heavy indictment against the intervention of government beyond what he considers its legitimate sphere. Briefly stated it amounts to this: All parts of Socialism hang together. One measure of government interference leads to another, and both together make necessary a third; and so, the course once fairly entered on, there is little possibility of turning back. The nation is rushing headlong with an ever-increasing momentum towards Socialism; and Socialism to Mr. Spencer is just another name for slavery.

There are men who would gladly welcome the regulation by government of one class of affairs, but would reject its interference in another. Perhaps no individual is absolutely without socialistic leanings in one or more directions, and scarcely any one would welcome government interference in everything. A would have the telegraphs managed by the State, but would leave the railways to private enterprise; B would have just the reverse; C (probably a Liberal) would allow the State to provide free secular, but not religious education; whereas D (an old-fashioned Conservative) would maintain an Established Church, while insisting on each man paying for his own children's secular training; E would have the government regulate the sale of drink; F would have compulsory State insurance for old age; and so on. Each man has his own special object that he wishes the State to effect for him; but he would not approve of the schemes of the others. Such men are not thorough-going Socialists, and it is to them that the present argument specially appeals. It says, in effect: "In helping forward your own end, you are helping forward all the others—in inviting the government to control and oust individual effort in one case you invite it to interfere in all. Before you know where you are, you will have a complete system of Socialism established where you only wished a remedy for one comparatively small evil. You cannot stop the train you have put in motion. If the State interferes in one place, it produces consequences which would not otherwise have existed, and for which it is therefore responsible. In dealing with these, a further set

of effects are produced, and the province of the executive
is increased without limit."

The man **who** maintains that all things should be
owned and managed by the government, may not **wish to**
interfere with personal liberty and individuality or with the
sanctity of family life. It is pointed **out to** him, however,
that government cannot regulate property without regulating
wages; nor can it pay these without satisfying itself that
work **has** been duly done. The government becomes the
sole employer of labour in the country, and **dictates to** each
man **how** much work he is to do, and **of what kind it** must
be. Each individual finds himself compelled to **work at**
an appointed task or starve, and to surrender entirely **the**
fruit of his labours to the State, his master.

Property is the natural medium through which the individual develops to a full maturity. When private property
is struck at, then personality suffers too. The Collectivist
cannot systematically attack the one without the other. The
Socialist will naturally **refuse** to admit **any more** of this
argument than suits himself. **It is incumbent** upon him,
however, to point out clearly to what extent he **proposes**
ultimately to carry out his principles of State intervention,
and to show how it is possible to go so far without going
further. If he stops short of the ideal of Plato, where
marriage is abolished and children are reared by the State
in entire isolation from their parents, he must **show** how he
proposes to abolish property and yet maintain the family
intact.[1]

Upon him—as the would-be innovator—rests the *onus* of
meeting the argument of the **"thin end of the** wedge" by
proving to the satisfaction of the half-converted proselyte
that it is possible to go a certain length with Socialists
without being compelled to go beyond what his reason can
justify or his conscience approve.

(3) With a third important class of arguments, the theory
of the State is only indirectly interested—those drawn from

---

[1] **For proof of** the assertion that abolition of private property involves
the **abolition of** the family, *vide* W. **E. H.** Lecky, *Democracy and Liberty*,
p. 206, and the authorities there cited.

political economy. To estimate their value the entire range of economics would require to be exhausted. A thorough-going Socialism must take into its own hands the regulation of the laws of supply and demand. Government would require to interfere in trade and commerce not only here and there, but all along the line. This would mean an entire upheaval of the existing science of political economy which rests, as every one knows, on a systematic application of the principle of *laissez faire*. Socialism and Free Trade, whatever may be their relative merits, are necessarily opposed to one another. The universally accepted axioms of economics are all built on the principle that government (except in certain abnormal circumstances) does more harm than good by meddling. Socialism, on the contrary, requires the State to take all land, capital, and machinery into its own hands, and to regulate everything. The present conclusions of economics may be wrong of course, however widely accepted, but Socialists are under the necessity of formulating an entirely different science of economics, and of satisfying themselves that it will work in practice. Individualists hold that this is not only a gigantic task, but one impossible of fulfilment. They say that no central authority can ever regulate production so as to meet the constantly varying demands of every part of a great nation. They hold that its calculations will constantly be upset—that even if it had all-embracing wisdom to adjust everything perfectly to begin with, the mere operations of nature on the population through births and deaths would upset the scheme before it had even begun to work. Unless it could take nature itself, and the keys of life and death, under its control, it would necessarily fail. Only nature can adjust itself to the needs of nature infinitely varying through time and space. If government removes all artificial restraints and steps aside (say the opponents of State intervention) things will adjust themselves of their own accord. But government can never take the place of an omniscient and omnipotent providence controlling nature. It may do infinite harm, but not infinite good.

Political science must depend on the results of economics,

upon which it bases its own conclusions. It is not called upon to verify these economic data any more than to examine the truth of any dogma of medicine which it accepts as a basis for its doctrine of State-action in relation to health.[1] It must be prepared, however, to accept new discoveries in the other sciences, and to alter its own conclusions accordingly when these demand it. As soon as Socialists have formulated a coherent political economy consistent with the schemes they advocate, the theory of the State must reconsider its main positions with reference to them. Meantime the Individualists hold the field, and political science cannot be blamed for refusing to follow socialistic theories until their advocates have squared them with existing facts.

(4) It is necessary for completeness to give a separate notice to what is perhaps merely another form of the arguments already referred to, namely, that the scheme is utterly *impracticable*. Granting that the Socialist's ideals are sound and consistent with themselves, they cannot, for all that, it is urged, be put in practice. They are just as absurd as all the other fine schemes professing to hasten on the millennium, or to create a heaven upon earth. Indeed all socialistic paradises, from Plato's *Republic* to Mr. Bellamy's *Looking Backward*, make a strange omission. They draw alluring pictures of a world where the traveller will find all pleasures and blessings in rich store, but they fail to instruct him how to get there. They draw alluring ideals, but spend no time in showing how to realize them or even to draw nearer to such realization. Even Mr. Blatchford, a man of practical leanings as he is, makes no secret of his difficulty in this respect.

"The establishment and organization," he says, "of a socialistic State are the two branches of the work to which I have given least attention."[2] This is the case with most of them. They are so busy writing in praise of the charms of their ideals, that they have little time for studying how to attain them. On this point, however, the author

---

[1] *E.g.* political science may vindicate compulsory vaccination without investigating the scientific data on which it rests.

[2] *Merrie England*, p. 104.

of *Merrie England* is more sensible than many. He holds that "Socialism will not come by means of a sudden *coup*. It will grow up naturally out of our surroundings, and will develop naturally and by degrees. But its growth and its development may be materially hastened. . . . We have begun long ago. Nearly all law is more or less socialistic, for nearly all law implies the right of the State to control individuals for the benefit of the nation. But of late years the law has been steadily becoming more and more socialistic."[1] This language of one of the warmest friends of Socialism is strangely in accord with that of its strongest modern enemy, Mr. Spencer. In his opinion we are rapidly drifting towards Socialism. "Many concurrent causes," he says, "threaten continually to accelerate the transformation now going on. . . . Influences of various kinds conspire to increase corporate action, and decrease individual action. . . . The numerous socialistic changes made by Act of Parliament, joined with the numerous others presently to be made, will by and by be all merged in State Socialism—swallowed in the vast wave which they have little by little raised."[2]

If all this is true—if Great Britain is steadily and almost inevitably drifting towards universal Socialism—no further vindication of its practicability is needed. Men may endeavour to hasten or retard its progress according as they welcome its results or fear them, but they cannot prevent the inevitable.

In spite of the high testimony of Mr. Spencer, however, there is reason to doubt the truth of the prediction that a simple continuance of the present trend of politics will bring Socialism to pass. Opinions of a contrary kind are also to be found among both its supporters and its enemies. Thus "the Socialist of the street," so far from believing that his pet schemes are slowly and beneficently producing themselves in a natural manner, thinks that only dynamite is strong enough to help them towards fulfilment. His methods of realizing his ideals are summary and violent. Looking on the present structure of society and the State as hurtful to progress, and utterly hateful, he holds that

[1] *Merrie England*, p. 105.   [2] *The Man versus the State*, p. 33.

his first duty is to shatter the whole fabric completely and irrevocably, and he assumes that when the artificial barriers which prop up social and economic abuses have thus been removed, a better condition of things will somehow get itself into being. Such men certainly do not think that the trend of the century is inevitably towards Socialism. Indeed a majority of thinkers on both sides consider that the modern State (unlike the old Greek cities) is founded on an essentially individualistic basis, which becomes only more pronounced as the world progresses. Mr. Wordsworth Donisthorpe, whose individualistic views are not less emphatically expressed than Mr. Spencer's own, differs from him entirely in his reading of the present trend of society and legislation. He does not deny the undoubted fact that many socialistic items of government activity are showing themselves, but he is satisfied that these are isolated instances of back eddies, while the main strong current of Individualism is sweeping onwards with greater and greater power. On the whole, the course of events, he holds, is towards increasing freedom. There may be, here and there, relapses into Socialism, but the true principles of Individualism are bound to triumph in the long run. "This, then, is the observed fact," says Mr. Donisthorpe, "that as civilization advances, the State tends to throw off one claim after another to interfere with the free action of its members, while at the same time it becomes stronger, more regular, speedier, and more certain in performing the functions that remain to it. Where it interferes, it interferes thoroughly. At the present time the tendency is one of throwing off certain forms of State control." [1]

It is by no means, then, a settled point that Socialism is gradually approaching of its own accord. On the contrary, the balance of opinion is decidedly the other way. The problem of its practicability or the reverse must be worked out on other lines.

(5) Finally, it is urged against Socialism that, even if possible, the ideal would be a most undesirable one when actually realized. The sum and crown of all its evils may be put in one word—slavery. All Socialism, it is said, is

---

[1] *Individualism*, p. 300.

slavery. "Each member of the community as an individual would be a slave of the community as a whole."[1]

It is perhaps useless to follow in detail all the charges which are brought against Socialism. All the evils that slavery brings are said to be bound up within it. Thus whatever view we take of the ultimate end of the State (unless we limit that end to the function of maintaining *order* at any cost), it is said that Collectivism fails to attain it. Such a system is another name for despotism. For if all industry and commerce must be managed from a central authority which has to calculate and regulate everything, it follows that all deviations from the appointed and expected routine on which these calculations are based must be strenuously put down. The order of things established by the State must be maintained at all costs, and all opposing individual interests, wishes, or aspirations must be remorselessly brushed aside. Social, domestic, and individual life would lose all their elasticity and buoyancy were they robbed of all powers of initiation. Existence would become humdrum and monotonous, with all its spontaneity crushed out. With the elimination of the element of chance and also of the possibility of bettering one's material lot by one's own exertions, all *hope* and ambition would be eradicated as well. The State would sink to the level of an excellently managed boarding-school or poor-house, where the officials of the State would hand round with absolute impartiality as many material comforts as possible to each. All the bustle, joy, and excitement of an active life where each man could make or mar his fortunes according to his ability and luck, would be blotted out. The monotony and fixity of everything would become unendurable. Men would cry out again for the old order of things with all its risks and difficulties. All excessive interference of the government in the national life tends to produce a uniformity in the governed masses. It substitutes State-help for self-help and so suppresses all spontaneous activity and initiative effort, and finally even all wish for such. Thus it brings in its train results disastrous to the moral character of the individual. He feels that the strong arm

[1] *The Man* versus *the State*, p. 39.

of the government undertakes the duty of protecting and
feeding him, and looking after his interests and those of
others. He loses all feeling of responsibility for his
own lot or his neighbour's. He becomes careless of himself
and callous towards others. Individuality is crushed out
by the greater power of the State narrowing the sphere
of personal effort till no space is left to move or breathe.
The free, spontaneous, healthy life of the citizen is sapped
and absorbed into the bureaus and functionaries of the
central government where it becomes hard and dead and
petrified. All its vital energy is sucked out of the mass
of the nation, and becomes stagnant and inert in the veins
of an all-devouring government. The greatness and life-
energy of the individual and the nation are poisoned at their
sources.

So far we have looked chiefly to the condition of the
subjects under a socialistic regime. It is still necessary
to inquire into the condition of the regulators or governors.
It will probably be said that in a democratic State—it is
assumed that Socialism and Democracy will go hand in
hand—the governed and the government are one. The
fallacy here is, however, very easy of detection. It is
hidden in part under the ambiguity occasioned by the several
meanings of the word "government" and partly under the
confusion between actual administration and indirect control.
No form of Democracy, of a practical nature, can possibly
mean that each individual is equally free to act as the
recognized agent of the State in every kind of work. That
would be Anarchy not Democracy. The Democracy must
appoint officials to act for it. These may be one or many.
They may be mutually independent or arranged in an ordered
line from highest to lowest. They may be appointed for
longer or shorter periods, or for life, and their spheres of
action may be more or less extended, while the conditions
and restraints placed upon them may vary in effectiveness.
The control of the people may be intermittent or constant;
but however thorough-going the Democracy may be—however
narrowly it watches its servants and scrutinizes their minutest
actions—however mercilessly it punishes their faults or

N

omissions, it can never dispense with agents altogether. It might, if it were foolish enough so to cripple its own powers of action, appoint new agents every week and bind them by laws and conditions so tightly that they could hardly move at all, even during their short tenure of office; still, agents of some kind it must have. Further, the more numerous the duties which the government undertakes, the more officials it requires: the more important these duties, the more powers it must bestow if it wishes them well executed. Thus democratic forms in no degree obviate that necessity for a host of government officials which is inherent in Socialism. Indeed their effect is just the reverse. It is not the Democracy itself that acts, but its servants: thus the checks afforded by a popular resistance are much weakened. When the executive were truly servants of the monarch, the people devised checks to fetter the arbitrary action of Ministers of the crown. When the Ministers become the servants of the people, these checks disappear. An enormous increase of officials and officialdom is thus inherent in Collectivism. These servants of the State, when increasing duties and consequently extended powers are thrust upon them, will more and more become its masters. To prevent collisions they must be arranged in due subordination to one another as in all well-organized institutions, whether commercial, military, or governmental. The lowest grades or privates are under captains, and the captains under majors; over all stands the commander-in-chief. Thus we reach the conception of a regular official aristocracy where rank and power depend on the position held in the hierarchy of government employees. Those left outside the ranks count for nothing or very little; within, each man is valued according to his grade. Here, then, is a regularly organized army of officials, ruling all under them with despotic sway, and each obeying the orders of his immediate superior officer. The highest official would be a despotic commander-in-chief.

This is what was meant by Professor Huxley when he spoke of "regimentation" and defined it as a "quasi-military organization of society for the purpose of conquering the general welfare by means of that enforced apparent equality

which brings about the hugest of real inequalities."[1]   Nothing
short of "a quasi-military organization" could crush out
competition and individual self-seeking; and the aim at a
perfect equality would defeat itself through the officers of
this social army becoming the masters of all the private
citizens and the creatures of the commander-in-chief.

One of the principal errors of Socialism, indeed, seems to
be the unfounded belief that a host of officials, acting
professedly for the good of all, will do better in the long run
for the common good than if each man were allowed free
play to act for himself and those dear to him.   In the
necessary distinction, however, between those who are officials
and those who are not, class prejudices and interests would
necessarily clash with the rights of individuals.   The officials
would be tempted to act for their own advancement.   Only
within the charmed circle of government employees would
there exist possibilities of improving one's position by ability,
or by sycophancy to those higher in rank.   Each man within
the official army would naturally wish to ascend the scale:
many of those excluded would seek admittance.   Thus would
quickly disappear that boasted equality which (whether a
good or a bad thing) is claimed by Socialists as one great
merit of their system.   If private property was abolished
with the social inequalities which come in its train, a new
principle of grading society would take its place, closely
following the various ranks of the official phalanx.   Increased
wealth being no longer attainable by industry or skill, official
advancement would absorb the energies of all who had a
chance of promotion.

These five lines of argument, taken together, have a weight
which no one can afford to despise.   Those drawn from political
economy, in particular, if not unanswerable, have at least not
yet been answered.   Until a serious and successful attempt is
made to formulate a system of socialistic economics, moderate
men can hardly be expected to embark on a hazardous voyage
with all their old lighthouses destroyed, and their compasses
thrown overboard.

Weighty as these reasons are, however, the great test of

---

[1] *Natural and Political Rights* (*Method and Results*), p. 418.

Socialism, as of every other system, is actual experience. Before forming an opinion one way or another, it is necessary to examine the phenomena connected with all societies or nations which profess to include socialistic factors in their composition. Theories are all very well, but the politician not unnaturally asks, how the scheme has actually worked in practice.

The historical aspect of the subject thus presents itself. What are the schemes which have been formulated? and, still more, what are those which have actually been put in practice? This branch of the inquiry arranges itself under four heads: (1) paper constitutions and Utopias of a collectivist tendency; (2) the Greek States formed, or said to have been formed, on a socialistic basis; (3) small voluntary societies professing communistic principles; (4) the socialistic elements actually at work in the fabric of large, well-developed modern commonwealths, which are still partially influenced by individualistic tendencies as well.

This is a wide field, and the survey must be of the briefest. (1) The paper Utopias have already been alluded to, and their examination belongs more to the theoretical than to the practical side of the question. The study of their contents and historical context is however a duty incumbent on every one who wishes to exhaust the merits and demerits of Socialism. They, of course, differ widely from one another in every conceivable way: in the extent to which they go, in their self-consistency, in their aims, in their religious leanings, in their varying prejudices and sympathies, and in the literary ability and style and methods of treatment of their various authors. A refutation of one is by no means a refutation of the others. Each must be tried on its own individual merits.

They have, however, many features in common. An attentive survey leads to the conclusion that a consensus of socialistic opinion holds certain radical changes in the constitution of social and family life to be necessary in order to bring these institutions into line with the new system of government. These changes, good or bad, must be tried on their own merits. If they are thought to be evil, they must be

balanced against the expected good to be found in Socialism
as a whole. It is by no means a self-evident truth that
a community of property must be condemned because it
interferes with the purity of the family. Every one has
a right, however, to have explained to him the ulterior
consequences of a system before he is asked to countenance it.

An examination of these various schemes, even on paper,
will do much to make the benefits as well as the faults of
Socialism familiar to the mind of one who is able to separate
their essential from their merely accidental features. This
inquiry cannot be attempted here.

(2) A still more fruitful field for observation is found when
we pass beyond mere speculation to those actual experiments
in Socialism, of which history has kept the record. The
organized life of such commonwealths as those of Athens
and Sparta is full of interest and replete with suggestions to
the modern Communist, though for many reasons he would
neither wish to follow in their footsteps, nor could he do
so if he would. Varying in many ways from one another,
all the Greek City-States had strong elements of Socialism
in their composition; but of a Socialism intuitive rather
than self-conscious. State intervention regulated the whole
life of the Greek cities because the divorce between public
and private interests had not yet been effected. Organization was necessarily bound up with their civilization, but
that organization had never been clearly split into different
branches, such as legal, political, and social. Government
interfered as freely with private as with public interests. In
the best times of Athens the body of the citizens in their
popular assemblies were at once rulers and subjects. They
decided all causes brought before them, and in doing so
mixed up ethical with legal considerations, and thus invaded
domestic life, and imparted an element of instability to
individual rights. Early Socialism was unconscious and
immature, and existed because the processes of differentiation
had not yet been fully developed. Modern Socialism may
copy and incorporate in itself many of the features of the old,
but it can never exactly reproduce it, even if it would, any

more than an old man can make himself young again. The special features in the constitutions of all the Greek States marked out their civilization as in many ways precocious, depending on conditions merely transitory and exceptional, specially favourable and sheltered, and never likely to repeat themselves. These conditions were chiefly two—the small extent of area covered rendering it possible for the whole community to be present, and so to share personally in the entire life of the State in its every current; and the existence of a large slave population, outside the pale of the law, mere chattels finding no place whatever in the common life, and by their exertions giving their masters leisure to attend to the affairs of the commonwealth, and to acquire the needed culture. Thus, if the modern Socialist points to the high place in the world's history attained by Athens under a regime of State control, it is open to the Individualist to retort that the high development of the few was founded on the degradation of the many. The Individualist may add that the modern socialistic State would be as bad, since scope for individual effort and development within it would be confined to the regiment of functionaries, while the mass of unofficial citizens became the slaves.

(3) Passing over the traces of Socialism scattered through the Middle Ages—the whole feudal system, indeed, was in some aspects a vast scheme of Collectivism—we find that within the last two centuries various attempts have been made to produce socialistic communities on the basis of voluntary association. Such experiments have been generally confined to a comparatively small number of men and women specially chosen by a skilful leader, like the choice spirits of a pioneer band, among whom, in addition, a strong current of religious enthusiasm has usually prevailed to give vigour and stability to the movement. America has been the home of most of the experiments of this kind which in recent years have endured for any length of time or met with any special measure of success. Among such associations may be instanced the Shaker Community, the Ebenezer Community, the Skeneateles Community, the Janson Community, and—most important of all, perhaps—the

famous Oneida Community.[1] **Each** of these has features peculiar to itself, but it is instructive to note one or two of the most important characteristics which all of them possess.

These communities are all **based** upon the principle of voluntary association, and thus essentially differ from every system of universal and compulsory State Socialism. The minor elements of difference hence resulting include at least one that makes the task before **them** harder of fulfilment, and several that are specially favourable to their success. The chief element of weakness in the voluntary principle **is** easily seen. The communities are not independent States, and therefore their members can appeal for protection against their decisions to the wider community without. Hence a tendency to disruption is a constant menace to their stability. The various members have voluntarily banded themselves together, and they are free to break up by voluntary consent. Their origin was "a social compact," and this is the source of all the **characteristics in which** they differ from States. If an independent **nation ceased** to exist, either anarchy or foreign conquest would **be** inevitable. **If**, however, **a** community founded by **contract is** dissolved, its members are quietly absorbed in the **wider community of the** nation. The copartnery is at an end, and each man is free **to go** his own way. Thus many **such** societies have broken **up** almost of unanimous consent ; while in almost all a majority has continually to fight against the disaffection of individuals who are desirous of seceding. The great difficulty, then, for such an organization is to keep itself together. The cohesive forces which restrain the atoms from flying apart are usually two—religious enthusiasm, and the power of some dominating personality whose will and prestige overawe the rest into submission. **Such a man is** often the high priest and founder of a sect. **Special and** perhaps fortuitous circumstances are thus **required** to keep these associations together for any length of **time**. **From** this source of weakness a compulsory scheme **of** Socialism established by **an**

[1] An interesting and impartial account and criticism of these societies is contained in an essay by Mr. Goldwin Smith, upon "Communism in the United States," forming an Appendix to *Questions of the Day*, p. 338.

independent State would be entirely free. On the other hand, the voluntary communities possess counterbalancing advantages sufficient to make their prospects of success greater than those of States. While a universal scheme of State Socialism would compel the unwilling to submit to its control, a voluntary association includes only such as believe in the doctrines on which the association rests. At the inauguration of the experiment at least, the members are all more or less enthusiasts. Those who originally organize the adventure have it in their option to choose only such applicants for admission as seem suited to contribute to its success by their personal qualifications, or by the property they are willing to place at the disposal of the community. The rabble and riff-raff are excluded, and so is avoided the need to deal with the lapsed masses, whose existence is the worst problem to be faced by existing governments—the problem in the attempted solution of which Socialism has its best apology. Close corporations, like the Oneida community, are formed exclusively of picked men and women. Various principles of selection may be adopted, but the right to exclude undesirable members is always insisted on; and, as a matter of actual observation, no such society has ever thrown open its doors to all who chose to come. In most cases, indeed, the community has given an eager attention to the securing of wealthy members, or of men specially skilled in such arts as are likely to be useful to them. Only those communities have thrived whose members have been carefully selected. The difficulties of the ruling and directing power are thus made comparatively easy.

The government of a great State has to make arrangements for men of every variety inhabiting territories that lie widely apart. These small communities, on the contrary, have only to deal with men who, from the very fact of their membership, are of somewhat similar tastes and leanings. There is a uniformity of material which makes an orderly system of paternal government comparatively easy. A further aid is found in the limited extent of the field of operations. Such societies are small in number to begin with, and new members are afterwards admitted

only with the **greatest** caution **and** circumspection. The
extent of territory to which their operations are confined is
a material factor **in** the question, and many further points
of difference might easily be noticed.

In this **light it is** clearly impossible **to argue** even from
the complete success of such **small bodies** practising a
doctrine of **all** things in common, in favour of a national
scheme of compulsory Communism under coercion by the
State. Complete success, however, has rarely, if ever, crowned
the efforts of any one of these societies which **has kept** its
socialistic principles intact. Many of **them have suffered**
disintegration by a natural process of decay, and many **have**
only continued to exist by departing in practice, if **not in**
theory, from the doctrine to which they owed their **origin.**
Even where success has been achieved, this has been due
to specially favouring circumstances, and to the employment
of means that would utterly scandalize many of those who
are ready **to support Socialism** on other grounds. **The sup-**
pression of **the institution of** the family may **not be a logical**
necessity of the principles of Communism, but **in practice**
it has been invariably found that such societies have only
flourished on the ruins of **family life and purity.**

"That which is at once common," says Mr. Goldwin Smith,
"**to all** the successful communities, and peculiar to them, is
the rejection of marriage, whereby in the first place **they**
are exempted from the disuniting influence of the separate
family, **and in** the second place they **are** enabled to accumulate wealth in a way which **would** be impossible if
they had children to maintain. . . . **The** members of
Beizell's community are strict celibates; **so** are the Shakers;
so are the Rappites; so are the Snowbergers."[1] In the
Oneida community, in the opinion of **the same** writer, "we
have again the too familiar and simple conditions of success,
exemption from the **disuniting** influence of the separate
family, and **the** facility for the accumulation of wealth
attendant **on** the absence **or** paucity of children. Com-
munism, in fine, can be rendered practicable only by a
standing defiance of morality and nature."[2]

[1] *Questions of the Day*, p. 347   [2] *Ibid.*, p. 352.

Not only is the social life of the community made to take the place of the domestic life of the family, but the latter as an institution is utterly crushed out of existence. The extinction of the family removes the chief pillar on which both social and political institutions at present rest. It involves an entire reversal of our ordinary morality and current modes of thought, as well as a radical reorganization of society and of individual and domestic life. These changes, however undesirable, are possible in a small society of devotees who voluntarily adopt principles abhorrent to the average man or woman, but they could never be forced upon a whole nation. The law of succession and the principles on which capital is distributed depend likewise on the constitution of the family. It is equally clear that the entire questions of marriage and population are also involved, though these are topics which cannot be fully discussed with decency outside of a modern society novel. It is enough to note the fact that the family is suppressed in these socialistic societies of the nineteenth century as thoroughly as was proposed by Plato in his ideal republic of the fourth century before the Christian era. In this way only can Socialists rid themselves of the growth of separate interests tending to break up the community of property on which they rest.

By the same expedient the numbers of the community are kept down to a normal level. New members are admitted from without only when they can contribute to the selfish interests of the existing corporation by their wealth or otherwise, while the natural increase of population is suppressed or regulated. Thus almost invariably a gradual decrease in numbers takes place. The exclusiveness of all successful communities is indeed well worthy of careful notice. While within the charmed circle (the right of admission to which is so carefully guarded) the relations of the members are based on principles of all things in common, the attitude of the group towards the outside world exhibits all the worst features of the most selfish form of Individualism. Having carefully excluded all paupers from their midst to begin with, the community aim at the

aggrandisement of themselves **as a** close corporation, regard-
less of the poverty-stricken masses around them. But while
they neglect their duties towards the outside world, they
are willing to **take such** benefits from it as **they** can
absorb. The socialistic corporation **is not a** self-sufficing
independent **society in** itself; **but** merely an association
enjoying the protection of a State **which secures** it from
unlawful interference, while allowing **it to carry its** principles
into practice. Each community becomes **more** and more a
capitalist, and lives on the interest of the money **which it**
lends to outsiders. Thus it stands related to the **outside**
world as capitalist to labourer, **or as lender to borrower.**
The principle of Communism is adopted in so far **as it**
benefits the selfish interests of the community, and rejected
whenever it **is found** not to pay. Such one-sided adherence to socialistic principles is not unlike the way in
which free-trade is sometimes advocated by manufacturers
who possess mills **in Britain** and in America, and who
believe in free-trade here and protection there. The rich
communistic societies have no desire to have anything in
common with their poorer neighbours. **A** good example of
this position towards the outside world is afforded by **the**
Rappites, as this famous community is described **by** Mr.
Goldwin Smith: "The Rappites, a set of enthusiasts **who**
expected the speedy advent of the millennium, called their
first two settlements Harmony. Their third, by a signifi-
cant change of name, they called Economy. They are not
only wealthy, but millionaires of the first order We are
not surprised to learn that **they** do not proselytize, though
converts **enough** might undoubtedly be found **to** a doctrine
even more extravagant than Rappism, if it were endowed
with twenty millions. The Silver Islet **Company** would be
about as likely to desire proselytes. **Those** who have
visited the community report **that all** its members are
advanced in years. The end of Rapp's millennium is **in**
fact a tontine, which will terminate in a Rappite Astor."[1]

Communities such as this cannot be considered as **apostles**
of a creed for equalizing national wealth and **eradicating**

[1] Goldwin Smith, *Questions of the Day*, p. **349.**

poverty from the **world**. **On the** contrary, they carefully wall themselves round from contaminating influences, shutting all poverty outside, and thus **contrive** to succeed not by defying the laws of political economy, **but** by eliminating the elements of society which make these difficult of application, and by adopting within their own narrow circle extreme remedies, such as the suppression of marriage—remedies difficult to enforce even under favouring circumstances, and absolutely impracticable **in a** larger and more heterogeneous society. Communists succeed only because they are inconsistent with **their own principles** in **their** dealings with outsiders, and **because within their own** dominions they do violence to **human nature** in its most sacred development—the family. **The objections raised by** political economists are not over-come. **They simply do** not apply

(4) **There only remain to** be considered the socialistic **elements and tendencies actually at** work in the institutions **of** modern nations. **It has been** said already that every society must contain **factors of two** sorts, individualistic and socialistic. Thus it is not surprising that the extreme votaries **of** either system, looking **chiefly upon** such tendencies as work in the opposite direction **to what** they desire, find much they cannot approve in the methods of procedure adopted by the government they are forced to **obey**. **Many** Individualists, shutting their eyes to the factors **that make** for freedom, neglecting **all** contradictory evidence, and looking only on such phases of modern politics as seem to increase the scope **of** the government's solicitude for the positive welfare of **its** citizens, declare that our system of policy is already socialistic, **and tends** to become more so.

Without stopping to criticise the one-sidedness of this **line of** argument, it is sufficient to admit **its** validity so **far as to allow** that society as at present constituted does **contain** many traits pointing in the direction indicated. To examine these exhaustively would involve a survey of the institutions of every country in **the** world. In England itself, for example, very many such features could readily be found. **It is** more instructive, however, to select for examination **some** country where collectivist ideals have obtained a greater measure of practical recognition. In this way the benefits and the evils of the system—assuming that, like all human inventions, it has both—may be more clearly observed. Many agencies which are seen tentatively and timidly at work in the mother-country have made bold strides in the colonies. In new countries there is less inertia to be overcome before advanced theories can receive a fitting embodiment. Many schemes have been put to the test of experience in the colonies, and there brought to complete success or signal failure, while in Great Britain itself they have not even entered the arena of practical politics at all. It is in respect of socialistic tendencies that Australia is most clearly seen to be "in advance" of the mother country. Victoria, in especial, is a particularly favourable field of observation; because there these various socialistic tendencies are all to be found in an exaggerated form. "In Victoria State Socialism has completely triumphed." Such was the opinion of Sir Charles Dilke,[1] after his visit to the antipodes. In one of our chief Australian colonies, then, in the opinion of an acute observer, Socialism had not only been established by the Colonial Legislature, but had signally succeeded. Sir Charles Dilke, however, wrote before the financial disasters of the last four or five years had swept over Australia, making their devastating influence most cruelly felt just in these colonies where socialistic ideals and methods had been most uncompromisingly adopted. There may be room for doubt how far a consistent Collectivism was really established by the Victorian Legislature, but no one can deny that its whole tenor was clearly in that direction, and that Melbourne put to the test of experiment, in an exaggerated form, every socialistic tendency that can be traced in the mother country. It is equally clear that, whether established or not, Victorian Socialism cannot now (in 1896) be said to have "completely triumphed." Australia, and in especial Melbourne, has not only engulfed itself in general bankruptcy, but has brought wide-spread ruin among thousands of English and Scottish investors who have embarked their savings in colonial banks and mortgage companies. The natural complexity of social

[1] *Problems of Greater Britain*, I., p. 185.

and political phenomena renders it extremely difficult to connect any two facts together as cause and effect; but if it
is ever possible to arrive at any definite conclusions within
this sphere, Individualists have every justification for blaming
socialistic principles as the cause of the financial upheaval
that has dislocated the commerce of the world.

Before attempting to draw conclusions, however, it is well
to state, as clearly as may be, the undisputed facts of the
case. Two propositions are generally admitted. In the first
place, the theory of legislation, and the entire methods of
administration throughout the Australian Colonies, and in
especial in Victoria, were based upon collectivist rather than
individualistic ideals, although it may be incorrect to say
that a complete and consistent system of Socialism was
actually established. In the second place, whatever may
have been the cause, the methods of government prevalent
in Victoria have not "completely triumphed," but have
upon the contrary brought about (or at least failed to avert)
disasters, involving in a wide-spread ruin not only the
entire colony, but also its creditors in every part of the
world. These seem to be the outstanding facts; but it
does not follow, without further proof, that the two are
connected together. While both parties admit that government interfered to secure, by positive legislation and a
regime of regulation, the material welfare of its subjects,
it is yet *possible* to deny that this policy was directly
responsible for the misery that seemed to result. Other
evil factors, such as extravagance, were at work, to which
part of the blame may be due. How far are the socialistic methods directly connected with the economic
failure? How far (if at all) are they responsible for the
borrowing and extravagance which have brought (tardily,
it is true, but surely) in their train, such wide-spread
ruin? To answer these questions fully would be to write
the history of the colony, but a few salient facts may
be briefly mentioned. Before Victoria and the other colonies
obtained constitutions and responsible governments of their
own, the Colonial Office at home had indicated the lines
on which the development of Australia was in future to

proceed. With the annexation of that continent to the British Crown a vast extent of unoccupied land had been placed in its hands to be distributed among claimants, or to be kept for the use of the settlers as a whole. Government became a great landowner, and so Socialism in one of its chief features was a fact accomplished. Other socialistic features naturally resulted. A tendency to throw the burden of the development of the country on the State as the greatest landowner was established, and the sphere of government activity was rapidly enlarged. The habit of dependence upon government was in part also the result of the transportation of criminals to Botany Bay, and the consequent treatment of the whole of New South Wales as a convict settlement. The only labour obtainable was penal labour. This was necessarily directed by government; and the works of various sorts thus constructed naturally continued under the management of the central authorities by whose commands and under whose direction they had been made.

In 1855, Tasmania and Victoria became self-governing, and next year New South Wales and South Australia followed;[1] but the new colonial authorities succeeded to the methods as well as the powers of the home government. The principle of State intervention was continued, and indeed received a new impetus. The sale of land to new immigrants supplied for a time great riches to the colonial governments, and money was spent freely in developing the country by means of harbours, railways, and public buildings, all belonging to and managed by the executive, and paid for from the public purse. The results of this policy were two-fold—the extension of the sphere of government action in initiating and maintaining works of every kind, and the habit of liberal or even extravagant methods of expending public money. The habit thus acquired by government of lavishly sinking capital in railways and harbours continued long after the original source of revenue had dried up, with the exhaustion of the more desirable portions of unappropriated

---

[1] *Vide* Alpheus Todd's *Parliamentary Government in the Colonies* (2nd Edition), p. 84.

land.   It was soon found, however, that want of money need
not hamper the benevolent care of government for the rapid
development of the colony and the improvement of the
condition of its people of every grade and class.   A plethora
of capital existed in the mother country seeking investment,
and this was readily diverted to Australia in the form of
loans granted upon terms which every year became more
favourable to the borrower.   New public libraries and
museums continued to be built by the colonial governments
out of money supplied by English capitalists.   As long as
new loans flowed in there was no difficulty in paying the
interest on the old ones, while a good balance was left
with which further to advance the welfare of the colonists.
The Socialism of New South Wales and Victoria was thus
founded on borrowed English gold—on money which had
been made in Britain on the principles of economics there
acted on—free trade and *laissez faire* and the individualistic
haggling of the market-place.

No more than the communistic voluntary societies of
America could this Australian Collectivism be called self-
dependent.   It rested at first on the sale of unappropriated
land, and afterwards upon the borrowed money which it
succeeded in attracting, but which it was quite unable to
repay.   The time for meeting this debt arrived when the
credit of the Colonies—the flimsy support upon which the
whole socialistic fabric rested—began to be called in question.
Only then did Victoria realize that she had still to pay the
heavy bill incurred by her socialistic tendencies or else own
herself bankrupt.   The easy doctrine of repudiation is fortunately repugnant to the public conscience of the Colonies.
An honest attempt is being made to meet the burdens
brought about by their own extravagance, and this has caused
the present acute distress at the Antipodes.   That colony
where Collectivism has gone furthest, where State Socialism
was said to have "completely triumphed," is the one where
the financial panic has been sharpest, and where the resulting
distress has been most severe.   Melbourne is the city which
has suffered most, and which has entailed misery on the
greatest number of creditors in Britain.

The particular directions taken by socialistic legislation in the various colonies, and the measure of success (permanent or temporary) met with in each, supply fertile fields for investigation to students of such phenomena, but we must confine our attention to one of these. The eight hours' system —that central plank in the labour platform, and the object of so much discussion in this country—has actually been established by the Victorian Legislature.

That the basis of all such legislation is socialistic requires no explanation. If the State does not interfere, the hours of employment will regulate themselves according to the contracts made between capitalists in need of men and labourers in need of work. Hours of labour will, therefore, vary according to individual and local circumstances. Under the eight hours' system the government steps in and lays down one hard and fast rule for all its subjects. No one, however willing, may work more than eight hours a day. This forcible regulation of labour runs directly counter to all principles of *laissez faire.* Advocates of a similar measure in this country have often pointed triumphantly to Victoria as a colony where all alleged difficulties had been successfully overcome, and where the system might be seen actually at work to the entire satisfaction of all concerned.

Such rose-coloured estimates of its success are not likely to find advocates at the present day among those who see that the eight hours' system, as established in Victoria, was an integral part of the socialistic methods of government there put in practice, the complete and dismal failure of which we have just been tracing. Those who boasted of its complete triumph five years ago may have seen cause by this time materially to modify their views. Indeed, before the financial break-down of the colonies, many observers questioned even the temporary success which for a time seemed to be achieved. Thus, before the catastrophe had occurred, Mr. Charles Fairfield[1] had expressed the opinion that the scheme was at all practicable only because of the abnormal and specially favourable conditions under which the experiment was tried.

[1] *A Plea for Liberty,* p. 163.

o

These conditions of a spurious success, as he gives them, are chiefly four: (1) A protective tariff; (2) the absence of such keen competition for work as has to be faced in the home market; (3) the employment of labour on State-owned railways and other undertakings; and (4) a process of unlimited borrowing from creditors outside the colony. These four conditions, then, represent the price which Victoria had to pay in order to effect the apparent success—provisional as it has after all turned out to be—of the eight hours' system.

Much food for reflection is suggested by the whole of Mr. Fairfield's essay upon State Socialism in the antipodes, although the force of many of his arguments will be weakened upon those who have greatest need to listen to them by the bitterly partisan tone which pervades it. When due allowance is made for the bias of the writer, there is still much truth contained in the picture which he draws of the working of Collectivism in Victoria.

"Colonial State Socialism," he says,[1] "revolves in a sort of circle, and the same sequence appears to present itself at whatever point we inspect it. Politicians sanction and float loans to provide employment for their patrons on pleasant terms, local banks and credit institutions make use of the proceeds of State borrowing to 'finance' building societies, importers, manufacturers, tradesmen, and private speculators, who in turn give credit to working men for goods, or for land and houses bought by them at inflation prices out of their savings. Neither shop debts, interest, nor instalments on purchases of land and houses can be paid unless wages are good, and work on political railways and 'useful public works' plenty. These pleasant practices grow upon the community like opium-eating. Ministers therefore dare not now hold their hand, calculate ways and means closely, or stop borrowing, lest the whole top-heavy fabric of State Socialism should come toppling down about their ears." . . . And again, "State Socialism to-day in the Antipodes seems to me to preach to willing disciples the despicable gospel of shirking laziness, mendicancy, and moral cowardice. The further consciousness among all classes there, that triumphant and popular State

[1] *A Plea for Liberty*, p. 166.

Socialism depends for its existence on absorbing money from abroad, without reasonable prospect of ever being able to repay it, seems to me bad also." [1]

It is possible to accept the undoubted truth of much of what Mr. Fairfield has here so graphically expressed without entirely sharing his sentiments or approving the forcible language in which he conveys them. The most casual reader can hardly fail to be struck by the forcible comment on his criticism, furnished by the disasters which have overwhelmed Australia since he wrote. Wherever the boasted success of Socialism was greatest, there the crash has been correspondingly severe. If the collectivist experiment of which Melbourne was the headquarters has not conclusively proved the impracticability of the economic basis of Socialism, it has certainly done nothing to make good its claims. It is, of course, open to its adherents to urge that it failed so utterly not because it went too far, but because it did not go far enough.

The result of the entire inquiry, then, would seem to be that history has furnished absolutely no evidence that Socialism as a scheme of government is either practicable or desirable, while on *a priori* grounds there are strong reasons to show that it is inadequate as a complete solution of the problem it has set itself.

The questions at issue between Socialists and the defenders of the present organization of society are vital ones. It is remarkable indeed that the two institutions which Socialists are forced by the logic of their position to attack most uncompromisingly—to wit, property and the family—are the very factors in modern civilization which all " orthodox " writers on social and political subjects combine to praise. Conservatives see in them twin pillars of stability, while Liberals count them among the most effective engines of further progress.

If we turn to any one of the old-fashioned school of political writers, we shall find the two institutions of property and marriage, in the exact forms sanctioned by existing law, spoken of as the chief prerequisites, not only of all government, but of all morality as well. Sir James Mackintosh,

[1] *A Plea for Liberty*, p. 198.

for example, in his once famous essay on the " Law of Nature and Nations,"[1] declares that " Almost all the relations and duties of human life will be found more immediately, or more remotely, to arise out of the two great institutions of property and marriage. They constitute, preserve, and improve society. Upon their gradual improvement depends the progressive civilization of mankind, in them rests the whole order of civil life. . . . Around these institutions all our social duties will be found at various distances to range themselves."

The vital nature of the warfare waged by Socialists against the foundations of existing society is thus brought into clear consciousness when it is realized that these two central institutions are the special objects of their attacks. Their hostility to all rights of private property is openly avowed as their chief merit ; while willingly or unwillingly all communistic schemes have come into violent collision with the family

---

[1] *Miscellaneous Works*, Vol. I., p. 372.

CHAPTER XIV.

INDIVIDUALISTIC SOLUTION CONSIDERED GENERALLY.

THE broad ground of distinction between **ancient** and modern States is frequently expressed by saying **that** the former were essentially socialistic **and** the latter individualistic. The same principle of contrast is perhaps involved in the formula of **the** late **Sir Henry** Sumner Maine, that "society progresses from *status* to contract." In the **earlier** stages of civilization a man's rank and mode of life **are** determined chiefly by forces over which **he has no control.** Caste and custom regulate everything. Among modern nations, **on** the contrary, every individual has wide opportunities of bettering his lot or of making it worse, according to his ability and perseverance. Within certain limits his position in life **is** just what he has made it. In other words, he determines his own lot by the *contracts*, express or implied, into which he voluntarily enters. It is still a third way of expressing the same truth to say that "regulation" **was** the watchword of the old **world** and "free competition" of the new, or that, as Mr. Herbert Spencer puts **it, we** have passed from the "militant" to the "industrial" type **of** social organization, and from the system **of** "compulsory co-operation" to **that** of "voluntary co-operation."[1]

This statement of the law of progress **will** probably be found somewhat one-sided and inadequate, for there are integrating as well as disintegrating **forces** at work in all stages of the world's development. New forms of compulsion and regu-

[1] *The Man versus the State*, p. 1.

lation take the places left vacant by the old ones, though, fortunately, they leave within themselves more scope for the free play of individual liberty. It is untrue to represent the whole trend of history as sweeping uninterruptedly from State coercion to individual freedom. It is an unfounded and false assumption that these are necessarily opposed to each other.

It is possible to hold that they may yet be combined in a less imperfect future organization; and that society may yet escape the limitations that hampered both past and present States in so far as they favoured one element at the expense of the other. Progress has not followed any one straight line—as for example, that leading from bondage to freedom—but has been (as Mr. Spencer himself frequently insists in other connections) a combination of integration and differentiation by which the homogeneous and simple has become the heterogeneous and complex. Coercion and liberty have existed in close relations at every stage of this process. While it is true that sometimes one and sometimes the other has been chiefly emphasized, neither of them has ever entirely vanquished the other. Subject to this explanation, however, it is undoubtedly correct to hold that in the ancient State the individual on the whole suffered; while in modern theories at least the powers of State control have been comparatively curtailed.

If it be true, then, that our present civilization is founded on an essentially individualistic basis, this fact may explain to some extent why the word "Individualism" is less familiar than "Socialism." A thing of every-day use is little noticed, while a change attracts attention. Doctrines long received pass unchallenged, unnoticed, and unnamed, while a *bizarre* opinion by its very uncouthness will ensure a fuller criticism and a closer attention. It may be because the mass of modern men are all Individualists together that they find it unnecessary to adopt a special name to call attention to the circumstance. Whatever the explanation, it is an undoubted fact that while the name Socialist is one commonly in use, its opposite, Individualist, is rarely heard in ordinary conversation and would convey no definite meaning to the average mind. Socialism is a creed with which certain tangible ideas are closely and familiarly associated; while Individualism is a term known only to theorists. Yet every man who **is out** and out opposed to Socialism—and there are many such—is an Individualist, whether aware **of** the fact or **not**.

Other influences work in **the** same direction. Socialism is constructive—the creed of the enthusiast "in the street" is not here spoken of—while its rival is destructive. The one would build up a complex fabric **of** State control; the other would reduce it to its narrowest limits. The theoretical Socialist is under the necessity of creating ideal pictures or architects' plans of the building he proposes to erect; and thus definite Utopias are created to catch the public eye. This gives rise to comment and notoriety. The Individualist, on the contrary, has no simple universal panacea to offer for inspection.

This difference of method is, however, not altogether adverse to Individualists. If the creation of Utopias attracts admiration, it also invites criticism. If government is to regulate property and trade and commerce, **it is incumbent** on **those** who wish this, to show that **it is practicable.** They are not allowed to rest content after simply demolishing existing institutions. Individualists, on the other hand, do not profess to lay before **their** constituents any legislative measures guaranteed to cure all the ailments of **society.** On the contrary, they declaim against the interference of laws and legislation in these matters altogether. The height of human wisdom in their view is to let nature alone, for it knows its work better than man ever can. Thus, when you ask such a theorist for a sample of his wares, and insist on an explanation of his own scheme which he would substitute for the present social organization, he is free to answer: "I have no system. I would substitute nothing. It is the business of nature to work out its own destiny through its own laws. **All** I can do is to remove the artificial barriers that interrupt its course and **warp** its handiwork. I cannot even trace exactly what that course will be. I can only trust that all will go well, and am sure at least that the meddling of government will only make things worse."

Such an attitude of mind explains naturally enough why no individualistic *News from Nowhere* or *Looking Backward* has been given to the world. What is more important, it shows why it is more difficult to point out the errors of the Individualist. It is impossible to know where to have him. He is always busy waging war in the enemy's country against existing institutions, and moves so rapidly from point to point that he exposes little surface on which he may be attacked himself.

The popularity of Socialism is increased from the fact that its adherents hold forth an almost immediate prospect of benefit from its adoption. The Collectivist believes that a government thoroughly imbued with socialistic theories, and above all with the socialistic interpretation of the laws of justice, will have sufficient power to overcome most of the economic evils of the present system and wisdom enough rightly to direct that enormous power. Human agency is to do everything by a strong system of regulation and control working outwards from a central sovereignty. If it can do this at all, why should it not begin at once? Thus near, if not immediate, prospects of relief are held out to the sufferers from present evils or to philanthropists who are willing to join its ranks. Most Individualists, on the other hand, are more modest in their expectations and less impatient of delay. Their enthusiasm for the curative power of nature—acting through its "laws of evolution," "survival of the fittest," "supply and demand," or what not—is alloyed by the knowledge that her operations require a long expanse of time. Centuries perhaps must pass before evolution, acting on natural lines, can do much to alleviate present distress. "Slow but sure," is their motto; but the hope that future generations may be better off is cold comfort to the man whose soul is wrung by the present sufferings of humanity, or to him whose wishes are directed to the immediate bettering of his own condition and who cares nothing for posterity.

There are, of course, many different degrees and phases of Individualism as well as of Socialism, varying from a praiseworthy but ill-defined desire to protect the liberty of the subject from unnecessary interference on the part of a fussy bureaucracy, to a deliberate attempt to abolish government and even the State itself altogether. While a few of the most extreme and least enlightened among the latter class demand its *immediate* abolition, most of them are content to enter upon a course of policy with that object in view which will require several generations to mature. Even Anarchists themselves admit of degrees of intensity within their councils. " The abolition of the external State," says Victor Yarros,[1] " must be preceded by the decay of the notions which breathe life and vigour into that clumsy monster, in other words, it is only when the people learn to value liberty, and to understand the truths of the Anarchist philosophy, that the question of practically abolishing the State looms up and acquires significance."

It is unnecessary to point out that it is as impossible to abolish " the State " as that term has been here defined, as to abolish the Individual, for it is clearly the government that is alluded to and not the State at all. In addition to those Individualists or Anarchists who are willing to wait until the masses are educated to their views before they seek to abolish all systems of national organization, many disclaim all intention of uprooting either the legislative, the administrative, or the judicial functions of the central authority, and propose merely to confine the organs that respectively exercise them to their normal spheres. Moderate Individualists desire only to decrease the limits of the State's active interference with the rights of its members. The advance in democracy, which during the last half-century has been a prominent feature in the history of all progressive nations, has given a fresh impetus to every form of government activity, and it is to a natural reaction from this socialistic spirit of interference that the renewed agitation in an opposite direction is due. The nobles and people in earlier ages set strict limits on the prerogatives of the monarch when he enjoyed the power as well as the name of sovereign and personally directed the administrations of his realm. With the advent of the impersonal sovereignty of parliament, the democracy has now no master but itself,

[1] Cited in *A Plea for Liberty*, p. 67.

and in this is seen a new and more deadly menace to individual liberty. "It will be a wise precaution," says Mr. Wordsworth Donisthorpe, in emphasizing the danger of this tendency, "to guard democracy from its own defects by limiting the powers of the State however constituted, and to enact, while yet it is day, that all interference of government in matters outside its normal duties shall be a violation of the constitution."[1]

Here we have, then, a clear statement of the aims of Individualism by one of its most moderate and enlightened exponents. Apart from the opinions we may hold of the desirability of the end thus proposed, two difficulties in its accomplishment readily suggest themselves, of which one is theoretical and the other practical. It is necessary in the first place to define wherein the "normal" duties of the State consist; and this we shall find to be an impossible task, for what is abnormal in one age or country may be indispensable in another. Even if such a criterion could be found, it would be necessary in the second place to devise an expedient whereby the sovereign and all-embracing State *could* "limit" its own powers or suffer them to be limited, and yet remain a State. This would be to place political restrictions upon the political sovereign—which is, by definition, impossible, so long as it remains independent. Parliament, which is the legal sovereign, might, of course, place legal restriction upon itself, but this could be done only by abrogating its sovereignty and placing the sceptre in another's hand. It is impossible "to enact" that the legislative activity of government be subject to any restraint without altering the central principle of the British constitution. Before advising this, Mr. Donisthorpe must suggest some new constitution to take its place, and be prepared to show how this will be better able to keep government to its "normal duties"—whatever these may be —than the old one.

Parliament has on several occasions—notably in framing the Acts of Union with Scotland and Ireland respectively— sought to set limits to the powers of future Parliaments, and has signally failed. The statutory enactments and the public

[1] *Individualism*, p. 70.

opinion of a calm to-day afford no protection against the over-government of a passionate to-morrow. Even moderate Individualists thus set themselves a problem that can never be solved. It is impossible to do what John Stuart Mill asserts to be necessary, viz. to limit the power of the people over themselves. Society cannot effectively do what he says it must do—guard itself against "the tyranny of the majority." [1]

If individualistic friends of liberty are wise, they will confine their efforts to more practicable schemes. There are two ways in which they may guard against encroachments on freedom. (1) They may take care that reforming zeal does not remove the wholesome restraints placed by existing constitutional law upon the arbitrary power of executive officials; (2) though without altering the fundamental principles of the constitution they cannot fetter the legislative powers of Parliament, they may effectually provide against the hasty or unfair use of these powers. Those who apply the maxim "Let alone" to the restriction of undue interference with individual rights ought to increase the checks on the despotism of a bare parliamentary majority by the addition of a third legislative chamber, rather than join in any attempt to abolish the somewhat weakened bulwark at present afforded by the House of Lords.

There are dangers on both sides, however; for if you render difficult or impossible all legislative interference with the existing order of things—whether that order rest upon a collectivist or an individualistic basis—you increase the likelihood of revolution. It is dangerous to block up the legitimate channels through which the will of the nation may legally force its way, but it is impossible to limit that will itself.

All Individualists, however they differ in methods and in degree, are resolved to cut down government interference to some extent. They are far, as yet, from agreement as to what constitutes this "government interference" to which they object. They are equally far from unanimity as to the extent to which they are prepared to go. Indeed by piecing

[1] Mill, *On Liberty*, p. 12.

together the various functions and duties of government that
one or other of the most enlightened among Individualists
would tolerate or even encourage, a whole might be constructed comprising a fairly thorough-going system **of** govern-
ment control.   All Individualists agree in assuming an
absolute antithesis between the powers **of** government and
the liberty of the subject, and also in the opinion that
where these are likely to **collide**, there **is a** strong *a priori*
presumption in favour **of the** latter.

CHAPTER XV.

INDIVIDUALISTIC SOLUTION—ARGUMENT FROM
ABSTRACT RIGHTS.

THE ground common to all Individualists is the necessity of putting some limits to the sphere of the government's activity. All aim at protecting the individual from the State. Their arguments fall naturally into two great divisions according to the line of attack adopted. It is maintained, on the one hand, that there are certain spheres marked off by nature or justice into which government has absolutely no right to intrude. Such interference is objected to on the ground that it would violate certain abstract principles or natural rights which are so sacred and absolute that no State has a justifiable warrant to infringe them. On the other hand, it is urged alternatively that, whether or not the government can justify such powers on a speculative basis, it is always *inexpedient* for it to employ them. It always does harm where it seeks to do good by extending its functions beyond their normal limits. The problem, then, is to define the proper sphere of activity, beyond which it is inexpedient and wrong for government to step. Many of its votaries adopt both lines of argument; but, though these may be consistently held by one man, they are essentially different, and will accordingly be treated here in separate chapters. The essence of the argument from natural rights lies in the supposed existence of some abstract principle of justice—of some abstract rights—which

are outside of and greater than the State. Certain hard
and fast barriers are constructed in imagination, and it is
said that the State cannot, without doing violence to itself
and to its duties, climb over these. It is not merely that
it is inexpedient for the State to allow its officials to interfere in this or that direction. Something more than mere
good policy is at stake. Eternal principles, absolute and
fundamental rights, are assailed if the government dare to
go beyond its appointed sphere. " The violation of the
rights of a single individual," it has been forcibly said, " is
an act of treason—is an act of war against humanity."[1]

Too often the issues are confused by jumbling the two
lines of argument together. The harm wrought by such
and such a law working in a certain way is first referred
to. Insistence is laid on its stupidity and its maladroitness,
and how worse evils are caused by it than those which it
sought to remedy. Then, when a successful defence has
been made on those same grounds of expediency, the attack
is suddenly shifted. The emphasis is now laid on the injustice and the violation of natural rights of property or of
freedom, caused by the statute complained of. The double
line of attack is not, of course, in itself unfair, but it may
be used (and often is used) in a manner most unfair.

For a clear understanding of the points in dispute, then, it
is necessary to make—provisionally at any rate—a distinct
separation between the two lines of argument. The question
asked in the present chapter is a very simple one. Are there
any absolute principles or rights which the government acting
under proper authority from the State cannot invade ? Are
there *any* rights inherent in any persons or groups of
persons within the State which may be called absolute ? Is
there *any* limit at all to the right of the State to do anything whatsoever, if that course is advisable for the welfare
of itself as an organic unity comprising all of its members
as component parts ? The answer here given is equally
simple. There is no such absolute, indefeasible, inviolable right which can justly defy the State acting for the
common good. Such a right would be inconsistent with the

[1] See *Justice* for 29th August, 1885.

sovereignty of the **whole,** and would render the efficient
organization of the State impossible. An absolute right
would introduce a dualism—a second sovereign power equal
in dignity to the State itself or superior to it. There is no
so-called fundamental right so intimate or **sacred that the**
law cannot **invade it** if only the need is proportionately
great. For example, to take **an** extreme **case,** if the continued existence of the nation were threatened by invasion
of a barbarous power, to repel such **an** enemy every right
of the individual, the family, and the locality might **be**
trampled under foot. All houses might be **burned, and every**
citizen forced by a universal conscription **to abandon his**
entire liberty and fight against the invaders, even although
his conscience disapproved of war. This **is an extreme**
case justifying extreme remedies; but it is all a matter of
degree. Less violent infringements of so-called natural rights
of freedom are justified by less pressing emergencies. If
the evil to be so avoided **is** only proportionately great,
the government **is not** only justified, but is morally bound
to make such encroachment as the public welfare needs. It
is, further, in every case, the right of the State to judge
for itself when such occasion **has** arisen, and what amount
of interference with private rights or vested interests is
necessary. It cannot wait to take the opinion of the
individual who suffers, or of the section of the community
whose rights are invaded.

No member of the body politic can **be allowed** to arrogate
to himself the right of private judgment as to the duties of
the State. If the interests **of** the community conflict with
those of any private citizen, and if the rule of right as to
their relations admits of different interpretations, the opinion
of the individual must give way before that of the society of
which he forms part. It is for the State itself to judge
what is just and what is unjust, and in making this estimate
it must balance the **good of one** factor with that of another,
and see that each is kept subordinate to the good of the
whole. No part can be allowed selfishly to set up its self-
arrogated rights so as to wrong the whole.

If Mr. Spencer is not the sole living exponent **of the**

doctrine of natural rights which are absolutely valid against
the State, he is at least its best known and most brilliant
adherent. " Has the individual," he asks,[1] " some rights which
are valid against the community?" In his opinion, the individual has such rights.

In the *Social Statics* he speaks of the "right of the individual to ignore the State," a phrase sounding like a *reductio
ad absurdum* of the entire doctrine. The inherent absurdity
is, however, deftly concealed in the more recent exposition
of the objection contained in *The Man* versus *the State*. Here
the theory makes what is (it is to be hoped) its last stand
on British soil. At the outset, Mr. Spencer clearly acknow-
ledges the fact that in England there is a complete consensus
of opinion against him both of statesmen and of lawyers, and
he quotes in particular from Stanley Jevons and Matthew
Arnold.[2] He might have added the names of writers of
such widely differing schools as Sheldon Amos, Sir Frederick
Pollock, Sir James Fitzjames Stephen, Professor Ritchie, and Mr.
Donisthorpe. He consoles himself, however, with the thought
that his view is borne out by the whole current of German
opinion as embodied in the doctrine of *Naturrecht*. That this
consolation is founded on an entire misunderstanding, is the
universal verdict of his friends and adversaries alike. Mr.
Wordsworth Donisthorpe, himself an Individualist, and in
some respects Mr. Spencer's own disciple, declares that in
no recognized sense of the German word *Naturrecht* " is
there any resemblance to the natural rights championed by
Mr. Spencer, who is, of course, aware that although ' Recht '
may be translated by ' droit ' or ' jus,' it cannot be translated
into English by the term ' right ' or ' rights,' or any other
single word; and furthermore, that although ' Recht ' and
' droit ' are fairly synonymous, ' Naturrecht,' on the other
hand, cannot be rendered into French as ' droit naturel.' Mr.
Spencer's natural rights are the ' droit naturel ' of Rousseau,
the ' jus naturale ' of Ulpian, the inalienable right of 'every
man born into the world' of Mr. Henry George; but not the
' Naturrecht ' of Savigny. So that the appeal to the root
idea of German jurisprudence (which is, above all, historical

---

[1] *The Man* versus *the State*, p. 83.   [2] *Ibid.*, p. 87.

in method) to shore up the justly discredited card castle of 'natural rights,' is, to say the least of it, unfortunate."[1]

A still graver difficulty meets him when he descends to particulars, and endeavours to draw out a list of assumed natural rights that are "valid" against the State. He is forced to the somewhat extraordinary device of reviving the ghost or shadow of the exploded social compact theory of Locke and Rousseau. The contract, with Mr. Spencer, is no longer (it is true) an actual one, but only a tacit or implied agreement. Now every contract must contain specific provisions, which are binding on all the parties to it, and the clear inference is that no other conditions are binding at all. Thus if you are only careful enough in the manufacture of your imaginary contract, you can triumphantly draw out of it one by one in the form of imaginary clauses the various pet themes which previously you have stealthily smuggled into it, just as a conjurer brings eggs out of an empty hat. While, with Hobbes, the contract led logically to an absolute tyranny, with Locke it pointed to a mixed monarchy limited by strong aristocratic influences with a dash of mild democracy thrown in, assuming the exact form of the Whig doctrine of the Revolution Settlement of 1689. Under the skilful legerdemain of Rousseau it became the most powerful support of an unrestrained democracy. It is scarcely to be wondered at, then, that a dialectician of Mr. Spencer's experience, once forced to resort to such a weapon, uses it with deadly effect to prove exactly what he wants. He compares the body politic to an association incorporated for the purpose of effecting certain specific objects, capable of definite enunciation. All that is required is to find exactly what objects were included in this incorporation, and the inquirer knows at once beyond a doubt the exact sphere and duties of government. When the great unfounded assumptions involved in this premiss of an actual incorporation of society for specific purposes have once been swallowed,

---

[1] Wordsworth Donisthorpe, *Individualism*, p. 270. See also Professor D. G. Ritchie's *State Interference* (pp. 33 to 35) for his criticism of what he calls "this quaint invocation of the wisdom of the Germans"; and also Sir Frederick Pollock's *Science of Politics.*

P

it is comparatively easy to convince ourselves that all other objects are beyond its proper sphere. "The members of an incorporated body are bound severally to submit to the will of the majority *in all matters concerning the fulfilment of the objects for which they are incorporated, but in no others.* And I contend that this holds of an incorporated nation as much as of an incorporated Company." [1] This position is perfectly unassailable *if* the nation is incorporated, that is to say, if the exploded social contract theory is founded on fact. When an imaginary incorporation is postulated, imaginary articles of association follow as a matter of course. Mr. Spencer, after declaring that there is no actual deed specifying the purpose of incorporation, goes on to supply this defect by a series of rules framed by himself in accordance with his general philosophy, specifying what such a deed would have been if it had existed. We need hardly be surprised, then, when we find those imaginary articles contain all his favourite tenets, and prove his entire case beyond any shadow of doubt. For example, to cite only one of these *a priori* articles, " In the absence of an agreement the supremacy of a majority over a minority does not exist at all." An imaginary agreement to this effect is, it seems, embodied in the imaginary deed of incorporation ; but under certain important limitations. The power of the majority is only warranted for certain specific purposes, and these turn out to be exactly such as suit Mr. Spencer's theories and prejudices. Thus "subordination of minority to majority is legitimate" only for (1) "defence of society as a whole against external invaders," and (2) "defence of each citizen against internal invaders," because these ends are "obviously" desired by every one except the criminal. " Such subordination is not legitimate beyond this." [2]

The natural rights of each man, then, would seem to preclude all interference of law and government, except on the plea of defending against invasion the natural rights of other men. To prove his case, however, Mr. Spencer has to prop up the universally discredited theory of absolute individual rights by the equally exploded doctrine of the social

[1] *The Man* versus *the State*, p. 83.   [2] *Ibid.*, p. 103.

contract. "The original contract was slain by Hume, and trampled upon by Burke,"[1] and with it have fallen all natural rights of man to defy society.[2]

No theory, however, is harder to kill outright. The doctrine of natural rights tends to reappear in a new phase immediately it has been rebutted in its old one. A few of its best known forms must be briefly enumerated, and, if possible, refuted. Absolute claims to exemption from the control of government have been set up on behalf of (1) rights of individual liberty, (2) rights of conscience, (3) contractual and proprietary rights, (4) rights of the church, the family, and the voluntary association, (5) rights of subject nationalities, and (6) "the rights of man" considered generally.

(1) Individual freedom is the first of these principles for which Individualists demand exemption from the province of law. Mill is the apostle of liberty, and it is in that sacred name that he wishes to thrust aside all outside restraints that tend to fetter the development of every citizen. He wishes to protect man from social as well as political tyranny—from public opinion as well as from law and government.

Liberty is to be fenced about from the invasion of other forces as well as from the interference of government. With these motives he institutes an inquiry into " Civil or Social Liberty, the nature and limits of the power which can be legitimately exercised by society over the individual."[3] The problem is (still in his own words) where to draw the line " between individual independence and social control."[4] His conclusion appears on the face of it a very simple one. Only one aim, he finds, can ever justify such interference either by the State or by the various forces of society, and that aim is " self-protection." The sphere of the government, then, is just so much territory as can be fenced off on the plea of self-defence.

It would be difficult to improve on the clearness and force

---

[1] *Vide* Sir F Pollock, *Science of Politics*, p. 113.

[2] With the criticism of Mr. Spencer, which is here hazarded, may be compared that of Mr. Donisthorpe (*Individualism*, pp. 260-275), who views the subject, however, from a different stand-point.

[3] Mill, *On Liberty*, p. 7.   [4] *Ibid.*, p. 16.

of the actual words in which he has explained his own principle. "The sole end for which mankind are warranted individually or collectively in interfering with the liberty of action of any of their number is self-protection. The only purpose for which power can be rightfully exercised over any member of a civilized community, against his will, is to prevent harm to others. His own good, either physical or moral, is not sufficient warrant. The only part of the conduct of any one for which he is amenable to society, is that which concerns others. In the part which merely concerns himself, his independence is, of right, absolute. Over himself, over his own body and mind, the individual is sovereign."[1]

In these sentences is contained Mill's complete solution of the problem he set himself in his *Essay on Liberty*, namely, to find a definite settled principle of government action applicable to all circumstances, times, and countries. He professes to find the absolute criterion he is in search of in " self-protection." If the motive of any action of society or of any law which restricts freedom can be shown to be the desire to protect, it is justified. If not, no other plea will be sustained. Now this seems at first sight to possess the qualities of certainty and simplicity—the two things needed in a good working criterion. On closer examination both of these quickly vanish. It breaks down when applied to any of the difficult questions that arise in practice. The best way to watch its collapse is to follow Mill himself in its application to a few practical cases. We are surprised to find that this " one very simple principle," which we are told in one page is " entitled to govern absolutely the dealings of society with the individual,"[2] is declared in the very next page not to apply at all to a numerous and important class of cases. "It is, perhaps, hardly necessary to say that this doctrine is meant to apply only to human beings in the maturity of their faculties."[3] The simplicity of the one principle has already vanished, and the certainty is following fast; for it is extremely difficult to determine what " maturity of faculties " means, and still more difficult to judge in whom it resides. Children are of course excluded. But who are

[1] Mill, *On Liberty*, p. 27.   [2] *Ibid.*, p. 22.   [3] *Ibid.*, p. 23.

children ? **Positive** law in this country terminates minority
at twenty-one, **but** this is merely an arbitrary provision made
for purposes of practical convenience. Even allowing that
all under twenty-one are children, what principle is to apply
to them ? Are **those who are not of age** to have no protection
against society **at all?**[1] Maturity **is a thing** gradually reached,
and not suddenly jumped into at an age which society fixes
beforehand. Further, one individual **reaches it** sooner than
another. Children, however, are not the only class excluded.
The criterion does not, it seems, apply to barbarians either.
"Despotism is a legitimate mode of government in dealing
with barbarians, provided the end be their improvement, and
the means justified by actually effecting that end." **The**
introduction of these two provisos still further increases the
complexity. But the vagueness of the test is a worse fault
than its failure in simplicity. The criterion becomes utterly
useless, for who is a barbarian ? A second **test** is needed to
point **out those men whose** faculties are mature. Who **is**
judge ? Are **the** Zulus barbarians ? Are the Boers ? Have the
millions of India come to maturity, or only some of them ? No
nation or individual is safe from the imputation of immaturity
being pled by enemies who wish to justify undue interference.
Some men would question whether the inhabitants of **Ireland**
or the Highlands of Scotland had come to their majority. John
Stuart Mill might have looked on Collectivists as barbarians,
while they might have invaded his rights under a similar plea.

The complexities only increase when the inquirer passes
from a consideration of the various classes **of** individuals to
whom the rule applies, **to** an enumeration **of** the kinds of
actions which it regulates. The application of the criterion
of self-protection leads to the rule that neither the society
nor the State has a right to interfere as long as a man's
"conduct affects the interests of no person besides himself."[2]
A new difficulty here **presents** itself, which Mill clearly
enough perceived. "**The** distinction here pointed out," he

---

[1] Apparently not ; for, in another part of his essay, Mill says, "Society
has had absolute power over them during all the early portions of their
existence " (Mill, *Liberty*, p. 147).

[2] *Ibid.*, p. 140.

says, "between the part of a person's life which concerns only himself, and that which concerns others many persons will refuse to admit."[1]   He states the difficulty fairly enough; but never answers it.   He merely confuses the issue by making a distinction between "actual" and "constructive injuries," the latter of which do not count.   This is only to create a need for still another criterion to decide what actions are merely "constructive."

Indeed, there is no part of a man's life which concerns only himself: with every advance in science comes a deepening sense of the solidarity of the race to strengthen the conviction that there is no action, however private, of any man which exclusively affects himself.   No one can even breathe without affecting currents of air which may bear germs of disease fraught with death to others.   To be perfectly safe from hurt by our neighbours is impossible.   *Any* measure might be justified on the ground of self-protection.

It is, however, in its application to special cases that the arbitrary nature of the principle shows.   It is necessary either to abandon it altogether or to twist it backwards and forwards to make it tally with observed facts.

Mill's one simple principle of action then turns out to involve a whole series of other principles, even when applied to such specially favourable cases as he actually chooses. It breaks down even more completely before a more thoroughgoing analysis of existing society.[2]   In one sense the criterion includes too much, and in another too little.   If the life of the individual is only possible in that of the State—if man is a πολιτικὸν ζῶον—then the State does more for him than merely protect him from his neighbours.   It gives him a field for development and supplies him with everything that distinguishes him from the brutes.   Thus to reduce the relations between them to the thin limit of Mill's criterion, is to give a wrong impression altogether. Government may best help a man by leaving him to help

---

[1] Mill, *Liberty*, p. 143.

[2] Individualists themselves admit that it fails to work.   Thus Mr. Wordsworth Donisthorpe (*Plea for Liberty*, p. 71) sums up his examination: "On the whole, Mill's test will not do."

himself; but surely if it *can* help forward his **highest**
interests it ought **to** do so. There is no inherent absurdity
in the State doing more than protecting him. On the other
hand, self-protection leaves too wide an opportunity for State
interference, because any act can be justified on the grounds
of self-defence. In Mill's own words, "It is one of the undisputed functions of government to take precautions against
crime before it has been committed, as well as **to** detect
and punish it afterwards." There is no arbitrary measure
of the executive government; no harsh and repressive
criminal law; no interference with the **liberty and rights of**
the subject; no invasion of the privacy and **sanctity of**
family life; which cannot be justified on the ground of self-
protection. Not to multiply instances unnecessarily, was it
not in the **name of** self-protection or of the public safety
that the worst crimes **of the** French Revolution were
perpetrated?

Thus Mill's criterion signally and utterly breaks down. It
cannot fulfil **its** professed purpose of supplying one test which
supersedes all others. An almost parallel course of reasoning
would show that all other tests proposed are equally delusive.
Indeed, the pursuit of such a **principle is a hopeless task.**
No such criterion exists. Neither "self-protection" nor any
other principle of division can define the exact extent to which
the natural right of liberty can **justly defy** the government,
for the simple reason that no such natural right exists at all.
Freedom is possible only within the law, and not against
the law.

(2) Rights of conscience are the most sacred possession of the
individual man. Here, at least, it may be said, neither the
living agents of the State nor its laws can intrude. The
influence of the State is at once so powerful and so penetrating,
however, that it is not safe to jump to any such conclusion.
A preliminary inquiry into the nature of these rights is
necessary. The question arises, What makes any opinion a
right of **conscience?** Two answers are possible. (*a*) It
may **be said** that each man must be the sole interpreter
for himself of his own conscience. No earthly adviser, no
church, and **no** State can stand between him and his Maker.

(*b*) On the other hand, no man can be allowed, on the plea of conscientious scruples, to set aside the law of the land. Even if the legislature laid down the rule that no statute was to be allowed to invade "rights of conscience"—granting for the moment that any Parliament could so far neglect its duty as to use so vague a phrase—even then, if a dispute arose as to what constituted such rights, the determination would lie with the State by the mouth of its Courts of Law, and not with the individual. Such rights of conscience, then, as are an effective bar to the interference of the government must be granted by the State itself. From the legal stand-point it is the State that determines rights of conscience ; while from the moral side (as we have already seen) each must judge for himself. The final and complete answer must probably combine both elements, but its solution lies beyond the scope of this Essay. The important point is that, in a question between the individual and the State, the final decision lies with the latter.

The individual conscience, then, if it would escape the pressure of State law, must conform itself to that law. Rights of conscience, like all other rights, are subject to legal control. Conscience is in one sense absolutely dependent on the community, in spite of the fact that it is in another sense free; for it is moulded by the sentiments of sur-rounding society and the laws of the State. Heredity, education, and environment all have their bearing upon it. As long as the individual is so closely bound up in society his conscience cannot shake itself clear of trammels. When a State, then, recoils from violating such rights, it is not because it recognizes in them some principle equally or more powerful than its own sovereignty, whose precincts it dare not invade. No; its abstention arises from quite different reasons. These are chiefly two. In the first place, it judges, in the special cases where it abstains, that it would be inexpedient or unjust to interfere; and, in the second place, in the innermost sanctuary of conscience it *cannot* interfere. It may compel a man to perform evil acts. It may stigmatize and punish him as a criminal when he is a saint, but it cannot by compulsion make his

conscience alter its judgment between right and wrong. There
is a last resort of freedom where despotism can never intrude.
In this sense there *is* an absolute and inviolable right of
conscience ; but this is not the sense in which the phrase
is used by those who wish to restrict the province of government. The State is powerless to make the meanest slave
believe that wrong is right against his own conscience, as it is
powerless to make him believe that night is day, or that two
and two make five. Outside of this its power is irresistible.
It can withhold the necessaries of life from those who
refuse to subscribe to its tenets. It can reduce man almost
to the level of the brute. It can, finally, put the individual
conscience at rest, as far as this world is concerned, by putting
the individual to death for refusing to accept the interpretation of religious dogmas promulgated by its authority.
When its duty calls it to determine on a line of conduct
involving a breach of what are said to be rights of conscience,
it approaches this consideration just as it would approach any
other question. It is all a matter of degree. The pressing
nature of the occasion varies, and therefore the solicitude for
the preservation of rights of conscience must vary too. A
man's conscience may demand " peace at any price," but
this cannot exempt him from the payment of a war tax.
A still greater necessity may demand a forced conscription.
This violates his conscience even more vitally. Here a new
element of the problem comes to light. Rights of conscience
seem to vary in degree, and it is possible to do greater violence
to them in one way than in another. In fact, a close survey
shows that rights of conscience, in so far as they affect the
relations between the man and the State, are simply one aspect
of the general rights of man. To infringe rights of conscience
comes to mean simply to infringe other rights, such as
property, liberty, or life. Thus, while on the one side a
subject could justify every act of rebellion against the government by pleading that he acted in defence of what is a
right of conscience on his own interpretation ; on the other
hand, government can hardly take a single step, pass a
single law, or impose a single tax without outraging the
religious or moral scruples of some of its subjects.

From all this reasoning three principles emerge: (i.) It is difficult to determine what are "rights of conscience," and still more wherein their violation consists. They are not *sui generis*, but only aspects of ordinary rights, and differ from one another in degree. (ii.) It is the State and not the individual which must finally pronounce judgment on what are and what are not such rights. (iii.) Even if it admits a right of conscience, it does not bind itself to regard that as *absolute* against itself in all possible contingencies, for such rights are essentially relative in their nature.

Individual rights of conscience, then, are no exception to the general rule. They cannot fence themselves in security from invasion by the State. The oppressed individual has only one resort—that of martyrs in all ages—he can die for conscience' sake. He cannot set up the law of his moral nature as a sanctuary from which to defy the majesty of the State.

(3) Similar claims are often made on behalf of contractual and proprietary rights. "Freedom of contract" is often spoken of as a principle of such sanctity that it is unholy, if not unlawful, for the legislature to interfere with it. The Factory Acts, the Bank Holiday Acts, the Crofters' Acts, and the Employers' Liability Acts, are all frequently condemned because they place limits to the right to make and to enforce certain classes of contracts. The American Constitution has so far accepted this theory of the sacred inviolability of contracts as to prohibit all interference with them on the part of the various States now federated together. The Parliament of Great Britain, however, has shown itself of recent years more and more disposed to restrict contractual rights.

The subject of rights of property is of even more vital interest. The cry that vested interests are at stake is often raised by men who would reject any natural rights of liberty, though of late years the two interests have been brought into somewhat unusual contact under the auspices of the Liberty and Property Defence League, whose object is, generally, to protect personal freedom and proprietary rights against socialistic legislation.

The case against "vested interests" is admirably put by

Prof. Hoffman.[1] " The doctrine of the inviolability of **vested rights** rests on **a** false conception of the State, and **before the** true conception has no foundation whatever. The **true** State will **never** allow any individual, or collection of individuals, to hold and use any given property any longer than such holding contributes to the common good. The moment it ceases to do so, that moment the vested right becomes violable. The government of one generation can never unalterably bind a future generation as to its use of property. **It** can never grant a franchise for the use of property that a future generation cannot annul, or **make a contract that** a future generation **cannot break.** The word ' forever ' in any document concerning the possession and use of property is a fiction. The sooner it is **read out of** court the better. Because a government has once allowed corporations to **be** formed for the investment and use of property is no reason why they should be continued in existence when they cease to promote the public welfare. It is not only the right, but the duty **of the** State to legislate them out of existence when it becomes clear that some other method of holding and using property will better further the well-being of the people. The laws concerning the use of property are just as subject to change as those concerning the acquisition of property, and it is the duty of the State through its government to have them changed whenever it is evident that the good of the organism as a whole requires it."

All rights and interests are only relative ; but this by no means prevents them possessing a certain weight which must be estimated with reference to the good of the whole. In the interests of order, permanence, and stability, great, perhaps paramount, importance should be placed upon the protection of the property of individuals. When vested interests are invaded, compensation should always be given, assuming that what is infringed is really a right ; but the State must emphatically deny all assumption of an absolute inviolability **for** any personal or property right.

(4) Natural rights of an inalienable kind have also been demanded on behalf of the Church, the family, and the voluntary

[1] Hoffman, *Sphere of the State*, p. 60.

association. It is claimed, in particular, by churchmen of almost every denomination that the exclusive care of spiritual affairs belongs to the Church, while the civil government must confine itself to temporal matters.

Though the two theories have much in common, this claim is not a mere repetition of the doctrine of the absolute rights of conscience, because the Church has too often shown itself the most intolerant infringer of those rights. The State has very often had to exercise its powers of sovereignty over the Church to prevent the invasion of the "natural" rights of individuals. No such claims of the Church can be admitted.

(5) One form of abstract rights yet calls for brief consideration. It is interesting, if only as showing how hydra-headed and hard to kill the monster is. It is brought up by Bluntschli in defence of the claims of different nationalities where more "nations" than one are included within the same State. Two instances will explain the difference between a Nation and a State, as it presents itself to Bluntschli. Austria and Hungary are separate in race, language, and traditions, and yet both are bound together into the Austrian Empire by subjection to a common sovereign. Ireland, again, although inhabited by a different race with different sympathies, is bound into one state with England and Scotland, and finding itself in a minority, must often submit to measures of which it disapproves. It is on behalf of such nationalities as Hungary and Ireland that Bluntschli sets up the plea of abstract rights. The chief among these rights is the title to existence as a nation.[1] From this source flow a number of derivative rights : (i.) The State cannot deny a nationality its language, or prohibit its literature ; (ii.) a people has a right to its own customs; (iii.) to its own laws; (iv.) also to its own moral and intellectual life. "Man," it seems, "can have no juster cause for resistance to tyranny than defence of nationality." It might be sufficient answer to those theories to show (as could easily be done) that Bluntschli admits important exceptions to each of his own rules in other portions of the same valuable treatise in which he propounds them. But this would be merely an argu-

[1] *Theory of the State*, p. 89.

ment *ad hominem* after all. The real ground of objection
holds good as before. When he says that the State "*cannot*
deny a nationality its language," the word "cannot" is not
only confused with the meaning "ought not," but even "ought
not" will not apply, for the State *ought* to do everything to
further its highest end, in acting for the common good. If
that is best served by a separation between two nationalities,
a repeal of the union ought to be insisted on, but not otherwise. It is the whole nation, however, and not the seceding
part, which must decide; and as long as the two nations form
one State, the sovereign will must be absolute within its every
corner.

(6) The last form of this claim set up for the individual
which needs consideration is the most general of all. It
came into prominence in the eighteenth century, under the
name of the Rights of Man. The phrase has a history of
its own: it has played an important part in helping more
than one revolution to alter the destinies of the human
race, but its career cannot here be traced.[1] Its importance
culminated when it was embodied in the principles of 1789
by the French Constituent Assembly, and formed the foundation upon which its members attempted to build their new
constitution. The doctrine of the Rights of Man obtained
a great impulse from Rousseau's system of political science,
and received a solemn endorsement by the assembly entrusted
with the sovereignty of the French State, when it was made
the foundation of the whole fabric. Thirteen years before,
the same doctrine had formed the basis of the American
Declaration of Independence, adopted by Congress on the
4th of July, 1776; and almost a century earlier it had
occupied a prominent place in the discussions of the English
Convention Parliament, preliminary to the framing of the
Bill of Rights, though fortunately the builders of that last
of the three great bulwarks of our constitutional liberties
were too shrewd and practical men to endanger its stability
by basing it on any theory, however fashionable at the time.
They built on history and precedent, and not on vague
philosophic platitudes.

[1] See Prof. Ritchie's *Natural Rights*, chapter i., for a detailed account.

What is this theory of the Rights of Man which has played so distinguished a *rôle* in English, French, and American national progress? It naturally assumed various forms according to the times and places of its appearance; but its essential feature is everywhere the same. Man as man has certain rights which no State or government dare attack. Every man, because of his own separate individuality, has these rights.

Catalogues of these naturally vary, but they usually include freedom of thought, speech, and action; rights of public meeting, of combination, and freedom of the press, and so on. All of them are excellent things in their proper places. Nor is there the least objection to calling them "natural rights" if any good purpose is thereby served; though it is incumbent on those using the term to explain exactly what they mean. Danger arises only when they are spoken of as "absolute" rights.

All these so-called Rights of Man found their extravagant demands on the assumption that they were prior to the existence of the State, and therefore above and beyond its proper jurisdiction. They are overthrown when the fallacy of the social contract is exposed.

The conclusion of the whole inquiry then is that the argument for inalienable and absolute rights valid against the State cannot stand in any one of its many forms. Whatever is included in the State is subject to its political sovereignty, and therefore can ground no claim to any rights which are absolute. Further, it can have no *legal* rights even against the legal sovereign or chief part of the existing government. Parliament is legally above association and family and church and individual.

The State is absolutely (as well as legally) above them all. In determining the proper functions of government, " the first step," said the late Professor Jevons,[1] " must be to rid our minds of the idea that there are any such things in social matters as abstract rights, absolute principles, indefeasible laws, inalterable rules, or anything whatever of an eternal and inflexible nature." Man has assuredly rights,

[1] Stanley Jevons, *The State in Relation to Labour*, p. 6.

but a true doctrine of these rights must regard them as existing only in and through the State, and never apart from or against it. They must be based upon the sovereignty of the body politic. This is at once the most immovable foundation on which they can rest, and a guarantee that they will not be carried to excess and so pass into wrongs. Law, as defined by a perfect State, cannot clash with the individual rights of any of its subjects when their differences are reconciled in the light of a truly organic theory of mankind. "Individual and private rights," as has been forcibly said, "have their root in a social authority; the individual possesses his rights, not because of any divine and eternal claim to them, but because they have been given to him and confirmed to him by the State. . . . The rights of man give no actual vantage for urging a claim, but the rights of an Englishman born are clear and defined against encroachment, because he is not merely a man, but a man born to the freedom for which his forefathers struggled."[1] Man's rights become actualities only through the State, and the legitimate sphere of the individual is also the legitimate sphere of the government.

The truth is that the whole discussion is at bottom—as is, unfortunately, too often the case with such discussions— a mere battle of definitions. There are several senses—too obvious to need to be dwelt upon—of the words "natural rights" which every one would admit—rights which most men actually have; rights which they ought to have in a perfect world; and so forth.[2] The one important question is: Are these rights *absolute*? If we once admit (and how can we help admitting?) that there are emergencies under pressure of which the community is justified in invading these, we have admitted all that is required. To this the Individualist may answer: "If that is all you want you have it, because no one would deny this for a moment. Every

[1] William Cunningham, *Politics and Economics*, p. 137.

[2] The various ambiguities with which the expression "natural rights" is positively bristling are admirably explained in Prof. Ritchie's most recently published work, especially in chapter ii., where the different meanings of "natural" are explained, and in chapter v., where the various meanings of "Rights" are given.

Individualist admits that necessity has no law, and that in extreme circumstances, where absolutely necessary, you may infringe an absolute right." Such an admission, indeed, involves all that is contended for; but what is wanted is not a bald acquiescence in an evident truism, but that the varied aspects of truth which it contains should be understood and acted on. Unfortunately the same Individualist who makes the admission on one page appears on the next, and argues away as if he had never admitted anything. The dogma of absolute rights is hard to kill.

The conclusion has been well expressed by Prof. Hoffman.[1] " It is easy to see the falsity of the doctrine of 'inalienable rights.' The signers of the Declaration of Independence declare that 'life, liberty, and the pursuit of happiness' are such rights. They are, to be sure, the natural rights of every individual; but a natural right is not of necessity an absolute right."

The common fallacy is to prove the existence of a "natural right" in the sense of a relative right, and then assume that it is therefore inviolable and inalienable. Man, however, is by nature a social and political being; therefore his natural rights must have a reference to the State, the need for which is included in his nature. His rights in particular come to him only in and through the State. He has "natural" rights at all only because his nature binds him to the State which makes their realization possible.

[1] Hoffman, *The Sphere of the State*, p. 6.

CHAPTER XVI.

INDIVIDUALISTIC SOLUTION—ARGUMENTS FROM THE FUTILITY AND INEXPEDIENCY OF OVER-GOVERNMENT.

To dispose of the argument from natural rights is only to reject half of the Individualist's case. Indeed, Mr. Wordsworth Donisthorpe has not only discarded all connection with absolute rights, but has with incisive and unanswerable logic annihilated this argument with overwhelming vehemence. This always interesting, and at times brilliant exponent of Individualism tries to found his system on inductions from experience. The substance of his argument is that all government action beyond its own normal functions is inexpedient and hurtful, and defeats its ends either by failing in the object aimed at or by producing worse evils in room of those removed. This line of argument is, of course, by no means confined to him. All Individualists hold to the same central principle just enunciated; but most of them use it in conjunction with the untenable argument from absolute rights already discussed and found wanting.

Simply stated, the argument is this, that (whether just or unjust), over-government is always futile or inexpedient or both—that to extend law or administration beyond their normal limits is necessarily to hurt both national and individual welfare.[1] If it can be proved that government

---

[1] J. S. Mill states the argument from inexpediency more moderately and modestly. Interference may, in his opinion, be inexpedient on three grounds, viz.: (1) Many things are better done by private

always does harm when it so interferes, and is always
entirely wrong, no stronger ground can be occupied. The
Individualist, for example, tries to prove from history that
every law passed by Parliament to regulate trade, to co-
ordinate supply and demand, or to make a debased coinage
legal tender, has been a blunder and source of distress
even to those whom it sought to benefit. Having amassed
as great a number of favourable instances as possible, he
draws the sweeping conclusion that Parliament ought *never*
to interfere with any branch of trade. Several difficulties
suggest themselves, however, inherent in the nature of such
an argument. In the first place, it is extremely difficult to
make a sufficiently wide collection of data to work upon.
The position is only secure when the consequences of *all* laws
have been examined, and this is quite an impossible task.
In the second place, in making an induction from so wide a
field, with the desire to prove a position already taken up,
it is almost impossible to avoid the fallacy of neglecting
contradictory evidence. In the third place, even if the
generalization has been successfully and fairly made, and has
satisfactorily proved the position for the past, it is liable to
be overthrown in the future whenever new circumstances
arise. If the objection to a certain kind of government
action is merely that it is generally inexpedient, it is open
for its advocate to offer to show that the present instance
is an exception to the general rule. If he can do this, the
argument from expediency is his. Thus Individualists who
rely only on such considerations can never feel their position
impregnable. They are liable to new attacks at any moment,
and from every side.

individual action than by the government; (2) power of initiation
and action unfettered by authority is the best education for the
people; and (3) if government officials have a hand in everything,
the State becomes stereotyped and fossilized—a rampant bureaucracy
tyrannizes over a stagnant nation. See *Essay on Liberty*, p. 196. These
are indeed weighty reasons; but we may allow them their full force
without becoming Individualists. They warn us against the abuse of
Government interference in all spheres; but do not exclude it from its
proper place in any one sphere.

" Never " is difficult to prove, and when the Individualist seeks to show that government can *never* do any good by meddling, he undertakes a gigantic task. If the doctrine of absolute rights, however, deserts him, this is the only ground left him by the logic of the position. He tries in various ways to make the burden lighter, with what success we must see. He usually hedges the full difficulty of his position in three ways. In the first place, ultimate results, he says, must be looked to as well as immediate ones. Even if those nearest effects which we can see are good and practicable for the State to accomplish, still there are ultimate consequences which are evil. " The practical politician," says Mr. Spencer [1] (he is never tired of showering abuse on this inoffensive gentleman), " who goes on thinking only of proximate results, naturally never thinks of results still more remote, still more general, and still more important than those just at hand." When it is remembered that the ultimate results of the simplest act of every private individual, as well as of every State official, have absolutely no limit at all, the boldest man will hesitate to assert that no evil has ever resulted from any one given action. No one ought, of course, to effect a small present good at the expense of a great future evil. Even the " practical politician " who has read of Esau and his mess of pottage is not entirely ignorant of this truism. He would call it in plain English "short-sighted policy," and this is just the same thing which Mr. Spencer prefers to call by longer names. Unfortunately the appeal from immediate to ultimate effects may operate both ways. The Socialist may say that when the Individualist objects to a small proximate evil resulting from government action, he is stupid not to see the ultimate results which are good to an extent quite out of proportion with the present evil.

In the second place, Mr. Spencer and others of his school would argue that although no evil (direct or indirect) can be shown to result from the particular act of government intervention, yet this action will form a precedent for other things which will lead to evil. This contention, however, if pushed to its logical conclusion, involves the doctrine that

[1] *The Man* versus *the State*, p. 25.

the State can never do anything for any one without doing everything for every one, which is a manifest absurdity.

In the third place, Individualists—most of them at any rate, for Mr. Auberon Herbert is a notable exception—would admit that government has a legitimate sphere and legitimate functions of its own. Thus the task is made still easier. It has only to be proved that a balance of benefits (ultimate and proximate) never results from the extension of government intervention beyond this sphere.

The Anarchist, indeed, is the only consistent Individualist, for he alone follows where the logic of his position leads him. To admit that government has any province of its own at all, wherein it may absolutely control the individual, involves a complete departure from the purely individualistic stand-point. Such an admission is essentially of the nature of a compromise with Socialism. " You keep on your side of the fence, and I shall keep on mine," the individual seems to say to the State. It is true that he places the fence to suit his own theories, very far away from the abstraction to which he reduces himself, and very near that other abstraction to which he reduces the State. Still the compromise is there, though it is one which is all in favour of the individual.

Here we come within sight of the problem of Individualism. There is a definite province, it seems, for government intervention. There is also a province for self-government, into which the State has no right to intrude. If, then, there are two spheres of influence thus mutually exclusive for all practical purposes, some scientific frontier must be constructed between their alien territories. Individualists have not failed to see the need of such a careful delimitation, and each of them has attempted to supply it. Unfortunately no two of them have been able exactly to agree as to the lines it ought to follow.

The most noteworthy efforts in this direction are those of Von Humboldt, John Stuart Mill, and Mr. Herbert Spencer.

Von Humboldt's guiding principle [1] for mapping out the proper province of the government is " the security of others."

[1] Von Humboldt, *Sphere and Duties of Government*, translated by Joseph Coultard, p. 19.

The object of his essay upon the *Sphere and Duties of Government* is to show that the State has no concern with the "positive welfare" of its members. "A State, then," he says, "has one of two ends in view; it designs either to promote happiness or simply to prevent evil; and in this latter case, the evil may be that which arises from natural causes, or that which springs from man's disregard for his neighbour's rights. If it restricts its solicitude to the second of those objects; it aims merely at security; and I would here oppose this term security to every possible end of State agency, and comprise these last under the general head of positive welfare."

To look after their own comfort and well-being is the province of the individual citizens. The government has no right directly to promote happiness, and no right to try to counteract the evils springing from natural sources. Its sole function is to see that each man has *security* from his neighbours, and to force him to allow the like to them. Here, then, is a clear antithesis between the province of the State and that of the individual, and the former is narrowed down to play a very inferior *rôle*. The individual has apparently a right to object to all interference with him or his affairs of whatever kind, unless the security of others demands it. Even his own security is no warrant for meddling with him, still less the desire for his advancement.

Von Humboldt's chief follower and exponent in this country was John Stuart Mill, whose strong personality, colouring every theory that passed through the medium of his mind, gave to the *Essay on Liberty* a distinct individuality of its own, though the general point of view is the same as that of Von Humboldt.

How Mill's attempt to sketch the exact limits of individual liberty by means of "self-protection" utterly breaks down, has been already explained in criticising the doctrine of natural rights. Mr. Spencer's efforts are equally unsuccessful. Sometimes he declares that defence against internal and external invasion is the only guide; sometimes he contends that while the State has a right to coerce each subject "negatively" it cannot coerce him "positively."

It would be most instructive to ascertain how far the detailed conclusions founded on these two principles of delimitation coincide.   It is also open to question if it is really possible to discriminate between negative and positive coercion, or if the one does not rather shade into the other imperceptibly.   Meantime, it is sufficient to notice that Mr. Spencer's second definition restricts the sphere of the State to whatever it can do by negative compulsion alone without resorting to positive compulsion.   In plain language, it can compel no man, but only forbid or prevent.   There are thus at least four competing principles in the field, each professing to be what Mill calls "a settled principle of action" to guide the government in knowing its own province and mapping it off from that of its private citizens.   Von Humboldt states it as security from the evils "which spring from man's disregard for his neighbours' right"; Mill, as "self-protection"; Mr. Herbert Spencer, as "defence against external and internal invaders," and again as "whatever can be done without positive compulsion."

Now each Individualist is only responsible for his own principle; he has only to protect from attack by the State the bulwarks with which he has surrounded the exclusively individual sphere as marked off by himself.   Thus the fact that each of them has fenced off a differently bounded territory is no argument against him ; yet it shows that there is a total want of consensus of opinion in the Individualists' camp as to first principles.   What is more, not one of these principles is sufficient to accomplish what it professes.   Each of them, when examined and applied to particular cases, turns out to be too vague to be of any practical use ; while again it is at once too narrow and too wide to square either with philosophical principles or with observed facts.

Individualists have, indeed, set themselves an impossible task by first assuming a division which does not exist between the whole and its members, and then trying to find where it is.   They all agree that it is on their own principles *theoretically necessary* to fix a hard and fast line, and the more candid (who are usually the most clear-sighted as well) admit that this is *practically impossible*.   Two quotations will show the existence of this logical inconsistency in the individualistic position.

The Earl of Pembroke—the founder of the Liberty and Property Defence League—expresses this theoretical necessity as follows:[1] "There must be some sort of promise or compact existing between the individual and the society, and that compact must contain the principle, if such a principle there be." Here is the recognition of the need of a hard and fast line of demarcation. The practical impossibility of fulfilling his lordship's own condition is well expressed by him in the same pamphlet: "We must make up our minds to give up the idea of discovering any single principle that will enable us in all cases to set the proper boundaries to State action, and protect the province of individual freedom."

Mr. Donisthorpe finds the same impossibility of squaring practice with the logical requirements of his individualistic position. "The problem is," he says,[2] "What are the proper limits of liberty? and if these cannot be properly theoretically defined, what rules should be adopted for our practical guidance? . . . Where in theory shall we draw the line, which in practice we *have to draw somewhere?*" After showing in detail the fallacies of all attempted principles of division, he gives his own view: "We cannot draw a hard and fast line between the proper field of State interference and the field sacred to individual freedom. There is no principle whereby the effective majority can decide whether to interfere or not."[3]

His conclusion is perfectly true, but it carries with it a deeper meaning than he would admit. It sweeps away the logical basis of abstract Individualism altogether. The reason why we cannot fence off the "field of State interference" from the "field sacred to individual liberty," as we can fence off two actual fields containing different breeds of sheep, is simply because no such separate fields exist. Every part of the "field" of the one is a proper "field" for the other. Individuals have *no* field sacred from the State, and the State

[1] *Liberty and Socialism*, p. 57.   [2] In the *Plea for Liberty*, p. 70.
[3] *Ibid.*, p. 74.

necessarily interferes with everything and everybody within it, though it need not do so in a stupid or unjust or arbitrary manner, or by means of meddlesome officials. Thus the reasoning of Lord Pembroke and Mr. Donisthorpe (and others might be quoted to the same effect) contains a tacit admission that they have built their theories on a false philosophy.

Collectivists declaim against existing institutions on the ground that they are too individualistic, but Mr. Spencer and his friends attack them on the opposite ground, that they are too socialistic. It will help to a clearer understanding of their stand-point, to mention the chief objections set forth in *The Man* versus *the State* against the existing social and political system.

(1) Mr. Spencer's first charge may be dismissed as hardly a serious one—that all Liberals who countenance State interference are Tories in disguise. This is the doctrine of "the new Toryism." Stripped of all unnecessary verbiage it simply means that Tory and Socialist are identical, while every Liberal is necessarily an Individualist if he is consistent with himself,—which is simply absurd. As this argument is practically an appeal to Liberals, he assumes of course that all Toryism is bad. It is strange in this light to read (as one sometimes does) that Mr. Spencer is himself the most deadly enemy of modern Radicalism, and therefore the staunchest of Tories.[1]

(2) The second argument is drawn from the inherent stupidity of legislators, which is indeed only a necessary inference from the imperfection of human nature—though the legislator seems to absorb a greater share of folly than his fellow-men. Nature, if only let alone, knows better than man. Many instances are given of the mistaken principles upon which lawgivers have interfered with freedom, and the inference is drawn, not that these legislators were specially stupid or rash, but that *all* legislators are necessarily equally bad. This is the doctrine of "The sins of legislators."[2]

---

[1] Cf. Ritchie's *State Interference*, p. 3. "Mr. Spencer is perhaps the most formidable foe with whom the New Radicalism has to reckon."

[2] *The Man* versus *the State*, p. 44.

(3) Then follow a number of special applications of this doctrine affording particular instances of the harm done by government action. Some of these are appalling enough. The list is a long one and not exhilarating reading. But the conclusions are quite unwarranted. For example, government interference, it seems, is at variance with all the recognized doctrines of political economy. "Interferences with the connection between supply and demand, given up in certain fields after immense mischiefs had been done during many centuries, are now taking place in other fields." "Supply of houses for the poor" is instanced.[1]

(4) All unnecessary government action is unjust, it is urged, because the persons who pay for it are not those who reap the benefit. It is unjust to tax A (who never reads) to provide free libraries, where B may pollute his mind with novels of which A does not approve; or to tax C, whose small income keeps him a bachelor, to provide free education for D's twelve children. This argument deserves very serious consideration. Its force, however, may be modified by the thought that no tax can be absolutely just to every one. Yet no individual (except Mr. Auberon Herbert) would on that account abolish all taxes together. Some government functions are necessary and yet cannot be supported by voluntary subscriptions like a charity school. The statesmen who are responsible for spending and levying the taxes should be as just as possible. It may turn out that taxation for certain objects is unfair, but no sweeping application of the principle to all payments from the public purse can be allowed.

(5) "Every extension," says Mr. Spencer, "of the regulative policy involves an addition to the regulative agents—a further growth of officialism and an increasing power of the organization formed of officials."[2] This is true, so far as it goes. It merely amounts to this, however, that a tendency to excess should be avoided, because there may be too much of anything—good as well as bad.

(6) In increasing the powers and duties of officialism and bureaucracy, habits of self-help and personal responsibility

---

[1] *The Man* versus *the State*, p. 51.   [2] *Ibid.*, p. 29.

are weakened. " Increasing power of a growing administrative
organization is accompanied by decreasing power of the
rest of the society to resist its further growth and control."
This is true, but only shows once more that excessive
government action is mischievous, not that all of it is bad.

(7) Progressive government action, it is further urged, means
reckless expenditure of public money. This fact, combined
with those above enumerated, tends to pauperize the nation,
and leads to national bankruptcy. All free gifts given to
the people, whether by the State or by wealthy individuals,
are of the nature of alms. Whether the charity takes the
form of money, or of food and clothing, or of free education or free libraries, or free concerts, it is charity all the
same. Alms are evil when a private man gives them. Still
no one can object. They are doubly evil, Mr. Spencer holds,
when given by the State under forced taxation, wrung from
the pockets of the unwilling. To give alms at all is to sin
against the Ricardian law of wages, as it is virtually an
attempt to raise wages artificially above their normal level,
which is as impossible as to raise the level of the sea.
Sooner or later the old level is restored, and the amount of
the charity ultimately finds it way into the pockets of the
employers of labour in the form of increased profits. It
does not relieve distress; it adds to the luxury of those who
have already too much. Such is the result of the Ricardian
law of wages, as interpreted by both Individualists and Socialists.
The latter would cure it by abolishing property altogether ;
the former by abolishing, as far as possible, government interference. Now there is much truth in the Individualist's
contention : whenever the State does interfere by giving
charity, it undoubtedly does tend to pauperize the nation. It
does not follow, however, that therefore the State should
never do anything for fear that it may be so entrapped into
virtually giving alms to some one. If free education is almsgiving, it is inconsistent with received political economy.
But that is just the point in dispute. Is it almsgiving ?
A similar question might be asked of each of the other acts
complained of.

[1] *The Man* versus *the State*, p. 33.

These last five heads are all instances of the application to special cases of the doctrine of " the sins of legislators."

(8) Then there is the cumulative argument (already referred to). The amount of government action increases like a rolling snowball, or rather like an avalanche. The fatal course once begun, no power on earth can stop it. We have started already, it would seem, on a journey which must end in State Socialism. The principle of " political momentum " shows that escape is hardly possible. This is the doctrine of " the Coming Slavery." [1]

(9) The last argument of Mr. Spencer that need here be given is that Parliament has no right to pass statutes authorizing government interference in certain cases at all. Mr. Spencer puts to himself the question: " Is Parliament omnipotent ? " and answers it with an emphatic " No." The divine right of " Parliaments means the divine right of majorities," and there is no such right, he adds, because, it seems, individuals have never acquiesced in it. This is, of course, simply a return to the old doctrine of absolute natural rights from the other side. Parliament cannot invade the rights of man. To take this view is to deny both the political sovereignty of the State itself and the legal sovereignty of Parliament. The former doctrine is the basis of every system of public law, and of every science of politics, while the latter is the theory laid down with unanimity in every legal treatise on the constitution, both ancient and modern, from De Lolme and Blackstone to Mr. Dicey and Sir William Anson. Mr. Spencer, in stoutly denying it, is in a minority of one. He refuses to accept the lawyers' dictum as to what is the law of England on this point. When statutes and decisions of our law courts are referred to, he replies by producing his imaginary deed of incorporation of the English nation, of which he as the inventor alone holds the key. This consensus of opinion against him, which single-handed he defies, is what he calls the doctrine of " the great political superstition." [2]

These nine lines of argument, then, are the chief pleas put forward by counsel for the plaintiff in the great case of

[1] *The Man* versus *the State*, p. 19.   [2] *Ibid.*, p. 78.

" *The Man* versus *the State*."   They are urged with vehemence
and fertility of resource; and as the appearance in court of
witnesses for the defence is strictly forbidden, the first effect
produced on the impartial mind is apt to be an overpowering
one.   A second perusal of the evidence modifies, in some
measure, the effect of these arguments upon the reader.   Some
of the considerations which tend to break their force have
already been adduced, and more will follow in their proper
place.

When all is said, however, great weight must still be
allowed to them.   If they do not prove that all government
intervention is bad, they sound at least a salutary note of
warning against the dangers of an extreme or ill-devised
system of Collectivism.   They discredit Socialism if they fail
to establish Individualism.

If it be true that Parliament is at present prone to indulge
in meddlesome and mischievous legislation in some directions—
and there is ground for the belief—then the protest of the
Individualist is surely not without its value.   The legislature
has done much harm in the past, and will probably do more
in the future.   Free discussion of the principles on which
it ought to work cannot possibly do evil, and may do good;
and Mr. Spencer's contribution to the debate is certainly of
the highest value.   In defending us from one extreme, however, he is hurried toward principles which logically land us
in the other.   While many of the lines of argument followed
in " *The Man* versus *the State* " deserve consideration, and may
well give pause to those who are consciously rushing or
unconsciously drifting in the trend of Socialism, such brief
criticism of them as has been already given tends to show
that their force is effective *against the abuse of government
in every sphere, not against its proper use in any sphere*—that
while they teach us that Socialism is wrong, they fail to prove
that Individualism is right.   Certain general considerations
modify the strength of Mr. Spencer's exposition of Individualism,
considered as a consistent system of politics.   Three lines
of defence against the indictment of government interference
may briefly be suggested.

(1) The field of observation, from a survey of which con-

clusions antagonistic to State control are drawn, is too narrow. It is exclusively based on economic considerations. Now, political economy is a useful branch of knowledge, but it is only one restricted science after all. It rests on an abstraction which is only relatively true, and if pushed to excess becomes an untruth. It considers the world and man exclusively from the point of view of material wealth. In the eyes of economic science man is merely a being who produces and consumes. The "dismal science" looks only at the material side of man as a producing and produce-devouring machine. Man has, indeed, hands to work with and a mouth to feed, but he has more. The philosopher and the statesman dare not neglect the other factors in his composition. Hence there are other aspects of human life and other phases of the mutual relations of men which must be taken into account as well as the economic ones, and spiritual needs frequently outweigh material interests. In the world of reality all kinds of relations are inextricably bound up with one another, and it is true to say that you can never have a state of things whence economic conditions have been eliminated. Though always there, however, they may be of comparatively little importance alongside of other relations, moral, hygienic, or domestic. When principles, founded on an induction from exclusively industrial phenomena, are applied to questions of an entirely different nature, careful examination is required to see if they hold good in the new field as well as in the old. Individualists too often neglect this distinction.

(2) Even in purely economic considerations many important exceptions from the principle of non-intervention are insisted on by authorities of an individualistic bias. John Stuart Mill, in the fifth book of his *Political Economy*, after instancing and denouncing several forms of government interference founded on erroneous theories (such as the protection of native industries and the repression of usury), goes on to argue that none of the grounds of *laissez faire* apply to six classes of cases which he there specifies. These are briefly as follows: (*a*) Things in which the public as consumers are not the best judges, *e.g.* education; (*b*)

cases of infancy, idiotcy, the labour of children, and cruelty to animals; (c) cases of contracts for a prolonged period, *e.g.* marriage; (d) things which would otherwise fall to be controlled by joint-stock companies ought to be regulated by the State; (e) cases where one man cannot take the initiative unless government enforces the same course on all: this would justify compulsory early closing of shops; and (f) actions performed by one set of people to benefit another.[1]

These exceptions to the province of *laissez faire* are very wide and sweeping. Indeed many moderate Socialists could build their systems upon them without asking wider concessions. It would be extremely instructive to analyze each of these exceptions in detail, to discover the underlying principles and to test how far their consistently logical extension would carry us. Even at a glance it is evident that the doctrine of Mill on Political Economy gives government far wider powers than that of Mill on Liberty, which has been already discussed. It might further be shown that each of these differs from the doctrine of Mill on Representative Government. Mill's mind was essentially analytical. He selected one abstract principle, such as Utility or Liberty, as the basis of each of his works, and kept that principle exclusively in sight throughout. Thus he rendered a priceless service to everything he touched. But unfortunately he left each abstract principle by itself, never performing the complementary task of synthesis, which is the chief duty of philosophy in reaching its ultimate goal by "thinking things together." As a consequence Mill too often puts abstractions in place of realities, while the conclusions founded on one isolated principle are at variance with those based upon another. The government, for example, could do many things under the principles of the *Political Economy* which it could not under those of the *Essay on Liberty*.

Mr. Herbert Spencer is not, of course, liable for the opinions of his fellow Individualist, Mill; but it would be interesting to ask how far he agrees to the specific exceptions allowed in the *Political Economy* to the doctrine of

[1] Mill's *Political Economy*, chapters x. and xi.

laissez faire; and, where he does not, how he proposes to get over the difficulties which Mill recognized when he frankly made so many wide concessions.

(3) A third line of defence is competent against the Individualist. Mr. Spencer, it may be urged, is not sufficiently explicit as to the enemy he attacks under the names of "over-government," "State coercion," "Socialism," "corporate action," and "compulsory co-operation." He is not content with making temperate and specific charges against definite agencies, but confuses the issues by launching his thunderbolts at all the structures and organizations upheld by our present system of polity. "Over-government" is accused indiscriminately of every existing evil. His position seems to be that all existing evils of society are due to government interference; but he fails to distinguish between some eleven or twelve different senses in which that term may be used.

His arguments may be effectually met, or, at any rate, their force may be considerably broken by the reply that many of the evils complained of are not due to government action at all; and that others are caused by the abuse of administrative authority or by the use of defective and foolish methods capable of improvement in the future. The great complexity of the phenomena dealt with by political science makes it dangerous to point dogmatically to any one factor as the cause of the evil in an event which is the resultant of so many agencies. It is difficult to apportion accurately the shares of blame attaching to the forces of nature, to the actions of individual men, and to the conscious intervention of government respectively, in regard to a social evil to which each has contributed something. It is not fair for the man to blame the State for misfortunes inseparable from his earthly lot. The Socialist is equally unjust, though he accuses not over-government, but *laissez faire* for every form of evil.

Mr. Spencer, though he falls into a similar mistake on the other side, is keen enough in detecting the weakness of the Socialist. "There is a notion," he says,[1] "always

---

[1] *The Man versus the State*, p. 19.

more or less prevalent and just now vociferously expressed that all social suffering is removable"; but while he laughs at pretensions of Socialism to remove these social ulcers, it seems at times as though he thought that Individualism could. "Over-government" is made the scapegoat for the effects of its own misdeeds along with those resulting from the unlicensed acts of individuals and the operation of natural laws. It is as foolish for the Individualist to blame government control for causing those social sores which are nature's handiwork, as for the Socialist to believe that government control can cure them.

In estimating the force of the indictment against "over-government," the difference between legitimate government action and its abuse must further be kept in mind. The blunders of a foolish ruler, and the persecutions of a cruel one, do not prove all governors bad. Imperfect tools must be retained with all their dangers till better ones are invented to take their place. Some of "the sins of legislators" have been caused by the adoption of the crude doctrines of contemporary science. Parliaments in the past relied on the skilled opinion of the experts of their day, and caused often wide-spread misery. Who was to blame for this? The physician who employs all his skill in the light of the defective medical science of his day may cause his patient's death; and yet no one will accuse him of manslaughter. Society cannot do without doctors, and must not blame them because science is not yet perfectly matured. No more can government action be dispensed with, though it cannot always act on perfect knowledge. If experience proves its theories wrong, it is necessary to discard the theories, not the government that has adopted them. It is an encouraging fact rather than otherwise that this course has often been promptly followed, as, for example, in the reversal of the Poor Law administration subsequent to the failure of the allowance system as in force prior to 1832. The break-down did not prove that the relief of the poor lay outside the normal functions of government, but only that its methods had been wrong and wrongly directed.

Before we condemn "over-government" for all the current

troubles of the age, we must deduct the share of guilt of other agencies. When this has been done, it is still necessary to inquire exactly what is meant by " government " and what constitutes its excess. There are at least eleven different meanings or shades of meaning in which the phrase " over-government " may be used.

(1) It often means an undue extension of the province of authority, and therefore (since this doctrine is commonly accompanied by a dualistic view of things), a corresponding diminution in the legitimate province of liberty.[1] It signifies then, in the first instance, an invasion of what is considered the proper domain of " freedom."

(2) The same phrase may be applied to a country where there are thought to be too many laws. It would thus be equivalent to " over-legislation." The number of statutes passed would here be the chief object of attention, and " over-government " would be least felt in primitive tribes where everything was regulated by unchanging custom.

(3) It is possible to emphasize rather the quality than the quantity of laws, and while still identifying over-government with over-legislation, to define the latter not so much as an excessive number of changes in the statute law, but as a system of meddlesome interference by Parliament with matters better let alone. It now means " inquisitorial legislation " rather than " too much legislation."

(4) Over-government again may signify " too much State management " in place of State control. Many who would object to all trade and commerce being taken from the sphere of competition and private enterprise, and placed under various administrative departments, would gladly see the control of the central government tightened upon limited companies, and especially upon their most recent development called " trusts," which for want of proper regulation dislocate from time to time the entire economic well-being of the United States. Such heightened indirect control would be stigmatized as " over-government " by all fraudulent company promoters, and by those who enrich themselves through

[1] This is the sense in which it is used by Sir John Seeley, *Introduction to Political Science*, p. 120.

R

" trusts "; while others would reserve the term for the actual absorption of all such corporations by the State and their subsequent direct management by executive officials.

(5) The name may be reserved for government monopolies like the post office, by men who would not object to a fair competition with private letter-carriers.

(6) A collectivist scheme for the appropriation of land and capital by the State, and the abolition of the rights of private property might be, with more or less propriety, called " over-government," which would thus mean State ownership as opposed to private ownership.

(7) It might again mean nationalization as opposed to municipalization of such necessaries of modern life as roads and bridges.

(8) Even this does not complete the list. This much-used word " over-government " sometimes means centralization— that local government has been elbowed out by bureaucracy, or has sunk into undue insignificance.

The logic of the Individualist would seem to hold equally against local government as against central government. Now there are many things which each locality is best able to do for itself. For example, cities like Manchester, Glasgow, or Birmingham should be left to make and enforce regulations for paving and lighting their own streets, unmolested by Parliament, as long as they break no law of the land. These things would never be done at all upon any uniform plan, unless the municipal authorities enforced compliance with their wishes. Here, to many minds, municipal action is good, but national action bad ; yet from the point of view of individual liberty it matters little whether the power which compels a man to keep his house to the line of the street is a Corporation bye-law or a statute of Parliament. In each case the principles of Individualism are set at defiance.

(9) Another use of the word is perhaps merely another aspect of bureaucracy. It denotes, however, not so much the substituting of central action in the place of local government as the prohibitions or unnecessary restrictions placed in the way of individual initiation. In some countries a subject

cannot change his address or start on a journey, without first obtaining the consent of some State official. In others he is left free to act on his own responsibility, subject only to his liability to punishment if he invades his neighbour's claim to similar rights. The position of the press in various countries affords good examples of the two systems. In Russia the press is gagged in case it should do harm. In England it is free; but if any publisher abuse this liberty he will be punished. Where a license, or the *imprimatur* of a *bureau* is required before a man can act in the ordinary affairs of life, "over-government" may justly be charged against the State.

(10) Another phase of the evil complained of arises from the adoption of a special method of enforcing laws. When a law is passed, it is the province of the State to see that its provisions are not set at defiance. There are, however, two courses open for preventing it from remaining a dead letter. Individuals may be allowed to enforce such of its provisions as they think will benefit themselves by applying to the law courts to protect their rights as defined by the new law. On the other hand, its enforcement may be entrusted to an executive department or an official.[1] For example, if a law prohibits the sale of "margarine" as butter, two courses are open. Private individuals, who are wronged by its infringement, may be given a right of action, or alternatively a series of inspectors paid out of public rates may be appointed to inspect all dairy produce before it can be lawfully exposed for sale at all. The second way of enforcing the law is clearly unnecessarily burdensome, expensive, and provocative of arbitrary interference with liberty of action and initiation. The evil here lies not in the law itself, but in the provision for its enforcement. "Over-government" would here mean an executive as opposed to a judicial method of affording to subjects the protection of the laws.

(11) It may also mean the endowment of petty administrative officers with excessive powers of an arbitrary and discretionary nature in the discharge of their duties, and might thus be called "officialism." In this sense all con-

---

[1] Cf. Lord Farrer, *The State in its Relation to Trade*, p. 9.

tinental nations, such as France, where a special law known as *droit administratif* exists for the protection of the executive, would be "over-governed" as compared with Britain.

It is not necessary to maintain that all the various uses of the word included in this long catalogue are equally legitimate; nor that Individualists in attacking the abuse of government always confuse all of them with one another; but it is here asserted that writers like Mr. Herbert Spencer are not sufficiently explicit in defining what they attack, and that arguments which are valid against one phase of government intervention are often used without formal proof as though they applied to all.

A detailed refutation of Individualism is impossible and unnecessary, until the evils complained of are stated with less ambiguity. The arraignment of existing systems and institutions must break down, unless it is made more specific. The Individualist must be asked to state in black and white to what phases and degrees of "over-government" he objects, and then he is bound to explain how he proposes to get on without them. When he has complied with this not unreasonable request, moderate politicians of all schools will be in a position to say how far they agree with him, and to frame definite arguments in support of their conclusions when they make bold to disagree. We must know definitely what Individualists want before we can decide how far they can safely be allowed to get it.

CHAPTER XVII.

THE SOLUTION BY COMPROMISE.

WHEN Individualists, forced by the stress of hard facts, are compelled to allow a certain province, however limited in extent, to government intervention, they really adopt a compromise with Socialism. Only Anarchists avoid this necessity. Socialists, on the other hand, when they admit any sphere as inappropriate to government interference, are to that extent temporizing with the enemy. All the solutions already considered, then, unintentionally partake more or less of the nature of a compromise. Various direct attempts, however, which cannot be described as distinctively either socialistic or individualistic, have been made to effect a compromise between the opposed doctrines of *laissez faire* and regimentation. It is proposed to group these together, and briefly glance at the chief features of a few of the most important among them.

(1) It is sometimes maintained that the legislature is justified in restraining individual freedom on moral grounds, but never on purely economic ones. This attitude of compromise towards the old-fashioned Liberal views of a thoroughgoing policy of *laissez faire* was well expressed by the Duke of Argyll in his speech on the Agricultural Holdings Act of 1875. He maintained that, while there are circumstances " which compel us frequently to interfere for moral ends " with freedom of contract, for all that " restrictive legislation for the attainment of purely economic ends is not only needless but injurious."[1]

[1] 3 *Hansard*, ccxxiii. 949, cited Cunningham, *Politics and Economics*, p. 146.

In this view, while *laissez faire* ought to rule the economic relations of the citizens, their moral relations are within the sphere of government control.

(2) A line of argument that seems the converse of this was taken by Mr. Goschen in his Edinburgh address, when he insisted on the danger of a system of official inspection acting as a substitute for the moral responsibility of individuals. " We should exhaust," he said, " every means of enforcing personal responsibility before we substitute public responsibility." [1] We must struggle to resist a condition of public morality " when due preparation for an inspector's visit would represent the discharge of all obligations and the fulfilment of all claims." [2] In this view, one of the chief dangers of legislative interference is the risk of undermining individual responsibility by invading the sphere of the moral relations of the citizens. All legislation would thus stand condemned if it tampered with or weakened the moral tone of the community.

(3) It is sometimes argued that all legislation that interferes with freedom of contract is bad.

(4) Others find the criterion of which all are in search in the effect which a proposed law is likely to have on the self-reliance of individuals. Each man, it is said, knows best what he wants, and is best able to provide it for himself if only let alone. His moral fibre will be weakened if a parental or rather motherly government does everything for him. In especial, all laws are utterly bad that provide the necessaries of life.

It would be easy to multiply examples of similar attempts at compromise. It would be easy, too, to point out objections in detail to every one of them. While, on the one hand, it is impossible to divide absolutely economic from moral ends, on the other hand, the risk of weakening individual responsibility must sometimes be incurred to avoid graver perils. It is difficult, again, to know what constitutes undue freedom of contract, and therefore so vague a principle cannot be used as a basis of compromise. Lastly, the necessaries of life are exactly what every one agrees that the Poor Laws

[1] *Addresses on Educational and Economic Subjects*, p. 77.
[2] *Ibid.*, p. 84.

must provide. These and many more detailed objections
show that each of the four compromises above suggested is
open to special objections of its own. Their chief defect
lies deeper, however, and applies equally to all. All compromises are false in principle, and, though often valuable
in practice as affording a *modus vivendi* for the time being,
must never be regarded as final or treated as absolute.
Between two things so intimately and organically connected
as the State and the individual, it is impossible to make
any compromise as to their respective spheres of action,
for wherever the one is there must the other be also. This
is the philosophical objection to the solution by compromise.
The practical objection has been well expressed by Professor
Jevons :[1] "This question involves the most delicate and
complicated considerations, and the outcome of the inquiry
is that we can lay down no hard-and-fast rules, but must
treat every case in detail upon its merits." A compromise,
then, is too clumsy and mechanical a contrivance to satisfy
political science, or to square with actual social phenomena,
and so form a working basis for a theory of legislation.

[1] *The State in Relation to Labour*, preface.

CHAPTER XVIII.

THE ORGANIC SOLUTION.

THERE are, apparently, insuperable difficulties of both a philosophic and a practical sort to adjusting the province of government upon lines exclusively socialistic or exclusively individualistic. To make the State everything and the individual nothing leads to absurdities on one side; while the subordination of the State to the individual leads to disaster on the other. Attempts at compromise, too, have been seen to be futile. All three solutions then have completely broken down; yet the problem need not be despaired of. The discussion of the elements of truth contained in each unsuccessful attempt has already shown where the ultimate solution must be sought. The conclusion to which everything points is, indeed, only a development of the principle from which this Essay started—the essentially organic relations between the State and the individual—the fact that the one without the other is a lifeless and indeed meaningless abstraction. All societies and all institutions are both socialistic and individualistic in their nature. What is wanted is not a mere compromise, but a principle which combines and transcends both classes of tendencies in a higher and nobler unity.

Some of the Individualists whose insight is clearest seem to come near this position. Mr. Donisthorpe, in explaining Individualism as he understands it, really develops this theory far beyond the mere individualistic basis from which he starts, and by which he professes to abide. "The whole history of civilization is," in his opinion, "the history of a struggle to establish a relation between society and its units, between the whole and its parts, which is neither absolute Socialism nor absolute Anarchy; but a state in which, by action and reaction of each upon each, such an adaptation shall take place, that the welfare of the whole and that of the units shall eventually become coincident and not antagonistic. Such is the problem of civilization, of the development of the hyper-organism; integration without impairing the individuality of the component units. The final result to which we shall ever approximate, but never attain, will be perfect civil liberty, or the greatest liberty which is compatible with the utmost well-being of society as a whole; and perfect law, or such subordination of the individual will to that of society as may be compatible with the utmost well-being of the individual."[1]

Mr. Donisthorpe has here formulated his belief in a golden mean, and is, so far, worthy of all support, though he may have placed it not in the middle, but considerably further to the side of the individual than he ought. Instead of calling this mean by some neutral name, however, he dubs it Individualism—a word usually reserved for one of the two extremes which he agrees in thinking that all sensible men should shun—while the two extremes are, in his opinion, Socialism and Anarchy. There is no good purpose to be served by disputing about a mere question of nomenclature, and if Mr. Donisthorpe is prepared to throw overboard under the name of Anarchy the evils which this Essay finds in Individualism, there would be no real difference left about which to argue. Individualism, however, as he expounds it, is not such a golden mean as it professes to be. On the contrary, when carried to its logical conclusion, it is identical with that extreme which he calls Anarchy. While Mr. Donisthorpe, in the passage just cited, really abandons his original position as a pure Individualist, he yet fails to shake himself free from the idea of a dualism between State and individual, and so the desire for a compromise is always present, and tends to set limits to the comprehensiveness of his aim.

[1] Wordsworth Donisthorpe, *Individualism*, p. 303.

The doctrine of even the most moderate among the Individualists differs, then, materially from the solution here proposed. It not only emphasizes unduly one factor in the problem to the detriment of the other, but it assumes an absolute dualism between them that has no warrant in fact, and proceeds to build all its conclusions on this erroneous foundation. The organic theory alone fully explains all the problems of society and government, while it finds a place within it for the apparently conflicting tendencies of a socialistic and individualistic nature respectively—tendencies which are equally indispensable for the welfare of mankind, and equally ineradicable from the life of every community.

Socialism and Individualism are, in the political world, what the forces of attraction and repulsion are in the natural world. They seem opposed, and yet neither could exist without the other, while in the final unrestrained triumph of either, the whole established order of things would dissolve and pass away. The two together form what Kant has described somewhat clumsily as " the unsocial sociability of men "—the fundamental contradiction of human nature which forces men to seek one another's society, and yet causes each one to endeavour " to direct everything merely according to his own mind." [1]

Political science can neglect neither the forces of integration nor those of differentiation. While maintaining the sovereignty of the whole and the coercive powers of government, it must avoid all systems of slavery, and again, without neglecting the liberty and right of initiation of the social atoms, it must provide against anarchy and disintegration. Nothing short of the organic theory can reconcile these contending interests and tendencies.

The conception of an organic State involves two fundamental principles. In the first place, as nothing that affects the part can be indifferent to the whole, the State is bound by its laws and government to aim jointly with the citizens at the perfect development of every individual in the community. Nothing is beyond the proper sphere of

[1] See Kant's *Principles of Politics*, translated by Professor Hastie, p. 10.

government in pursuing this high end. In the second place, while nothing is suffered to remain outside the State, fit provision must be made for every individual enjoying a full free life within it.

Each of these propositions requires some explanation : (1) No one insisted more strenuously than Bluntschli on the essentially organic nature of the State ; yet almost all the defects of his political philosophy may be traced to the inadequate way in which he applies this conception to practice. He excludes various spheres of influence from the legitimate province of the State ; and thus contradicts his own definition of it as an organic unity including all its parts. At the same time, he imposes limits on the power of the State inconsistent with the doctrine of its sovereignty. He draws, for example, a distinction (quite untenable when taken as absolute and final) between public and private law within a community, and declares that, while the State is absolute over the former, the latter is the domain of the individual.[1] Society, again, is differentiated from the State, and the absolute control of the latter over the former is denied. The knowledge of this distinction, he says, "protects society against the tyranny of the State." [2] In some connections the State seems to be further denied by him the right to interfere with, morality ; [3] with the church and religion ; [4] with education ; [5] with property, [6] with the family ; [7] with the prejudices of subject nationalities ; and lastly, even with the pursuits of individuals, for it cannot control private life "in what is essentially individual." [8] It would be unjust to exaggerate the amount of force given by Bluntschli to these various exceptional cases ; but it is evident that a truly organic State must exclude none of these things from its all-embracing sphere. It may refrain from unwise interference in special cases, but it has the *right* to interfere in all.

(2) On the other hand, a proper place must be found within the State for all those organizations which are not

---

[1] Bluntschli, *Theory of the State*, p. 228.
[2] *Ibid.*, p. 102. [3] *Ibid.*, p. 37. [4] *Ibid.*, p. 39.
[5] *Ibid.*, p. 301. [6] *Ibid.*, p. 234. [7] *Ibid.*, p. 182.
[8] *Ibid.*, p. 301.

allowed to stay without. The family and the Church must be properly protected and cared for. In especial, there follows from the organic theory the necessity of providing for each individual the possibility of sharing in the life of that State to which he is forced to yield obedience. In an ideal commonwealth every citizen should be able to earn an honest livelihood of so adequate a nature as to enable him to secure the necessary conditions of physical health, to participate in the influences of family life, to enjoy some measure of political rights, and to obtain " some living contact with the things of the mind."[1]   Every current of the national life must flow freely within reach of every citizen before the relations between them can be looked on as the perfection of organic union.

This is merely a theoretical solution, however, it may be said, which brings us no nearer any tangible results. The sequel must show how far the theory leads directly towards rules of a practical usefulness, but its indirect benefits are obvious at a glance. If true, it destroys at once all extreme systems, whether collectivist or anarchical, founded on inadequate theories. In especial, it would show the folly of the endeavour to find a boundary which has no existence between the individual and the State, and to devise expedients to prevent the government from crossing a line which does not exist.

Two distinctions may afford a partial clue to a practical solution—the difference between legislation and administrative interference, and that between government management and government control. It is not necessary for an administrative department to undertake directly the performance, or even the supervision, of all industries and arts of the nation. Indirect control, wherever possible and equally effective, is to be preferred to direct management. It is possible, indeed, to imagine a State of the future in which both the socialistic and the individualistic tendencies of the present are exaggerated, and yet robbed of their evils through the operation of an increased government control, and a diminished government management.

[1] John Maccunn, *Ethics of Citizenship*, p. 69.

That benignant deity or malignant demon "the State" must not undertake to perform the duties of its citizens while they sit and read novels and grow fat. It ought rather to leave each man free to labour in his own way so long as he does not shirk his legal duties; and to pounce on him with punishment for the past, and compulsion for the future, when he has deliberately neglected these. The government must not relieve individuals of primary responsibilities, though it ought to accept an ultimate responsibility of compelling them where they have failed to comply voluntarily with the minimum of obligation which the State demands. It may be wise to punish citizens criminally for non-performance of duties, where it would be foolish to send a government official to act in their stead.

The directions and limits of this government control will require to be carefully examined, but it seems clear that, in many cases, the substitution of indirect forms of interference for direct government management affords a basis for realizing many of the advantages of the competing systems, while escaping some of their dangers. It gives room for free initiation and the free play of individual responsibility, without relaxing the power of the government in its duty of furthering the general welfare. On the other hand, it makes the citizen independent *within* the State, though not *against* the State.

It is upon such general lines as these that an ultimate solution may be looked for; but its final statement must be the outcome of an exhaustive analysis of the results of history and the experience of actually existing States, and not a deduction of a series of abstract propositions from any *a priori* doctrine. A few suggestions derived from some of the more outstanding facts are all that can be attempted here.

CHAPTER XIX.

AN ANALYSIS OF ACTUAL RELATIONS BETWEEN THE GOVERNMENT AND THE INDIVIDUAL FROM THE POINT OF VIEW OF THE LATTER.

A COMPLEX network of relationships binds men to one another and to the State. An analysis of these relations may be approached from the side of the sovereignty of the whole or of the liberty of the part. It is convenient to take the latter aspect first.

The abstract doctrine that every man should be free is apparently a very simple one ; but as a matter of fact every individual is subject to a great number of restraints in the exercise of this so-called "liberty." The absolutely unrestrained freedom of one man would mean the absolute dependence of his neighbours and the annihilation of the sovereignty of the State, unless that sovereignty were centred in the unrestrained individual, who would then be an irresponsible despot. This is only one application of the maxim *summum jus summa injuria.*

Special restraints are placed upon children, lunatics, and criminals, partly in their own interests and partly for the protection of the public. These are exceptional cases which may be eliminated in the meantime from the scope of the inquiry. The members of each of these classes are not considered individuals by the State. In legal phrase, neither a minor nor a lunatic has a full *persona.* He is not capable of enjoying or exercising the full rights of a citizen.

It must not be thought, however, that, when a child has

reached the age defined by law as man's full estate, all restraints immediately slip off him. He is, and must always be, subject to innumerable forms and varieties of external control.

What are these restraints or limitations? They may be divided for our present purpose (though without any claim to exhaustive enumeration or scientific accuracy) into three classes: (1) physical, (2) social, and (3) legal.

(1) No man can shake himself free from the fetters imposed upon him by time and space, and the limitations inherent in his own nature. He cannot dive into the past or project himself into the future. He must walk along the surface of the globe. He can neither descend into the earth nor fly above it. His freedom is limited by his own powers of locomotion; and he has to contend with the force of nature in supplying every wish, and even in sustaining bare life within him. These are some of the most obvious of the physical restraints that hem him in on every hand, and he can make but little headway against these elemental forces by his own unaided energies. Any partial conquest he can effect is possible only through the co-operation of his fellow-men. The united efforts of generations have produced railways and phonographs, steam-engines and electrical machines, which have enabled men to gain a partial triumph over space and time, and over nature herself by directing her energies to the accomplishment of their own ends. It is, then, by his power of association, or by what may be conveniently termed his social nature that man gains a little freedom from a complete dependence on the blind forces of nature that imprison him.

The saying of Rousseau, " Man is born free, and everywhere he is in fetters,"[1] is the exact reverse of the truth. We should rather say, " Man is born a slave, and it is only by the help of his fellow-men that he can throw off a single chain."

He ought therefore to think twice before rebelling at the milder limitations which society puts upon him in return for freeing him from a more cruel master.

[1] *Contrat Social*, I. i.

(2) The basis of social restraints, however, lies deeper than any principle of returning a payment for benefits received. Diogenes might pride himself on his independence by affecting to set society at defiance. In reality he merely refused the benefits it could give him, without freeing himself from the chief of its restraints. He could not cut himself adrift from the rest of humanity by living in a tub, or by retiring to a wilderness. In his solitude many voices would haunt him. The terrible principle of heredity, the ideas derived from former contact with his fellow-men, and (unless he did violence to his nature) the longing for human sympathy and love would follow him. Social restraints bear harder on some men than upon others, but they exist for all. At present, in civilized society, these restraints seem to sink into comparative insignificance as compared with strictly legal bonds. This is not because they have disappeared, but because they have been strengthened and confirmed in receiving the stamp of positive law. Even yet, however, there are many social restraints which, though not illegal, are still unendowed with the authority of law. Thus a man who would not be shunned by his fellow-men is subject more or less to the restraints placed upon him by the moral sense of the community in which he lives. He is subject to public opinion under penalty of losing much that he values in life. He is subject to "the laws of good society" under penalty of social ostracism. Even in this narrowest sense of society, then, the individual is bound to submit to various limitations on his liberty. Such restraints are not enforceable in the law courts, but they compel obedience under sanction of some form of "boycotting." This method of punishing an individual who refuses to submit to the usages of his own neighbourhood or society is liable to many gradations of intensity. In its mildest form it means the interruption of social relations, but may rise by gradual steps to the ruin of a man's business connection, or the refusal to supply him with the necessaries of life in return for his money. In its ultimate form it becomes "lynch law," still prevalent in some parts of the United States of America.

In its lowest stages, then, this principle of the boycott is perfectly legitimate and lawful; but at a certain point, not always easily determined, it comes into conflict with the positive law of the land. The government will interfere to protect the individual from the excessive tyranny of society when that passes a certain limit. The practical difficulty of determining this exact point need not detain us here, for the general principle is sufficient to give a good illustration of how the individual escapes to some extent from the tyranny of society by an appeal to law, in a similar way to that in which he escapes from the tyranny of nature by allying himself with society.

(3) In addition to physical and social limitations to freedom there is yet a third class imposed by the will of the State. These are legal restraints. To examine into their nature and origin would be to write a complete system of jurisprudence and a complete history of law. In a modern State, such as England, it is easy to understand the difference between a restraint which is legal and one which is merely social. The practical test lies in this, that the law courts will enforce the one but not the other. This is the ultimate criterion of positive law for lawyers and business men, whatever theories philosophers care to make.

There are many acts, then, to which a man's unlimited freedom would naturally lead him if he were not forbidden by law. Now these legal restraints confront him in three distinct forms.

A simple instance will illustrate this. A wishes to take a short cut to his home. He leaves the high road and proceeds across the fields. He comes to the property of B, who objects to the public walking through his grounds. Suppose that the law endorses B's objection—in other words, that B has an undisputed legal right to forbid A's entrance, there are three ways in which B may enforce his rights, and therefore three ways in which A's liberty of action may be impeded. A ten-foot wall may be built all round the property, a policeman or a gamekeeper may be placed with instructions to turn all-comers out, or a simple notice may be posted stating that there is no legal right of way,

s

with or without the addition that "Trespassers will be prosecuted."

These three are simple types under which all methods of enforcing legal restrictions may be brought. When the State gives to one of its subjects a right against another, it may (a) leave him to protect it by making its violation physically impossible, (b) appoint a number of officials to guard it for him, or (c) simply open the doors of its law courts to award him damages in case of its infringement. The first of these methods is comparatively unimportant, since its application is limited to a few exceptional cases. The distinction between the remaining methods, which may be respectively named the executive and judicial methods of enforcing rights, is a vital one. Many of the arguments which the Individualist directs against legal restrictions upon liberty, apply rather to the way in which these are enforced than to the restrictions themselves. The judicial method is free from the dangers of the executive system, which requires to appoint a host of inspectors and officials, with wide arbitrary powers and the right to interfere when in their judgment the law is likely to be broken.

The dangers of the latter way of enforcing rights are twofold. Carried to excess it would not only hamper trade unduly, but would soon sap the self-reliance and power of initiation of the nation. Again, all such methods tend to leave too great arbitrary powers in the hands of individuals whose imperfect moral nature is open both to bribes and to prejudices, and whose judgment is liable to error. Every traveller in Russia is liable to be stopped and summarily expelled from any district, according to the groundless suspicions or mere caprice of any superintendent of police. Even in England, where a jealous eye has always scrutinized the conduct of officials, the police force have certain arbitrary powers at their disposal. They may (though at their peril) arrest a man for an imaginary disturbance of the peace, or accept a small gratuity for overlooking a minor breach of law. All such powers are bad without exception, if they can possibly be dispensed with. In criticizing them, every argument is sound and appropriate which Individualists direct more loosely against government interference in general. State action is not (as they think) an evil in itself, but the arbitrary action of State officials is. Unfortunately it is not possible to do without the latter altogether. While all meddlesome official interference with private citizens is to be deplored, it can yet never be dispensed with altogether. The practical conclusion is that it should be reduced to a minimum. Now this is exactly the result at which all practical English statesmen and lawyers have long since arrived. It forms an essential principle of the British constitution. Englishmen were fighting for the abolition of arbitrary powers in the executive government, so as to make of practical value such rights as were possible, while Frenchmen were enunciating grand but unrealizable theories of the rights of man. Jealousy of the arbitrary powers of the executive is in part a legacy from the misgovernment of the Stuarts, but it expresses at the same time a deep accord with the whole history and disposition of the Anglo-Saxon race.

On a retrospective survey of the restrictions placed by law on individual liberty of action, three propositions come to light. In the first place, some such restrictions are indispensable. In the second place, they are not necessarily evil in themselves, but only in the method of their enforcement, when arbitrary powers of prohibition are vested in public officials or private individuals, or excessive penalties are inflicted out of proportion to the offence. In the third place, such arbitrary powers can never be altogether dispensed with, though they may be and ought to be abridged as far as possible. The existence of legal restraints on himself and others gives each man more true liberty than would be possible in the absence of law. "The more law the more liberty" is true, if the law is of the right sort. The imposition of national legal restraints on the citizens saves the individual from the tyranny of local society; while social influences help to free man from the tyranny of nature. The function of the State, then, in defining and enforcing law is necessary not only for preserving order and maintaining the permanence of the whole, but even for the liberty of the individual. The chief end of law is to make men free.

Social influences and tyrannies, however, are not the only evils from which the intervention of the State protects the individual. The same power saves him from the despotism of all voluntary associations and local authorities. The power of positive law is always an ultimate court of appeal from injustice done by any minor authority.

This suggests another most important aspect of the relations between individuals and States. It is true that in many cases they come face to face. But in many other cases—more numerous and more intimately associated with the daily routine of life—the connection is not direct, but through some intermediary.

Every British citizen is necessarily a resident in a parish, and in some town or county, and he is a member of a family. He is generally also connected with various corporations, as for example a Trades Union, a Masonic Lodge, a Friendly Society, or a Club, and perhaps with one or two commercial associations incorporated under the Companies' Acts. All of these subordinate groups come between the man and the State. Each of these local authorities or voluntary associations has certain powers over its members, but each of them is subject to the sovereignty of the law. Thus the State and its hand-maiden the law must decide between two possible lines of policy. They may either stand aloof, leaving each of these bodies to manage its own internal affairs (including its quarrels with its members) in its own way, or step in to protect the individuals in the minority from the tyranny of the majority who compose the rest of the society. It is the second attitude which all existing States more or less consistently adopt. In this policy, it is here maintained, the government is not only justified, but bound in duty to per-severe; because in doing so it not only secures its own stability, but protects and actually increases the freedom of its citizens. If government interference with corporate bodies is unwise or excessive, the rights of individuals, it is true, must suffer; but if wise and moderate, the more State inter-vention there is, the more freedom will accrue to its citizens. It is usual to consider government and coercion as synony-mous, and as together constituting the direct antithesis of individual liberty. We must remember, however, how many other forms of restraint men are subject to, and that government (if itself a tyrant) strikes all other tyrants down.

Numerous voluntary associations, corporations, and local authorities stand between the State and the individual. In controlling any one of these the government indirectly affects the individual. In all of them it seems that its interference makes, on the whole, for liberty. It would be possible, of course, for the State to abolish all or any of these intermediate bodies, or without destroying them it might so paralyze their powers of action and particularly of initiation, as to render them quite useless and inert. If government interference took anything approaching this form, individual liberty would undoubtedly suffer along with corporate privileges, since the freedom of association is one of the most cherished rights. But the State does no such thing. It allows every lawful form of voluntary combination full scope, and only intervenes when its forbearance is abused, and injury done to its citizens.

The " Trust," or Corporation, or Trades Union would often crush the individual into powder, if that ogre of the Individualist's imagination—the State—did not extend its all-powerful arm to strike the oppressor down.

CHAPTER XX.

AN ANALYSIS OF THE ACTUAL RELATIONS BETWEEN THE GOVERNMENT AND THE INDIVIDUAL FROM THE POINT OF VIEW OF THE FORMER.

WE have hitherto looked with the eye of the citizen on the complex relations that connect him to the State, and have found that the laws and government are not his oppressors, but his guardians and friends. It is necessary to change the point of view, and to approach the analysis of the same relations from the side of the State. Before seeking to determine what extent or methods of government interference are justifiable in an ideal State, it is well to ascertain the facts applicable to existing governments, such as that of England at the present day.

Now the first step in the analysis is to emphasize an obvious distinction. The difference between legislative interference and executive interference is too often neglected in speculative writings, perhaps from its very obviousness. The State acts by two agencies—impersonal laws and living officials. Thus State intervention may mean either an alteration of the existing law, or the active meddling of an administrative officer, such as a sanitary inspector or policeman. It is incumbent on every Individualist who would alter the existing organization of society, to declare clearly whether his objections are equally strong against both classes of intervention. Does he object, for example, to all statutes attempting to define family relationships, or would he only oppose the intrusion on domestic privacy involved in the

visits of inspectors to enforce them ? This is exactly **what** the average Individualist fails **to** do.

It is proposed now to disentangle **these two** essentially distinct questions ; **to** inquire (first) **into** the sphere actually influenced by legislation at the present day, and (secondly) into the duties actually performed **by the executive.**

(1) *THE SPHERE OF THE LEGISLATURE.*

It is perhaps impossible to devise an absolutely satisfactory basis of classification for the various forms of legislative activity ; but laws may be arranged in some such **order as** the following when viewed according to the chief object which they may be presumed to seek :

(1) To define, **protect, and enforce rights.**

(2) To define **and punish crimes.**

(3) To **alter the form of** government, and **regulate the** mutual relations of its parts.

(4) To confer such powers and authority upon the various government organs and officials as are necessary to enable them to fulfil their duties, executive and judicial.

(5) To confer special powers or immunities on corporations **or** individuals, or to inflict special disabilities on individuals **as** a means of furthering the public good.

(6) To provide for the poor and **protect** the **weak.**

(7) To promote the material prosperity of the nation.

(8) To develop the intellectual faculties and resources of the citizens, and to elevate their moral and spiritual nature.

(9) To impose taxes to **meet** the needs **of** government.

How far is it right or advisable to set limits to the power of Parliament in seeking each of these ends respectively ?

(1) To define **the mutual** rights **and** obligations of individuals; **to prevent these** rights when **so** defined **from** being invaded or defied ; and to provide **reparation or com-** pensation where they have been violated; **these** are clearly the duties of the central government, if **they are** the duties **of** any one. Laws may be inexpedient, **unwise,** or unjust in principle or in detail ; **but it cannot be said** that any *sphere* is alien to **Parliament as** long **as it** confines itself **to** these objects.

Obviously the **liberty of British** subjects would **not be** increased by imitating the provisions of the constitution of the United States of America restricting Congress to eighteen topics of legislation ; for the practical effect of thus narrowing the sphere of Congress is only to place **elsewhere the** right **to legislate** on all excluded **topics.**

The practical effect is **not** to liberate **the** individual American, even in part, from the control of government, but **rather to** subject him to two law-making masters instead of **one.** The partial independence of each member of the Federal **Union is** preserved, but the citizen is to that extent deprived **of the** protection that **the united wisdom** of the nation **might** otherwise afford **him from the tyranny** of the locality. The practical **result is not** that legislation **is** excluded **from any topic,** but that a different law prevails **in every district, and the local** law-making body will often impose petty restrictions that Congress would refuse to sanction.[1]

Evidently the method adopted in America of limiting the **sphere of** the central legislature would not satisfy the average Individualist. If legislation were to be confined to any special province in **defining the** mutual relations of individuals, all other **legal** rights **of the** citizens would require to be regulated **in one of two** ways, (*a*) by contract or (*b*) by custom. Each of these modes is entirely inadequate.

(*a*) There are **whole** classes of obligations (such as those **arising** *ex delicto* or *quasi ex delicto*) that cannot be explained **on the** principle that the parties have expressly **or** tacitly **agreed to them.** Contract is by no means sufficient to define **all** the rights of individuals. The utter inadequacy of the doctrine as a complete theory of the State will be shown **in a** separate chapter.

---

[1] A press cutting will illustrate what is meant better than many arguments : "The Ohio legislature has passed a law forbidding women to wear **large hats at theatres,** and imposing a fine of ten dollars upon any **manager for each hat** he allows to be worn in his theatre obstructing **the view of the** audience of the stage. The measure is applicable to **headgear of any** kind."

(*b*) In a civilized and advancing country like England, it is equally impossible to leave to custom the duty of defining any important portion of the rights of individuals. The legislature must be ready when required to interfere with every branch of the national law, civil and criminal. It should not, indeed, pass a statute one day and repeal it the next; but there is absolutely no sphere to which the law does not extend. There is no relation so intimate, no right so intrinsic, no obligation so binding, but that law gives it its ultimate sanction. Law is everywhere, and wherever law is, there is the sphere of the legislature. Parliament cannot excuse itself from responsibility for a bad law on the ground that it never made it, since it tacitly approves what it fails to condemn.

Now as a society advances in civilization, or even when its circumstances change without any distinct advance, either its laws must alter too, or become a drag upon it. Where there is no existing law to meet the new circumstances, custom of trade may grow up to take its place, but this is at best only a transitory and imperfect expedient. The legislature should follow in its wake with a declaratory statute, pruning and defining custom where it is too vague to be serviceable, and eliminating local divergencies to keep one uniform law throughout the land. Where a body of old laws exists to hamper new conditions to which they are unsuited, custom can give but little help. Legal fictions and judge-made laws on equitable principles are devised, but these are only artificial aids. Custom cannot prevail in opposition to statute law, though it may supplement it where deficient.

Thus a constitutional method must be found to bring the dead law to life again by contact with the conditions of the new national life. If the recognized legislature refuses to perform its duties, revolution will take its place. All rights, civil and political, must be subjected to the defining power of Parliament.

(2) The definition of what constitutes a crime must also be left to Parliament. No practical man will seriously advocate the abolition of all criminal law. It is possible, of course, to imagine an ideal State where perfection is secured

not only by the excellence of its institutions, but by the absolute sinlessness of all its citizens. In such a community no punishments would be needed, for no one could ever commit a crime. Even then, criminal law (since it is unquestioningly obeyed) must exist, though as a natural, or moral, rather than a positive law. Until human nature is utterly transformed, however, wrongs will be committed, or kept in check only by coercive criminal enactments. Whatever theory of punishment we adopt it seems necessary that felonies and misdemeanours should be repressed. The received doctrine is that all crimes should be punished. But what is a crime? Who is to define it? Surely neither the criminal nor the individual judge or jury. The State alone can undertake that solemn task, for by sternly forbidding all individuals to avenge wrongs done to themselves or their relatives—in putting down all vendettas and rights of private warfare—the State must charge itself with the duty of revenging individual injuries, and therefore of defining what constitutes a crime.

Unless the State appointed a separate organ for the regulation of penal laws (a dualistic system which would never work in practice, from the difficulty of differentiating between criminal and civil injury), it must entrust this duty to the ordinary legislature, that is, Parliament.

In defining, then, the various kinds and degrees of crime, Parliament may be guided by diverse principles according to the theories of crime and of legislation current at the time. Modern public opinion leans to the side of leniency. Our present code may not suit all tender-hearted philanthropists, but it is certainly not exceptionally severe. Parliament could, however—and this is the important point—without unduly extending its proper functions or illogically widening the notion of crime, reduce human liberty almost to vanishing point. It could, too, quite well defend this line of action on the purely individualistic grounds of "protection" or "negative coercion."

It would be possible to abolish all public health officers and sanitary inspectors, and in their place to construct a whole code of criminal law assigning graduated penalties to the breach of regulations laid down with painful minuteness. Every man then would be "free" in a sense to break this code, for no inspector need interfere with him beforehand, but he would be liable to take the penal consequences of his act. The public prosecutor would proceed against him on information laid by any private individual. Whether our penal laws are merciful or severe, numerous or scanty, no other organ save the central legislature can be entrusted with the power of defining crimes.

(3) The function of Parliament in altering constitutional law need not be discussed here.

(4) When Parliament enacts statutes conferring new powers upon the executive government, the liberties of the nation may be seriously endangered; yet the evil in that case does not consist in the legislature as such stepping beyond its proper sphere, but in the impetus given to unwarrantable interference by administrative officials.

(5) The policy of granting special immunities to corporations by private Acts of Parliament is difficult to vindicate on principles of abstract justice. Compulsory powers of purchase are conferred upon railway companies whereby vested interests are invaded. This comes dangerously near favouring one class or group of individuals at the expense of another. Similar theoretical objections seem to apply to acts of attainder and acts of indemnity. Justification of such legislation must be sought in their necessity for the common good, and in the principle that the so-called right of the individual is not really a right if it conflicts with the welfare of the whole. All such measures may be dismissed as exceptional.

(6) While to provide for the poor and to protect the weak cannot be justified on a purely individualistic basis, no one at the present day seriously contemplates the abolition of all poor laws, and it is therefore unnecessary to prove that Parliament is within its proper sphere in enacting such measures. In giving charity, however, the legislature has passed, it must be noticed, beyond the mere definition of rights, strictly so called, and has entered on a policy of tempering justice with mercy.

(7) and (8) The next two classes of laws may be grouped together, as they have much in common, and are equally exposed to the extreme vigour of the Individualist's attack. The course adopted by Parliament with increasing consistency throughout most of the present century, of directly furthering the material prosperity of the nation and the intellectual and moral welfare of the people, is at variance equally with the principles of Von Humboldt, Mill, and Mr. Herbert Spencer. Two lines of argument minimize the force of their objections.

(*a*) In attacking all such legislation, Individualists are forced to take up a position that deprives their protests of all practical value. Their objections are grounded on the presumed *motives* of the various measures. It would be impossible to adopt a criterion either more flexible or more vague. One motive shades into another. The alleged object of any Act of Parliament may be very far from that which actually influences the votes of a majority of the 670 members of the House of Commons. Even the legislature itself is hardly in a position to judge of its own aims and intentions. Almost any motive might be advanced in favour of any law. As long as presumed motive is the criterion whether or not Parliament has gone beyond its proper sphere, the supporters of any measure have only to declare that its object is the "protection of rights" to disarm the criticism of Individualists.

(*b*) Legislation in promotion of national wealth or intellectual progress or the interests of posterity, however, need not be made to depend on such technical arguments. If the good of the community is the sole criterion of legislation, no valid objection can be taken to any law on the ground that its avowed motive is directly to promote the intellectual advancement of the whole community. On the contrary, no aim can be more praiseworthy. It is, of course, open to Individualists to argue that all such laws only defeat their ends; but that is to adopt an entirely different attitude, and to rest on an unwarranted assumption.

(9) The last class of laws requiring comment are those that impose taxes. Mr. Auberon Herbert is in a minority

of one in holding it possible to conduct all the necessary business of government on voluntary subscriptions in place of taxes extorted by force if need be. Taxes of some extent are necessary, however they may be minimized. Now there is no doubt that the power to levy them is safer in the hands of the central legislative organ of the State than in any narrower and more local body. "Taxation," it has been well said, "is always an act of sovereignty, and belongs to the State as a whole."[1] The question is thus reduced to one of degree. Parliament is undoubtedly within its proper sphere in imposing such just taxes as it deems necessary.

The result of the entire survey of the objects of legislation under these nine heads shows that there is no sphere alien to the action of Parliament in performing its proper legislative functions. Legislative interference is objectionable only on one or other of the following grounds: (a) that it is unwise, inexpedient, or unjust; (b) that it imposes excessive penalties; (c) that it unnecessarily vests arbitrary powers in the executive; or (d) that it lays on excessive or unjust taxation. There is no sphere from which it can be legitimately excluded.

Thus, for example, protective legislation is wrong, not because it is an attempt to define by statute the respective rights of producer and consumer, but because it defines these on a false basis or under an inequitable bias. The old law of treason and the multiplication of capital offences were open to reproach, not because the State had no right to punish crime, but because it did so with savage and excessive brutality. Some provisions of the Factories and Workshops Acts are open to objection, not because they define the relations between masters and employees, but because they place too wide discretionary powers in the hands of inspectors. Lastly, the old Poor Laws were iniquitous, not because the legislature had no right to provide for the destitute, but because it did so unwisely and at a ruinous cost to the nation by means of an ever-increasing taxation which threatened to reduce even the rich to the level of paupers.

It is impossible, then, to exclude legislative action from any sphere which is ruled by law; and law in a thoroughly

---

[1] Prof. F. Hoffman, *The Sphere of the State*, p. 114.

civilized State must define all relations between man and
man. Where the law leaves room for doubt, it opens a
door for quarrels, breaches of the peace, and the oppression
of the weak, which is the worst of all possible "sins of
legislators."

As long as Parliament confines itself to purely legislative
business the outcry against "over-government" is meaningless. The Individualist may here interpose, however, that
hardly any Act of Parliament is without some provisions
which involve either executive action or taxation. Parliament in England is, by its legislative supremacy, in a
position to dictate orders to the executive and also to direct
the finances of the nation. In exercising either of these powers
it may unwarrantably interfere in a wrong direction. This
is true; but in doing so it steps beyond the region of legislation proper, and acts as the ultimate controller of the
administration. If this is what the Individualist really objects
to, it is important he should realize that his argument is
directed, not against the legislative functions of Parliament
at all, but against the exercise of its other function of
controlling the executive.

(2) THE SPHERE AND DUTIES OF THE EXECUTIVE.

The ambiguity of the charge of "over-government," even
when confined to purely administrative action or interference,
has already been explained. It may mean an excess of
government management as opposed to government control;
State ownership substituted for the rights of private property;
centralization as opposed to local government; a bureaucracy
which numbs the energy and sense of responsibility of
private citizens; or a system of excessive police supervision
working through an elaborate apparatus of licences and
checks, prohibiting free discussion and gagging the press.

These are merely a few of the widely different things,
stigmatized indiscriminately by Individualists as the abuse of
government, under the general description of State intervention.

The extreme indefiniteness of all such vague condemnations
of the intervention of the State beyond its normal sphere

frustrates all attempts to carry on the discussion with any hope of attaining useful results. If the Individualist wishes his weight to be felt in practical politics, he must discard vague generalities and ambiguous phrases, and point out accurately the specific sins of government to which he objects.

It should be his task to draw up an exhaustive list of the functions which the executive actually performs, and to state clearly those that he would immediately abolish, and those that he regards as evils necessary for the present but to be gradually got rid of. It does not seem unfair to ask him further to meet the difficulties to which these changes would give rise, either by argument or by some practical substitute for government control. It is no part of the scheme of this Essay to relieve him from this duty, but some indication may not unnaturally be expected here as to the nature of the chief duties actually performed by the executive authorities in most modern European States. A good basis for such an attempt is to be found in two admirable works of the "English Citizen Series": *The State in Relation to Labour*, by the late Professor Stanley Jevons; and *The State in Relation to Trade*, by Lord Farrer. The analysis ought to be undertaken, in the first instance, by practical business men working in the various administrative departments, who are content to record the facts observed as they occur, without selecting them in the light of any preconceived theory with either an individualistic or collectivist bias.

All that can be here attempted is a mere jotting down of a few of the most obvious of the functions of the administrative government; and for the present the distinction between such acts as are directly performed by the central government and those done by local authorities, must be ignored.

The "facultative" or abnormal functions performed by the administrative machinery of government are so numerous and complex that they almost defy classification on any satisfactory principle, but they may be roughly grouped under the following heads:

(1) It directs wars and foreign diplomacy; and is responsible for the continued efficacy of army and navy.

Where such a course is thought advisable or necessary, the government builds its own forts and warships, and manufactures its own guns and ammunition. Its diplomatic agents abroad perform many duties of a somewhat miscellaneous nature, such as protecting British trade in foreign countries, keeping up lines of communication, and collecting statistics.

(2) It undertakes to defend its citizens against the lawless aggression of their fellow-subjects. A police force is maintained, and riots are suppressed.

(3) It provides for the relief of the poor and the health of the people, and performs many services with the view of promoting their comfort and physical well-being. These duties are usually performed through local machinery, the ultimate control, however, resting with departments of the central government. The making of roads, bridges, and harbours, the supply of water, sanitation, the providing of artisans' dwellings, the erection and maintenance of model lodging-houses, compulsory vaccination, State-aided emigration—all these may be grouped under this general head.

(4) It provides education for all children beneath a certain age, and compels their attendance at school. It adopts an attitude of encouragement towards all arts and sciences; establishes museums and art galleries, and stocks them with specimens chosen by its officials appointed for the purpose; grants charters to bodies like the Royal Academy; appoints a Poet-Laureate and an Astronomer-Royal; confers titles and dignities on those it considers worthy; and undertakes scientific expeditions.

(5) It maintains an Episcopalian Established Church in England, and a Presbyterian one in Scotland.

(6) It supervises and controls the powers conferred on municipalities and other local authorities, and also on voluntary associations, civil and religious.

(7) It performs all such miscellaneous functions as are deemed necessary for the progress of the nation, and yet cannot be equally well accomplished by private or corporate enterprise. It acts, for example, as a carrier of letters and parcels; a banker of small savings; and a transmitter of telegrams.

(8) It maintains registers **and** grants licenses. **Thus registers of** births, deaths, and marriages, and of limited liability **companies** are kept by the State; and licenses **are required by doctors,** solicitors, **and** others before **they can enter on their** professional duties.[1]

(9) **Lastly, the** government of **Great Britain, as** is to be **expected** amidst a " nation of shopkeepers," **performs** an enormous amount **of** work of a miscellaneous **nature,** with the view **of** supervising and aiding the trade **of the** country. It determines standards of value and the **medium of** exchange, institutes inquiries into the causes of explosions **and accidents, collects** and disseminates **useful** information, **grants letters** patent and copyrights, **places** restriction on various **classes** of dealings, refuses **to enforce** immoral contracts, regulates **all** partial monopolies such as railways (where competition had previously failed),[2] tests the safety of ships, confers trade-marks, suppresses adulteration, and interferes generally **in** mines, factories, **and** elsewhere to secure **the** health and **safety of those employed.**

---

[1] **For a** detailed **list of such minor functions of** government see the *Fabian Essays,* pp. 46 to 52, **and the volumes of** the "English Citizen Series" already alluded **to.**

[2] **Cf.** Lord Farrer, *The State in Relation to Trade,* p. 69.

T

CHAPTER XXI.

LOCAL AUTHORITIES AND VOLUNTARY ASSOCIATIONS.

THE direct relationships between the State and the individual are not the only ones. There are many smaller groups or quasi-States within the larger group, which serve as channels of communication between the political unit and the body politic. These may mostly be arranged under two heads—municipal, county, or other local governments, on the one hand, and voluntary associations on the other. There are indeed two groups within the State, each of which is of a nature so entirely special and *sui generis* that it can be classed with none of the others. These are the institutions of the family and the church, which will require separate treatment.[1]

Much has been written on the relations between central and local government. The problem is a wide one, and a full consideration of it would fall naturally into three branches, treating of legislation, administration, and the dispensation of justice respectively. This would include a complete analysis of the entire machinery of the various civilized States of the world. A few special aspects of this wide inquiry are all that can be here discussed. The first question relates to the right of making laws. Should legislation be a national matter, or a local one, or partly both? Some thinkers, realizing the importance of the reign of one universal law over all the territories of a State as an element both of national unification and of practical convenience, but

[1] *Vide infra*, chapters xxiv. and xxvii. respectively.

at the same time conscious of the difficulties of a central legislative assembly making regulations suited for widely distant and diverse localities, suggest that law should be partly national or imperial, and partly local.

Others say that all law ought to be national, but that none of its provisions should descend to matters of detail, as that would prevent their applicability to the diversities of local usage. This opens up the whole question of the nature of law. How far should it confine itself to general principles ? Is it possible to legislate at all without descending to details ? One phase only of the general question as to the delegation of power by the British Parliament can be here discussed, viz. the advisability of granting separate legislative organs to Ireland and Scotland. " Local government," as the phrase is now used, is not confined to the right of every district to " manage its own affairs." It includes in the popular mouth the power to make laws as well. The discussion of the rights of subject nationalities comes in here still further to complicate the inquiry as to how far law ought to be uniform throughout the territory of one body politic.

The views of society and of the State expounded in this Essay would seem to favour conclusions such as these :

(1) The central legislative authority must retain the clear right of overturning any laws made by every subordinate institution within its sphere. Otherwise disruption of the State is already effected in a latent form, and only requires opportunity to break the commonwealth forcibly in pieces.

(2) The advantage of having uniform laws is so important to the whole empire as to outweigh any minor hardship that a particular district might suffer through the failure of the law to adjust itself to local peculiarities.

(3) Wise and well-framed laws, keeping to the function of defining, enforcing, and protecting rights and duties, and involving no administrative orders, are equally applicable to all parts of an empire, and unjust to no one.

(4) The power of making laws proper should never be delegated to any district or locality. " Local legislation is absurd."

(5) There is no harm, but on the contrary much good, to be expected from vesting every district, large or small, as well as every voluntary association, with the right to make bye-laws or administrative regulations according to their several needs. To every municipal corporation may well be entrusted, along with the right to manage its own internal affairs, the power to issue such bye-laws or regulations as are necessarily involved in its local autonomy. But no town ought to be allowed to determine, for example, what class of private contracts should be enforceable within its jurisdiction, or to alter the law of succession or the law of divorce. The same applies to larger divisions such as Scotland or Ireland. As long as these remain parts of one State, they must be subject to one law as far as possible. There is at present a rapid assimilation going on between Scots law and English law. No powers should be allowed to either Ireland or Scotland which would introduce conflicting rules of law within the empire. Each of them, however, must be endowed with the fullest powers to manage "its own business" after its own methods. The difficulty is to define (in the lights which modern science and philosophy have thrown on the solidarity of the race) what is, in the case of any town or any district, "its own business." It must be left to the Imperial Parliament to determine what is an exclusively Irish or Scottish affair, and what affects the commonwealth as a whole. Further, no local majority must be allowed opportunities of coercing local minorities in such a way as seems unjust to the moral sense of the whole community. Under these limits full powers of "local government" or district administration should be given to each locality, and with these executive powers the right to make bye-laws would naturally go; but no rights of legislation properly so-called could be entrusted to any power save the legal sovereign—Parliament.[1] Such an arrangement would not imply any diminution of the sovereignty of Parliament. It would merely mean that the central government is willing

[1] Cf. Wordsworth Donisthorpe, *Individualism*, p. 25 : "If local authorities are to be permitted to legislate independently, it is clear we are brought back to the original position of local anarchy."

to allow the local authorities of each subject nation, province, county, or parish to perform such local work as it
is fitted for, and that these powers will be conceded as long
as they are not abused. The individual, however, has the
better chance of justice, the wider the majority is to which he
appeals. It is the duty of the State never to diminish its
power to protect the aggrieved individual from the tyranny
of the parish, county, or province wherein he happens to
reside. The central government must not only jealously
preserve its theoretical rights of interference, but must
keep the machinery for enforcing these in good working
order and under its own immediate control. The electric
chain between the central authority and the citizen must
never be broken in passing through any of the smaller
organizations.

These results, then, point to an allocation of the administrative duties of government between the central and the local
authorities. Many of the objections urged with point and
success against the imperial government undertaking certain
classes of work for which it is totally unfitted are quite
inapplicable to a system under which these duties are performed by local authorities. It would be stupid, for example,
for Parliament to occupy its time with the consideration of
the best method of lighting the streets of each city in the
kingdom, and for the Home Secretary to travel about the
country to collect local information in the various towns.
Such work can be more efficiently and cheaply performed
by the mayor and aldermen of each city, to whom the
work will probably be a greater pleasure, and in whose
wisdom (rightly or wrongly) the body of the townsmen will
have greater confidence. The central government is thus left
with more time to perform the important duties which it
dare not delegate to any one.

The bulk of the arguments brought forward by consistent
Individualists, however, are intended to bear against the
interference of local authorities of every description with as
great force as against the interference of the State itself. It
is true that they are usually reticent or remiss as to the
exact list of offensive actions to which they object; but the

principle of their reasoning would seem to extend even to the enforcement of a general scheme for lighting and paving the streets of a city or for supplying water to a whole community under a compulsory assessment. It would be difficult to prove that the placing of a row of lamp-posts along the streets of a town in a certain definite order is necessary for "self-preservation" or for any of these "normal" functions of government for effecting which coercion and interference with liberty are alone justifiable on individualistic principles. Yet by merely voluntary action or association, even so simple a measure as this could never be carried out. Power of coercion, though never actually enforced, must be there; for without it any ordered city life would be impossible. One man maliciously inclined, sordid, or eccentric might defeat every project set on foot if all power to coerce him were denied to the authorities or the majority who favoured it. It is coercion to put a lamp-post opposite the house of a proprietor who objects to it; and it is coercion to make him contribute towards the remuneration of the watchman who interferes with his natural right to remove it. There is thus no denying that every duty performed by the municipal authorities, as well as by those at Whitehall and Downing Street, limits a man's freedom *in a particular direction.* But the question remains, Does it limit his freedom considered as a whole? Such restraints as those here spoken of are of so trivial a nature, and the inconvenience (if any) to the individual is so slight, compared with the benefit to the community at large, that no reasonable man would for a moment object. No individual is less free because he has to acquiesce in an orderly arrangement for lighting and cleansing the streets and to pay his just share of the expense, than if he lived in a town without lighting or cleansing at all, or one in which such matters were badly managed by competing joint-stock companies.

Some Individualists have a definite remedy to propose for what they consider the evils of local government: they would substitute voluntary association. "Private enterprise," to quote from Mr. Donisthorpe, "can, and will, effect all that is good and lawful for any local area which is ripe for

it."[1]   And **again** : "The highest form of local government is one
of complete and unqualified private enterprise."[2]   **Now, most**
people will be **inclined** to agree with Mr. Donisthorpe **that**
when any public **or** individual want **can** be better (or even
nearly **as well)** supplied by **private** enterprise than under a
regime **of** municipal interference, the authorities should stand
aside.   The majority of thinkers, however, would not be
prepared to concede to him that **all beneficial** undertakings
can be carried through in this way better than in any other,
or even that any beneficial measure not so realizable must be
delayed in the meantime because of **the loss of** "liberty"
involved in coercion by government administration.   **On the**
contrary, while there are **many** departments of industry **in**
which both central and **local** authorities would merely make
trouble by interfering, there are others which can be **a**
thousand times better performed under their official initiative
and management than **by** private enterprise.   There are, **in**
addition, **some benefits to** a whole community, **and these of a**
most fundamental and normal kind, and **necessary** to every
form of civilization, which could never be effected at all,
even in a rude and unsatisfactory way, without **the coercive
power** of an executive of some sort, either local **or central.**[3]
There are, on the other hand, many cases in which the
restraints placed on private liberty are more galling and
coercive under a regime of voluntary association than under
one of municipal authority.

At first sight there seems **to be a** strong antithesis between
the principle of local **government** and that of association
on a contractual basis.   **The one,** it is often said, depends

---

[1] *Individualism*, p. 25.   [2] *Ibid.*, p. 26.

[3] **Cf. Dr.** Henry Dyer, *The Evolution of Industry* (p. 157). Speaking
of the supply by local **authorities** of commodities "of a simple and
uniform nature, the **quality of which can be** easily tested, and about
which there is likely to ·be little **difference** of opinion, such for instance, **as water,** gas, and electric light," Dr. Dyer rightly says that
"from **their nature** it is highly desirable that they should be monopolies, **for it would** not only be very inconvenient but wasteful and
absurd to have **our** streets invaded by companies which claimed the
right **of** free competition."

exclusively on compulsion, and the other on voluntary co-operation. The citizen cannot escape from any particular local authority without leaving the district, nor from all local authorities without leaving the country. He is compelled to submit to the mandates of some local government. With voluntary associations it is said to be entirely different. The citizen may either join them or leave them alone. Within the association he is subject to no restrictions save those to which he has expressly assented, to wit, the conditions of membership. In conforming to these, he is merely carrying out his own contract. The extent of authority possessed by a local magistracy over the same man seems at first sight very different. It is generally much wider in scope, and indeed may be extended to any degree under powers conferred by Parliament. Its orders and regulations are backed by the coercive power of the State. It is founded on authority and not upon contract. The one seems a regime of compulsion, the other of free-will. A more thorough analysis, however, clears away a great part, if not all, of this absolute contrast. A working man, for example, may often be more free to choose his place of residence than to choose between being a member of a trades union or not.

On the one hand, every citizen of any town may be said to have placed himself willingly under its protection and authority. When a new Police Act is passed by the legislature, endowing the city magistrates with increased powers of dealing with individual rights, if the citizen remains voluntarily where he is, his consent to the changes is naturally presumed. Although the powers of local government, then, proceed from authority, they afterwards obtain the express or tacit consent of the citizen. On the other hand, every individual who enters an association—indeed every one who becomes a party to a contract of any sort—makes himself subject to coercion, and to coercion enforced by government. Thus by buying a few shares in a joint-stock undertaking you may become liable to a very great measure of coercion—more in fact than is incurred in taking up your residence in a special town. If the Articles of Association—which you may never have asked to see—contain obligations with which you cannot comply, you may find yourself coerced to the extent of the confiscation of your shares. The voluntary principle is only made effective by the action of government through its compulsive power.

The State-will and the individual-will, authority and freedom, are really combined in both cases, although these seemed at first the very antithesis of each other. There are some institutions, in fact, which possess so equally the more obvious characteristics of both that it is difficult to decide to which they belong. Of this type any railway company is a good example. In its origin a voluntary association of individuals for the purpose of enriching themselves, it has yet applied to Parliament for special powers, exactly as a municipality might do. Railways are always looked upon in Britain as public institutions, upon which special privileges have been conferred and from which special duties and public services are in return required. The power to compel private individuals to sell such lands as the railway needs is granted by Act of Parliament, along with the privilege of making bye-laws and regulations. But the government insists in return upon submission to many restrictions imposed by statute, such as the inability to raise passenger fares beyond a certain specified rate, and the effective control of the Board of Trade. Thus, though railways are not conducted by an administrative department, they are subjected to control (legislative and executive) just like local authorities. Other classes of corporations might be cited partaking partly of the nature of one kind of association and partly of another, and thus formed on a basis at once voluntary and compulsory.[1]

The real difference between the two is one of origin.

---

[1] Mr. Chamberlain in the *Forum* for November, 1892, has laid emphasis upon the points of analogy. "The leading idea of the English system of municipal government may be said to be that of a joint-stock or co-operative enterprise in which every citizen is a shareholder and of which the dividends are receivable in the improved health and increase in the comfort and happiness of the community." Cf. also Dr. Dyer's *Evolution of Industry*, p. 161, where the above opinion is cited.

Local government as it exists in England to-day—the institutions of that nature under the so-called Anglo-Saxon system are not here alluded to—owes its existence to the delegation of powers from the central government; whereas the origin of voluntary associations depends upon the initiative of individual citizens. Each class is a connecting link in which both the State and the individual acquiesce, and which combines the elements of consent and coercion; but the one proceeds from the State downwards, the other from the individual upwards.

There are two further principles of difference: (a) the nature of the sanctions by which the association can enforce its commands; and (b) the fact that local authorities are necessarily formed on a basis of contiguity or neighbourhood.

(a) The municipal or county authority is allowed by the central government to enforce its will upon the recalcitrant citizen by methods denied to the voluntary association. This is not open to objection, on the ground of invidiousness, unless it can be shown that the need of the voluntary body for coercive powers is as great as that of the local authority, and that the functions of the one are as important and necessary as those of the other. It is small consolation to the aggrieved individual to be told that it is a voluntary association which coerces him. The valid grounds of complaint are either that the sanction is a disproportionate one or that it is unjustly applied.

(b) The fact that the powers of each local government are confined to a specific territorial division of the country, is of even more importance. Some public benefits must be organized on a local basis or remain altogether unperformed. While a Yorkshireman may insure his house from fire, through the medium of a London insurance company or a Scotch one, it is impossible to arrange sanitation or police organization on such a basis. Wherever an undertaking can only be performed by those who live in one neighbourhood acting together and with practical unanimity, it is necessary to entrust its conduct to a local authority. Otherwise the opposition of a small minority of unreasonable individuals might ruin the whole scheme. Private enterprise means competition, and while it is well carefully to avoid **condemning all competition as** unhealthy, there are undoubtedly certain classes of work from which it must necessarily be excluded. Large cities like Glasgow, Birmingham, or Liverpool can be supplied with water only through powers specially conferred by Parliament upon local authorities. **If two or** three private companies had insisted on competing to supply Glasgow with **water,** not only would the cost to **the community** have been enormous, but the supply would have been much worse both in quality and quantity than at **present. What private com**pany could have obtained powers to **turn Loch Katrine into** a reservoir for Glasgow ? or have justified **the priority of its** claims ?

Such schemes, necessary as **they are to our** modern civilization, **can** only be carried out by the agency of a local authority acting under special powers conferred by Parliament and under **its control.** Where natural resources (water, for example) are **capable of** exhaustion, the system of competition involved **in** voluntary association is entirely inapplicable.

The argument against local government, grounded on the liberty of individuals, breaks down as completely as that based upon expediency ; for certain forms of **voluntary** associations **are** worse enemies to freedom than any **local authorities at** present in existence. Despotism **may exist** within every description of club or free combination of **men,** but the best (because the most exaggerated) **example is to be** found in the trades unionism which forms **so** marked a factor in our present labour system. **On this subject it is well** to rely on the testimony of Individualists whose prejudices are all in favour of voluntary associations as opposed **to local government.** The following passage by Mr. George Howell **is taken** from the symposium written in favour of Individualism under the name of *A Plea for Liberty.*[1] **"Recently, as** late as August, 1890, the newly-formed **Dockers'** Union, led by the men who claim **to be the originators of** what they are pleased to describe **as the 'new trades** unionism,' decreed that their books should **be** closed ; that no new members were to be enrolled ; that they **were** now sufficient in numbers to perform the work at the

[1] *Plea for Liberty,* p. 138.

docks, and that any addition would but impede their progress, by being brought into competition with the accredited members of the union. Any departure from this decree was to be left in the hands of the executive of the union. This autocratic ukase is worthy of the most unscrupulous despotic tyrant that ever disgraced the pages of history : no parallel for it can be found in the annals of labour, except perhaps in the more degenerate days of the trading corporations of the middle ages, or possibly in some of the commercial 'rings' of modern times. It says in effect, 'We, the members of the Dockers' Union, are quite sufficient in number to do all the dock work of the port of London or other ports; we only are to be employed; no other men shall come into competition with our labour, and we will dictate the terms and conditions upon which we shall be employed. If you don't like it, we will stop all industry until you cave in.' Supposing all other unions adopted the same policy, and shut out all labour except that which had been enrolled in the books of the union, what is to become of the unemployed? Beggary or the workhouse is to be the lot of all newcomers into the field of industry, unless they can be banished into other lands. If any doctrine so abominable had been propounded by employers the world of labour would have been up in arms. The monopoly of the land, or the upper chamber of the legislature, sinks into insignificance by the side of this unexampled piece of wicked stupidity on the part of the new leaders, the apostles of the New Trades Unionism."

Thus, while the old unionism confined its energies to forcing men to join or starve, the new unionism, while it continues to boycott and thus to starve those who are left outside, refuses to admit them except at the arbitrary will of the executive committee which forms the irresponsible government of these "voluntary associations." Once inside, the member finds himself under an absolute despotism. Valuable testimony to this tyranny is borne by that apostle of Individualism, Mr. Herbert Spencer :[1] " 'Be one of us or we will cut off your means of living' is the usual threat of each trades union to outsiders of the same trade.

[1] *Plea for Liberty*, p. 22.

While their members insist on their own freedom to combine and fix the rates at which they will work (as they are perfectly justified in doing), the freedom of those who disagree with them is not only denied but the asserting of it is treated as a crime." Again, still to quote from Mr. Spencer :[1] "The coercion of outsiders by unionists is paralleled only by their subjection to their leaders. That they may conquer in the struggle they surrender their individual liberties and individual judgments and show no resentment, however dictatorial may be the rule exercised over them."

He goes on to ask what will happen when the State under a socialistic regime becomes one vast universal trades union. The possibility of that event, however remote, is certainly one fitted to make prudent Socialists pause and think, but it is not the only, or even the chief lesson to be learnt. The despotism of trades unions has its message to Individualists also. It warns them that the true liberty of the individual can only be protected by the interference of the State, for only the State itself is powerful enough to defy a league of trades unions. Government must limit the misused liberty of such voluntary associations or there will be no room left for the liberty of the individual. Such interference is not socialistic, but proceeds along the *via media* endorsed by common-sense, the principles of which, properly rationalized, must be, after all, in harmony with those ultimately formulated by a true philosophy.

Protection from the socialistic tyranny of trades unionism can only be sought through government intervention, whether that take the form of legislation or of action by the imperial or the local authorities. Individualists who are consistent advocates of self-help and freedom ought to insist upon increased government coercion to prevent trades unions from forcing communism on their unwilling members, and to protect " blacklegs " from being compelled to join such " voluntary" associations under the penalty of starvation. Still, with all its defects and limits and liability to abuse, the voluntary system is excellent in its own place. Its adherents only injure its claims to perform those duties for

[1] *Plea for Liberty*, p. 23.

which it is by nature fitted, by urging it to usurp all the
duties of government. There are many functions which it
can undertake not only as well as but infinitely better than
any government or local officials. Parliament has not only
to protect individuals from being coerced unreasonably by
voluntary associations, but to prevent the latter from being
unnecessarily meddled with by local government.

A number of interesting questions arise as to the relations
of Individualism and Socialism to local government and to
voluntary associations. The system of Rousseau, professedly
on an individualistic basis, was really a municipal, though
not a national, Socialism. He advocated that the whole of
France should be split up into small quasi-States or communes,
each of them complete in itself and as nearly as possible
independent of the others, though he failed to give any indication of how this independence was to be secured consistently
with his principles. A question of greater practical interest
is, how far it is possible to realize the chief benefits claimed
by Socialism, or rather to overcome the chief evils it laments
in the existing order of things, by means of associations
conducted exclusively on a voluntary basis. By making a
free use of the two principles of co-operative production,
and of mutual insurance against loss of various kinds, individuals who believe in certain of the advantages of Socialism
(such as the absence of competition and the equal distribution
of the burden of an unavoidable loss upon all the members
of a community), can secure for themselves such benefits as
they value. Those who do not believe in these principles are
under no coercion to join.

It would be impossible, without swelling this chapter to
an undue extent, to seek to apply its principles to particular
cases. Many volumes have been written to show to what
extent, on grounds of justice and expediency, railways, telegraphs, roads, or museums, should be regulated by the nation
or managed by private enterprise exclusively. It is sometimes insisted that they should be subjected to a more
or less close supervision of an administrative department of
the imperial government, and sometimes that they should
be taken over altogether by the municipality or by the State.

These questions cannot be here discussed in detail. It may be again pointed out, however, that each case is to be decided on its own merits. There is no absolute presumption in favour of a so-called "coercive" regime over a "voluntary" one, or *vice versa*.

In conclusion, it may be said that the respective claims of central and local government must be carefully weighed and balanced one against the other. The health of the State depends on the preservation of a proper equipoise between them. Much has been said—and wisely said—upon the evils caused by the encroachment of central organs upon the duties of localities. This is the bureaucracy of the German system. It seems to be an evil inherent in every socialistic scheme yet invented or put partially into practice. The evils of such a system are incalculable—sapping as they do the vigour and self-resource of the nation. Self-government and local government have always been features of the British constitution, which has thus escaped the evils of a too centralized system. It must never be forgotten, however, that there are evils equally dangerous to the safety of the commonweal on the other side. Where the powers of local government grow out of proportion to those of the central authority, the balance necessary to a healthy action is equally destroyed. The chief duties of government must never be left for either local authorities or voluntary associations to take up. If the chief agent of the State steps back from its proper place, as the ultimate and highest power in the State, as the supreme lawgiver and last court of appeal—if it shirks the duty of supplying command and guidance to its subjects when they look to it for help or encouragement—other authorities will be only too willing to step in. If the State will not govern when called on, the reins will be taken from its hands. If the government ceases to be the centre and focus of the national life, taking the foremost place in all important works and interests in the commonwealth, the sovereignty will pass from it to those who both can and will lead the citizens; but with the fall of the effective power of the central authority, will come the disintegration of the nation, which will cease to be a harmonious and united body, and become either a congeries of districts ruled over by local authorities or a series of classes warring against one another, and subject to the dictation of such bodies as trades unions on the one side and commercial "trusts" or "rings" on the other.

The State must preserve its sovereignty and leadership intact, and this involves its stern resistance of all attempts to oust it from its legitimate share of the control of the local bodies, associations, and individual interests. It must keep itself in touch with every smaller power within it, and keep every such power in clear subjection to itself.

Imperial federation approaches the same question from the other side. The problem is to find machinery to join each colony in constitutional and organic union with the mother country, and to preserve intact the effective sovereignty of the latter without unduly interfering with the just rights and liberties and power of action of the colonies. If the Imperial Parliament fails to enforce its will upon its dependencies, these will become States. Similarly, if it allows any municipalities or chartered companies or trades unions to shake themselves free of all coercion, their own coercion will become unbearable.

CHAPTER XXII.

LIBERTY AND COERCION.

It has been one of the main objects of this Essay to combat the antithesis between the individual and the State in the abstract and unbending form in which it is often formulated. The two are necessarily bound together, and it is therefore impossible to differentiate their respective spheres. In systems of philosophy where this antithesis is insisted on, it does not stand alone, for it is logically connected with various other dualisms that a too abstract philosophy seeks to establish between principles essentially related. It is associated in particular with the opposition between liberty and coercion. It emphasizes the difference between the inner and the outer law.

Now, it is undoubtedly of great importance to see clearly that the true nature of liberty and coercion can only be understood with reference to each other, and it is quite true that they seem, as manifested in life and history, to be constantly at variance. The opposition, however, is only relative. The atoms are indeed always chafing against restraint, struggling for a negative liberty which in its extreme form would be anarchy. The central power is always striving for order and coercion, which in its extreme form would be slavery. A state of practical equilibrium is the resultant of conflicting forces ; but it is not a dead equilibrium. The element of strife on which it is built is really an element of life. It is the constant struggle between the central authority and the constituent atoms that keeps the body politic healthy. The

U

energy thus expended promotes motion and life. It is said that under a democratic form of government there is urgent danger of the equilibrium being upset, because the units think that they constitute the government, and naturally have no fear of themselves. This confidence, it is held, is the foundation of a tyranny. Whenever a want is felt, the friendly government is appealed to to supply it, and increased powers are gladly bestowed to enable it effectually to fulfil its ever-increasing tasks. According to Mr. Spencer, a Frankenstein is being called into existence and endowed with earthly omnipotence. Democracy has thus a bias towards both Socialism and despotism. If this be true—and it contains an element of truth, though not the whole—neutral individuals would do well to vote for *laissez faire*, wherever government meddling fails clearly to prove its case. In this respect Mr. Spencer's warning may do good service.

But there is another side to the picture. Under a well organized democracy the coercive action of the whole on the parts is to some extent counteracted by the freer action of each unit upon the whole. For this purpose the mere vote of any individual is a secondary matter. The main thing is that he should be able to air his own grievances and to state his own rational arguments clearly before the central authority, and to ensure in this way that he will not be coerced by a mechanical external power, but only by a sympathetic force guided by the common will and common reason of the nation, to which he has been permitted to contribute his quota, and upon which he has been allowed to exercise freely all his arguments.

Mr. Spencer begins his essay on the "Sins of Legislators" with these striking words: "Be it or be it not true that Man is shapen in iniquity and conceived in sin, it is unquestionably true that government is begotten of aggression and by aggression."

Now it is a mere truism that coercion or efficient force must be at the command of every government, but to call that force "aggression" is to apply an abusive epithet, calculated to make an unfair impression on the mind of a careless or ignorant

reader. It is like calling a soldier "a hired cut-throat" or a
barrister a "paid liar." It is a perversion of a certain
aspect of truth. But there is a further and graver objection
to Mr. Spencer's way of stating his argument.[1] The passage
cited insinuates that coercion or "aggression" came into
existence with government. Now, if a man could pass
at once from being a member of a savage tribe, that owned
no authority at all, into the status of a full citizen of a
civilized State, he would not jump—as Mr. Spencer's sentence
would have us believe—from freedom into aggression. On
the contrary he would escape from the aggression of anarchy
to an ordered force on whose moderation and rational principles
of action he could depend. The offensive term "aggression,"
if applicable at all, refers to the savage tribe and not to the
nation which is "over-governed" on principles of right.

Subject to this explanation, however, the fact must be
faced that coercion is the basis of all government. The
legislature—where the constitution secures to it the legal
sovereignty—is the ultimate director of force in the commonwealth, while the executive is its ultimate applier. The
object of government in thus regulating and using coercion,
is not to deprive its subjects of freedom, but to secure their
freedom. It does not create force, but only collects, directs,
and applies existing forces. By so doing it makes irresistible
the restraints imposed on individuals, but it also frees these
restraints from all that is arbitrary, and makes them regular
and rational. The one coercion of the resultant is substituted
for the thousands of isolated and conflicting coercions of an
unorganized society.

When the individual man, in the person of Von Humboldt,
John Stuart Mill, or Mr. Spencer, cries out against the
coercive authority of the State, philosophy seems to answer
him that he is foolish to revolt against his own true nature
as embodied in a higher form and degree in the rational State.
To the business man, who finds obedience injurious to his
abstract view of his own isolated interests, and who cares little
for the consolations of philosophy, a more practical answer
may be given. He may be reminded that it is only by the

[1] *The Man versus the State*, p. 44.

coercion of the State that he is saved from a much more galling system of restraints.

Those who oppose the liberty of the individual to the authority of the government absolutely, proceed on two false assumptions, viz. (1) that liberty is always a good thing in itself, and coercion a bad thing; and (2) that to increase the one is necessarily to diminish the other. Each of these requires some examination. To say categorically that coercion is bad and liberty is good, is to make them ends in themselves instead of merely means to ends. Before a State endows the individual with full social and political rights, it is surely competent to ask what he will do with them when he has got them. It would be foolish to present full rights of citizenship to any foreign anarchist who landed on our shores with the avowed intention to ruin England. Whenever he has broken the law, or has incited others to do so, he is at once deprived of that freedom which has become a menace to the welfare of the State. Liberty is here clearly enough seen not to be a good thing for the State. It is, perhaps, not so obvious that it would be evil for the individual as well; but when we admit the essential dependence of even a criminal upon that society against which he lives in chronic rebellion, we see that in sinning against the law he sins against himself. Liberty to commit a crime is to him not a benefit but in every way a curse.

Again, it is difficult to see how it is right or expedient to allow a man liberty to hurt himself. Suicide is prohibited among all civilized nations. Sir James F. Stephen, in his criticism of Mill, eloquently maintains that liberty is either good or bad according to the use to which it is put, just as fire is good or bad according as it warms or burns us.[1] Similarly, in his view, coercion is to be praised or condemned according to the object for which it is resorted to. It seems, however, unnecessary to go quite so far as this to establish the main truth that Sir James contends for. Nor is it necessary to say, as he does, that coercion is only a form of persuasion. Liberty may be invariably a better thing than coercion, *caeteris paribus*, and yet not co-extensive with

[1] *Liberty, Equality, Fraternity*, p. 48.

the supreme good of humanity. No one would deny that
if a man can be induced to do right willingly and of his
own initiative, this is better from every point of view than
that he should act grudgingly because he must. Sir J. F.
Stephen, indeed, confesses this when he allows that coercion
may be evil when *more of it than necessary* is used; for if it
were neither good nor bad in its essence, a little more or
less would not matter. The highest stage of moral grandeur
is reached when a man does noble deeds freely and joyfully,
and not through dread of punishment, or under the actual
sting of the lash.

That liberty cannot be made an absolute end in itself is
borne out by the theory on which all education proceeds,
for otherwise why should society inflict education or discipline
of any kind on an unwilling child—and what child is not
unwilling, more or less, to learn? The State educates the
child before it makes him free.

The second individualistic assumption which requires
examination is that whatever is gained to authority is lost
to freedom and *vice versa;* just as one vessel might be
emptied by pouring its contents into another. In reality
the facts are exactly the reverse. The stronger the government becomes, the greater, *caeteris paribus,* is the liberty of
its subjects. It has been already pointed out that the
coercion of government is a way of escape from the worse
coercion of unorganized society, of local prejudice, and, worst
of all, of anarchy.

All England rejoiced in the greater liberty enjoyed under
the despotic Tudor rule established by Henry VII., because
the "lack of governance" of the Lancastrian and Yorkist
period had allowed true liberty to be trampled under foot
in the anarchy of the Wars of the Roses. In the first
half of the fifteenth century the coercive power of government had entirely broken down, with the loss of prestige
and dignity of the crown. Henry of Richmond placed both
again on a firm basis. In doing so, he notably illustrated
the truth that to establish a strong government is not to
diminish the individual's freedom.

All must submit to coercion of some sort, or, worse

still, suffer it without submission. Subjection is the natural lot of men. Now, government simply takes this business of coercion into its own hands. It regulates the degree and method of its application to each individual. The ultimate right of coercion flows into a strong government. The force at the command of government is the resultant of the forces of the whole community, which neutralize one another in this universal "clearing-house" of a central authority. Government controls the stored-up force of the commonwealth. The coercion of government is in this way the high road to liberty.

All rule implies both submission and consent. It implies either that every private citizen is contented, or that he cannot make good his discontent. This is the valid aspect of the truth presented in a distorted form by the Social Contract theory, and by its weak reflection the "incorporation of society" invented by Mr. Spencer. The aggrieved individual finds himself unable either to obtain redress by altering the law or constitution to his own ideal or to rebel effectually against the form of authority to which he objects.

It is not a "contract" in the same sense in which we speak of a "contract of sale" or a "contract of marriage."

An established government may enforce any law against a recalcitrant individual without pausing to ask him politely whether he has openly or tacitly, directly or implicitly, agreed to that law—or even (more generally) agreed to the right of the government to make laws at all. The *onus* is all the other way. It is the business of the individual (1) *to justify his dissent*, and (2) *to make that dissent effective*. This he may do in either of two ways (*a*) by obtaining through his eloquence, his arguments, or the enthusiasm caused by his martyr sufferings, the repeal of the obnoxious law, or (*b*) by refusing to comply, and successfully defying the government to compel him. The first course is quite lawful and constitutional; the second course is flat rebellion against the government.

Where national institutions are established on a democratic basis this question of the opposition of coercion and liberty takes the form of the conflicting rights of majorities and minorities. If **every** Act of Parliament required the **consent** of every member of the House of Commons, all **legislation** would obviously become impossible. The votes of **the many** must be allowed to outweigh **those** of the few. **The** only question is, What is to constitute **an** effective majority? It would be quite possible for the legislature as a whole to decree that no measure should become law **until a two-thirds** majority of the Lower House had agreed to **it.** It would be possible even to require a different majority for one class of laws than for another.[1] As things stand at present, **however, there is** nothing either in the law of the realm, in **the conventions of the** constitution, or in the customs and procedure or standing **orders** of the Commons' House to prevent any bill being **accepted** by that House by a bare majority of one vote. **As** the Speaker **does** not take part in the division—except in giving a casting vote—335 votes, or exactly one-half, or less than a numerical majority of the whole House, could **coerce** a compact **minority of 334 members, and** commit the whole House to any principle **whatever—even to** the entire abolition of the existing **laws and** constitution *en bloc.* If **the** Lower House of Parliament were the sole **depositary of** the legislative power, there would **be no** check whatever on this divine right of majorities. As it is, the House of Lords **and** the legislative rights of the crown **stand as** the champions of minorities. The barriers so imposed, however, are good only in certain circumstances and up to certain limits. These are nowhere precisely defined, but it is admitted on all hands that a clear majority of **the** House **of** Commons, *when it has without doubt the voice of the nation at its back,* **can** sweep all opposition before it. The rule **or tyranny of the** Lower House of Parliament means at bottom **the rule or** tyranny of the majority of the nation over the minority— that 51 per cent. of the people may coerce the remaining 49.

It is evident **that** there will always be a minority dissenting from every **measure.** The rule of the majority **in some** form is a necessity inherent **in** every society. It only remains to be asked: Is this rule of the majority necessarily the

---

[1] The provisions of the constitution of the United States for its own amendment are an interesting commentary on this.

tyranny of the majority? Suppose a hundred men adrift on a raft with no land in sight. Surely it is not tyranny for ninety-eight men to insist on steering east when the remaining two believe that safety lies in the west. It is not tyranny, again, for the city magistrates to compel one recalcitrant individual to keep back his building line from blocking the entire traffic of a busy thoroughfare. Where the common good demands some course of action, any plan adopted must displease some one, and it is no tyranny to prevent a minority from forcing *their* schemes on an unwilling majority. Tyranny, then, does not consist in the use of coercion by majorities, but in its abuse. It is not easy to define what constitutes this abuse. Some would place the criterion in the intention of those who coerce, others in the methods employed—such as the gagging of free discussion, of which the application of the " closure " in the House of Commons is a good example. A suggestion towards a better test may be got from the organic conception of society. If the majority applies its right of compulsion in a mechanical rather than in an organic way, this is the essence of oppression. The criterion thus suggested is necessarily a somewhat elastic one. It implies in a general way that the ruling power should never act harshly or unsympathetically towards the coerced minority. These considerations point once more to the old conclusion that coercion is not absolutely bad, but only its excess or misdirection. In other words, the rule of the majority is not necessarily the tyranny of the majority.

When all is said, however, there is generally something harsh in coercion which cannot be altogether eliminated. It is a very important practical question, then, to inquire how this harshness may be reduced to a minimum, consistently with the maintenance of the unimpaired sovereignty of the central government.

John Stuart Mill, with his usual penetration, saw that the coercion of government was only one side of a wider question, and that the coercion of society and public opinion were even worse evils. " Protection against the tyranny of the magistrate is not enough ; there needs protection also against the tyranny of the prevailing opinion and feeling." [1] He adds that in England " the yoke of opinion " is perhaps heavier than that of law. The conclusion he draws is that in democracies it is necessary to limit the power of the people over themselves.

Now it is hardly necessary to inquire whether such a limitation would be desirable, because it is self-evident that it is impossible of accomplishment. The sovereign people of to-day who support individualistic theories cannot limit the sovereign people of to-morrow, who may all be Socialists. It would be an attempt of democracy to dethrone itself, and put up a dictum of John Stuart Mill to reign in its stead. There is no practical safety to be looked for against the tyranny of majorities on the lines laid down by Mill.

Indeed there is no safeguard anywhere except in the diffusion of enlightened views as to the nature of society and of a spirit of justice and public morality. These qualities cannot be forced by one generation upon the next, though, of course, the handing down of traditions and institutions and the principle of heredity may do much in that direction.

The tyranny of the State, of society, or of the majority, can be guarded against only from within, not from without. An enlightened view of the nature of society is what is wanted —not as a mere tenet of speculative interest, but widely diffused among the people, and used as a rule of action in practical politics.

Tyranny is only possible in a commonwealth based upon an arithmetical or mechanical theory, regarding itself as an aggregate of individuals with isolated interests, or drawing a sharp line between the ruling body and the subject masses.

Under popular forms of government this danger shows itself whenever the principle of representation is allowed to become merely quantitative. The old anomalies of the franchise, as they stood prior to the Reform Bill of 1832, were undoubtedly a disgrace to a civilized country; but there may be a danger also in carrying the principle of equality in voting to extremes. To divide the nation into arbitrary but equal divisions for polling purposes, and to take infinite pains that each man has the same infinitesimal

[1] *Essay on Liberty*, p. 13.

fraction of a joint representative in Parliament, tends to disseminate false ideas as to the nature of the State. The evils of this system would be ten-fold aggravated if taken in conjunction with a principle the advent of which it perhaps tends to hasten—the degradation of representatives into mere delegates. A delegate is a puppet who can only move according as his constituency pulls the strings. Delegation is the essence of a mechanical theory of democratic organization, and a mere mockery of representative government. If a majority in Parliament were to build upon these principles, its want of liberty of action would necessarily involve a want of sympathy with opponents, and minorities would be subjected to an unreasoning tyranny like that of the blind powers of nature.

The good citizen ought to be a member of the State first, and only secondarily a member either of a political party or of a majority or minority. If this were realized, tyranny within a State would be impossible. The organic unity of an individual with something outside of himself should draw him into close relations with the whole body politic and not with a sect or party.

The oppression of the majority can be avoided only by rising in practice above the idea of the State as a sum of units. We must get beyond the conception of sovereignty as the resultant of conflicting wills. In reality the voice of the majority is the voice of the nation. It is the rational general will, and not merely the sum of the individual wills of the " ayes " minus the sum of the wills of the " noes."

If the individual is allowed a fair chance of bringing the whole weight of his personality to bear on the discussion before the matter is settled, he has afterwards no right to object to his views being overruled by the voice of the nation. History affords several fine instances where the exponent of a new theory began in a minority of one, made a bold stand, and ended by conquering a whole nation originally opposed to him. Truly, in Mill's noble words, " One person with a belief is a social power equal to ninety-nine who have only interests."[1]

---

[1] *Representative Government*, p. 14.

A recent and powerful commentary upon the doctrine of the so-called tyranny of majorities was afforded by the career of the late Mr. Bradlaugh. Beginning in a minority of one, he ended by forcing the whole nation to agree with him. The solution of the mystery is quite a simple one. Reason was on his side. He was right and the majority was wrong. In admitting this it is not necessary to endorse either the wisdom of Mr. Bradlaugh's conduct or methods of procedure or to express any opinion of the personal dignity of his action, nor, on the other hand, to agree that the treatment accorded to him was either just or generous. There were faults on all sides; but Mr. Bradlaugh triumphed, and his success is a good illustration of the rights of minorities.[1]

These conclusions would lead to the adoption in practice of such rules as the following: (*a*) The dissenting individual or party ought to be allowed freely to plead every argument against the disputed measure, and "closure" ought to be applied only when liberty of discussion has been clearly abused or used as a mere engine of obstruction. (*b*) The majority should endeavour honestly to sympathize with the point of view of the minority before overruling it by sheer force of numbers. (*c*) An attempt should always be made to convert the minority by persuasion before applying force. A majority, it has been well said, comes near tyranny "when it neglects available means of justifying its action in the eyes of its opponents."[2] (*d*) More force than absolutely necessary

---

[1] Cf. Prof. Ritchie, *State Interference*, p. 73. "As to the rights of minorities, it may be enough at present to point out that the most important and valuable right of a minority is the right to turn itself into a majority if it can, *i.e.* the right of freedom of speech and freedom of association, not the impossible right of the member to exist apart from the organic whole."

[2] John MacCunn, *Ethics of Citizenship*, p. 119. On the whole subject of the rights of majorities and minorities, in addition to the authorities cited by Mr. MacCunn, the following works may be consulted: Sheldon Amos, *Science of Politics*, p. 198; Sir J. F. Stephen, *Liberty, Equality, Fraternity*, p. 22; Herbert Spencer, *The Man versus the State*, p. 103; Prof. Bryce, *American Commonwealth, passim*; Wordsworth Donisthorpe, *Individualism*, pp. 25 and 260; Prof. D. G. Ritchie, *State Interference*, p. 73.

should never be applied. (*e*) The minority on its part ought
in turn loyally to acquiesce when fairly beaten; accept the
conclusion arrived at as its own; and work for its success,
thus rendering coercion unnecessary.

Those who object to the rule of majorities must direct
their efforts towards regulating its abuse, since it is
impossible to abolish it except by substituting the rule
of minorities—the tyranny either of the one or of the few,
which would not suit democratic ideals. All governments
must aim at keeping intact their powers of coercion, but
that does not imply that they must also aim at subverting
"liberty." On the contrary, the object of all legislative and
administrative activity ought to be to raise men to the
highest level of freedom, according to their nature as rational
beings, by means of such restraints as are necessary.[1]

The sharp antithesis between coercion and liberty thus
breaks down on a close analysis of the aims and uses of
government; and the same result will be found to follow
from any attempt to give an exact definition of what is
meant by "liberty."

The absolute freedom of frail finite man trembling before
the energies of nature, the mysteries of life and death, and the
conflicting interests of his brother men, is unthinkable and
absurd. The sum of the forces arrayed against the individual
is infinitely greater than he, and therefore the more such forces
are reduced to order and subjected to the guidance of justice
founded on reason, the better for him and his "natural rights."
Even the strong man needs to shelter himself behind the still
stronger arm of the law, and in the rush for wealth the weak
without its aid would be trampled to death. If freedom
means merely the absence of all restraint, it is as unattainable
as omnipotence or omniscience. Man is, in this sense, always
a slave—the slave of destiny, of circumstance, or of his own
evil passions, if not of society or the State. Every man,
says Mr. Herbert Spencer,[2] "must have a master, but the
master may be nature or may be a fellow man. When
he is under the impersonal coercion of nature we say that

[1] Cf. Kant's *Principles of Politics*, translated by Prof. Hastie, p. 34.
[2] Introduction to the *Plea for Liberty*.

he is free; and when he is under the personal coercion of some one above him we call him, according to the degree of his dependence, a slave, a serf, or a vassal." The choice of masters, however, does not lie between nature and man, for each individual must at every moment of his life be subject to both. The rule of a majority representing so wide a community as to become "impersonal" is the alternative to that of a despot or a feudal over-lord. Liberty means the sovereignty of laws as distinct from the sovereignty of individuals. Under an individualistic regime man, it is sometimes asserted, in partially shaking off the rule of government, would to that extent fall under the despotism of a wealthy few rather than of nature, becoming thus the servant of a harder master.

Coercion in some form thus imposes its sway upon the individual. In a sense, therefore, he is never "free"; but the word liberty has two meanings, and these must be carefully kept apart. Negative liberty is impossible. "The condition of human life is such," it has been said, "that we must of necessity be restrained and compelled by circumstances in nearly every action of our lives."[1] Positive freedom, however, is a different thing. "Know the truth and the truth will make you free." This is positive liberty in the moral or spiritual sense. That man is morally free who is the bond-slave of reason in place of selfish passions and desires. Is no similar conception of positive freedom possible in the sphere of the State? Undoubtedly it is, for political freedom means subjection to the laws of a rational government, which frees individuals from subjection to a chaos of warring wills. It means the substitution of the coercion of Parliament for that of free competition, of the national will for that of the county or parish or trades union, of wisdom for ignorance. It is only when a negative and abstract conception is formed of liberty, that government is necessarily its foe. It is by taking this inadequate view of freedom that Sir John Seeley is led to make the opposition final and irreconcilable. "Liberty, in short," he says, "in the common use of language, is opposed to restraint, and as government in the political department is restraint, liberty

[1] Stephen, *Liberty, Equality, Fraternity*, p. 11.

in a political sense should be the opposite of government. . . . Liberty being taken as the opposite of government, we may say that each man's life is divided into two provinces, the province of government and the province of liberty."[1]   Such reasoning, founded as it is on individualistic assumptions, would lead to the conclusion that the savage is more " free " than the subject of a civilized State, because the number of restraints placed upon him is less.

Mr. Herbert Spencer's definition may be profitably compared with Professor Seeley's, as both have fallen into the same error. "The liberty which a citizen enjoys is to be measured, not by the nature of the governmental machinery he lives under, whether representative or other, but by the relative paucity of the restraints it imposes on him."[2] Now, this is to take an artificial and mechanical view of liberty, and to determine the degree of freedom or of bondage by merely adding up the sum of restraints irrespective of their character. It is, however, the nature and not the number of these restraints that is the important point. To obey the uniform laws of a rational government is freedom, whereas to be at the mercy of the capricious dictates of a Nero is slavery. Freedom, when understood in a positive sense, is not lawlessness.

"The modern English citizen," says Professor Jevons, " who lives under the burden of the revised edition of the statutes, not to speak of innumerable municipal, railroad, sanitary, and other bye-laws, is after all an infinitely freer as well as nobler creature than the savage, who is always under the despotism of physical want, far freer too than the poor Indian, who, though perhaps unacquainted with written law, is bound down by the most inflexible system of traditional usage and superstition."[3]

Law and political freedom, rightly understood, are thus seen not to be mutual enemies, but rather necessary counterparts which cannot exist the one without the other. The important thing is to understand wherein true liberty is to

[1] *Introduction to Political Science*, p. 119.
[2] *The Man versus the State*, p. 15.
[3] *The State in Relation to Labour*, p. 14.

be found. Its **real** nature has been well expressed **by Dr.**
Hutchison **Stirling in** explaining the place it occupies **in the**
Hegelian system. " Freedom," he says, " ought not **to be**
taken abstractly as the freedom of subjective self-will. Legal
restriction **ought to be** seen **to be the true** freedom, and
formerly precisely such restrictions **used to** be called *the*
freedoms, *the* liberties. In effect, **every veritable** law is a
freedom, a liberty, for it is a result **of** objective reason. In
the best sense it is not true, then, that the **State** is but the
mutual limitation of each others' liberties ; **in** the best sense,
on the contrary, the State is **a realization of liberty, for,** in
reality, to restrain particular or **formal** will **is to emancipate**
universal and substantial will."[1]

But it is not enough to know from what the individual
desires to be **free,** before we can judge if his liberty is a good
or a bad thing for himself **or for** the State. Even its negative aspect **(which implies** nothing more than the absence of
restraint) **is meaningless** apart from a knowledge of the bonds
to be shaken off ; **but in** real or positive conceptions of liberty,
the relativity of the term is still **more obvious.** The important **question is :—What things ought a man to be free**
to do ?

Freedom, then, is not the absence of all restraints, but
rather the substitution of rational ones for irrational. Positive
freedom implies the removal of all restraints that hinder the
attainment of what is excellent. In a word, he is free who
enjoys the opportunity of self-realization according to his
highest nature as a rational being. Governments ought to
grant freedom to each of their subjects to further his own
development, and to help forward the good of humanity ; but
not to brutalize himself and others, or prove a danger to
the stability, health, or **moral vigour** of society. The true
freedom of the subject lies **in** the right to enjoy the
full life of the **State in** all its phases—economic, social,
and political. **This is** the meaning of organic. Allow all
the currents **of** man's life and opinions, **in** so far as these
are healthful and **rational,** to flow into and influence the
State ; **take** him along **in** the full current of the common

[1] *Lectures on the Philosophy of Law,* p. 39.

life, and let the government he must obey be one of light and persuasion, not of darkness and oppression; then, and only then, he will be fully free.

It seems after all, then, that coercion and liberty are friends not foes; and when the absolute barrier raised by an abstract philosophy between them is broken down, other dualisms fall with it. John Stuart Mill's plea for liberty is joined with one for individuality or originality. To the opposition he sets up between freedom and government, he adds another between originality on the one hand, and authority or education on the other. Here, as before, abstractions, useful as stepping stones, are dangerous as final resting places. True originality can never be independent of discipline and dare not despise the attainments and teaching of others.

"There is nothing new under the sun" is itself an old saying. If true, originality would seem impossible. It is perhaps safer to say that originality is only a relative thing. There can be no "creative genius" able to make something out of nothing. Genius can only rearrange and view old facts under new relations.

Originality is not exclusively an emanation from the inner consciousness of the individual. To gain it he must first absorb all that lies around him, falling under the sway of the ordinary recognized rules. Only when he has mastered them can he hope to rise beyond them. In Carlyle's phrase, his first step is to "swallow all formulas." To despise authority is to aim at originality and to achieve eccentricity —to become a mountebank instead of a genius. "True originality," it has been said, "does not consist in living in a world of one's own, but in making the common world new by a fresh interpretation of it, and such a fresh interpretation of it no one could give unless he knew it."[1]

Genius means an advance beyond the ordinary position attained by the average of mankind, not a falling behind it. The man who insists to-day that the sun goes round the earth is not an original genius, but an ignorant blockhead.

[1] The Master of Balliol, address on "The Relation of Culture to Knowledge," delivered at Aberystwith, October, 1895.

To be original he must first learn all that others have to teach, and then pass beyond them if he can. Before he takes the first step, then, he must submit himself to others, accept restraints, curb vain imaginations, and in a sense lose his own individuality to find it in a higher form. Eccentricity is not originality any more than caprice is freedom. Liberty and individuality depend on authority and the solidarity of the human race.

Individuality has its own place in the State, but it is only one of two factors. Its due subjection to the laws imposed by the sovereignty of the community must be recognized. "If individuality has no play," says Professor Huxley, "society does not advance; if individuality breaks out of all bounds, society perishes."[1]

The result of the whole inquiry seems to be that all absolute dualisms between State and individual, coercion and liberty, authority and originality must be abandoned.

When government is attacked on the ground that it is an aggressor, several replies are open: (1) Coercion is not the whole of government, but only one element. The consent of the governed is always to some extent implied, as Rousseau, the enemy of all arbitrary authority, clearly saw, though he expressed it in a distorted fashion in his social contract theory. (2) Coercion is not necessarily evil if directed to a good end and not employed in excess of what that end justifies. (3) The coercion of government is an immediate escape from the tyranny of less rational powers. (4) Lastly, an apparent encroachment on liberty in one age has often, as a historical fact, paved the way for an advance in rational freedom for the next.

These considerations seem sufficient to make the individualistic indictment against government break down, along with the false assumptions upon which it rests.

[1] *Method and Results*, p. 277.

CHAPTER XXIII.

EQUALITY.

THERE is no more obvious phenomenon of human nature than the radical fundamental inequality of men. No two men are, or ever have been, exactly equal in any one respect since the world began. Human beings differ enormously from one another in characteristics of every kind—moral, intellectual, and physical. They are unequal in animal strength, in bodily proportion, and even in the capabilities of physical pain. They are still more unequal in respect of intellectual endowments—in breadth of mental horizon, in capacity for study, in natural bent of mind, and in wealth of imagination. If moral worth be taken as the test of equality, as is sometimes done, the result is still more pronounced. Men differ in moral worth from the Apostle Paul to Judas Iscariot, as they differ in intellectual calibre from Shakespeare to Mr. Martin Tupper, or in strength from Goliath to a newly-born child.

The radical inequality of men, then, is a fact which it is madness to dispute, however bitterly it may be deplored. Every true theory of government must take as one of its axioms—if not its very starting-point—the *fact* of the inequality of men.

It may be said, however, that no sane man seriously doubts this. The fallacy lurks, all the same, in the background of many average minds as an imperfectly formulated preconception; and equality is tacitly assumed to be the loftiest social and political ideal. In one form or another it **consciously or** unconsciously tinges many otherwise **diverse views of society** and theories of government.

To most men the idea of equality is rather a prophecy for the future than a generalization from the past, a statement of what ought to be rather than of what is. Equality is, however, as delusive an ideal as it is unreal as an established fact. Its inherent absurdity is disguised only by the prudence of its advocates, who refrain from clearly defining what they mean. It is allowed to colour men's thoughts, while it refuses to come to clear consciousness itself. If the statement that all men *are* equal is as erroneous as that the surface of the earth is level, the assertion that all men *ought to be* equal is as absurd as that the earth ought to be one vast plain. An attempt to reduce the earth to a dead level would be no whit more stupid or mischievous than the endeavour to force all men to be equal.

Inequality is a law of nature, and can no more be ignored than the law of gravity or the principle of cohesion. The forces of nature may be partially controlled and tamed to work in man's service, but its laws can never be reversed.

Neither by leaving men to the unfettered liberty of their own Individualism, nor under a thorough system of Collectivism, is it possible to eradicate their essential inequalities. If all mountains were levelled with the valleys the world would be one dull, uninteresting, universal plain. If the inequality of existence were abolished there would remain none of the poetry and none of the lights and shadows of human life. This world would not supply the discipline needed as a preparation for a higher form of existence.[1]

Absolute equality is evidently as impossible of attainment as absolute liberty; therefore the science of right cannot postulate either one or other as a practical rule for the guidance of legislators or rulers.

Liberty and equality, to have any definite meaning in the

[1] Cf. Sir J. F. Stephen's *Liberty, Equality, Fraternity*, p. 235. "Men are fundamentally unequal, and this inequality will show itself arrange society as you like." And Prof. Flint's *Socialism*, p. 320. "Mankind must develop or die, and development involves differentiation, unlikeness, inequality."

political world, must be used as relative terms, and therefore defined with reference to ends outside of themselves. When this is forgotten the theorist is landed in the usual dangers and insoluble problems which beset the abstract thinker. The Individualist and the Socialist alike profess to search for principles of abstract justice. The former identifies it with liberty and the latter with equality. Thus, using these rival clews to guide them when they step from the region of abstractions to the world of realities, the worship of the same deity called "justice" leads them by absolutely opposite roads.

The root of all well-ordered social action is declared by Mr. Herbert Spencer to be "a sentiment of justice which at once insists on personal freedom and is solicitous for the like freedom of others."[1] To the average Individualist, then, justice means liberty. Those of its worshippers who have socialistic leanings, on the other hand, would identify justice with equality. Now, *abstract* liberty and *abstract* equality may well be identical while they remain empty universals, for all zeros are the same. But they clash immediately they find a content from the empirical material of experience. *Laissez faire* is called on to realize the individualistic conception of practical justice embodying "freedom," while the coercion of the State in every department of life is required for the attainment of socialistic justice as "equality" on a communistic basis.

The problems which present themselves for solution are: (1) Does strict justice demand equality (in any definite meaning of that word) among the fellow-citizens of a State? and (2) how far is it the duty of government to see this equality realized?

The first step in the inquiry is obviously to determine what is really meant by "equality" in the region of practical politics, when we have once laid aside vague generalities and

---

[1] *A Plea for Liberty*, p. 25. Cf. Kant's *Philosophy of Law*, translated by Prof. Hastie, p. 45. "Right, therefore, comprehends the whole of the conditions under which voluntary actions of any one person can be harmonized in reality with the voluntary actions of every other person, according to a universal law of freedom."

empty universals. It is necessary to be definite; for it will not do to prove that abstract justice implies abstract equality, and then to jump to the conclusion that within the family circle the son has equal authority with the father, or that the tenant has an equal right to the rent with the landlord, or that every male adult has an equal claim to a ruling voice in the Cabinet with the Prime Minister. Abstract and actual equality are very different things.

It is thus useless to demand that men be made "equal" without specifying clearly what is meant. There are obviously certain kinds of equality that may be at once dismissed, since neither government nor any other human agency can affect them. It is as impossible to make men equal in wisdom or in happiness, as in age or stature. After such conceptions have been eliminated, at least seven distinct varieties of equality remain. It is necessary to separate these clearly from one another before asking how far the State may be bound, in the name of justice, to secure their realization in the mutual relations of its citizens. (1) "Civil equality" requires that all men should be equal before the law. Justice demands that its courts, in dispensing law, should treat all over whom their jurisdiction extends absolutely without fear or favour. This is clearly not the kind of equality for which Socialists clamour; for judicial impartiality is already sufficiently secured in countries like England where the reign of law brooks no rival; sets aside all class privileges and official immunities; and puts the highest and the lowest on the same level in the courts of law.

It is easy, however, to misunderstand what this species of equality means. It merely implies that all men have an equal right of standing in a Court of Law to make good the inequalities which nature and their own exertions have procured for them. The dispensation of equal justice to all men does not imply that when a case of disputed inheritance is brought before the courts, an equal distribution of the subject of litigation will be made among the claimants. It merely means that each claimant will receive an equal and impartial hearing for every legal argument he can bring forward to establish his rights as the law defines them.

"An equal law" is a just law, and not one which recognizes the equal rights of every one to everything. This extremely abstract meaning of equality—according to which each citizen is the possible subject of rights—is perhaps the only one which justice categorically demands. "Equality," says Sir James Stephen, "has no special connection with justice except in the narrow sense of judicial impartiality."[1]

(2) "Political equality" is of a different nature, and though possibly a wise thing, its absolute necessity in a well-governed country cannot be said to be so axiomatic as that of civil equality. It is easy to distinguish between the two. The relations of individuals to the government, and their rights against it, are of two kinds, civil and political. The first class defines the position of the citizen as one of the subjects of government, fixing the extent of the control that can be legitimately exercised over him, laying down rules by which that control will be guided, and specifying the measure of protection which he is entitled to demand. The second class defines the position of the citizen as a part of government, or at least as having upon it an indirect influence, fixing his share in the election of rulers, his right to strive for the alteration of the constitution, and his eligibility to be appointed to a direct position in the government.

The sum of a citizen's civil rights or *jus privatum* is the counterpart of the control which the government has over him; whereas the sum of his political rights or *jus publicum* is identical with the control which he has over the government. From this distinction it appears that civil or legal equality does not necessarily involve political; for it is quite consistent to hold that the law should have equal control over all, including even the sovereign, along with the doctrine that all have not an equal voice in the making of laws or the choosing of rulers. Indeed, the formula of equal political rights in its extreme form is not only inconsistent with the existence of a hereditary monarchy and a second chamber of any sort, but even with the existence of representative government; for if all have equal political rights why should there be any division into representatives and represented?

[1] See *Liberty, Equality, Fraternity*, p. 238.

Equality of political rights, to have any sensible meaning at all, must be restricted materially. It means in practice little more than an universal franchise. "One man, one vote," is quite a logical contention, running counter to no "law of nature." It falls far short of political equality, however, and its realization would make men equal at the polling booths, just as they are already equal in a court of law. It would in no way imply the equal political influence of the most illiterate voter with Mr. Gladstone, nor the right of every citizen to interfere in naval affairs with the same authority as the first lord of the Admiralty.[1] One phase of the general question of the equality of the sexes centres round the possession of the franchise. It is the State which in all such matters must finally decide; and it ought to do so, not on the ground either of a "natural right" of man to rule, or a "natural right" of woman to equality, but on the general grounds which regulate all its decisions. It must decide in favour of whatever course will best further the various proximate objects for which it exists in the light of that ultimate end which includes and transcends them all.

(3) The only equality which the Individualist insists on is "equality in freedom." This claim is put forward, it is true, rather in the interests of liberty than of equality. The only limit in this view to the right of all men to be free —absolutely free—is the equally absolute right to liberty of every other man. The only legitimate business of the State is then, it would seem, to see that this empty freedom is distributed equally among all its citizens, and to perform the duties necessary for the attainment of this end, such as the prevention of foreign interference or domestic disorder from interrupting its universal reign.

(4) "Religious equality" is a phrase often used, but rarely analyzed. It may mean either an absolute toleration by the State of all religious and irreligious sects equally, with the absence of all restraints direct and indirect (an ideal utterly unattainable apart from anarchy), or merely the absence of

---

[1] Cf. T. H. Huxley, *Method and Results*, p. 308. "'Political inequality naturally dogs the heels of 'natural' inequality."

an established church. It might even mean the equal establishment of all churches of whatever creeds or ceremonies.

(5) "Moral equality" might be made a party cry. If the criterion is to be applied by individual consciences, however, toleration of differing codes of morality must imply toleration of immorality as well, for what the community condemns the individual may approve. To allow conduct to pass uncensured and unrestrained only when it confines itself within those lines considered not immoral by the community, is intolerance and the reverse of equality. The adherent of religious equality may be more willing to tolerate the dissemination of heresy and atheism than the believer in moral equality to allow the propagation of gross immorality. The difference seems to be that religious dissenters form a large minority, and bigamists a very small one. It is difficult to see why bigamy should be punished and atheism go free—*on grounds of equality alone.* It may easily be proved, of course, that one is more injurious to the community than the other.

(6) "Social equality" is another ideal which commends itself to many minds. Society, as it exists, is founded on inequality. No two families moving in the same circle are exactly on a par. Society is a chain extending from the sovereign downwards—each link hanging on to the one immediately above it, and supporting in turn one a little lower than itself.

How far is the State responsible for this inequality ? How far should it interfere to alter it ? The provisions of English law have a two-fold bearing on the subject. In the first place, the law allows no class privileges or invidious distinctions of any kind to interfere with the impartial dispensation of justice. Neither hereditary nobility nor high officials of State have any licence to break the law of the land, and even the prerogative of the sovereign is subject to its sway. This is, however, rather equality of the first sort—an equal standing before the law—than social equality in the sense under discussion. The one, however, tends to bring the other in its train. In the second place, the Queen is the fountain of honour ; and by conferring through the appropriate constitutional channels, peerages, baronetcies, knighthoods, and other distinctions, Her Majesty, as head of the State, can greatly

affect the relative social positions of her subjects. **This is**
only one element in determining social position; but so far
as the State **confers honours at** all, it gives its **voice in**
favour of inequality. Beyond this somewhat unimportant
interference, it leaves each individual to sink or rise to his
natural level in society as best **he may.**

(7) There is still another **form of** inequality towards
which the government must **assume an attitude** of some
sort. Is it the duty of the legislature to **aim** at establishing, as far as possible, **a** complete equality of material wealth
or of the enjoyment of its fruits? **Ought it** to attempt any
modification at all of the extreme inequality **that divides**
the rich from the poor?

This field **of inquiry is a** wide **one,** and it is well to
limit it wherever **practicable. It** cannot be the duty of **the**
State to do what is impossible; therefore the issue may be
at once **narrowed by** discarding all attempts to produce a
dead **uniform level. Absolute** equality of wealth or **of its**
produce is impossible **in a** world where **men** grow old and
die in varying numbers that cannot be calculated beforehand,
while the ratio of these deaths **to the births** of children
destined to fill their places is equally uncertain. The laws
of supply and demand, too, insist on asserting themselves in
spite of all State regulation of labour, and so continue to
upset the best laid plans. **There are, besides,** innumerable
differences of bodily organization, of mental endowments, and
of taste, which make the **needs of** individuals for the various
forms of wealth **unequal—and this** difficulty would certainly
not be diminished by the abolition of "money" as a medium
of exchange. **It is** difficult to understand how even an
omniscient and omnipotent government could superintend a
distribution of the **natural** good things of the world in a
way that would be "**equal**" or successful in satisfying the
needs of any one **man, or** in advancing the well-being of
the community **as** a whole.

The demand for absolute material equality may then be
dismissed **as** at once unattainable and undesirable. Some approximation to equality may be made, however, or rather some
modification of the more **glaring** inequalities of life. Equality,

as a term of practical politics, is only a matter of degree.
When this is granted, there is nothing inherently absurd or
illogical in the demand that the law should do something
to lessen the hardships of the poor man's lot and to compel the rich man to contribute from his superfluity towards
that desirable end. But while such a proposal cannot be
summarily dismissed as ridiculous on the face of it, weighty
questions yet require to be answered as to its justice
and expediency even in the interests of the poor themselves. To adopt the only criterion at once safe and definite,
Will such a course advance the highest ends for which the
State exists? or, as the question comes to be one of degree,
How far does a due regard for that end justify the government in going?

Different theorists have adopted as an ideal almost every
gradation from extreme communistic doctrines to the plausible
and praiseworthy though indefinite claim for what is vaguely
called "an equal start in life."

The present law in England makes no direct attempt
towards even an approximate equality of wealth. The Poor
Laws might be pointed to as a possible exception, but their
object is not to raise the poor to a level with any other class,
but to provide out of the common purse the bare necessities of
existence for those who are utterly destitute. Much modern
legislation, it is true, aiming at other objects (such as the
promotion of education or safe-guarding the health of localities), by putting increased taxation chiefly on the well-to-do,
unconsciously tends in this direction.[1]

In estimating the merits of any of the theories which
advocate a forcible readjustment of wealth and poverty, one

---

[1] Cf. Dr. Henry Dyer's *Evolution of Industry*, p. 158, where the
whole of the present scheme of levying local rates is declared to be
socialistic, "for they fall much more heavily upon property and on
the incomes generally of the well-to-do classes than upon the poor,
thus helping to equalize the distribution of wealth and forcing a
practical recognition of the fact that the community is a social organism."
It must not be forgotten, however, that part at least of the taxation
thus expended on local improvements comes back indirectly to the
owners of local property in the form of increased rents and what is
often called "*unearned* increment."

principle **seems** certain. No moral State can select arbitrarily any **one class** of property, and confiscate it without
compensation. Even if private ownership comes to be ultimately
condemned, **and** even if it were to be considered equitable to
abolish it by one stroke, and not gradually through centuries
of slow approximation to new conditions, it would still be
utterly contrary to the science of right and the true interests
of humanity to select arbitrarily one victim **of the** change in
public sentiment, and let others go **free.**

It is true that the unreasonable interests **of** individuals
cannot be allowed to block the advance of the State, and
so-called natural rights of citizens must often be **invaded**
against the will of those affected; but this should never be
done arbitrarily, **and** never without giving as full compensation as is consistent with the nature of the property of
which they are deprived, and with the resources of the
nation. This **is not** a limitation upon the power or the
abstract rights **of the State,** but an ethical **maxim** which **it**
cannot ignore without injury to its **own** highest interests.
It does not deprive it of the right to punish a citizen for
a crime or misdemeanour by the deprivation of part or
of the whole of his possessions, nor of the right to compel
a man to fulfil all obligations incurred by his contract or
quasi-contract, delict or quasi-delict, nor of the right to coerce
the rich man to contribute a **greater share** of taxation
than his poorer neighbour for the **general** ends of the
State.

It does limit, **however,** a justice-loving nation from stepping in and appropriating summarily possessions which an
individual has acquired in strict conformity with law. It
forbids the State, on grounds of public morality—in plain
words, under the penalty of being considered by more
equitably minded States and individuals, a thief and a breaker
of faith—from forcibly taking one kind of property from A
and **leaving B** to enjoy the fruits of an equally large income
derived **from** property of another class.

If **the** present law allows private ownership of land,
houses, machinery, trading companies, mortgages, personal
debts, and ships as all equally legal, it ought never to select

one of these kinds of property as more subject to confiscation without compensation than another.

It is unjustifiable to attempt to shelter the expropriation of a citizen who is innocent of offence *in the eyes of the existing law*, under the pretence that that law is bad.

If the legislature is convinced that the old law is immoral, it should undoubtedly make a change as soon as possible, but it cannot repair its old sins by committing new ones of a more heinous nature. Thus Mr. Henry George is entitled to convince the conscience of Great Britain (if he can) that private property in land is immoral; and if the community sincerely forms the opinion that he is right, the law ought to be altered at once, making it illegal for any one to hold land in the future. But to refuse to give to each proprietor from whom property has been so taken a full compensation for its market value (and also, if possible, for any sentimental considerations attached to it) is to punish him by the new law for doing what the old law protected and encouraged him in doing. If the abolished system was immoral, the whole community which was responsible for the wicked law shared in the sin. It is unjust to single out the actual holders of land at the time when the change is made, to act as scapegoats for the sins of all. The law ought only to punish individuals for breaches of its mandates, not for its own former imperfections as judged by a later standard. Mr. Henry George's system is open to all the usual objections to which retrospective legislation is always exposed, and that in an exaggerated degree, while it has special objections of its own.

This is only one instance of a principle of quite universal application. Even if it were possible to sweep poverty for ever from the land by seizing on the surplus riches of any one class, and applying them to relieve the crying necessities of the many, the State ought still to pause before committing itself to such a course, in case, by so doing, it should interfere with the eternal principles of justice, or (if the phrase be preferred) with the rational basis of a utilitarian system of ethics. Confiscation is too severe a remedy to be applied to the body politic, to alleviate even the frightful evils which Socialism professes to cure.

If a man has once made a fortune under the protection of the law and without violating its provisions, it can never be to the ultimate good of the community to prevent his enjoyment of what the past law has encouraged him to call his own for the natural term of his life. Accumulated wealth in the hands of individuals must be respected, unless contemporary law has branded as illegal any particular type of property or the methods by which it has been acquired or the uses to which it is put.

The aim of absolute equality and the methods of confiscation must then be alike discarded by every system of political science with truth and justice before its eyes. Apart from socialistic Utopias founded on a complete abolition of private property, only two schemes have come definitely before the public for lessening material inequalities—a graduated income tax and an ascending scale of death duties. These proposals seem at first sight to have much in common—to hold out the same inducements and to lie open to the same objections. But there is one cardinal point of distinction; for the first would debar the comparatively rich capitalist from enjoying part of what he had himself acquired, whereas the latter would keep from the expectant heir something which had never been his.

Strong reasons may be urged against both schemes, but the future may evolve means of overcoming the practical difficulties. It is only their theoretical aspects that can be here discussed.

It is only fair that the heaviest burden of providing benefits wherein the whole community participates should fall on those best able to bear it, especially when it is to those favourites of fortune that the greater share of the benefit accrues in proportion as they have more at stake. Thus, if increased taxation is essential for purely national needs—these are of course difficult to define—it is not necessarily unjust that the rich man out of his abundance should pay one shilling in the pound, while only one penny is taken from those to whom a decrease of revenue will mean a deprivation of many of the small comforts of life. Such a graduated taxation is justifiable on these two conditions: first, that the sliding scale be really a fair one (though the difficulty here comes in of determining what is fair), and, secondly, that it is really levied for *bona fide* purposes of taxation (though here again comes in the new difficulty of providing a criterion to determine what such purposes are). But if the whole scheme is merely a cloak for partial confiscation, then it only adds hypocrisy to theft. If A's ability and industry have enabled him to lay aside a few hundred pounds for a rainy day, while B has squandered all he earned, it would be iniquitous under the name of graduated taxation to allow B to enjoy a half or even a smaller portion of the produce of A's store.

A thorough-going scheme of graduated death duties escapes some of these crucial objections, though it has difficulties and dangers of its own. In a "state of nature"—if that phrase is used for the impossible condition of human life from which even the rudiments of social and political organization are entirely wanting—when a man died, all his possessions would become *res nullius*, to be scrambled for among the first-comers, and to be borne off by the strongest or most cunning. In early times it is the family which determines how the deceased's property shall be divided. The peaceable possession of those who take either by bequest or by intestate succession, is at a later stage secured by the government. There is no such right apart from positive law; and ancient systems of jurisprudence have not always recognized either the right of testation or the right of blood relations to divide the inheritance. It is open for the State, then, to determine how far it will allow a man, with or without children, to exercise free rights of testation, and also how far it will allow the family in testate or intestate succession to absorb the whole of the wealth accumulated by the deceased in his lifetime. If the State thinks it expedient and just—which are, of course, exactly the aspects of the question on which it is difficult to decide—it may say to the heirs and successors of the man who leaves two millions behind him, " I take one million for the community and

leave the balance to you," and to the representatives of him
who leaves one million, " I take £30,000 for myself," and
so on, on whatever descending scale may be reckoned fair
and expedient.

Such a scheme has many and obvious difficulties in its
way ; but it could not be justly branded with the name of
confiscation, for the following reasons : In the first place, you
cannot take from a man what has never belonged to him ;
in the second place, without laying any emphasis on the fact
that the wealth of the deceased was accumulated through
the instrumentality of the community in which he lived,
it may be urged that it is only through the good offices of
law and government that the heirs and successors are
enabled peaceably to enter upon their inheritance, and that
therefore the State is justified in taking a part in payment
for its services in protecting the rest. It would be necessary,
however, that such a measure (even if all theoretical and
practical objections to it were successfully overcome) should
be entered upon very gradually, and that due notice should
be given of the intended changes so as to prevent undue
interference with the reasonable expectations of children or
other presumptive beneficiaries. Such a measure of reform
(if possible at all) would not only place in the hands of the
State a fund for carrying out the various ends for which it
exists, and which, for want of money, it is often unable to
fulfil, but would also help to keep within due limits a
danger to the national welfare which becomes every year
more threatening in the United States of America—if not
yet in Great Britain—from the vast accumulations of millions
in the hands of a few rich families.

The object of graduated death duties is not to produce
absolute equality, but only to ameliorate great inequalities
that threaten to grow so large as to menace the sovereignty
of the State itself.

It has been frequently pointed out that even an approximation to equality of material well-being is impossible,
however uniformly wealth may be distributed among individuals, as long as these are grouped in families, for the
man who has twelve children to support is not as rich as

his neighbour who has only one, and the child of squandering parents is not "equal" to the child of wise and frugal ones.

The claim to equality of happiness or the means of happiness may be considered merely as a phase of the claim for equality of wealth, so far as it has any definite meaning at all. It seems to be tacitly implied in the theories of the school of Bentham, in the "greatest happiness of the greatest number," where "each is to count for one, and nobody for more than one." Few faddists either of the individualistic or socialistic type are likely seriously to hold the government responsible for providing all its subjects with an equal amount of happiness, or with equal means for its attainment in a world where each individual must seek happiness in his own way.

The Declaration of Independence by the United States of America, incorporating the wisdom of Jean Jacques Rousseau into the primitive Puritan theology, holds "these truths to be self-evident, that all men are created equal, that they are endowed by their Creator with certain unalienable Rights, that among these are Life, Liberty, and the pursuit of Happiness." The equal right to pursue happiness is thus substituted for the equal right to obtain it. It would be beside the mark to estimate how far the laws of the United States have successfully realized this ideal; for the important point to note is its vagueness and impracticability. If it has any definite meaning, it must resolve itself into a claim for equal opportunities. Life is looked on as a race, and each child is entitled to a fair start with all the others.

When theorists have settled how far this is desirable and just, then the practical question will arise: What ought the government to do towards its advancement?

The whole question of the relations of government and legislation to the ideal of equality illustrates the dependence of political philosophy upon the results of all the other sciences. Much preliminary work has to be done before the theory of the State can take the matter up. Before Parliament can interfere it ought to have weighed the results of specialists in economics, sociology, and the science of right. It is for

the first-named to say how far the economic well-being of
the nation demands a more equal distribution of wealth. It
is for sociology to correct the too abstract conclusions of
political economy by showing the relation of mere material
wealth to all the other phases of social welfare, such as enjoyment, art, and virtue. It is for the science of right (in the
Kantian sense, which includes jurisprudence and ethics under
one conception) to determine how far the ideal can be attained
without violating the principles of truth and justice. Only
after all these have given their verdicts can political science
declare how far it is wise for government to interfere. It
is only after social well-being has been defined that statesmen
can step in as Individualists or Collectivists with their rival
schemes for its realization.

Those who hold the organic theory of society refuse to
assume with the Socialist that, *a priori*, governments are
bound to accept the sole responsibility for whatever is amiss
in the distribution of wealth, or with the Individualist that
the State's only duty is to let things drift on as best they
may. Indications indeed are not wanting that under the
present system of industry, we are moving towards a
"coming slavery," where, however, the slave-owner will not
be the State but the wealth of a few individuals.

The philosophic justification of property is that it is needed
for the development of personality.[1] Now, in certain diseased
conditions of society, wealth may defeat its own end by
crushing out the persons of the citizens instead of developing
them. When danger arises from this source, the legislature
in a civilized State is bound to interfere. Thus when the
old debtors' law was abused, imprisonment for debt had to
be abolished to free those who had become the slaves of the
proprietary rights of others pushed to excess. Similarly
where "trusts" or trade corporations insist on urging their
rights of property to extremities, the State may be compelled to step in, to prevent the reins of government being
dragged out of its own hands, only to be seized by industrial
associations representing either capital or labour, or perhaps
both.

[1] Cf. W Galbraith Miller's *Philosophy of Law*, Lecture v., and also p. 304.

Y

In flying from the extreme of individualistic indifference it is not necessary to rush to another, and to attempt to distribute all **property equally.** The wise course lies in the centre, in a reasonable extent of State interference judiciously applied.

Government *must* interfere if it can **further the** "**good**" of mankind—remembering always that that end combines the **universal** principles of right with those practical conditions **of a** healthy life of which happiness **is the outward sign. In** this aim, as in others, **it** is absurd to expect an **absolute** criterion by reference to which the legislature can at once know whether **or not** to interfere. A few practical suggestions may be made, however, in summing up the **results of the** discussion. (I.) **It is** quite possible, without **injustice, to** reduce **the excessive** inequalities of existing fortunes, by extending **the principles** already at work, such as the graduated **scheme of death** duties, or **even the** sliding scale of income **tax.** **No such** scheme ought, however, **to be** extended **so as to act as a cloak** for what is practically **con-fiscation.** There is a **danger in** introducing the principle at **all,** as it admits **so readily of abuse.** Prudence alone would dictate that all taxation **should stop** clearly short of such interference with private **property** as would destroy "the incentive of gain."

(II.) The ideal of "an equal start **in life,"** when once its vagueness and difficulty of realization **are clearly** grasped, is not without its value. All artificial restraints, whether the **creations of law or** of social arrangements and prejudices, ought to be **removed** to allow free play to every individual **to rise to such a** position in the State as he **is** fitted to fill. **He** should enjoy such opportunities of development as **may be** given him without injuring the rights of others. To express this ideal **by** the word "equality" is, however, **a** hindrance rather than **a help.** Children, despite the Declaration of Independence, **are not born** naturally equal. The race **is a handicap from the first. At** least three different views are possible **as** to what is the proper meaning of "an equal **start in life."** (*a*) The State may aim at giving equal advantages **by law to all** alike, both weak and strong; (*b*) it may consider that more should be done for the stupid boy than for his brighter brother, who needs it less; or (c) it may hold that artificial advantages should be proportionate to natural ones, and that therefore the best opportunities should go to those best able to use them.

Free education is the practical shape which this theory has recently taken in Great Britain. An uniform minimum of education is forced upon every child between certain ages. This is in reality far from securing to all "an equal start in life," for the stupid boy who is less able to benefit will not unnaturally receive less attention from his masters. Bursaries again are open to those who excel their fellows, and thus even a university education is within reach of a talented few, and will still further increase the inequalities of life by giving to him who already has. All this is contrary to the gospel of equality according to Rousseau, who maintains that " it is precisely because the force of circumstances tends always to destroy equality, that the force of legislation ought always to tend to maintain it."[1] To give effect to Rousseau's doctrine it would be necessary for the stupid child to receive twice as much education as the clever one.

(III.) The third practical suggestion is that the legislature (if dissatisfied with the present unequal distribution of the good things of this world, but yet unwilling to interfere with fortunes already amassed) should aim at so altering the economic conditions of commerce that it will be impossible in the future for one man to amass by speculation an amount of wealth greater a thousand-fold than that of his more industrious neighbour.

The law may be changed to meet the requirements of a more developed public opinion or more equitable national conscience so as effectually to prevent new accumulations of capital being made under the old conditions. Thus, if the opinion comes to prevail that the existing relations between capital and labour are iniquitous and pernicious, the duty will arise of changing them for the future by means of new legislative definitions of the respective rights of employers and workmen; but this would not justify

[1] *Contrat Social*, II., xi.

interference with fortunes **made under the** old system.   The question **of how** far such new **definition is** called **for** must be answered **on** the usual grounds of justice and expediency.

(IV.) The most important suggestion of **all** is that **it** is better to **awaken** the owners of property to **a due** sense **of** their responsibility than **to** endanger the stability of **the** State **by** unnecessarily attacking vested **interests.**   "More **good will be done,"** to quote **Professor Jowett,**[1] "by awakening in rich **men a sense of** the **duties of property,** than by the violation **of its rights."**   Inequality, according to the same authority, may **not be** altogether a bad thing even **for the poor;** for it cannot "be denied that great inequalities of property, by **giving a** stimulus to increased production, may give a larger **share of the goods of life to** the poor than could be **obtained by any system of** distribution however just."[2]

[1] Introduction to Aristotle's *Politics,* p. 28.   [2] *Ibid.,* p. 34.

CHAPTER XXIV.

THE STATE AND THE FAMILY.

AMONG the most prominent features of this last decade of the nineteenth century must be ranked the various processes working together for the disintegration of the family. The most obvious, though not perhaps the chief of these, is the movement for what is called the enfranchisement of women, of which the claim on behalf of wives as well as spinsters to equal political rights with men is one of the most familiar symptoms.

The social system of the past, throughout all its triumphs and its failures, has held fast to the principle that politics and the heated discussions they usually engender ought to be jealously excluded from marring the harmony of domestic life. The husband, as the acknowledged head of the family, has hitherto been entrusted with the political rights and duties deemed essential for the representation of the interests of his home in the councils of the nation. If politics and the family are brought into closer relation in the future, the results will probably be mixed. While the conservative desires to preserve the privacy and sanctity of home life, the advocate of change may urge that the acerbity and one-sidedness of political discussions would be softened by contact with the pure influences of the family. Much might doubtless be said on both sides, but the fear seems to be not unfounded that the adoption by two spouses of different political creeds accompanied by active electioneering efforts, would bring an element of discord into the sanctuary of home.

The possibility of a career for women independent of the vicissitudes of their husbands' lives opens up even a wider field for reflection. If married women are to aim at developing their own capacities for trade or literature, disturbing the monopoly hitherto held by men, it will be necessary for them to follow their careers into whatever social circles and parts of the world these summon them. Under the existing organization of society a wife is content, as a general rule, to subordinate her own personal inclinations as to place of abode and social surroundings to the requirements of her husband's business, to which he likewise has to sacrifice his own preferences for particular climates and localities. All minor considerations are planned in conformity with the movements of the bread-winner of the family. Now, if a woman also is to have a career of her own, one of three things must happen. She may follow a trade or profession as a pastime or as an auxiliary employment; she may force her husband to make the requirements of his business subservient to her own; or she must be prepared to separate from him when their careers summon them to different towns or countries. If the husband is engaged in cotton spinning in Lancashire, and the wife receives the offer of a professorship in Sydney or Cape Town, the prospects and perhaps the invested capital of one must be sacrificed to the ambition of the other to save the family from being broken up.

If marriage remains a tie "till death do us part," and human nature physical and moral does not materially change, married women cannot follow their careers like married men. A wife may enter tentatively on a line of her own, prepared to consider it as of merely secondary importance to her husband's labours, to be taken up or laid aside according as circumstances allow, leaving these, as at present, dependent to a great extent on the requirements of the business of the husband. This course is not likely to recommend itself to the more ardent among the advocates of a complete equality between the sexes; yet it seems the only logical solution of the difficulty, having regard to the interruptions which a married woman's business career must suffer, through her more onerous share in the toils inseparable from the rearing of a family.

If the woman is not willing to follow a career rather as a secondary than as a primary pursuit in life—rather under the *rôle* of an amateur than that of a professional—the disintegration of the family seems an inevitable consequence. A woman has the option of course of refraining from entering into the married state altogether, but if once this becomes the rule rather than the exception, the family would be saved from disintegration only by ceasing to exist. It is difficult to find to what extent "the subjection of women" may be removed or ameliorated in the future; just as it is hard to tell where a stone once set in motion will stop, but undoubtedly the legislature has already done much to readjust the relations of husbands and wives. One instance out of many may be referred to—the recent modifications of the law of property in both England and Scotland, which allow a wife to acquire and manage an estate in land or movables in practical independence of her husband's control.

The claim of women to extend the legitimate sphere of their influence beyond the little affairs of the home to the world of trade and the world of politics, is by no means the only aspect of the disintegration of the family. The institution of marriage itself is boldly attacked. All the wild modern theories as to freedom of relations between the sexes, the alleged injustice of marriage vows being permanently binding on either party desirous of breaking the tie, and the claims put forward to greater facilities of divorce, point to the break-up of family life. Again, advocates of the rights of children to rebel against parental control are not wanting. Boys and girls put forth claims to lead their own lives in their own way without let or hindrance. There have always been rebellious children at all stages of the world's progress; but the peculiar feature of to-day lies in the systematic nature of the revolt from authority, and in the attempt to justify it on sober scientific principles. It is claimed that even young children should not be biassed either one way or another by their parents and guardians. Each child should, it is said, be encouraged to develop himself according to his own nature, apart from the family traditions of politics, morals, or religion. He is to fulfil the law of his own being, free as far as possible from correction or reproof. Strangely enough, the individuals who put forth these claims to be relieved from the restraint of family life, are by no means prepared to renounce its advantages. While they shake themselves free from inherited traditions and beliefs, they usually claim, as an inalienable right to be received as a matter of course, and without any necessity of returning thanks, the best maintenance, education, and start in life which their family can possibly afford to them. The decay of reverence for parents is thus undoubtedly an important factor in the break-up of the family. A number of miscellaneous items might be dwelt upon, all pointing in the same direction. Thus when the State steps in to educate children it helps to diminish the dependence of the child on the father, while it removes the feeling of responsibility of the latter for the welfare of his offspring. Then, the spirit of unrest and cosmopolitanism of the present day is not without an important bearing. The monotony of family life is irksome to a generation that loves excitement. The desire for travel and change of sensation in parents who can afford it, makes them more ready to entrust the training of their children to hired service, and to send them at an early age to school. In America, again, the difficulty of obtaining domestic servants has extended to great proportions the boarding-house system, which is quite incompatible with true family life.

These tendencies—and more could be added—show that the family is being attacked both from the inside and from the outside.

It is maintained, and probably with truth, that some of these features are merely temporarily antagonistic to the true unity of the family—that they break it up relatively, not absolutely, and in order to consolidate it again on a nobler and more equitable footing. Speaking of one of these tendencies, Professor Flint has well said:[1] "The movement towards securing to women equal rights with men, and free scope to exercise all their faculties, although some have regarded it as likely to endanger and disorganize the

[1] *Socialism*, p. 286.

family, really tends directly and powerfully to its consolidation and true development. It favours the formation of a better class of women. It contributes largely to increase the number of women who are not necessitated to enter into loveless marriages." This is undoubtedly true, but even the forces which tend to build up the nobler family of the future help to break up the family of to-day. To that extent their immediate effect is to be deplored, though the present loss should be discounted by the future gain.

Other of the elements at work, however, seem essentially, and not merely relatively, hostile to the family, and these are necessarily evil.

When we inquire into the reasons of all this decay of the family coincident with the great advance of science and civilization, it is not difficult to form a conclusion.

The family is being attacked from two opposite sides at once. Socialistic and individualistic influences alike are sapping its foundations. There is a sense, of course, in which every family, like every society and every State, must include both of these influences. There is a true Socialism in the community of interests and comforts and sympathies of home life; while, at the same time, the family is the sanctuary that protects the individual at all times, and especially during the tender years of his immaturity and growth, from the hostile influences of the outside world. Society would crush the immature individual if the family did not guard him, and thus secure the very basis of Individualism from overthrow.

Abstract Socialism and abstract Individualism are, however, alike the enemies of the family. Here, perhaps, the weakest spot in both systems is laid bare. Each extreme theory fails to solve the problems involved in the existence of the family. Each of them is unable to find an adequate place for domestic life in its ideal system. To take only one problem, the relations of a young child to society cannot be explained exclusively on the lines of the Socialist or on those of the Individualist. The latter claims for the father the right as against the community to educate and train his

own child as he chooses. The State has no title to interfere in any way. The father, who is responsible for the
very existence of the child, and who has its best interests
presumably at heart, is surely the best judge of what is good
for it. To push this doctrine to extremes, however, would be
to reduce the child to the level of its father's chattel or slave.
This was the original theory of the older Roman law, and
apparently the logical outcome of the rights of the father on
a purely individualistic basis. But the child too is an individual, potentially if not actually, even at the earliest moment
of its existence. The Individualist must preserve him from the
tyranny of his father, taking care that development of the one
being is not stunted or dwarfed by the overshadowing of the
other. The child must be protected in the rights of his nascent
individuality as well as the father in those of his maturity.
The budding genius of the son must not be crushed out by the
narrow prejudices of the father. If he cannot do without a
guardian he must at least be allowed to choose one after his
own heart. Thus the claims of the father and child become
mutually irreconcilable on a purely individualistic basis.
The logical absurdity of the position lies in this, that on the
lines of an abstract division between the unit and the
group there is a stage somewhere in the development of the
child when he can be properly described neither as possessing
nor as wanting an individuality. Some attempt may be made
to disguise the difficulty by fixing by law arbitrary ages at
which the child gains partial emancipation from the *patria
potestas*. But this is merely a make-shift, and affords no solution.

If an equally extreme Socialism tries to escape this
difficulty by swallowing up both individual and family
in the State, it does so only to fall into other dilemmas
peculiar to itself, which are absolutely insurmountable on its
own principles. It is perhaps possible for the State, by the
exercise of an unlimited and despotic force, to compel all
parents to hand over their children to an administrative
department or Board of the executive government whose
business would be to rear and educate them. Such a scheme,
however absurd it may seem, is exactly what was proposed
by Plato for his ideal republic.

In this way a socialistic government might make secure its tyrannical sway over the minds and bodies of children as soon as they are born; but it could never get beyond the individualistic basis on which they are ushered into the world. It might be partially successful in smothering all motherly instincts in its women; but it could never get beyond the fact of motherhood itself—that no man can come into the community except on an individualistic basis as the individual son of an individual mother. But the philosophic or logical difficulties (great as they are) are less than the practical ones. The family proper cannot exist under a regime of pure Socialism, any more than under one of pure Individualism. All consistent and thorough-going attempts in either direction have begun by annihilating the family. Yet, as the existence of individuals and of States in the future is dependent on the population of the world, each of them has been forced to substitute some caricature of the family in its place. Professor Flint, in giving a partial assent to the hostile criticism passed by Socialists on the structure of the family as at present constituted, maintains that the only substitutes offered have faults a thousand-fold more radical and horrible. When " we ask them how they propose to get rid of, or at least to lessen, the evils which they have indicated, they have virtually no other answer to give us than that they would introduce evils far worse—the absorption of the family in the community, free love, the separation of spouses at will, transference of children from the charge of their parents to that of the State."[1]

Some of these results, it is interesting to note, come strangely near the ideals reached by purely individualistic thinkers. Both schools logically require to annihilate the family; and this is impossible in practice. The result under either regime would be not to crush it out, but simply to degrade it.

The family is historically the germ from which the State developed. It is still the ordinary source through which the ranks of citizenship are filled. "The three institutions

[1] *Socialism*, p. 283.

of which every man is born a member are the Family, the
State, and the Church.   Fly to whatever corner of the earth
he chooses," it has been said, "he is still a member of a
Family, a citizen of a State, and a subject of an Almighty
Power." [1]   However the atheist or sceptic may question
the necessary though unrecognized connection with a church,
he cannot deny that no man is born except through the
agency of the family, if not in its noble purity, then in
some mutilated and degraded form.

Marriage and the family are under the special protection of the government.   Is this as it should be?   Ought
the law to take cognizance of such matters at all?   Undoubtedly it should; for the State cannot, if it would, leave
alone the family which is its prime factor and in a sense
its source.   In four directions, in especial, are the interests
of the two bound together: (1) population; (2) education;
(3) social status; and (4) distribution of wealth.

(1) The question of population depends on that institution
which commands the gates of life.   Even on that purely
industrial side of the State to which Socialists are apt to look
chiefly if not exclusively, production, distribution, and exchange are only one half of the problem, of which population
forms the other.   Material prosperity varies directly with the
amount of wealth, and inversely with the population.   The
law of wages, as expounded by Malthus and Ricardo, by Marx
and Lassalle, turns chiefly on this question of population.
Government, then, by encouraging or discouraging marriage,
may vitally affect the welfare of the State.   If the State
refused its countenance to every form of permanent union,
and at the same time undertook the free education, training,
and maintenance of all children of transitory connections, the
number of births would probably increase in an appalling ratio
to the number of existing citizens.   Such fluctuations in the
population of a State necessarily affect all its interests intimately.   The England of the future might for want of citizens
become too weak to protect itself from invasion.   On the
other hand, the resources of the country might be unable
to sustain the advent of an enormous horde of children,

[1] Hoffman, *The Sphere of the State*, p. 207.

especially during the time of their helplessness or non-age.

(2) The whole moral and intellectual training of society depends on the family. In the earliest and most impressionable age of every individual he is subjected to the discipline and example of home. The citizen begins life as a member of a family. "The family," as has been well said, "is the nursery of the State. . . . The character of the family determines the character of the State."[1] Under a system of Mormonism like that recently abolished in Utah, or under a regime of polygamy like that of Turkey, the training of the citizen is entirely different from what it would be if monogamy prevailed. Nor can it be denied that in the long run, whatever system rules, it must be established or tacitly sanctioned by law. Either the law will be altered to suit the practice, or the practice will mould itself into conformity with the law.

(3) Wisely or unwisely, public opinion places a stigma on the offspring of parents not united in wedlock in the usual way recognized by society. Wisely or unwisely, the State gives its authority towards strengthening this praiseworthy sentiment or silly prejudice of society. It does this by bestowing its special countenance on those who are married according to the legal methods, and by specially favouring their children in questions of succession and also of such social distinctions as are regulated by the State. In these ways the State favours the formation of permanent unions and discourages all such as are branded by popular thought as clandestine or immoral. No society is likely to exist wherein the law looks with equal favour on the life-long marriage of one man with one woman, as upon polygamy, polyandry, or free love. A State where "religious equality" is the rule is at any rate possible, but a State where morality and immorality in the family life are equal before the law is barely conceivable. The Anglican Church may be disestablished, but not the monogamic family. When political and social influences are becoming more and more closely blended, as is the tendency in England at the present day,

[1] **Prof.** Hoffman, *The Sphere of the State*, p. 207.

the structure of the family cannot fail to affect materially the structure of the State.

(4) The family further affects the State by influencing the diffusion of wealth and regulating the distribution of property. Great fortunes are sometimes amassed in a life-time; but more often they are accumulated only in the course of two or three generations. In any case the inequalities of wealth would be materially reduced if such fortunes were always scattered at the death of the individual who amassed them. As it is, when a millionaire dies without leaving a will, the members of his family inherit his possessions in certain proportions defined by the law of intestate succession. It is only through the action of the commonwealth, then, that a dead man's capital is secured to his heirs. This right of inheritance reacts upon the State. It influences the distribution of riches among the ranks of its citizens, and this is a noteworthy factor in that evil which Socialism is chiefly anxious to overcome. Unless the State made some legislative provision for the settlement of disputes as to the succession to an intestate individual—in addition to allowing such rights of testation as seem good to it—the relatives of the deceased would require to settle the matter by club-law or superior cunning. The State is under the necessity of declaring either for or against the right of testation generally: if it does not regulate the division of the dead man's goods, it will simply leave those included in the will and those passed over to settle the matter by force.

The State, therefore—as appears from these four instances —cannot leave the family alone, however desirous it may be to do so.

In abandoning a policy of *laissez faire* towards this most important social institution, what attitude ought the legislature to adopt? It is impossible to prescribe a complete code of rules equally applicable to all States at every stage of their history; but a few general suggestions may be made.

(1) The State must rule every institution within it; therefore it can never allow the customs or institutions or arrangements of the family to set its central authority at

defiance. Whatever rights are conceded, and however **much these are based on** "nature," in any one or more **of** the **many meanings of** that word, natural family rights **must never be made** absolute against **the** sovereign rights of the State. Whatever sphere is fenced **off for** the family with its domestic affections and sympathies **to** regulate, the government must never, either in theory **or in** practice, abdicate its ultimate right of interference and coercion, and must never allow any customs **to** arise likely to impede its free exercise, when required, of these reserved **powers.** The limits of family life within which **the** State does not **interfere,** by legal restrictions or otherwise, must be defined **by** Parliament in making laws, and **by the courts in** interpreting **them.**

(2) **The government** ought scrupulously to respect **the** *privacy* **of the family.** Legal restraints should be carefully regulated with a **view to** strengthen and supplement rather than to **weaken and** supersede natural affections and the duties that are spontaneously performed as the highest form of domestic happiness. Fatherly love should be allowed to act according to its own promptings, **and** in such varied channels as it tends naturally **to make for itself.** Only when these natural affections have failed signally to act, is **it wise for** the State to step in **with strong** compulsion.

(3) A State **with** political institutions planned on a rational basis need have no jealousy of the family. On the contrary, the **true interests of the** two never clash. It is only when it is sought to construct the constitution on extreme individualistic or extreme socialistic lines that a collision with **the** family is inevitable. In a healthy social and political life, where the individual and the State are not conceived **as two** antagonistic bodies, the end of the family is perfectly **in** harmony with the common ends of all the citizens and **of the** body politic.

(4) When the **family,** however, fails spontaneously to **attain** its ideal, or such **a** minimum of approximation towards **it as** the present state of society and civilization demands, **then the** government **must be authorized to** interfere. An **ideal family should** have no conflicting interests within its

bounds. While this is too high a level for almost any group of sinful individuals to reach, an ordinary well-conducted family should arrange its differences and disputes amicably within itself, without either the use of violence by one member to another or an appeal to any outside authority. Where this is impossible, however, the State must take the matter up, and arbitrate between them. Thus the government must protect the individual from the tyranny of family authority, even when that authority is exercised within the proper sphere of home influences as defined or tacitly approved by the law. Parents must be prevented from making an unreasonable or cruel use of the powers vested in them. Even in such cases, however, it is not always easy to say how far the law is justified in interfering, for acts of parental tyranny may often be enforced by means in themselves perfectly lawful, for example, by the threat to disinherit a disobedient child. The law of Scotland affords children some measure of protection even here; for each son or daughter has a right to a share of the father's movable or personal estate, which cannot be defeated by any exercise of testamentary powers. The law of England contains no similar provision.

The State is wisely abstemious in the exercise of its rights of interference either in favour of the family group against the undutiful individual, or to protect him against the group. In particular it is chary of meddling between husband and wife; although such a policy is sometimes provocative of hardship in individual cases, as where a wife has difficulty in obtaining protection from her husband's ill-usage unless that is of a pronounced and indisputable nature. Here, as elsewhere, the convenience or even the happiness of individuals must be sacrificed to the good of the commonwealth.

(5) The State must fix, either definitely or vaguely, how far the duty of education and of moral and physical training lies within the province of the family. It may do this in many ways—by determining for example: (a) that up to a certain age the family trains the child, and then gives place to agents appointed by the State; (b) that all education is primarily a family matter, whatever the age of the pupil; or

(c) as some Socialists hold, that all training, physical, intellectual, and moral, falls within the functions of the government. If any conflict of opinion should arise, it is undoubtedly for the State itself to decide, and not for either the parent or the child.

One of the chief functions of the family is undoubtedly to care for its children in their early youth. The influence of the training thus received will be subsequently seen in every phase of the national existence. "The first seven years of life are," in the opinion of Comte,[1] "the most decisive, because a mother's discipline lays so firm a foundation that the rest of life is seldom able to affect it."

If the legislature, after mature reflection, concluded this maternal influence to be on the whole an evil to the true welfare of the individual and the State, it would become its duty to suppress it. If, on the other hand, it is thought to be the best training for a child up to a certain age, it is the duty of the government to ward off (forcibly, if need be) all influences hostile to the mother's influence during that period. It is equally open to the State to interfere either positively or negatively with the later processes of education with the view of bringing the boy or girl more or less closely or exclusively under the care and influence of home. A statute might be passed that all children up to twelve or fifteen, or even eighteen years of age, should be educated by private tuition at home, or on the contrary, that all children after their tenth or eighth or sixth birthdays should be sent to boarding-schools, or, lastly, that day-schools should be the only legal form of education. The first plan means a complete subjection to home influences; the second a complete break in them; and the third a combination of the care of the family with the harder training of the outside world. While it is certain that the first system would tend to make boys effeminate, the practice of sending very young children to boarding-schools is communistic in its tendencies, though not necessarily collectivist. The world is made up of men and women, and contains hostile interests and home sympathy, so that to cut off a boy at once from family life

---

[1] Cited by Professor Flint, *Socialism*, p. 282.

z

and female influence is to deprive him of one-half of the world in which God has placed him ; while to confine him to the enervating atmosphere of too comfortable a home is to deprive him of the other.   On these principles, the day-school, combining home life with school discipline, realizes the golden mean which is the safest guide in the practical affairs of life. However this may be, the State wisely refrains from prescribing an uniform system of education, and leaves each family to decide under which of the three systems its children shall be reared.   It merely makes provision that all of them shall be educated somehow.

The law as to very young children is somewhat different, for the mother is confirmed by positive law in her natural right to act as sole guardian of her offspring during the years when they are absolutely dependent on the care of others. The attitude of the State towards little children, indeed, illustrates well how it is possible to avoid both extremes of Collectivism and Individualism.   It secures the full advantages of government control without resorting to government management, and of wise laws without arbitrary interference. Mothers are left to rear their babies as they individually think best, within reasonable limits.   The State does not institute a central administrative department charged with the duty of rearing them, nor authorize local authorities to interfere.   It does not prescribe a system of nursing, or lay down strict rules as to diet and hygiene.   It wisely realizes that nascent individualities will have almost infinitely different requirements, and that the individual parent is best suited to discover these and minister to them.   So far its policy is individualistic.   With this *laissez faire* attitude, it may without inconsistency combine the advantages of Socialism by a rigorous system of State control, kept in the background, but well within call whenever the natural duties of the parent are grossly neglected.   Statutes may be passed authorizing health lectures in every district, paid for by the community ; compelling vaccination ; prohibiting unnaturally severe chastisements ; and punishing breaches of parental duty.

(6) The management of the property of the spouses, and its

distribution when the family is broken up by death or divorce, are other matters which the State is required to regulate. Until quite recently the law of almost every European country handed over the wife's property to her husband during the marriage in a wholesale way. In Scotland and elsewhere, where the principles of the Roman Law prevailed, the real nature of this transaction was disguised under the specious name of a "*communio bonorum.*" The legal fiction held that all property which originally belonged to either spouse was after marriage the common possession of both; but the practice was very different from the theory. During the husband's life he had complete control over this so-called common fund, which he could alienate or consume in any way he chose, quite irrespective of the wife's wishes; while at his death it went to his representatives and not to hers. Such share as the widow got was taken by her as relict of the deceased, and not in her own right at all. In both England and Scotland this state of things has been altered, and the law now secures to the wife the exclusive property in her own effects, in addition to allowing her a share in her husband's estate at his death. Whatever plan has been adopted, it has always been the State acting through its ordinary legislature which has defined the respective rights of the spouses. It would be interesting to know whether the individualistic theorist would resent this as an unwarranted extension of State interference, and, if so, what better manner of settling the regulation of property within the family he would be prepared to substitute. Apart from law, the more selfish and arrogant of the two spouses would probably always usurp the control. The private means of both would be controlled by the more masterful or the more artful. The division of the family property among the children on the decease of the parents is an even more vital matter, in which it is difficult to see how an arrangement could be arrived at without the powerful intervention of positive law. The influence of the law of testate and of intestate succession on the unequal distribution of wealth in the State has been already mentioned.

(7) The last aspect of the relations between the State and the family is the most important of all. Has law any right

to intervene in the formation or dissolution of the latter ? Should the State take any part in marriages, and should it permit divorces ?

The extreme individualistic view is that all relations between the sexes should be treated as ordinary civil contracts between two individuals who have a perfect right to make any arrangement, temporary or permanent, which commends itself to both of them. On this theory the State has really no concern in the matter more than it has in a contract for the sale of a house, or a contract of insurance. Yet, in either of these latter cases, the law does interfere in many ways. It will not allow one of the parties to use fraud or force to coerce the free consent of the other. After the contract has been concluded, with all necessary legal formalities, it will insist on its terms being observed, as long as this is possible without violating law.

Even Individualists, then, would allow the government to interest itself to the same extent in the contract of marriage. They hold that the law should prevent either party being forced to marry, or induced to do so by fear, fraud, or essential error, but that, when the bargain is once struck, the government should force either spouse to observe the exact terms of the original contract. They might further concede that, where the bargain was left incomplete or ambiguous, the law might lay down presumptions as to the supposed intention of parties, subject always to amendment on the production of contrary evidence. They might even allow, for the convenience of all concerned, that certain forms of evidence of the ceremony should be required for certain purposes, as, for example, that contracts of marriage should be in writing, just as is at present required for contracts with respect to real property. Some of them might even go so far as to concede to the government a right to establish a register of such marriages, provided no one was compelled to make use of it who objected to do so.

Even ordinary contracts—of sale, hire, or insurance, for example—are not merely private arrangements between two persons. The State is tacitly a party to every lawful agreement, which it permits and enforces when called on. Every valid contract when analyzed contains four elements or moments: (*a*) the persons contracting; (*b*) their mutual consent; (*c*) the State, without whose express or implied recognition all idea of *legal* obligation would be absent; (*d*) the approval or at least toleration by the State of the terms agreed on.[1] Every legal agreement is in a sense both a private and a public contract. Under the latter aspect the State has a right to interfere in what concerns itself.

But the share thus taken by the State is not sufficient in the case of marriage, which is not only the most important of all agreements, but is essentially *sui generis*, because its chief object is the bringing of new individualities into the world. It prevents the extinction of the State by the gradual operation of death.

The law is thoroughly justified in imposing more stringent regulations on marriage than on any other form of agreement. It is not impossible to justify this on a purely individualistic basis, for the individualities of unborn children have rights that call for intervention. Children ought not to be summoned into existence under such conditions, physical, moral, and intellectual, as to render life a burden to them. It is upon the plea of vindicating the rights of such helpless individuals that the State's strongest claim to interfere is grounded.

As far as the fact of marriage goes, legal regulations should be entirely negative, not positive. "Marriage cannot be directly enforced," says Bluntschli, "because the freedom and will of the parties are essential to it."[2] Most people will be prepared to give a hearty assent to this, while they reject the further opinion of Bluntschli that all "restraints put upon marriage" by law "are prompted by an unsound condition of society," and to modify his statement that "to make marriage conditional on the arbitrary consent of the State is an unjustifiable infringement of individual rights." Of course, all "arbitrary" restraints are bad; but to prove an interference unjustifiable you require to prove that it *is* arbitrary or unnecessary, or both.

[1] Cf. W. Galbraith Miller's *Philosophy of Law*, p. 211.
[2] *Theory of the State*, p. 187.

The only difficulty is as to what constitutes a sufficient reason. Many men argue that the law should prevent all marriages likely to deteriorate the race, including those of near relatives, or of those who are criminals or drunkards or are afflicted with incurable or hereditary disease of mind or body. But this ground is always combined with another— the individual rights or happiness of the children of the marriage. " The State is the only power that can in any effective way guard the natural rights of unborn generations." [1]

Undoubtedly the State ought to continue to do what it has always done in civilized communities—absolutely refuse to recognize marriages wherever it sees sufficient grounds for interference.

It must always exercise some extent of control over marriages. It is a matter of degree. Each extreme must be avoided. Thus the law must neither force all its citizens of a marriageable age to enter into the bonds of matrimony, nor yet emulate the example of some communistic societies and forbid it altogether. Two intermediate lines of policy are open. The law may define the only terms upon which two individuals can marry at all, or it may leave each pair to make their own contract exactly as they please. In the early centuries of the Christian era the regulation of marriages was handed over to the Church, and the formalities essential to the union of wedlock were made a religious sacrament. At present the State treats the question of marriage very much as it treats that of an established church. It forces no one to marry. The confirmed bachelor is not even taxed by the State. He can stay outside the pale of married life if he choose, just as the Methodist need not attend the Established Church unless so inclined. Similarly the law tolerates, if it does not encourage, certain other forms of quasi-marriage, just as it tolerates other forms of religious worship, or even atheistic associations. It does not however tolerate connections repugnant to the moral sense of the community. It forbids marriages between near relatives and sternly represses bigamy, which it not only stigmatizes as immoral but punishes as criminal.

[1] Hoffman, *The Sphere of the State*, p. 211.

The consistent Individualist labours under the necessity of objecting on principle to two features in this existing order of things. He ought to forbid the State to interfere with the free right of any subjects to marry if they choose. If marriage lies outside the province of government, the law has no right to prevent even bigamy or polygamy, or unions between near relatives. On the same assumption it is wrong for the law to put a premium, as it were, on the orthodox or established form of union between the sexes. Why, it might be asked, should the State give special encouragement to those citizens to adopt the sentiments and practices on the marriage question which happen to suit the majority for the time being? Why should the wife receive more rights and protection than "The Woman who Did"? Why should the children of the latter be cut off from an equal share in the intestate succession to their father's estate? If the State is an association for the protection of liberty and property, the conclusion is obvious.

Most people will, however, apart from special theories, consider that the State is wise in laying down an uniform marriage law for the whole nation; in assuming that all respectable people will conform to it; and in adjusting the rights of members of the family upon this assumption. There can be no doubt, on the principles laid down in this Essay, that the State has the right and the duty to make such regulations for marriage as seem to itself to conduce most directly to its own ultimate end. Experience seems to have proved that an uniform law encouraging wedded life on the old basis of "for better or worse, till death do us part" in the long run contributes most to the welfare of the State, and to the "greatest happiness of the greatest number," and more particularly to the peace of mind of those who (however unwilling to admit it) most need the protection of the law—women. The revolt of a certain modern and probably limited type of woman against the family law is a rebellion against a system which has been framed to protect her weakness from abuse.

The State is justified in prescribing the form of the contract of marriage, then, as well as in forbidding unfit individuals to enter on the relationship at all. It is justified further in making that form in essentials the same for all—in not allowing optional systems. It fixes, then, the main terms of the only contract between the sexes which it recognizes as legal. It leaves individuals free, however, by written contract of marriage, to regulate certain important though subordinate details, especially those connected with money matters. Where the privileges of private contract are not exercised, the law provides a scheme which regulates these relations, to which spouses are presumed to have tacitly consented in the absence of express stipulation to the contrary.

After marriage is entered into, the law still retains the right to interfere whenever the necessity arises. Bluntschli lays down the rule that "the State cannot properly interfere with the private relations of man and wife," and then proceeds to enunciate a number of exceptions which it seems impossible to vindicate without overturning the basis upon which the rule rests, such, for example, as that "it may punish breaches of conjugal fidelity."

Now this is to reverse the natural order of things. The rule is that the State *may* interfere whenever and wherever it thinks there is a necessity, and of this it is sole judge. It must protect, if necessary, the wife from her husband's ill-usage or *vice versa*; but it should do so in such a way as least to interfere with the spontaneous performance of mutual duties by the spouses. The qualification of the rule, then, is that it is wise to interfere as little as possible. The law is slow to interfere between man and wife. Until quite recently English law upheld the right of the husband to the assistance of the State in compelling a wife to return under his roof.

The important question of divorce has still to be considered. Some Individualists would have all marriages perfectly free, so that the spouse who got tired of the other, or met a new mate more to his or her liking, would be entitled at once to break up the partnership, on giving perhaps a week's notice, and probably on making some small pecuniary compensation to the deserted spouse where that seemed advisable. Others would hold that, while one of the contracting parties cannot dissolve it against the wish of the other, marriage may be annulled by the mutual consent of the two individuals chiefly interested, while the State has no right to say a word on the subject.

The principles already explained leave no doubt that the State has something to say in the matter, has indeed the chief say. It is perfectly within its rights in placing a complete veto on all divorces or in handing over the regulation of the matter either to the Church courts or the civil courts to determine each individual case, either on its merits or in accordance with rules laid down by the legislature for that purpose. It has a right, in fine, to treat the question of divorce in any way it considers best suited to further its own highest interests, in which, of course, the interests of every individual are necessarily involved. This right needs no justification apart from the sovereignty of the State; but the use made of the right requires to be justified on grounds of morality, experience, and expediency.

Such grounds are chiefly four: (i.) Where one spouse has entered into a family relationship, understanding that it was for life, and has sacrificed all other interests and means of livelihood to fulfil his or her part of that contract, the State is more than justified in forbidding the other spouse lightly to refuse adherence to its original terms. This assumes, of course, that these terms were clearly understood originally. Faith must always be kept. (ii.) Even apart from contract or quasi-contract, a man may be forced to fulfil obligations beyond what he promised. The weak and confiding must be protected against the strong and designing. If an ignorant and inexperienced girl were induced on marrying to agree that her husband should have the option of renouncing the tie, the law might well interfere and set aside that part of the bargain. (iii.) The rights of children have to be considered. (iv.) The State has to protect itself from disintegration by the weakening of the family tie.

These reasons must be weighed by the State in considering any proposed amendment of the law of divorce, either in the direction of greater freedom or of greater restraint. It is not necessary here to pronounce a definite opinion either way.

It is sufficient to assert that the State has a right absolutely to prohibit divorce under any circumstances if it thinks fit.

One aspect of the socialistic idea has a noble element—the conception of the State itself as one great family. Here the aspiration is to extend the sphere of the domestic affections to embrace the whole nation, and so to make sympathy take the place of competition, and realize the reign of fraternity. In abolishing the natural family, however, the original sphere and the source of all such brotherly affections, it is to be feared rather that they will die altogether than bear transplanting to an alien soil so unsuited to their growth. The idea of brotherhood, however, as a watchword for members of one State is a very noble one. The only difficulty is as to the means of realizing it. Communists, in seeking to establish an universal reign of fraternity on earth, may end in annihilating it completely.

Fraternity, as an ideal of revolutionary politics, is not confined to professed Socialists. It is the third part of the composite motto of "Liberty, Equality, Fraternity," which has played so wide a part in history. Two criticisms suggest themselves. In the first place, the idea of Fraternity is entirely inconsistent with those of Liberty and Equality as these are currently understood. In the second place, in limiting the selected watchword to only one of the family relationships, it is doubtful whether the one chosen should not have been rather that of paternity, as the father is the head and chief bond of the family circle, and from him flow both authority and practical care for those who cannot protect themselves. In framing an ideal picture of the universe as a vast territory peopled by one great family, it seems arbitrary to choose only the relationship between brother and brother, excluding that between father and child, or husband and wife. At the bottom of the selection lies, of course, the huge assumption—the fallacy that vitiates many false systems of politics, both individualistic and socialistic—that all individuals are equally able to care for themselves, and therefore need only the sympathy and love of a brother, not the guidance and care of a father.

CHAPTER XXV.

THE STATE AND EDUCATION.

THE child comes into the world a bundle of undeveloped potentialities, void of experience and thought. The environment and external circumstances necessary for the growth of his mind and body are all supplied by the State. This is true, although not all nor even the chief part of them are imparted to the child directly by the officials of the government or by the laws or other organs of the State. The immediate environment depends on the influence of the family and of other institutions and agencies included in and controlled by the State. The child may have "innate ideas" in the sense of that *a priori* element which is one of the prerequisites of all conscious existence ; but the equally necessary *a posteriori* element can be got only from experience; and the sphere of the State, or of various parts of the State, is the only school where experience is possible for him. He is born into the commonwealth, and from the day of his birth the rights of citizenship, which he cannot actually enjoy till he has acquired full age, are held in trust for him by the State. It is true that it is the family whose influences at first surround him, moulding his earliest tendencies and aspirations after its traditions, but the family itself would be empty of content except for what flows into it from society and the State. The community as a whole, then, is the environment of the individual. It is the State which fills him with its own ideas and moulds him after its own pattern. The English youth grows up with habits and ideas quite absent in the Zulu or even in the Frenchman. Allowing all due claims for heredity—though this too has been indirectly supplied by the State through ancestors who were themselves its members—his environment has made him what he is.

The State then—using the word in its widest sense— puts its stamp on the young individuality before he has reached manhood and acquired the ability to choose his own surroundings. Willingly or unwillingly, it educates the individual and so has a terrible responsibility thrust upon its shoulders. The young mind as well as the young body is thrown upon its care during the important and impressionable years fated to mould the development of an immortal soul for time and for eternity. This trust, burdensome and disquieting as it is, is yet one which the State dare not decline.

Its duty to the young cannot be brushed aside or lightly treated. But it has also a duty to itself. In each helpless child lies a future citizen who will form an organic portion of the commonwealth, and may exercise a deep and lasting influence on its destinies. All children cannot become great statesmen, but all great statesmen once were children.

On these two grounds the State has both a right and a duty to include the education of the young within its proper province. Indeed it must educate whether it will or no. The only question is whether it will do so consciously or unconsciously, systematically or at random, well or ill. Government need not undertake the work of education, but the supreme legislative sovereign is forced to assume some attitude towards that all-important question.

There are three positions, any one of which Parliament may adopt. (I.) It may repudiate all direct responsibility, leaving each child to scramble for itself. (II.) It may compel parents to educate their offspring at their own expense. (III.) It may enforce education upon all and pay for it out of the national purse. Each of these three courses has its adherents. They must be examined in order.

I. The theory that the government and the law should leave the child alone in the matter of education is supported on behalf both of the family and of the individual. It is urged that the community has no right to interfere with the *family*, and that education is essentially a family matter. It is alternatively maintained that education is an *individual* matter, with which the government cannot meddle without unduly interfering with the rights of its citizens.

The arguments against these contentions have already been given in part. (1) The State has a duty to all children born within its pale, which it cannot shake off. (2) It has also a duty to itself to rear them as future good citizens. It has the most vital interest in the matter, for early education may determine whether a boy develops into a pickpocket or a "pillar of society." Whether a child is destined to become prime minister or a silent nameless voter, it is important that he should be duly trained to the fit exercise of his share in the power of the democracy. The nature and extent of his education will stamp his whole life, and thus materially affect the welfare of the nation and of every individual member of it. (3) The State cannot plead that the training of its future members is no part of the purposes for which it exists, since these purposes include the welfare and advancement of all.[1] Nor can it plead with relevancy that its government is not suited for the task, for it is not necessary that it should perform all its functions by its ordinary executive officials.

It thus seems tolerably plain that the State cannot, without derogating from its own dignity and neglecting one of its clearest duties, disown all responsibility for the training of its future members. "The ultimate control of and responsibility for the education of the people rests with the State."[2] We may agree with this sentiment without involving ourselves in the absurdity that the members of the Cabinet must personally superintend the teaching of the young, or that the legislature should appoint all the schoolmasters.

Though the impossible attitude of *laissez faire* towards education is associated with an individualistic philosophy, it does not follow that all Individualists object to the State

---

[1] Cf. F. C. Montague, *Limits of Individual Liberty*, p. 140. "The true function of the State is to make the most of the citizen."

[2] Prof. Hoffman, *The Sphere of the State*, p. 36.

superintending the training of its youth. The difference between the abstract theory of Von Humboldt and his practice in the concrete world of statesmanship has often been emphasized.

In his treatise on the *Sphere and Duties of Government* no principle is more categorically asserted than the necessity the State is under of observing an absolutely negative attitude towards education.

"The grand leading principle," he says,[1] "towards which every argument hitherto unfolded in these pages directly converges, is the absolute and essential importance of human development in its richest diversity, but national education, since at least it presupposes the selection and appointment of some one instructor, must always promote a definite form of development, however careful to avoid such an error. And hence it is attended with all those disadvantages which we before observed to flow from such a positive policy; and it only remains to be added that every restriction becomes more directly fatal when it operates on the moral parts of our nature—that if there is one thing more than another which absolutely requires free activity on the part of the individual it is precisely education, whose object it is to develop the individual." A few pages further on he reiterates, even more emphatically, the conclusion forced upon him by the logical necessities of his individualistic position. "I have only to conclude from what has been argued here, that national education seems to me to lie wholly beyond the limits within which political agency should properly be confined."[2]

Such was the solution given to the world by Von Humboldt the thinker in 1791; in 1808 he was appointed Minister of Worship and Public Instruction in the Prussian Reform Ministry, and the memory of Von Humboldt the statesman is kept green by association with the University of Berlin, founded by him as the crown of a complete system of national education, in the zealous furtherance of which he expended the best energies of the busiest years of his life.

With John Stuart Mill inconsistency takes a somewhat different form. He advocates boldly a theory of education

[1] P. 65.   [2] P. 71.

logically incompatible with the individualistic basis of the
rest of his philosophy. " The State," it appears from the
Essay on Liberty,[1] " should require and compel the **education**
up to a certain **standard of every** human being **who is born**
its citizen "—truly a **wise conclusion, but one** which it is
hard **to** reconcile with the general principles of a *laissez faire*
philosophy. Both the English Locke and **the** French Physio-
crats of the eighteenth century **have indeed** tried hard to
reconcile the limitation of the sphere **of** government to the
protection of liberty and property with a scheme **of** national
and enforced education.[2] Surely **this is** possible only by
straining the function of protecting liberty and property **to**
such undue proportions as would authorize any conceivable
course of coercion.

All the old individualistic arguments are brought by other
writers **to** bear against the interference of the State in **educa-**
tion : for **example, that** to train the young is to step **out of**
its legitimate sphere ; that provision for it is not included in
the imaginary articles of incorporation of the State ; that it
violates the natural rights and liberties of the father ; that
it is inexpedient, because the parents are the **best** judges
what education is required ; that it substitutes compulsion
for voluntary action and enforced obedience for virtue, and
so weakens the sense of parental responsibility. **All** these
objections and many more are brought **to** bear. The father,
it seems, has a natural right to think and act for his own
child until he comes of age, and no community can justly
deprive him **of it. In fine,** the enforcement of education by
the State, according to the Individualist, would be unjust to
both father and child, and **also** inexpedient and ultimately
productive of ruin to the State itself.

Most of the principles, of which these expressions are
merely applications to a special problem, have already been
criticised. A few further remarks, however, may help towards
an estimate of their practical value as bearing on the question
of education :—

(1) The abstract principle of individuality is here a **more**

[1] P. 187.

[2] Cf. Prof. Huxley's *Essay on Government* (*Method and Results*, p. 409).

than usually unsafe guide, since there are two individuals whose rival interests may clash. The child has a potential personality which must be considered as well as the father's developed one. Absolute non-intervention by the government between parent and child is utterly impossible in a civilized State. The Roman jurists looked back to a perhaps mythical age when the *patria potestas* included the right to put the child to death or sell him as a slave. But this power of life and death, if it ever existed unrestrained by law or custom, was lost by the Roman *pater familias* in prehistoric times. To throw the child back under the despotic power of the father would be a relapse to barbarism which no one seriously contemplates. The State must, and always does, interfere when necessary, and the only questions, as usual, are those of degree and methods.

(2) The argument that to interfere by law is to compel the father to do grudgingly and half-heartedly what he ought to do lovingly and happily is one which demands sympathetic consideration. The compulsion, however, need only be applied where the opportunity of voluntary action has been given and rejected. The spontaneous manifestation and tender beauty of parental love are not interrupted because the law forbids unnatural fathers to abuse their children; nor need the knowledge that neglectful parents are compelled to give a minimum of education to their offspring prevent the pride and pleasure with which true parents pinch and cramp their own lives to better their children's start in life by the best education to be purchased anywhere. The growth of virtue is not checked by the punishment of crime. The objection has thus no force at all, unless the State interferes unwisely and unnecessarily. It is not wise for it to usurp the father's place. But it does not weaken parental love if it stays in the background and interferes only on an emergency.

(3) A great proportion of the future members of every State are unhappily the offspring of utterly unworthy parents. These wretched children obtain a bad start in life, sadly handicapped by inherited vices and incapacities of every sort. Whatever education they receive can never make them equal

with the sons of decent, honest parents. To condemn them
to depend for education, as well as environment and heredity,
upon an unworthy father's want of love is to cut off every
hope of earthly salvation. They will be left remorselessly
by their parents, steeped in an atmosphere reeking with
every form of vice, and without a chance of knowing any
better. The voice of the State, demanding that a little light
be let in on these dark places, is the only chance the child
can have of ever becoming worthy of citizenship. Without
descending to such depths, the nominal heads of many homes
are themselves sadly in need of education. How far, then,
should the latent individuality of the child be measured by
the standard of the stunted personality and narrow views of
an ignorant father ? The day-labourer may think it education
enough if his son is trained to work his pick and shovel ;
and thus progress from generation to generation would be
made an impossibility and degeneracy would set in.

(4) Most of the Individualist's objections, so far as they
are valid at all, have force not against State intervention
per se but against the improper or extreme manner of its
application. Thus when he argues that each man is the best
judge of what is good for his child, the Socialist who would
have the State thrust the same education into all brains,
whether wide or narrow, would do well to listen. Yet ample
room is left for a father's care and right of private judgment
even under a regime where government insists on a minimum,
since not only may each father provide more, if he wishes,
but may even decide as to the manner and matter of
the modicum required by law.

All the individualistic arguments seem thus to break down
in a peculiarly signal manner when applied to the problem
of education. Here at least a consistent policy of *laissez
faire* is absurd and impossible.[1]

---

[1] Cf. Prof. Huxley, *Method and Results*, p. 288. "If the positive
advancement of the peace, wealth, and the intellectual and moral
development of its members are objects which the government as the
representative of the corporate authority of society may justly strive
after, in fulfilment of its end, the good of mankind : then it is clear
that the government may undertake to educate the people."

2 A

II. The second attitude which the legislature may adopt is one which is not exclusively either individualistic or socialistic, but is in complete accord with the organic theory of the State. The law may command that every child should receive a certain minimum of education as a legal right, and decree that it is the duty of the family, and especially of its male head, to provide this out of the family funds.

Education thus viewed would be primarily the business of the family. If the father had not the ability or the time—and he would not be likely to have either in a highly differentiated community where the principle of the division of labour had been carried to excess—he might appoint one or more competent substitutes—might, in fine, send his children to a respectable school and pay for the education there received. In this view the State would neither provide the schooling nor meet the expense incurred, nor would it undertake any responsibility for the existence of efficient schools, nor superintend the teaching. It would leave every father free to exercise his own discretion, to decide between board-school, day-school, and private tuition; and would give no advice as to the details of the instruction to be received, and support no national schools to supersede or compete with those conducted on principles of private enterprise or voluntary association. It would of course have some say in the matter, and exercise an indirect control, as it must do over every institution within its territory and over every person who owns its sovereignty, but would interfere only when other expedients had failed. This seems to be the position taken up by Mill: "The objections," he says, "which are urged with reason against State education do not apply to the enforcement of education by the State, but to the State's taking upon itself to direct that education: which is a totally different thing."[1] Having commanded a certain minimum of education, however, the law would require to see its command enforced. To determine the best means of doing this is a question for the

<hr/>

[1] *Essay on Liberty*, p. 190. This line of argument needed only to be generalized to have necessitated an advance beyond the individualistic stand-point.

practical statesman. It is obviously not possible in this matter simply to leave the wronged individual to obtain redress by application to the proper law courts; for the individual is not yet developed. The child cannot and dare not turn against its father to the protection of the State. The pupil has no *locus standi* in a court of law. Government inspection of some sort is evidently necessary. This may bring with it certain evils which wise legislation must modify and restrict as far as possible, eliminating everything that is arbitrary, and all unnecessary interference with the privacy of the family and the sacredness of home life. There are evils in every human scheme. The statesman has only to decide if these are greater or less than those involved in any possible alternative policy.

This second attitude may be summed up as follows: The State should command every man to educate his own children at his own expense up to a standard fixed by law, and ought only to interfere when this command is not voluntarily obeyed. This position is criticised from two sides, which may be called in a general way the socialistic and the individualistic. All the usual lines of criticism are called into requisition on both sides. There is one argument, however, of a novel kind which is often used by practical men who are neither Socialists nor Individualists, viz. that it is unjust to compel a man to educate his children without providing the schooling for nothing. Many men say that either the first or the third attitude is allowable, but that this second one is unjust to the parent. Now, there seems no good reason why the same principle, which already compels parents to care for the health and bodily welfare of their children, should not be extended to their intellectual and moral training as well. No man can refuse to be liable for the food necessary for his child's nourishment. Why, then, should he be allowed to stunt its mind? If he cannot provide food for mind and body alike, he has no right to paternity at all. *Primary* responsibility for supplying the wants and developing the capacities of children rests clearly with the individual father; the *ultimate* responsibility rests equally clearly with the State, which must compel the parent to fulfil his natural duties, having first given him an opportunity to do so of his spontaneous goodwill and pleasure. If the father is dead or disabled or utterly destitute, then the community must educate his pauper children as it must feed them, but this task it should undertake directly only when all other resources have failed.

III. Each of the political parties that divide the Great Britain of to-day has gone beyond the golden mean in the direction of State control of education. Conservatives and Liberals alike are committed to the third possible attitude of the law towards education. Great Britain as a nation undertakes a primary responsibility for the education of the children of every citizen, paying for it out of the national exchequer, insisting on the maintenance of an efficient staff of educators, and generally exercising a very minute and direct control over even the details of schooling. This may be called the socialistic attitude.

The chief arguments against free education may be enumerated as follows:—

(1) For the State to undertake the education of the child free of all expense to the family is to substitute State-love for father-love, to weaken the natural affections along with the responsibilities of the parent, and so to deteriorate the working classes, making them bad citizens in proportion as they become bad fathers. As parents become accustomed to look to the community to take from them their proper responsibilities for the intellectual welfare of the child they have brought into the world, they will begin to look to be relieved of the burden of feeding and clothing him as well. Human nature, even at its best, is ready to throw off a burden on to other shoulders willing to receive it; but it is in the bearing of one's own burdens manfully and uncomplainingly that the discipline of life consists. Such an effort lays the foundation of the self-reliant character so necessary for the administration of States. It keeps in check the discontent and grudging discharge of duty. "Free education," it is urged, "is an injury to the self-discipline of English character."[1]

[1] Thos. Mackay, *A Plea for Liberty*, p. 261.

(2) **It is** perhaps only another aspect of the same objection **to hold** that to relieve each family from the duty of **educating its own** young ones will produce a physical deterioration **of the race** by the avoidance of hardships and a moral degeneration by the **evasion** of duty. "Knowledge," it has been finely said, "has to be won **at the cost of** self-denial, being the best inheritance **a man can** bequeath to his children, as **the** fruit of the exertions **of** a life-time."[1]

(3) Free education, it is said, weakens the family tie. The **child** no longer needs to look **to his parents** with gratitude for the education their self-privation may have given **him.** Receiving his education from the bounty of the State, **he** feels emancipated from most of the duties of that family to which **he owes** fewer obligations. **If** the family suffers, the State will suffer **too.**

(4) **What is easily** got is lightly appreciated. The education thrust **upon every** unwilling recipient, without any sacrifice by **himself or** his guardians, is **apt to** be lightly appreciated. **There is** perhaps less weight **in this** objection, as **all** education is apt to be grudgingly received by the person chiefly concerned. The child, before he **has** learned its value, is rarely too keen at his work.

(5) The State, which pays for the training, will naturally dictate both its quality and quantity. There is thus a danger of the introduction of too great a monotony in the routine enforced on **all alike. Too** little regard is apt to be paid to the requirements of unique individualities. This objection is inherent, **perhaps, in** all schemes of education, but the **evils which are** found in centralized bureaucracies, are likely **to** attach **with** special force to **a** system of national education directed from a central department and conducted on uniform lines throughout the country. This danger is at present **kept** under check in some measure by allowing local **School** Boards the chief share in the management. It is not easy to see, however, how this can continue effectually to counteract the strong tendencies already manifesting themselves in the direction of a more thorough system of central control, which seems the legitimate out-

[1] Thos. Mackay, *A Plea for Liberty*, p. 272.

come of a scheme of education paid for out of the national purse.

(6) The responsibility of finding suitable employment for the boy when he is done with his schooling still rests with the parent. It may be argued, then, with much force that the father who has to choose for him, or to help him in choosing for himself, or who knows at any rate better than the government what sphere of life the son is likely to occupy, is the best judge of what amount and kind of education will best fit him for its duties. The farmer knows that his only son will succeed to his farm, and ought to be allowed to judge whether he should learn some smattering of agricultural chemistry rather than Latin or the elements of Euclid. If the State undertakes to educate the child to fill his station as a citizen, it may be argued that it should further determine what that station is to be, furnishing a situation in life in keeping with the education it has provided. Free schooling would in this light be merely a first step in the direction of a vast scheme of Collectivism reducing everything under the control of the State.

(7) As long as A is able to pay for the education of his own children, there seems no reason why the State should compel B to contribute towards that desirable object, any more than it should compel him to contribute to a fund for sending them to the sea-side for a holiday. It is sometimes urged by tender-hearted philanthropists that it is unjust for the State to compel A to fulfil his natural obligation by paying for the education of his own children, but surely it is more unjust to make B pay for them. It is unjust to allow the improvident father of ten children to burden the provident father of two with an equal *pro indiviso* share of educating the lot. It is still more unfair to compel the bachelor, who is too poor to marry, to pay for the education of the children of his wealthy and successful rival. "Free" education under compulsory taxation is unjust; but "compulsory" education, where every man is bound to support his own, but free to marry or to abstain from marriage, is open to no such objection.

(8) Free education is not only unjust to individuals: by increasing the rates, it is injurious also to the trade and commercial prosperity of the country. Every increase of taxation raises the cost of production. The assessment for education is itself a heavy item, and is felt more severely when taken in conjunction with others of a more or less socialistic tendency.

Every bale of cotton manufactured in Lancashire, and every ship built in the Clyde dockyards, is dearer because of free education. Thus British goods, already handicapped by dear labour, are being gradually elbowed out of their old chief place in the markets of the world. Goods of foreign manufacture are finding their way more and more into the home market. Taxation is, of course, a matter of degree; but free education is responsible for a heavy addition. Any further increase would probably give irresistible impetus to the cry already heard proceeding in a half-ashamed way from thinking Socialists, for a protective tariff for the products of British labour.

(9) It is further urged that the system will gradually pauperize the nation. Mr. Herbert Spencer draws a close analogy between the probable effects of the Free Education Acts and the proved results of the Poor Law as it stood prior to 1832. This is a question of economics, pure and simple, and, apparently, many arguments might be produced on both sides. Analogy is always a dangerous weapon; and there is certainly a difference between supplying food for adults and education for the young. It is open for argument, however, whether the difference is not one of degree rather than of kind. There may exist a pauperizing effect in free education, although the evil is less pronounced than in the case of the old Poor Laws.

(10) Lastly, and closely connected with the foregoing, comes the argument—perhaps the most important of all, though least suited for full discussion here—that to provide free education for all children—especially when accompanied, as it sometimes is, by a modicum of free rations—is to withdraw one of the most effective restraints on over-population. If a government rigidly enforces the principle that parents must accept a full responsibility for every child they bring

into the world, that world is less likely to become over-populated, than if the State shows a readiness to relieve the parents of any burdens which they ought individually to bear. Over-population, it is perhaps unnecessary to add, has been acknowledged since the days of Malthus to be the cause of low wages and the root of social distress.

Without speaking dogmatically, then, against that free education which has been adopted with acclamation through-out the land, it seems clear that there are grave dangers connected with it which its advocates have neglected or failed sufficiently to notice. The objections urged against it by Mr. Herbert Spencer and others cannot be easily brushed aside. On the other hand, these arguments, however far they may be good against "free" education, have no place against the compulsion of the State being brought to bear upon the father to perform his natural duties, by providing a modicum of education to every child, male or female. The State may have gone too far in its interference with education, but no arguments can prove that it should or can leave the matter altogether alone.

CHAPTER XXVI.

THE STATE AND MORALITY.

NOT only the prosperity of a State, but its very existence depends upon the stuff its citizens are made of—upon the moral fibre of its individual men and women, and the moral value of the ideas that animate its policy. In the words of Professor Jowett, commenting on Aristotle's *Politics:* "The State exists for the sake of a good life, and without virtue has no true existence."[1] It is, indeed, no accidental meeting of individuals who might instead have exercised an option of living in self-sufficing isolation. The reason why men must form a State of some sort, large or small, developed or embryonic, is that they are by nature moral agencies, knowing right from wrong. Thus the State itself partakes of necessity in that same moral nature of its citizens to which it owes its origin. Its official actions mingle with those of private individuals. In the resultant effects it is difficult to determine how far each agency has contributed to the joint result. The same world of men and things is affected by the actions of government and by those of its subjects. It is impossible to escape from the conclusion that the government is merely one moral agent among others. The same universal rules of right and wrong by which individuals are judged are applicable to governments as well. No power, whether executive or deliberative or legislative, can escape from the moral responsibilities attaching to its every act, decision, or law.

The government as a whole, then, and the State its master

[1] Introduction, p. lxix.

must accept responsibility for the ethical principles bound up in every act performed or statute enacted.[1] But the further questions still remain : How far is the State responsible for, and how far should it promote, the morality of its private citizens ? Has it a right to control individuals at all, on the avowed ground of their own moral good ?

The answer given by Individualists is that the government has no responsibility whatever for private acts of immorality or sin, and that it has no right to interfere with any man for his own moral good or advancement in the path of virtue. It must, therefore, leave him severely and absolutely alone, avoiding all action that will constrain his moral nature either for good or evil. Von Humboldt sums up his chapter on the *Amelioration of Morals* in the declaration " that the State must wholly refrain from every attempt to operate directly or indirectly on the morals and character of the nation, otherwise than as such a policy may become inevitable as a natural consequence of its other absolutely necessary measures ; and that everything calculated to promote such a design, and particularly all special supervision of education, religion, sumptuary, etc., lies wholly outside the limits of its legitimate activity." [2]

It is the object of the following pages to show that the opinion expressed in this extreme form is untenable in theory and impossible in practice, that the laws and administration of a country cannot, try how they may, avoid putting moral restraints upon individuals, and that they ought not always to refrain even where possible.

There are two broad grounds on which to justify a censor-

---

[1] It would be unnecessary to insist on what will to most men seem a truism, were it not directly denied by a writer of such weight as Mr. Auberon Herbert, who considers the whole foundation of all governments as essentially though unavoidably immoral. "I do not think that it is possible to find a perfect moral foundation for the authority of any government, be it the government of an emperor or a republic" (*The Right and Wrong of Compulsion by the State*, p. 22). If all compulsion were really a wrong to those compelled, it would be absurd to talk of guiding by moral rules what is essentially immoral.

[2] *Sphere and Duties of the State*, p. 113.

ship of morals. In the first place it may be urged that it is impossible for any government to avoid influencing, in one way or another, the ethical ideas, and controlling the actions of its citizens. In the second place, the plea that the highest interests of the whole community are at stake in the moral worth of the men who compose it, is of itself sufficient justification.

It is impossible for the government or the laws of a civilized country to maintain a strict neutrality in the war constantly waged between the powers of morality and immorality. No policy can be decided on, no treaty signed, no law enacted, and no tax levied, without the danger and even the certainty of doing violence to the conscience of some individual subject. Thus to some tender consciences all warfare is sinful, and every man who pays a tax that contributes directly or indirectly to its conduct is tainted with blood-guiltiness. To others, on the contrary, the duty of forcible intervention, even in foreign countries, to prevent gross Bulgarian or Armenian atrocities at any sacrifice of lives and money, is equally clear; and, to them, to submit tamely to a selfish government that ignores the sufferings of humanity is immoral. On whatever grounds a government may primarily see cause to act, as (for example) those of an economic or hygienic nature, conflicts are sure to arise sooner or later with the private morality of individuals. It is for the health of the community that compulsory vaccination is enforced; but this is frequently a violation of the conscience and the moral freedom of individuals. It is for the preaching of the Gospel of Christ that tithes or teinds are taken from the lands of men of all denominations; and this hurts the consciences of Jews and Mohammedans, as well as of those who believe in "religious equality." The national endowment of an opera-house might injure the moral sense of those compelled to contribute to the rates.

Sir James Stephen has illustrated, from our legislation in India, the impossibility of making laws for a people without thereby coercing the subjects for whom they are made into some degree of outward conformity with the moral and religious standards of those who make them. The policy o non-interference with native standards and prejudices was avowedly followed, but it was found to be absolutely impracticable.

This, then, is the negative justification of the intervention of the government in the private morals of its subjects—that it cannot adopt an attitude of *laissez faire* if it would. There is also a positive justification on the ground that it is its duty to interfere wherever such intervention is likely to do good. Any form of interference, whether direct or indirect, whether enforced by persuasion or compulsion, and to whatever extent it may be required, is justifiable on the ground that the highest interests of the community demand it. The mere plea of self-protection is sufficient; for it may be shown that when private morality becomes relaxed the bonds of society are loosened, and revolutions are more imminent. If the State is entitled to protect itself against danger of overthrow, it might on that plea alone institute a close censorship of morals, and punish any departure as a crime. It might do all this and still shelter itself with logical consistency behind the individualistic plea of self-protection. It has a still more clear title to interfere, however, on the ground not of self-defence but of advance and progress. Men are associated into States not merely for existence, but for the realization of such measure of perfection as can be attained on earth. The State is something different from the mere legal framework of its constitution. Its strength lies not in the material wealth of its territory or the accumulated riches that form the product of the labour of ages, but in the worth of its subjects. That worth rests upon moral forces. No institutions, however wisely contrived and deeply rooted in the history of the past, can enable a nation to continue its career of greatness or even to drag on an independent existence, if the vital forces forming its life's blood are tainted or enervated. If the sovereign State has a duty, and therefore a right, to alter its constitution, it has an equally pressing duty and an equally inalienable right to do what it can to stimulate the moral well-being of its citizens. The same life flows from the individuals to the central organs of the State and back again to every unit, and nothing that affects the individual is so trivial that it fails to influence the State. The government has then a right to interfere, and an interest to interfere, and a duty to interfere to promote the virtue of all its subjects, from the highest to the lowest.

It is indeed absurd to hold that the State must confine itself to law, while the individual attends to morality, for the distinction between law and morality must not be considered final or absolute : law loses its inner sanction and meaning if divorced from ethical principles. Man's moral nature is at once the basis of all his rights and the prerequisite of the existence of society—in so far as a society differs from a mere flock of sheep or band of apes. The State is an embodiment of the common will of individuals endowed with conscience or practical reason. This is the fundamental conception of the Hegelian philosophy, and has been well expounded by the late Professor Green. " The claim or right of the individual to have certain powers secured to him by society, and the counter claim of society to exercise certain powers over the individual, alike rest on the fact that these powers are necessary for the fulfilment of man's vocation as a moral being to an effectual self-devotion to the work of developing the perfect character in himself and others." [1] All legal rights and obligations are thus seen to be based on morality. It is this consideration which leads writers like Professor Green to the conclusion that the sphere of morality is not only a legitimate part of the province of the State, but the chief part and almost the whole, and that " the real function of government" is " to maintain conditions of life in which morality shall be possible." [2] Every organ of the government is bound to interfere (within the proper constitutional limits assigned to it) to help its citizens to realize

[1] *Collected Works*, Vol. II., p. 347.

[2] *Ibid.*, Vol. II., p. 345. **Cf.** William Cunningham, *Politics and Economics.* " The State is concerned with human conduct, its action is distinctly moral in character, it may be said that the business of the legislature is always that of enforcing morality in the widest sense of the term" (p. 141). Again, " Its business is to enforce morality as recognized by public opinion" (p. 144).

the virtuous life so inseparable from the prosperity of the community, *whenever such intervention is likely to accomplish its end.*

Such a line of reasoning, however, is very far from proving that all interference with private morality is sure of success. Stupid intervention must always do more harm than good , and there are cases in which no intervention of any kind is likely to effect anything but evil. Each question must be dealt with on its merits. Neither in the region of morality nor elsewhere is there any absolute presumption against State action any more than in its favour. The argument, then, merely proves that, *a priori*, there is no bar to such action on the ground that the State steps thereby beyond its proper sphere. The right and duty to interfere are established whenever the acts proposed are just and expedient.

Government interference with private morality is, however, condemned on very different grounds by the best friends of virtue, and by some of those who fully appreciate the vital interests that the State has therein at stake as well as its absolute right to interfere. They urge with great force that such interference will substitute an external habit of obedience for a spirit of free morality, and thus defeat its own designs. Professor Green was of this opinion. "The real function of government being to maintain conditions of life in which morality shall be possible, and morality consisting in the disinterested performance of self-imposed duties, 'paternal government' does its best to make it impossible by narrowing the room for the self-imposition of duties and for the play of disinterested motives."[1]

If this doctrine contained the entire truth, the State would best promote virtue by leaving it severely alone. This we have already seen to be impossible. The law cannot help influencing morality in a thousand ways. As a negative attitude is impossible, the only question is how its positive relations may be so extended as to do most good, or be so limited as to do least harm.

Five criteria have been suggested as affording a solution of the problem. (1) The State, it is said, ought never

1 *Works*, Vol. ii., p. 345.

directly to aim by its laws or its government at making men
moral, although no valid objection can be raised to any **course**
of **action** upon **which** it may have resolved to enter **for**
other motives (economic or hygienic, for example) **on** the
ground that it cannot effect this without putting moral con-
straint upon individuals. (2) No objection, **it is** said, may
be taken even to the direct interference **of** the State with
private morality by persuasion **and** education, *provided no
force is used.* (3) It is sometimes urged **that** the government may advance morality by removing obstacles **but** not
by furnishing positive support. (4) Public **opinion** is sometimes suggested as the only test. (5) Lastly, it may be held
that not only is direct and positive intervention **always**
allowable, but even coercion may be consistently applied,
provided it **is** likely to attain its end at a cost not
altogether disproportionate.

(1) It is obvious, to begin with, that the presumed motive
of the law or official **act** can never afford a practical ground
of complaint for **a** subject to adopt **when he** considers
himself aggrieved by a government anxious to shield itself
from blame. The makers of any **law and the devisers of**
any counsel are alone able **to** judge **of** the motives which
led **to** its enactment. **All** motives, **too, are mixed;** the good
with the bad; the **moral** with the economic; the selfish
with the unselfish. Thus it is often difficult for a private
man to analyze the motives of his simplest action; while, for
a complex body **like the** legislature dealing with **a** complicated code of laws, it would **be** simply impossible. Indeed,
it is difficult to see how any act can be divorced entirely
from moral considerations, though they may sometimes be
kept more in the background. Thus for example in legislat-
ing against overcrowding in lodging-houses, while the chief
object is to guard the health **of** the community, moral
considerations have also their place.

The criterion of motive, then, is of no practical utility;
but **it has** other and more vital defects as well. Is it never
right, it may be asked, to legislate avowedly with the object
of making men better than they **are?** The varied reasons
against such legislation may be reduced under two heads:

(*a*) morality is a matter of private judgment and should be left to the individual man, who is alone responsible for his actions; and (*b*) government should never interfere, in case it may be in the wrong and the individual in the right, as history has shown to have been the case in too many instances.

Now, the neutral man who wishes to find that golden mean which commends itself alike to philosophy and to common-sense, may accept both these arguments as containing sound *relative* truths, while he rejects them in their absolute form. Thus (*a*) it is quite true that each man's morality is primarily a matter for his own private direction; and there-fore all powers and authorities should think twice before interfering between him and his conscience. So-called external influences should rather stimulate him into obeying his own sense of duty than set up an external standard of conduct as its rival. This is the aspect of truth contained in the argument for private judgment in questions of morality. This criterion is only relative, however, not absolute; because all abstractions are false philosophically, and unworkable in practice. It is impossible always to distinguish between external and internal standards, and between private and public acts of the individual. No man's morality is "private" in the sense that it does not affect the public welfare, or that it is not in return moulded by the current estimates of the society of the age and country in which the individual moves. It is impossible, then, to draw any sharp line between what is and what is not private for the guidance of Parliament in deciding how far it may go.

(*b*) Similar considerations tend to weaken the alternative line of argument. Instances have often occurred—as for example in the often-cited case of Socrates—where the State has interfered in the name of morality, and has persecuted and attacked a higher standard of ethics than its own. Too great care indeed can never be taken to avoid the possibility of such isolated cases—though from the necessary imperfection of all human affairs the danger can never be absolutely obvi-ated, however it may be safe-guarded. This, too, is a relative truth. It does not for a moment prevent a raid by the officers of justice on a gambling-hell, or the immediate suppression of gross indecency, and the punishment of its perpetrators.

The **State can and** does hunt down and punish **vice.** It can **and** does encourage virtue. The **laws** that treat **certain** forms of immorality **as crimes cannot** be explained on any other basis; and while it is as difficult to prove as to disprove the presence of any one motive among others, it is probable that the suppression of immorality **or of** sin (if the **word** be preferred) is **one of** the objects of **all** criminal law. **In** preventing a man who is tired of life **from** committing suicide, the State is preventing **an act condemned** as immoral by the code of ethics on which its laws are, consciously or unconsciously, based. **Other and more** artificial motives **for** this branch of our **criminal law** may easily be **devised, but** most men will agree that this is the chief one. A desire to curb immorality **is at once the** only and the sufficient justification of the **State in** treating bigamy as **a** crime, where **all three** individuals immediately concerned are quite happy **and agreed, and no** force or fraud or concealment of facts **has been** used towards any of **the spouses.** The promotion of virtue is here as elsewhere a **most** praiseworthy motive of legislation. Indeed it might **be** well that, instead of eliminating this endeavour of **the** State **to** educate **its** citizens in morality, **the** whole of **our** criminal **law . were** based more consciously and consistently upon **this** theory. The convict should be **subjected to** wholesome restraint and discipline, less **as a punishment for** the past than as a training **to** enable him **to be, if possible,** a good citizen in the future. Only in "habit and **repute**" and hopeless cases **may** this object of amelioration **be** lost sight of. In the **reformatory** system, and the principle of the First Offenders' Act, the State **aims** at the moral welfare of its citizens as the direct and conscious motive of **its** legislation.

The assertion that the State ought never to interfere from motives of elevating the morals of its subjects seems thus entirely untenable. It **is** nevertheless true that in acting clearly **and** unambiguously from that motive it accepts a responsibility which should never be lightly undertaken, and runs a risk which can hardly be over-estimated.

2 B

(2) The second criterion proposed as a test for the legitimacy of State interference with private virtue is the absence of force—of positive coercion. The same arguments—or others very similar—might be used over again to show that this cannot be made a final and absolute standard. It is not always easy to know where persuasion ends and force begins, as Sir James Stephen has abundantly illustrated. It is not easy to see how it is possible for the State to carry out any reform or put into execution any law or regulation without the reserved right to apply that brute force without which all executive government becomes a farce. It is not easy to see why the State should hesitate to use such a sanction in furtherance of an end of whose desirability it is assured, provided it is likely to be effective.

For these and many other reasons which might be adduced, the application of coercion is not an absolute criterion. There are on the other hand at least two reasons that militate against the expediency of using force unless under very careful restraints and limitations.

In the first place, forced adherence to a moral standard not approved by the individual makes hypocrites instead of saints. In the second place, the highest form of morality must be spontaneous and joyous, not the grumbling obedience paid to a hated external law.

(3) We are thus led to consider the third suggested test, that of the late Professor Green. The highest object of human attainment is a "free morality," and the essence of this lies in the spontaneous action of a moral being "determined by a conception of the end to which it is relative." Thus every direct enforcement of outward conduct will only sap the foundation of all morality by destroying the basis of spontaneity on which it rests. "For this reason," concludes Professor Green,[1] "the effectual action of the State, *i.e.* the community as acting through law for the promotion of habits of true citizenship, seems necessarily to be confined to the removal of obstacles."

There is a valuable lesson embodied in this argument, namely, that legislators ought never to forget the danger of

[1] *Works*, Vol. ii., p. 514.

substituting a dead legality for a living morality; but viewed as the sole and universally applicable criterion of government action, it is manifestly inadequate. Not to insist on the practical difficulty of determining whether a particular law removes an obstacle from the path of virtue or affords positive aid, it is sometimes wise and expedient to enforce a formal and outward habit of good-living in the hope that it may lead some day to a truly inward and free morality.

The true test of the good or evil effects of any statute is how far it will ultimately stimulate a true vital and spontaneous morality. All interference which substitutes a hard metallic pharisaic observance of dead forms for the natural outcome in good actions of the pure heart within, is bad. All legislation which makes the compulsory compliance with the law one step in the progress of the moral agent towards a pure and spontaneous morality, is good. The cleansing of the outside of the platter must not be substituted for the purity of the inside. Enforced morality should be like a crutch that helps the injured man to regain his power of unaided locomotion. So far as it is serviceable at all, it is chiefly as a means to a higher end, and not as an end in itself. Even in itself, however, it is something to raise men from the level of swine to the standard of external and enforced respectability.

Much of the force of the Individualist's argument rests on the fallacious assumption that all men naturally strive hard to be moral, and err through defect in judgment rather than defect in will. Now the great mass of mankind are not so strongly rooted in virtue as to be insensible to all temptations and independent of all external supports. Morality is a thing of the inner man, but it is not independent of the material social and political environment. Socrates, perhaps, reached so high a level as to receive only hindrance instead of help from the manners and institutions of his country; but the ordinary mortal is kept from many a sin by the influence of his surroundings, by the knowledge of the standard of conduct that his friends expect of him, by the fear of public opinion, and the reverence for the traditions of his ancestors and the law of the land. Beneath this ordinary level of humanity there come the lapsed masses, who have no hope and hardly any desire of elevating their lives from their utterly debased condition, physical, mental, and moral. Coercive morality is for such men the only possible beginning, if not the end, of their salvation. If they are forced to comply with a moral standard, they may rise in time beyond it to a voluntary pursuit of a virtuous life; but humanly speaking, without such coercion, even the rudiments of morality are impossible to them. Even if such an expectation is groundless as regards themselves, it may help towards giving their children a start in life with fewer hereditary tendencies to vice. When the State merely insists that men shall not live like the lower animals, there is little danger of it persecuting what is in reality a higher standard of morality than its own. Certain forms of vice can be suppressed without the slightest possibility of doing harm to any one.

(4) It may be proposed again, that the State should interfere in moral questions only in cases where it is impossible there should be any doubt—that it should only suppress what public opinion with practical unanimity condemns, and only enforce by active coercion what the same opinion cries for with unanimity. This is the view of Mr. Cunningham—that the state of public opinion is the only criterion of such legislative interference. " From our point of view, then," he says, " no limits can be assigned to the sphere of action of the State: its business is to enforce morality as recognized by public opinion. . . . The State is concerned in seeing that every man performs that minimum of duty which public opinion demands of every citizen."[1] There is a very valuable element of truth in this, for no legislation ought to be in advance of the public opinion of the whole community, nor run counter to the scruples of any disinterested minority whose conduct and presumed motives are such as to entitle their opinions to any respect. It is, however, only one of many elements which we must take into consideration in determining the expediency of interference in any given case, although perhaps one of more than usual weight in questions of morality.

[1] *Politics and Economics*, p. 144.

Legislative coercion may bring up the stragglers into line with the ordinary rank and file, by whom public opinion is formed. Every important advance towards a higher standard must come from individuals, spreading gradually to the mass of the people, and last of all upwards to the government. The last stage in any enduring advance is the alteration of the law (if need be) to suit the new and higher morality. In this respect there is a notable difference between material and moral progress. Health regulations to prevent the spread of disease through infection or defective sanitation may be in advance of public opinion. They ought to work downwards to the people, proceeding from the initiative of the government, acting on the skilled advice of scientific and medical experts; but the progress of a new departure in morality must be all the other way.

(5) The fifth and last suggestion is that no *absolute* bar can be placed to the action of the State in the sphere of morality any more than in the sphere of health or of trade. It is always justified in interfering when its own conception of the public good seems to call for it. Its duty is to interfere in any direction required, and to use whatever force seems necessary. It must never act, however, where either it is likely to defeat the end it has in view, or to cause worse evils than it cures. A wise government will thus do well to allow their full relative weight to all the considerations suggested by its various advisers—to beware of degrading virtue to an irresponsive legality, to guard against the use of force where persuasion is equally effective, and to avoid the danger of reaction through urging the minimum of enforced duty beyond what public opinion warrants.

Each of those counsels, however, is a mere rule of expediency, not to be hardened into an absolute criterion.

This view of the duty of the State has perhaps never been more eloquently supported than by Sir James F. Stephen. "I think," he says, "that governments ought to take the responsibility of acting upon such principles, religious, political, and moral, as they may from time to time regard as most likely to be true, and this they cannot do without exercising a very considerable degree of coercion."[1]   Now, in his opinion, such compulsive authority may be applied by three methods, criminal law, civil law, and public opinion.   The substance of Sir James Stephen's argument is that it is impossible for any one of these agencies to act at all without coercion, and that it would be wrong of them to abstain from its use when necessary.   "Criminal law in this country actually is applied to the suppression of vice, and so to the promotion of virtue to a very considerable extent, and this I say is right."[2]   And the same holds good of the civil law, for the courts refuse to enforce immoral contracts, while the law of marriage and inheritance is based upon a well-formulated code of positive morality.   Thus "nearly every branch of civil law assumes the existence of a standard of moral good and evil, which the public at large have an interest in maintaining, and in many cases enforcing."   It is, therefore, impossible to lay down invariable rules as to how far the government may help and how far it will only hinder.

In no circumstances is there an absolute veto placed on the right of intervention.   The highest power in the State (that is to say, the nation acting through its accustomed constitutional channels) is the sole court of appeal on all such questions.

If it is urged that this vindication of the existing order of things—of this unfettered supremacy of the real "sovereign," which always does and must exist in every State— is a plea for persecution, several answers may be made.   In the first place, coercion in some form is a necessity, and the mildest form of it is that of a wisely ordered State which will permit no "persecution" but its own.   In the second place, in reserving to itself (as it cannot help reserving) the supreme right of intervention if need be, the legislative sovereign as the servant of the supreme people does not necessarily use that power for persecution.   There is no tyranny unless it is used wickedly and unwisely.   Lastly, in the only true sense in which morality is a private and not a public affair, the individual is invulnerable and can defy the State.   If he is forced into outward conformity with the code of the community, his soul is free.   Conscience cannot be coerced.

[1] *Liberty, Equality, Fraternity*, p. 53.   [2] *Ibid.*, p. 148.

CHAPTER XXVII.

THE STATE AND THE CHURCH.

WHEN the sphere of the State has been extended to embrace all the ends and aims of the lives of its subjects, no room for the Church would seem to have been left. The independent existence of the latter has been crushed out altogether. The truth is that in the modern highly developed State, in its widest signification, the Church is included as merely one factor in a larger whole. This doctrine is at variance at once with the claims of keen churchmen and with the popular notions as to the relations of the two.

The theory that the Church is simply a part or phase of the State, and therefore subordinated to the authority of the civil government, requires some explanation and vindication. Much light is thrown on the matter by an examination of the mutual relations of the two powers in the Middle Ages.

In theory all mediaeval Christendom was one vast territory, whose inhabitants owed a common allegiance to one God and professed a common faith in one Saviour. A theoretical division was made between the spiritual and temporal aspects of life. One ruler was recognized as sovereign over the former, and was called the Pope. Another was sovereign over the latter under the name of Emperor. These two potentates were intended to move hand in hand. The Pope undertook to lend the aid of his spiritual power to help the Emperor in his more mundane affairs, while in return the armed might of the temporal ruler was the natural

protector of religion. The Pope was head of the Church;
the Emperor, of the Empire-State.

As their jurisdictions moved in different planes and were
essentially distinct in kind, no one dreamed of asking which
was above the other. This theoretically postulated harmony
between two spheres of influence, one purely temporal and the
other purely spiritual, never held good in practice for a day.
The history of the Middle Ages is one long sad record of
discords and actual warfare between Pope and Emperor,
Guelph and Ghibelline, Church and State.

Now the spiritual power of the Pope over the nascent
nationalities of Europe was a very real one; whereas the
temporal power of the prince elected to the sovereignty of
the Holy Roman Empire was a mere shadow, unless he could
claim the support of hereditary dominions of his own. In
isolated England, in particular, his rights of feudal overlordship
were utterly ignored. While in theory one Empire-State
extended over Christendom, in reality a number of national
or dynastic States were growing up, each claiming and practically possessing independence of the Emperor and of one
another, but looking to Rome for spiritual guidance. It is
in this sense that one Church might be said in that age to
include all States. The only link that bound all peoples
together was Rome with its universal Church, its canon
law, its uniform ecclesiastical government and constitution,
and its hierarchy of priests, whose traditions and the Latin
language they used in common made them international
rather than national, and too often loyal churchmen rather
than patriotic statesmen. After the fall of the old Roman
Empire the only organization that deserved the name of
State was not the new or Holy Roman Empire but the
Catholic Church. The Church *was* the State. The organization and law of the Church were the only restraints
upon the anarchy and lawlessness always found in the train
of genuine feudalism. In each nation a branch of that
Church took root and would yield, only on compulsion,
a qualified allegiance to the State that sheltered it, while
it remained proud to own obedience to its spiritual head
at Rome. Thus there were men in England even, who looked

beyond their native island for the sovereignty before which they bowed; and continental churches were still more closely bound to Rome. Professing only to exercise spiritual authority, the canons of the ecclesiastical law usurped legislative weight throughout Europe; the Church courts obtained exclusive jurisdiction in various important classes of suits between man and man; and the decrees of the Pontiff, issued in papal bulls, found sanctions to enforce them in the power of excommunication and in the swords of the temporal princes who acted as "defenders of the faith." The Church, with its seven sacraments and its superintendence of education and relief of the poor, extended the province of the spiritual to embrace many of the most important social, domestic, and material interests of individuals. By pressing its jurisdiction over the sacrament of marriage, and by its control over the probate of wills and other matters where an oath was needed, the Church took into its own hands the law of succession, and the regulation of family relationships.

In those days many States were included within one church, whereas in modern England many churches are included within one State. Unfortunately ideas borrowed from a buried past are still used nominally to explain, but really to confuse, the facts of the present age, to which they are entirely inapplicable. Church and State have now, to some extent, changed places.

It is unnecessary to endeavour here to trace the steps by which, in countries such as England, a national ecclesiastical organization was gradually elaborated, beginning as a branch of the universal Church, and gradually tending towards separation from the parent stem. This tendency was due to various causes : partly to the growth of national feeling among the leading prelates; partly to the policy of kings in excluding the rivalry of the Papal supremacy from their dominions; and partly to the prejudice of the common people against foreign influences. When Henry VIII., with the formal concurrence of his Parliament, severed the connection of the Anglican Church with the Church of Rome, and placed himself as an insular Pope at its head, arbitrary and abrupt

as his innovations seemed, he merely put the coping stone
to a work that had long been in progress. Subsequently to
Henry VIII.'s day (except during the reaction towards Rome
at the accession of Queen **Mary), there has** always existed
a native English Church independent of the Pope, as well as
an English State independent of the Emperor.   Henceforward
the relations of Church and State, **so far as** England was
concerned, were exclusively to be determined by causes
beginning and ending **within** its own island territories.   Prior
to the Reformation the Church in England **had** not been
entirely subject to the civil power, but that was **only because**
the nation was **not fully** entitled to be called a **State.   As**
long as·Rome **had** a constitutional and acknowledged right to
meddle in English affairs, this country was not an independent
nation.

When **England shook** off the power of Rome, the **Church in**
becoming truly national, became subservient to the civil power.

The old dualism **did not** reappear—at least under the old
form in which it had torn Europe asunder in the early quarrels
between Pope and Emperor. From the first, Henry **VIII.**
made it clear that he, as head **of** the State, meant **to** be head
of the national Church as **well.   In** that age, **when** the
New Monarchy had attained its zenith—when the kingship
as the chief organ of the **central** government **had** absorbed
all political power and dictated its decrees **to Privy Council**
and Parliament alike—this supremacy of the **king over the**
Church meant **the** subjection of the latter to **the State.**

It was indeed no part of Henry's policy **consciously to**
subordinate the ecclesiastical organization **to the** Parliament,
since it suited him better to keep the two apart and play
off the one against the **other.**   Still, in making himself
(already the acknowledged **head** of both legislative and executive branches of the civil government) head of **the** Church
as well, he opened the **way for the** entire subjection of the
ecclesiastical to the civil authority. **In taking** even the
formal consent of Parliament to his Church reforms, he made a
further stride in the same direction. Thereafter the principle
of the sovereignty of Parliament over spiritual as well as
temporal concerns made steady progress, although as late as

the reigns of the first two Stuarts, we find attempts to deny
the right of the Commons to meddle with Church affairs.
The change was a gradual one. For example, the process by
which Parliament obtained the acknowledged right to tax the
clergy without the consent of Convocation, and which forms
one of the most curious chapters of our constitutional history,
was only brought to a close in 1664, by the arrangement made between Lord Chancellor Clarendon and Archbishop
Sheldon.

The Church of England is now, like the Church of Scotland,
an integral part of the British Constitution. All its affairs
are subject—just as the affairs of the individual, the family,
or the Trades Union are subject—to the legal sovereignty
of Parliament. In a word, the ecclesiastical, is bound to
obey the civil, government : the Church must bow to the
State.

The Established Churches of England and Scotland are by
no means the only ecclesiastical bodies within Great Britain.
The State extends its protection to and claims obedience from
two Established Churches, one Church which has been disestablished by Act of Parliament, various bodies of seceders
from each of these, and numerous congregations originally
formed on a purely contractual basis. All of these, whether
" free " or established, are subject to the sovereignty of the
State and its various laws and organs of control, the only
differences being that, while the members of the established
churches voluntarily associate themselves with an institution
which owns a special tie to the State, and whose relations
with that State are defined by a code of special customs
and laws, the members of the other churches refuse to
recognize such special ties, and leave the relations between
their church and the State to be determined by the ordinary
common and statute law of the land. Both classes of churches
are subject to the dominion of the State in both temporal
and spiritual matters.

This is a simple statement of the law as it stands—the
only interpretation consistent with the "reign of law" or the
"supremacy of Parliament," the two central principles of the
Constitution. The only point open for discussion is whether

such a condition of the law is right. Many distinguished churchmen of all denominations are prepared vehemently to argue on behalf of the claims of the Church to an equality with, or even to a supremacy over, "the State." A common misuse of words adds an unnecessary element of confusion to the discussion, and gives some colour to the pretensions of churchmen. The phrase "Church and State" brings with it a legacy of latent error in the associations borrowed from various periods of history. By taking for granted a necessary distinction, if not opposition, between the two, the expression seems, by a *petitio principii*, to assume the very point at issue, viz. that State and Church are mutually exclusive. The same phrase with the implied meaning contained in it has been in part to blame for the common solecism by which State is reduced to a mere synonym for Government. The real opposition is that between the civil and ecclesiastical governments.

The question, then, is not whether State or Church is supreme, but whether the civil or the ecclesiastical government ought to rule the other, or whether some compromise ought not rather to be made between them. When there is only one church and only one ecclesiastical organization, there is no immediate absurdity involved in the opinion that the chief legal authority should be given to some organ of the Church—say to Convocation—instead of to either King or Parliament; but when there are hundreds of churches in any country, the absurdity is apparent of proposing that the authority of the representatives of one sect should override the civil authority of the nation.

Churchmen support their claims partly by denying the statement of the law as expounded by lawyers, and partly by admitting it, while denying its justice. These two lines of argument are usually blended together in the hope that though neither stands by itself, they may shore up each other.

The answer to such a claim is simple enough. Each man is free to try to alter the present law and constitution, and to make the spiritual power supreme over the temporal if he choose. But until this is done the government of the day can claim to be both a temporal and a spiritual power, since it is vested with the supreme legal power in all things by the voice of the sovereign people.

The civil government, then, is the authorized agent of the community in all matters, spiritual as well as temporal. It possesses this double supremacy under mandate of the law. Here the churchman steps in with a new argument. The Church, he says, has its own law. Its canon law is founded on the law of God, and has superior sanctity and authority to either common law or statute law. This canon law rules within the Church as the civil law rules without. Neither can override the other; or if there is any inferiority in the case, it attaches to the secular law. This new argument —which is indeed just the old one in a new dress—is equally untenable. It is historically false, logically unsound. The course of English Constitutional History is a record of the triumph of the common law over all other codes, including the forest law of the Normans, the feudal law, the Canon law, all systems of special administrative law or martial law, and what may be conveniently called prerogative law. Various claims have been put forward at different epochs of English history for the independence of special courts claiming exemption from the principles, rules of evidence, and procedure of the common law. Thus the courts of the feudal barons, in early times, and the Court of the Star Chamber dispensing "prerogative law" as late as the seventeenth century, have claimed such exemption, while from the time of Thomas à Becket and his opposition to the Constitutions of Clarendon to that of Laud with his High Commission Court, the tribunals of the Church have struggled to dispense a special ecclesiastical law under various names and pleas. All these pretensions have long been reduced to mere empty theories. All tribunals, whether church courts, courts-martial, or local courts, must now humbly accept the ordinary law of the land and acquiesce in its definition of the extent of their jurisdiction and the limits of their power.

The law, indeed, allows that all exclusively church matters shall be decided by church authorities, exactly as it allows all the affairs of a limited liability company to be managed by its directors; but in both cases there are three important provisos: (1) That the civil power has the right to determine the province of the Church as of the company; (2) that even within the province thus limited and defined, the law of the land must not be infringed; and (3) that the legislative branch of the civil government has the sole right to alter the existing law as it thinks good.

All religious societies are not, however, in exactly the same position to the civil government. The relations of the Church of England to the State are of a specially intimate nature. Within the central government itself, representatives of this Church have a place assigned to them by law. The Archbishops and Bishops have seats in the House of Lords. The ecclesiastical organization of the Anglican Church has been built into the fabric of the State. This connection has two consequences. While on the one hand it gives this church a special constitutional means of influencing the policy and civil laws of the State by bestowing upon it a direct share in the legal sovereignty of Parliament; on the other hand, by the closeness of the tie and the clear enunciation of the fact that the Church is merely a part of the civil constitution, the temporal authorities are afforded a ready means of enforcing their will more effectually upon the spiritual. Churchmen can no longer proclaim an absolute dualism, while by their own constitution they are admittedly a mere part of the larger whole with which they would claim equality.

Before attempting to formulate the ideal relationship between Church and State in a perfect society, it is well to ascertain from history the various forms it has actually assumed in practice. It is not enough to decide categorically for either the establishment or the voluntary principle, since each of these contains several distinct species differing from one another in degree and perhaps in kind.

At least five solutions of the problem are compatible with an adherence to the principle of establishment, though some of these are of purely speculative interest.

(1) The State may establish one Church with or without endowments, insist on absolute uniformity of discipline and creed within it, and compel every citizen to become a member. This was the position assumed by the Tudor kings.

The system was completed and firmly secured on **an** orderly
and enduring basis by Queen Elizabeth. While the **Act** of
Supremacy made **her** head of the Church, the Act of Uniformity was intended **to** crush out all diversities and differences
within **it,** and at the **same** time to render it impossible
that either Catholic or Puritan should remain without. The
spiritual affairs of all England were to **be** managed by one
organization, on an absolutely uniform **plan to be** regulated
by .the church dignitaries and the Queen.

(2) It is possible, however, while maintaining and endowing a national Church, to which all citizens are welcome
and in which they have a right to **find a** place, **to allow
those** who object to the form of worship there insisted **on, to**
stay outside unmolested and in safety from any consequent
diminution of their civil and political rights. This is very
much the attitude of the present constitutional law of England.

(3) A **third course is** to compel membership **of the** one
church **which the** law recognizes, but to allow within it a
wide divergence of doctrine and of **service, and** even **of**
"local" church government, in so far **as that** is compatible
with the central management of **the whole as** really one
united organization.

(4) Again, both of these concessions may be made together.
While the **principle of** an establishment is still maintained
by the State, **a** wide latitude may **be** allowed within it,
and also full liberty to stay without.

(5) It is quite possible, however, for a State to support
and specially **recognize more** than **one** church. In Great
Britain, the episcopalian form of ecclesiastical government
is established throughout one part of the island, and the
presbyterian in the other. This is historically explained by
the fact **that** Great Britain arose from the union of two
States, each of which had its own national form of religion
before the amalgamation, **and** refused to **give** it up. An
example of a more curious nature is to be found in Switzerland, **where** the law establishes all religions alike.

Wherever there are two or more State churches, two courses
are open. (*a*) The one is to establish a number of churches
to one of which every citizen must belong, and to tolerate

no religious institution which is not so established. (b) The
other is to establish all churches that desire it, and to
allow voluntary associations as well.

All these systems have one principle in common—the
national recognition of religion—an acknowledged bond
between the State and a church or churches of some sort.
It is this principle which those who call themselves Liberationists attack, and they allude to the abolition of this bond
when they talk of the Church being " free." Freedom in
practical church politics means little more than disestablishment and disendowment. Many members of the voluntary
or dissenting communions are not satisfied, then, with liberty
to stay without the pale of the national church; they desire
to inflict compulsory freedom on all.

It must not be thought for one moment that all difficulties
are triumphed over by a simple declaration that the Church
is free, and by a dissolution of all official ties that nominally
connect it with the State. Although all religious associations were placed to-morrow upon a voluntary basis, the civil
government must still take up some position towards them,
and has indeed duties to perform in respect of them from
which it can never shake itself clear.

Three distinct positions are consistent with a purely
voluntary basis.

(1) There is no obvious absurdity in maintaining that the
Church needs no organization at all, but that every religious
individual, while placing his temporal interests under protection
of the State, should act as sole keeper of his own conscience.
The civil polity would thus be the only form of organization of
which he stood in need. Each man could, when he chose,
make his religious convictions the ruling motive in his
political actions, and so bring his influence to bear on the
policy of the nation, through the exercise of his ordinary
political rights and duties as a citizen, to wit, through
his franchise and rights of free discussion. Under this
theory, each man would be his own church, and would
minister to the necessities of his own soul as he thought fit.
Such a view would be only carrying to an extreme the right
of private judgment which led Luther and his fellow-reformers

to throw off the yoke of Rome when the needs of **their own** consciences required it. If all the individuals in a country **came to** think **like** this, there would still be religion, but no longer any visible church. In its regulation of spiritual affairs (if it decided on any intervention at all) the State would come face to face with the **individual.** No church or ecclesiastical organization would stand between. There **would** thus cease to be any relations between Church and State, because the former would cease **to** exist. The only problem to be solved would be that of **the right** attitude of the State towards the religious life **and actions of** each individual citizen.

(2) Those who think alike on the great mysteries of life and death and immortality will naturally draw together to help one another with sympathy, advice, and encouragement, and **so add** intensity to their common convictions and aspirations. To prevent such association is impossible, and the **laws** of all fully civilized States recognize it **as a** right. There seems no good reason why men should **not be** allowed **to band** themselves together for religious purposes as well as for those of pleasure, social intercourse, or commerce, as long as they break no law and injure no **one.** This, then, is the second of the relations possible between State and Church **upon** a voluntary basis—that religious associations, whether called churches or by any **other name, should** be treated by the law just like **any other** society **or** institution within the State; and that men should be allowed to organize themselves into just as many or as few churches as may suit them —each one owning **no** connection with the others except **such as is** determined by contract, mutually **and** freely entered into. Since association for religious purposes has a noble aim, churches would naturally be more dignified in their nature than, say, trades unions; but of this fact the State could take no official notice **without** in some sense "establishing" those of which **it took** such notice. The respective governments of **rival** churches would be not unlike the boards of directors of limited companies. They would neither have, nor **profess** to have, any special place as such in the constitution **of the** State, nor to have any special right to interfere with

2 c

the civil government. When an individual member came to differ from the doctrine, or to object to the discipline of one church, he would be free to join another.

The attitude of the civil government to these associations could never, of course, be a purely negative one, for that is impossible. The executive officials would prohibit them from performing illegal acts, and would, on the other hand, protect them from unlawful interference. The legislature would define, when necessary, not only the rights of each church with reference to outsiders, but also the rights of its members when the original contract was silent, or when lapse of time or other causes had rendered a readjustment necessary. Lastly, the ordinary law courts would have to decide how far such associations and their contracts were legal, to settle the meaning of their terms where ambiguous, and to arbitrate between the disputed rights of individual members, in the event of dissensions arising or a disruption taking place. Generally, the State would require to determine how far the sphere of each church extended, and the limits of the jurisdiction of its courts.

(3) Liberationists, however, while calling for " disestablishment," may not rest content that churches, or, at any rate, the particular one with which they are connected, should have no more share in the legal sovereignty than any other voluntary association. The Church may claim not only independence but a direct right of interference in the government of the State—a special share of influence in its corporate character, in addition to that exercised by its individual members, acting either of their own free will or under its direction as political agents. This is at bottom a claim to participate in the work of the civil government, but it is usually disguised under the form of a request for a voice in spiritual affairs, coupled with the assertion that " the Church " must have at least equal weight in defining the limits of this spiritual sphere. When a dispute arises between civil and ecclesiastical authorities as to their mutual boundary lines, some third principle or authority must be called in as umpire between them, if neither owns the sovereignty of the other. The search for such a principle is objectless to those who are convinced of the error

on which the distinction is based; but a short discussion of the solutions proposed may help to put that error in a clearer light.

It is necessary to remove an ambiguity lurking in the phrase "the Church." The member of any communion is apt to use the expression in a vague way to cover both the Church Universal and his own particular congregation. Thus a member of the Methodist Church or of the Free Church of Scotland pleads eloquently, on behalf of the true Church of God, for independence from all secular powers in the performance of the duties owed to its Divine Head. When he has established to his satisfaction these claims of the Church Universal, he identifies the latter with his own body. Now the immunities and rights thus demanded may be also claimed on behalf of the Mohammedans or the Positivists or the Buddhists. To favour Christianity more than Unitarianism is to decide between rival systems of theology. If the State were willing to afford special rights to "the Church," it would still be confronted with the difficulty of finding which of the many denominations could claim that title. If it must wait till all are joined together into one organization, like a federal republic of spiritual allies, it will wait long enough. If only a select few are to be admitted to a right to share in the Universal Church, who is to make the choice? To make any special compact with one or more churches to the exclusion of the others is simply to revert to the principle of an establishment in a more or less modified form.

When churchmen then propose that the dualism they have created ought to be bridged over by a series of conferences or concordats between the civil and the ecclesiastical authorities, the first difficulty presented to the statesman is to know where to find the latter. As long as the national church remains, the problem is easy; but in the absence of all religious establishments he has no right to decide between the rival claims of church dignitaries and synods. To decide between conflicting sects would make the temporal power a spiritual power as well, nor is the difficulty overcome by appointing spiritual advisers to decide for it, for in their appointment the same judgment is involved.

Until the "Universal Church" obtains the adherence of all the individuals in the nation to one system of ecclesiastical government (if not to one creed), the settlement of disputed boundaries and jurisdictions between Church and State by a solemn conclave between the representatives of the two is simply a dream.

A definite pronouncement in favour either of the principle of establishment or of that of voluntaryism would be here out of place, but it is idle to think that the State can shake itself free of all responsibility for, and interest in, the religion of its subjects by simply declaring itself in favour of the latter. A purely negative attitude is impossible, and that for many reasons; two of which may be briefly mentioned. (a) Morality and religion are so interwoven that the legis-lature cannot influence the one without also influencing the other, and it has already been shown that all laws have their foundations in morality. "All government," says Sir James F. Stephen, "has and must have a moral basis, and the connec-tion between morals and religion is so intimate that this implies a religious basis as well."[1]

(b) Education is another link between the civil government and religion, for it is impossible to draw a sharp line between intellectual and spiritual instruction. Modern Liberationists themselves begin to see this difficulty. The editor of a leading organ of Nonconformist opinion declares that in recent years "our idea of the State, its functions, and its responsibilities, has greatened," and frankly confesses that if we "admit, even in its most elevated form, the idea that the Church is an instrument of culture, be it intellectual or ethical or spiritual culture, the argument against establishment is gone."[2] It would seem, then, that the reasoning of the Liberationist must start from the assumption—humiliating as it is to clerical influence—that the Church is not in any sense "an instrument of culture." Dissenters of the old

---

[1] *Liberty, Equality, Fraternity*, p. 58. Even in India, he shows (a few pages further on) that legislation unintentionally coerces native religions by proceeding on the assumption that they are all false.

[2] Mr. Robertson Nicoll in a lecture on "The Church and the Press," read at the Free Church Congress, Nottingham, 10th March, 1896.

school held that the State had **no** right **to** meddle with **education,** and therefore none to control the Church. **Those of the new** school **draw** the same conclusion from the **premiss, that** the State *has* a right **to** meddle with **education. The** latter **assume the absence of** all direct relations between Church **and** education ; **the former,** their necessary connection. " To arrive at the conclusion," **says** Edward Miall,[1] " that it is the duty of **the** government **to** feed and clothe all the **people** of the realm, would be just about as logical as **to draw the same inference with** regard to education. Who **made it the** duty of the government **to** interfere with the direction **of** mind ? Whenever the rulers **of a people** get hold **of the** minds of the people, they **frame them** to patient submission, to oppression, and to sympathy **with** every **slavish** doctrine." Thus **the Dissenters** in 1847 opposed the regulation of education by the State **for** much the same reasons as led them **to oppose** the **regulation of** religion by the State. They **now acquiesce in the** establishment of education, while holding " with increasing clearness the necessity **for** the termination of all ecclesiastical establishments." To reconcile the two axioms, the Church has, **it** would seem, to renounce all claims to **act** as a medium of instruction.

[1] Quoted by Mr. Robertson Nicoll.

CHAPTER XXVIII.

CUSTOM, CONTRACT, AND LEGISLATION.

THE world's progress is many-sided, and its secret cannot be squeezed into an epigram. Sir Henry Maine assuredly did not intend to circumscribe the mystery of the universe within his well-known formula of the movement of progressive societies "from Status to Contract."[1] All such statements, however brilliantly expressed, are only half truths, and become dangerous if taken for the whole truth. Sir Henry Maine never meant that absolute freedom of contract was the only goal of progress, and the embodiment of every noble and desirable achievement of civilization. The extreme adherents of the doctrine of *laissez faire* are unfortunately less moderate, and are apt to insinuate into the formula a meaning that its author would have been the first to repudiate. Without undervaluing the boon of freedom of contract to a progressive community, there seems little doubt that it requires a supplement; for unlimited competition is anarchy. It is true that where custom and status imprison individuals within the walls of tradition, substantial advance

[1] Sir H. S. Maine, *Ancient Law* (tenth edition), p. 170. "All the forms of Status taken notice of in the Law of Persons were derived from, and to some extent are still coloured by the powers and privileges anciently residing in the family. If then we employ Status, agreeably with the usage of the best writers, to signify these personal conditions only, and avoid applying the term to such conditions as are the immediate or remote results of agreement, we may say that the movement of the progressive societies has hitherto been a movement from *Status to Contract*."

is impossible : freedom of contract is needed to open a door of escape. Progress cannot proceed far, however, before a new principle is needed to limit the licence of contract, and this is found in legislation enforced by the State. The will of the community must supplement the wills of contracting individuals. Thus to enunciate the law of progress as a movement " from status to contract " is to stop half-way. The formula should indicate *three* stages—custom, contract, legislation. Societies, then, which are destined to make any material progress in civilization, move from custom or status to contract, and from contract to legislation. **Several** explanations are needed to prevent misconception. Legislation, in supplementing contract, **does not by** any means supersede it, any more than the toleration of free contract deprives the individual of status. On the contrary, a fuller and more flexible legal status is founded upon contract. Where castes have **been broken up, and** the hard and fast divisions between classes inherent in feudalism have given **way** before the development of trade, and the liberal **ideas that** come in its train, then each man is free to regulate **his status** through the bargains he is able to make **with others. The day** labourer can, by his savings and judicious or lucky **investments, become** an employer, amass a fortune, purchase **land, and become** a county magnate **if** not a peer of the realm. Status acquired by contract is substituted for status conferred by birth. In a **somewhat** similar way, legislation in correcting **the** self-seeking tendency of a regime of *laissez faire* must **leave room** for **the free** play of contract. Parliament may limit agreements and define what provisions are legal without instituting a system of regimentation or socialistic State-management. Immoral agreements may be **suppressed** and fraudulent ones set aside without abolishing **freedom** of contract or forcing upon progressive societies a retrograde movement towards status, as defined by Sir Henry Maine.

The third stage of progress represented by the word " legislation," has features of its own, it is **true,** but it embodies those of each of the earlier stages in addition. The modern legislative spirit, with its unceasing activity, and its minute

and inquisitorial penetration into every aspect of the national
life, is essentially of recent growth. Parliament in the Middle
Ages has been described as a drag on the royal will in the
making of laws. The earliest statutes were tentative, temporary,
and timid.   Only during the last century have our statute
books swelled out to enormous dimensions with laws bearing
on every circumstance, relation, and pursuit of the people.
Legislation, as it is understood in nations like England of
to-day, is clearly a modern institution.   Yet the germs of
the principle it embodies were contained in the rudest beginnings of the State.   Even when the reign of *laissez faire*
was most undisputed, traces of legislative control were not
wanting, while during the period of status, neither contract
nor conscious law-making was altogether absent.   The earliest
laws were declaratory of status or custom.   When they
ventured openly beyond such mere registration of existing
practice, they tended to assume a contractual form.   Magna
Carta itself is a bilateral agreement between King John and
his Barons.   Real legislation, in its modern acceptation,
develops only at a comparatively late stage in a nation's
history.   It is not a mere arbitrary arrangement between two
or more beings endowed with reason and able to consent,
but a deliberate enunciation of a principle binding on all,
by the legal organ of the sovereignty expressing the rational
will of the whole community.   Only in legislation does the
rational nature of men, as associated in the State, reach its
highest development and most conscious expression.

If this view is correct, the doctrine often advanced by
Individualists, that the supreme and only duty of government is to enforce contracts and so leave its subjects free
to regulate their lives for themselves, is utterly inadequate.
Contract is only a stage and not the goal of progress, one
factor and not the sum of civilization.

The general argument against unlimited *laissez faire*[1] has

---

[1] *Laissez faire* has been defined by Prof. Sidgwick (*Elements of Politics*,
p. 137) as "letting people manage their own affairs in their own way, so
long as they do not cause mischief to others without the consent of those
others." Mr. Baden Powell (*State Aid and State Interference*, p. 29)
would reduce the functions of government even beneath what this meagre

been already sufficiently insisted on. The principle of contract carried to excess defeats its own end, which is presumably the freedom of individuals and their right to adjust themselves in their own way to the conditions of life that suit them best. Unrestrained competition, beginning in freedom, ends in monopoly, involving the worst slavery of all—the bondage of men to things, the subjection of persons to property. Thus a purely industrial society, founded on free contract, leads to materialism through excessive accumulations of wealth in the hands of individuals and the combinations of capitalists into "rings" and "trusts." Men are degraded to the mere instruments of production—are made means to the acquisition of wealth instead of ends in themselves.[1] Where two or three great firms combine their energies and capital, they can usually drive weaker competitors to the wall; and the reign of unrestrained competition brings about its own overthrow by the growth of monopolies that render all competition impossible. A new stage of status is reached which contract is powerless to break. Legislation, however, can succeed where the agreements of private individuals fail. The world fortunately is not doomed to stay where contract would leave it.

The terrible pictures drawn by Socialists of the state of England under a regime of freedom of contract cannot be controverted by impartially minded men, though some remedies proposed may be considered worse than the disease. Mr. Sidney Webb[2] has graphically described the "white slavery" that prevailed prior to the passing of the Factory Acts. "Women working half-naked in the coal mines; young children dragging trucks all day in the foul atmosphere of the underground galleries; infants bound to the loom for fifteen hours in the heated air of the cotton mill, and kept awake only by the overlooker's lash: hours of labour for all, young and old, limited only by the utmost capabilities of

formula would allow : "State aid should be utilized for the sole purpose of disestablishing State interference."

[1] Cf. Mackenzie, *Social Philosophy*, pp. 90 to 114; William Cunningham, *Politics and Economics*, p. 121 ; Professor H. Sidgwick, *Elements of Politics*, p. 142.   [2] *Fabian Essays*, p. 41.

physical endurance; complete absence of the sanitary provisions necessary to a rapidly growing population : these and
other nameless iniquities will be found recorded as the results
of freedom of contract and complete *laissez faire* in the
impartial pages of successive blue-book reports."

It is more pleasant to turn from the recital of such
horrors to the possibility of finding a remedy. Is the only
cure that to which Mr. Webb would point us, namely,
Socialism, as his friends of the Fabian Society define it,
or the State-ownership of all these mines and mills?
Surely not; for a more simple remedy has already been
found where (under our law of the three stages of progress)
we are prepared to seek it—in legislation. The Factory
Acts and kindred statutes have removed at least those evils
above enumerated, and are daily removing more; though a
terrestrial paradise has by no means been yet realized. Parliament has interfered ; but not by confiscating the property of
its subjects, and undertaking by its officers to perform their
functions and accept their responsibilities. On the contrary,
it has refused to meddle directly by its officials except where
absolutely necessary; and has simply by legislative enactment
brought home to the owners of factories and mines the responsibilities they had so long neglected with impunity. The
sacred principle of freedom of contract had been abused, and
was therefore subjected to control. The solution was found
in one word—legislation. Parliament enforced obligations and
imposed penalties without abolishing property. The State in
adopting this line of policy was assuming to itself no untried
or dangerous powers. It was only extending to contractual
relations its sovereign right of control to which all other
relations and all institutions had always been subject. Its
right to regulate contracts had indeed never been seriously
questioned, even when the doctrine of *laissez faire* was at
the height of its popularity. The principle of contract was
never considered absolute against the intervention of the
government. To begin with, it is the State that enforces
contracts. It does this by allowing any party to an agreement
to bring an action against the other party either for specific
performance or for damages as the case may be. The law

courts are thus afforded an opportunity of reviewing the terms and circumstances of all agreements before they enforce them. Now, **certain** contracts have always been considered illegal; and by **refusing to** recognize these **as** binding, **the** State has at all times possessed the machinery for a specially thorough control over the principle **of free** contract whenever it might be required. Two classes **of** agreements have always been either void or voidable at common **law: (1)** those to which **a** full and free consent had not been given; and (2) those which were immoral **or opposed** to public policy. Legal consent implies a *persona* capable of consenting, that is to say, a man or woman of **full age** and not incapacitated by reason of imbecility or lunacy; and it implies also **the absence** of fraud, force, and fear of violence, and that there is no **error** in essentials. Among contracts, on the other hand, that are ineffectual because *contra bonos mores*, may be instanced those **acting** as incentives to crime, conferring bribes, **or** out-raging the public sense of decency.

By developing either of these principles far enough, we might make considerable progress towards **a** thorough-going system of State control, if not actually towards Socialism. Thus, for example, a contract **made between an** employer **and a** starving man, binding **the latter,** in consideration of immediate relief, **to serve** the former **for** a term of years in return for the bare necessities of life, might be set aside either on the ground that a starving man is not free to consent, or that it is immoral for **an** employer to take advantage of such a misfortune. Recent legislation has—unconsciously to a great extent, it is true—adopted **both** principles. In pro-hibiting tenants from "contracting out" of the provisions made in their favour by the Ground Game Act, for example, Parliament must justify itself **either on** the plea that the tenant is not free to withhold his consent, or on the principle that such contracting out is immoral or opposed to public policy.

The Factory Acts can be vindicated more easily on the **ground that** they only enforce the equitable rights of the employees against their master. **Thus** the entire mass of recent statutes that have totally upset the reign of *laissez faire* can be justified as the extension of existing principles, well understood and widely enforced already. The era of legislation, then, is not sharply defined and marked off from that of contract. The two merge into each other almost imperceptibly, as do those of contract and status. In each of the three stages, obligations are enforced on the individual. In the first one, these arise out of the status into which each man is born. Penalties are inflicted on him for breaking through the established order. In the second or *laissez faire* era, each individual is supposed to create his own obligations. "In adopting freedom of contract," says Lord Farrer, "as the general principle governing mercantile dealings, what has been done is not to abolish obligation, but to substitute for an obligation devised by custom or law, an obligation self-imposed by the individual, and this obligation the State, not without many additions and limitations, undertakes to enforce."[1] It must not be forgotten, however, that in this second stage many obligations still exist based upon status; while it is even more important to note that in the third stage—that of legislation—obligations and penalties are directly imposed by the State itself as supplementary to, not in place of, those arising from custom and contract. To some extent this third principle of obligation imposed by Parliament seems to restore the regime of status, but there is really a wide difference; for a place is now preserved for the operation of all legitimate voluntary arrangements. Free contract breaks up the old synthesis of society, and legislation (civil and penal) must build a new one. The day when free contract was accepted as the whole duty of government has already passed away. All political parties combine to disclaim it. Mr. Thorold Rogers, for example, in the debate on the Irish Land Bill of 1881,[2] summarily dismissed this whole gospel of industrialism according to Bright and Cobden in a few contemptuous words, remarking that "much had been said about that three-legged horse, freedom of contract; but if they allowed persons to do just as they pleased in their relations with their fellow-subjects, the result would be universal

[1] *The State in Relation to Trade*, p. 14.

[2] 3 Hansard, cclx., 1135 (cited by Wm. Cunningham, *Politics and Economics*, p. 255).

swindling in the whole of society." Similar views are emphatically expressed on every side. We have already passed into the new era where conscious legislation of the whole State displaces the rule of private contract as well as that of unconscious custom. It is sometimes maintained that this is really the advent of Socialism. All legislation is sometimes said to be socialistic in principle. It is in this sense that we must explain the phrase of Sir William Harcourt so often quoted, "We are all Socialists now." All such phrases when seriously used, however, conceal a dangerous fallacy.[1] Legislation and Socialism are alike in one thing. Neither is consistent with the untrammelled license of a policy of *laissez faire*. The former, however, is able to remedy the evils of free competition without resorting to the methods of the latter. It is possible to subdue the anarchy produced by competition and free contracts by a system of indirect government control and the enforcement of individual responsibility, without absorbing all private property in the State. Socialism, properly understood, involves State-ownership; and when the same name is applied to the rigid enforcement of the duties of private ownership upon individual proprietors, a gratuitous element of confusion is deliberately introduced into the discussion. To punish a man for leaving a pit-head unenclosed, or for keeping unmuzzled a dog that is known to bite, is essentially a different policy from a scheme under which all mines and all dogs would be owned by the State.

Progress, then, cannot stop at untrammelled free contract. The new line of advance, however, is not that proposed by Socialists with their nationalisation of land and the instruments of production. Legislative definition of obligations and crimes, and the enforcement of damages and penalties for their infringement, afford all the supplement that is wanted. It would be absurd to claim that the whole law of progress is imprisoned in the phrase, "custom, contract, legislation," but it indicates, at all events, one necessary extension of the inadequate formula that progress is a movement exclusively "from status to contract."

[1] This fallacy underlies much of the reasoning of the first four *Fabian Essays*, viz. :—those on the *Basis of Socialism*.

CHAPTER XXIX.

THREE METHODS OF STATE INTERVENTION.

A COMPLETE scheme of *laissez faire* is unattainable. The closer we approximate to its only consistent ideal of unbridled competition and the survival of the fittest, the nearer we approach to anarchy. "Administrative Nihilism" is a dangerous motto; and indeed Individualists, however vehemently they declare their theoretical adherence to that formula, always qualify it in practice by the introduction of numerous exceptions, or by the surreptitious expansion of their superstructure in a way quite inconsistent with the narrow basis they profess to build upon.[1] *Laissez faire* and freedom of contract must be supplemented by legislation and State control, and the only questions open are those as to the extent of interference allowable, and the least objectionable methods of its application.

The Fabian Society and kindred associations welcome government intervention, and claim as their own each triumph won over unlimited competition; while Mr. Spencer and his followers are too ready to acquiesce in these claims of Socialism to an already half-achieved success. It is possible, however, to escape the anarchy of Individualism without resorting in any degree whatever to the drastic methods of Collectivism;

---

[1] Professor Sidgwick, for example, starting from the stand-point of Utilitarian Individualism and the "individualistic minimum" of State control involved, proceeds to supplement his results by admitting exceptional legislation with both "paternal" and socialistic tendencies. *Elements of Politics*, chapters iv., ix., and x.

for as one of the leading Fabians—for the moment off his guard—declares "it must not be forgotten that although Socialism involves State control, State control does not imply Socialism—at least in any modern meaning of the term." [1] The only cure for the evils of free contract is State intervention, but not necessarily Socialism; and State intervention may be either good or bad, according to its form and methods.

It has three phases which must be carefully distinguished from one another. I. State-ownership, or Socialism strictly so-called. II. Government administration, or regimentation. III. Legislative control.

It is quite possible that these three phases may be concurrently in force in one country, each in that sphere for which it is specially fitted. Further, each of them admits of several degrees and infinite variety in the methods of its application. Thus, for instance, while thorough-going Socialism would municipalize or nationalize all forms of property, Mr. Henry George would be content that the State should annex all land. This would be, strictly speaking, Socialism, though only a limited Socialism, since all movable or personal property would be still left to private ownership. While there is no *a priori* objection to any one of these three forms of State control in its proper place and subject to prudent conditions, the main object of this chapter is to show that (*a*) an excess of State control in any form is objectionable and dangerous; and (*b*) where two methods of its application are equally effective, the third is to be preferred, *caeteris paribus*, to the second, and the second to the first.

To prove these hypotheses, it is necessary to examine briefly each of these three methods of State intervention with its underlying ideas.

I. At first sight the surest remedy for the evils of the irresponsible private use of property, is to abolish it altogether; to allow the State to absorb all objects capable of appropriation; and to manage them directly by its officials or by government employees working under their commands. National or municipal ownership is the one point on which all Socialists are agreed.

[1] Hubert Bland, *Fabian Essays*, p. 212.

"What the achievement of Socialism involves economically," says Mr. J. Bernard Shaw,[1] "is the transfer of rent from the class which now appropriates it to the whole people. . . . The socialization of rent would mean the socialization of the sources of production by the expropriation of the present private proprietors, and the transference of the property to the entire nation." "Whatever State control may have meant fifty years ago," says Mr. Hubert Bland,[2] "it never meant hostility to private property as such. Now for us, and for as far ahead as we can see, it means that and little else."

Neglecting the more general bearings of Socialism—already sufficiently discussed—and neglecting also the justice and practicability of appropriating private property *without compensation*, it is proposed here to confine the inquiry to the merits and demerits of State-ownership as one of three competing methods of State control. It must not be forgotten that its advocates are not agreed as to what they want. (1) Consistent Socialists demand that all property (real and personal) should be owned by the county or the nation. (2) The land alone is claimed by some for the joint use of the people. (3) "All instruments of production must belong to the State" is the formula of a third sect. (4) Lastly, many politicians of all shades of opinion are declared Socialists to the moderate extent of desiring the State to own all telegraphs, and even all railways, and to work them for the benefit of the community.

It seems hardly necessary to emphasize the obvious fact (too often, however, ignored by Socialists) of the difference in principle and practice between advocating a State-monopoly of all property on the one hand, and allowing the State to become one proprietor having equal rights with individual proprietors, on the other. It is quite consistent to hold that each large town should own its own tramways, and yet to oppose the abolition of all private property.

The objections to the institution of private property are chiefly two: (a) Without its abolition "equality" is declared to be impossible. (b) It is said that it militates against the good of the community. The first argument is worthless,

[1] *Fabian Essays*, p. 179.   [2] *Ibid.*, p. 208.

since equality is in any case unattainable, and because it is doubtful how far it would be a blessing if attained. On the other hand, if the Socialist can only make good his second argument he has won his case. He must remember, however, that "the good" of humanity involves the things of the spirit as well as the things of the body, universals as well as particulars, justice as well as happiness. An unrighteous State cannot thrive, nor can its members. For those to whom more sordid reasons appeal, it may be urged that wealth is not happiness; and, further, that the socialization of the in- struments of industry might reduce the total production, thus impoverishing the wealthy without enriching the poor.

The doctrine here advocated as the true one is the regu- lation, not the annihilation of property—the enforcement of duties, not the invasion of rights. Although all rights of property must bow to the demands of justice and humanity as defined and enforced by the State, still it is here main- tained that the time-honoured institution of private property, when properly controlled and secured from abuse, is, on the whole, conducive and even essential to the well-being and development of every healthy community.

The arguments for and against State-ownership would fill a fair-sized volume, and cannot be given here. The place played by private property in a general system of philosophy may be profitably studied in the works of German idealists —especially in those of Kant and Hegel.[1] Its moral basis cannot be exhaustively considered apart from a complete system of ethics and theology. It may be allowable, how- ever, to quote a few sentences from the late Professor Green, in whose opinion property was necessary for the well-being of a community. "A necessary condition at once of the growth of a free morality, *i.e.* a certain behaviour of men determined by an understanding of moral relations, and by the value which they set on them as understood, and of the conception of those relations as relations between all men, is that free play should be given to every man's powers of

---

[1] English readers may consult Dr. Hutchison Stirling's *Lectures on the Philosophy of Law*, Prof. Morris' *Hegel's Philosophy of the State*, and Prof. Hastie's translation of Kant's *Philosophy of Law*.

appropriation."[1]   The only sense in which property is of value is, according to him, "as a permanent apparatus for carrying out a plan of life, for expressing ideas of what is beautiful, or giving effect to benevolent wishes."[2]   "The *rationale* of property in short," he goes on, "requires that every one who will conform to the positive condition of possessing it, viz. labour, and the negative condition, viz. respect for it as possessed by others, should, as far as social arrangements can make him so, be a possessor of property himself, and of such property as will at least enable him to develop a sense of responsibility, as distinct from mere property in the immediate necessaries of life."[3]   Now, Socialism, it is hardly necessary to point out, would only leave to subjects these "immediate necessaries of life."

The practical arguments against joint ownership, on grounds of common-sense and expediency, such as are likely to appeal to the average member of a British constituency, were perhaps never more forcibly or clearly expressed than two thousand years ago by Aristotle,[4] in his *critique* of Plato's *Republic*. The first five heads of his argument may be cited from Professor Jowett's summary[5]—(1) "When men have distinct interests, they will not be so likely to quarrel; and (2) they will make more progress, because every one will be attending to his own business; (3) there is a natural pride of ownership, and also (4) a pleasure in doing a kindness to others; these will be destroyed by communism; (5) the virtues of continence and liberality will no longer exist." Eleven other objections are added, but may be here omitted as they apply more closely to the scheme of Plato than to modern schemes, as, for instance, those of the Fabian Society. An universal (or even a general) system of State-ownership would involve difficulties, social, moral, industrial, and political, which are quite absent from the mild exceptional Socialism implied in the Post

---

[1] T. H. Green, *Works*, Vol. II., p. 524.   [2] *Ibid.*, p. 525.

[3] *Ibid.*, p. 526. Contrast Mr. Sydney Oliver (*Fabian Essays*, p. 114): "Socialists contend that the system of private property is actively destructive of the conditions in which alone the common morality necessary for happy social life is possible."

[4] *Politics*, II. 5.   [5] *Introduction*, p. xxxi.

Office and Telegraph department of government. Briefly stated, the chief objection to a general scheme of State-ownership **is** this : that it would force the government to act as a terrestrial providence, requiring omniscience and omnipotence to fulfil its gigantic task ; but omniscience cannot in fairness be expected, while its omnipotence would mean the slavish obedience of the governed. The barest outline of the argument is all that can be given.

If the State owns all instruments of industry and trade, it follows that the government must regulate all processes of production, and also distribute what is produced. No producer can find employment **save what** the government appoints. No consumer can possess any product of industry save what the government gives him. Executive officials, as the only employers of labour, must allocate tasks and see them accomplished to their satisfaction. Such despotic power **would** constitute a political danger of the gravest nature. The government would dictate to each citizen the nature and amount of the work he was bound **to do.** "In fact, work or starve will be the alternative set before each communal employee" says a prominent modern Socialist.[1] "The individual shirker will be warned, and, if he prove incorrigibly idle, discharged from the communal employ."[2]

The difficulties of distribution are, however, equally great. All the necessaries of life, when produced from the national workshops, would be the joint property of the nation. The invidious task of dividing these among the toiling millions would devolve upon the officials appointed by government to perform that office. "Socialism is the common holding of the means of production and exchange, and *the holding of them for the equal benefit of all.*"[3] The impossible task thus presents itself of providing equal benefits for unequal beings.[4] As every one would starve save for the portion doled out to him by the government, the State becomes primarily respon-

---

[1] Mrs. Annie Besant, *Fabian Essays*, p. 160.

[2] *Ibid.*, p. 166.

[3] Hubert Bland, *Fabian Essays*, p. 212.

[4] The difficulties of a fair distribution are well shown by Professor Flint, *Socialism*, p. 124.

sible for the up-keep of all its members, children as well as adults. Here a cruel dilemma meets it. It must either accept responsibility for what it cannot control; providing without limit for all children, legitimate or illegitimate, and thus abolishing the only effective check on the reckless increase of population, or else it must devise some scheme for effectually controlling the unlimited extension of its membership. This is the point where the abolition of private property comes into collision with the family and with morality.

Socialism cannot stop even when it has made the government the sole owner of all property, the sole manager of all production, and the sole employer of all labour. The government must go on boldly to undertake all responsibilities, to regulate all the affairs of the nation, to provide for every contingency, and generally to absorb the lives, interests, and endeavours of its citizens, and so to realize, as far as possible, its own ideal of a monotonous and stagnant perfection.

While totally rejecting all such schemes, we may without inconsistency cordially approve State-ownership of the property required for the efficient performance of such services as private enterprise has failed to render to the community. The nationalization of all the telephone instruments and wires in Great Britain does not bring us one step nearer a State Socialism properly so-called, any more than has the experiment already tried by several municipal authorities of owning and managing the local tramways.

II. Milder measures, however, are happily sufficient to effect any required degree of interference with individual actions, rights, and liberties. Government administration or regimentation may be resorted to without any State-ownership. Nationalization of property involves, of course, the most rigid and systematic form of regimentation, but the converse does not hold. The State may leave to every one full proprietary rights over the fruits of his own labour or other possessions, and yet control the use he makes of them by means of overseers or inspectors appointed to enforce its commands. Such regulation by executive officials may vary from a very mild form that can with difficulty be differentiated from purely legislative control, to a system of minute and constant supervision by government spies and inspectors.

Under this general head of government administration are here included all regulation by the State of individuals or of corporations, effected by means of licences and registers, with the restrictions these involve; all inspections of mines, factories, and schools; all orders issued by the Board of Trade for the regulation of railways, ships, and harbours; all measures taken by the Local Government Board to prevent the spread of infectious diseases and to improve the sanitary conditions of any district; and in addition all miscellaneous duties of administrative control, such as the hall-marking of gold plate, the testing of gun-barrels and chain cables, and the branding of herring, performed by Government officials for the safety or convenience of the public.

Some of the dangers of such interference, when in excess of what is absolutely necessary, have already been suggested. Lord Farrer [1] has reduced the chief among them under these seven heads: (1) "Any restriction is almost sure to bring some bad consequences on the persons restricted." (2) The indirect consequences may be bad though the direct are good. (3) It may be preventing good. (4) It negatives individual responsibility. (5) "The gain of a regulation enforced by law is often more apparent than real." (6) It makes persons less careful. (7) There are plenty of other objections, "such as the risk of corruption amongst a host of inspectors and administrators, the check of invention, ingenuity, and improvement, and so on." [2]

On these grounds Lord Farrer concludes, not in favour of unqualified *laissez faire*, but of the motto, " When in doubt, let the individual alone."

It only remains to be said that all these objections, in so far as valid against administrative interference, apply with added force to State-ownership, which, while necessarily involving administrative interference, with all the dangers that

---

[1] *The State in Relation to Trade*, p. 139.

[2] Compare Prof. H. Sidgwick's objections to "paternal" interference, (*Elements of Politics*, p. 37).

come in its train, has a host of even graver dangers peculiar to itself.

III. There still remains a third form of intervention—by simple legislative enactment unsupported by special administrative machinery—to which none of these objections can be validly applied. Unfortunately, however, it is not—in the present condition of society, at least—sufficiently effective in every case. It is not always possible to dispense with the official visit of the inspector, however much he comes to be regarded by an enlightened opinion as a necessary evil. The British public wisely view him with suspicion ; and it must always be remembered that the diminution of his powers and functions need neither weaken State control nor give rein to anarchy.

The difference between the second and third methods of State intervention may be best explained by two examples —the liberty of the press and the Merchant Shipping Act. There are two ways of preventing the dissemination in a printed form of sedition and libel. A rigorous censorship of the press may be instituted, or, alternatively, Parliament may leave every man free to take the risk of publishing what he pleases, subject to the penalties imposed for offences defined by statute. The first method represents regimentation, and the second legislative control. The respective merits of the two have been well expressed by John Locke. " I know not why a man should not have liberty to print whatever he would speak ; and to be answerable for the one, just as he is for the other, if he transgresses the law in either. But gagging a man, for fear he should talk heresy or sedition, has no other ground than such as will make gyves necessary for fear a man should use violence if his hands were free, and must at last end in the imprisonment of all who, you will suspect, may be guilty of treason or misdemeanour."[1]

A somewhat similar question was raised when Mr. Plimsoll first began his crusade against sending coffin-ships to sea. Shipowners were evidently grossly abusing the measure of liberty the existing law allowed them. Two

[1] Lord King's *Life of Locke* (Bohn's edition), p. 202.

rival lines of remedy offered themselves, corresponding more or less closely to the second and third methods of State control as here discussed. Socialists, indeed, would have cured **the** evil by making the State turn shipowner, and assume the entire control of all British ships, and therefore of more than half the carrying trade **of the** world. Such ownership, however, was not desired by **any** practical politician, and the choice lay between administrative supervision and stringent legislative definition of individual responsibility for loss at sea. The former course was chosen. Parliament laid down certain absolute rules with which all sea-going ships had to comply. Such compliance, however, at once put an end to all further responsibility of the **private** owners. In especial, each boat had to be **marked** with **a** "load line"—a visible mark showing the maximum freight it might legally carry. So long as this limit was observed, the owner was free from all responsibility, though his boat **were** actually overloaded. Many competent authorities seem **now** agreed that Parliament adopted the wrong alternative: that it should have avoided all unnecessary State manage-**ment**, and enforced, instead, personal responsibility more stringently by greater penalties where required. Mr. Plimsoll, it has been said, "recommended a **course** which, as he distinctly stated, would protect lives but diminish the responsibility of shipowners; he **thus urged Parliament to** neglect its proper function and **to expend the** energies of public officers on **work** which lies outside the sphere of State action. . . . His system was not carried out in its entirety, but it was so far carried out that the agitation which he **led** ceased; **and under the scheme he** accepted, overloading and faults in construction **have** enormously increased. It has been a terrible price for the **nation to** pay in order to exhibit the mischief which may be done by benevolent enthusiasm coupled with misconceptions as to the duties and powers of the State."[1]

These examples explain with sufficient accuracy **the** general distinction between the two methods of intervention here contrasted. So long as the provisions **of** a law can be

[1] Wm. Cunningham, *Politics and Economics*, p. 251.

enforced without hampering individual subjects in initiating or carrying out any schemes of profit or interest to themselves, and without subjecting them to supervision, or increasing the powers and functions of any administrative department, it is clear that none of the objections enumerated by Lord Farrer apply. If a law is objectionable, it is so because it is immoral, or ineffectual, or unwisely framed, and not because it can ever meddle where it has no business. While statutes are never to be condemned because they seek to enforce old responsibilities or to impose new ones of an equitable nature; there are, on the other hand, many burdensome and inexpedient methods of applying them, especially such as involve the conferring of arbitrary powers upon executive officers.

There are many spheres of life into whose privacy agents of the government must never be allowed to pry. If the impersonal law is outraged, it is true, the executive arm must in the last resort have authority to interfere; but such remedies are to be kept for extreme emergencies and fenced round with many careful restrictions, and never considered part of the ordinary routine of official duty. They are like medicines, welcome in cases of disease, but not meant for the healthy body's daily food.

A system of government management may be subversive of all self-reliance, while judicious legislative control acts as a stimulus. The ultimate right to interfere may, with the advance of civilization, be kept more and more consistently in the background, while the law is yet ready at a moment's notice to step forward to supplement the efforts of the weak or to force the unwilling to perform duties which they have refused voluntarily to fulfil. It seems probable that future progress may be at once towards a more minute State control and a diminution of administrative management.

The policy of a wise State ought to be to enact just laws defining mutual rights, and then to leave its citizens as free as possible to help themselves and one another within the limits thus defined, but to be ready to step in with coercive power to redress the wrongs which arise whenever this liberty is abused, or to prevent its abuse when imminent.

This way of viewing the relationship between the government and the governed may receive illustration from the relations which exist in Great Britain between the House of Commons and the members of the Cabinet; for we have established a system of Parliamentary control as opposed to Parliamentary management. When the Long Parliament, after its open breach with Charles, tried to take the reins of administration into its own hands, the folly of such a policy was soon disclosed. Now-a-days the House of Commons, while indirectly controlling every act of Her Majesty's Ministers, would never dream of directly meddling in any one executive matter. Laws are laid down for the guidance of councillors of the Crown, who are left free within defined limits to do in the Queen's name whatever they think best subject to ultimate responsibility to Parliament. Some such system of control, then, it is here suggested, is being gradually built up over every individual citizen, while, at the same time, direct management by government is restricted within narrower limits. Both tendencies, it is maintained, are signs of healthy progress.

On the one hand, the theoretical control enjoyed by every State has become more practically efficient. On the other hand, government is shaking itself free from such functions as can be performed equally well by private enterprise. The conduct of war—so long as brute force is recognized as a means of settling international disputes—is one of the clearest provinces of government action. The Admiralty is responsible for the efficiency of the navy, and the War Office for that of the army; while the naval dockyards are almost as much a part of the executive government as are the Treasury and the Home Office. In all these departments, however, a marked tendency has of late years been shown to curtail the sphere of direct government management. Cruisers and torpedo boats are built to contract by private firms, the work being subject to rejection if it fails to conform to the estimates.[1]

---

[1] A good instance of this tendency of government to delegate the actual performance of even its most normal functions is afforded by the part played by Messrs. Cook, the well-known tourist agents, in our recent wars in the Soudan. It is amusing to read in the newspapers

While the most public functions of government are thus delegated to private enterprise, there is no undertaking so private that the public interest in it is not safeguarded by numerous legislative enactments.

Another aspect of the distinction between the two forms of intervention by administrative management and legislative control respectively is afforded by the methods of redress open to a wronged individual. The State may either throw open the doors of its law courts to all its subjects, and leave them to come and claim their rights when they choose, or it may appoint official inspectors or other guardians to see that the ignorant and the weak are not wronged by superior cunning or force. Lord Farrer has explained these two methods of enforcing the provisions of a law,[1] and has pointed out that " the two forms of interference are generally incompatible." [2] The latter has at least three objections from which the former is free. In the first place, it is less thorough-going. In the second place, it is liable to jobbery and corruption. In the third place, it vests arbitrary power in the hands of one man and puts arbitrary checks on the actions of another. It may cripple private responsibility and initiative energy, and so injure both the trade of the nation and the moral stamina of its citizens.

It must not be forgotten, however, that in many cases individuals, from natural timidity, extreme poverty, social tyranny, or other reasons, are quite unable to protect themselves. In such cases, where there are no voluntary philanthropic agencies to afford such protection, government is bound to take the matter into its own hands, and arm its officials with the requisite powers. This is the principle upon which inspectors of factories and workshops act. Further, to leave it to the law courts to give redress is sometimes to prefer

of 10th March, 1896, the accounts of the arrangements made for the advance of troops to the front—how " Messrs. Thomas Cook & Son have contracted for the transport of these three regiments, and of the Surrey Regiment from Girgeh, whence they go from Cairo by rail to Assouan." Here we have, in a notable form, the substitution of indirect government control for direct government management.

[1] *The State in Relation to Trade*, chapter iv.   [2] *Ibid.*, p. 7.

cure to prevention. The injured individual may not desire compensation for wrongs done to him. He prefers that it should be made impossible for him to be wronged. When a man is killed through the reckless negligence of his employer, a sum of money paid to his widow may be a very poor consolation. Thus circumstances may very readily arise reversing the general presumption.

The lessons drawn from the comparison of the three forms of State control may be briefly stated. The first of these forms —State-ownership—is artificial, unnatural, and fraught with a thousand dangers, except when applied to limited kinds of property and under specially favourable circumstances. The second—administrative management—must always be looked on with suspicion, though it cannot be altogether dispensed with. The third—legislative control—in so far as its provisions are wise, just, and expedient, and involve no unnecessary admixture of either of the other forms, is open to no valid objection of any sort.

Legislation alone, backed where absolutely necessary by administrative machinery or official intervention, will form an adequate supplement to the doctrine of *laissez faire*, and go far to effect all that is practicable and just in the schemes of Socialists. Room will thus be left for the free play of the now mature principle of individuality and for the undisturbed enjoyment of property as the medium required for its development. Any system which crushes out the spontaneity and individuality of its subjects, robs the community of the most precious product secured through many centuries of growth and struggle. Socialistic commonwealths, by repressing many of the noblest and most energetic elements in human life, would establish an unstable equilibrium, in which stern coercion would need constantly to strive to suppress rebellion. No such danger would be encountered by a system of government that allowed free play to the individual tastes and habits of its citizens, while at the same time it defined legal obligations according to an advancing standard of equity and mercy, and rigorously exacted their performance.

PART III.

THE APPLICATION OF THEORY TO PRACTICAL POLITICS.

CHAPTER XXX.

SOME PRACTICAL CONCLUSIONS.

POLITICAL Science, wide as is its scope, does **not** include **the** arts of statecraft and politics. It treats of universal principles and leaves **in** other hands the *minutiae* involved in their application to particular cases as they arise. It does not profess to furnish the candidate for parliamentary honours with a ready-made code of electioneering axioms **or a** legislative programme that will tempt the votes **of** the constituencies. It is, at the same time, impossible to **make** an absolute line of cleavage between the theory **of** the State and **its** corresponding art; and, indeed, **it would** be undesirable **to rob** philosophic discussions of much **of** their vital interest **by** abstracting from them all reference to questions of the day. In this light it seems desirable to bring together in a concluding chapter a few of the practical applications of principles already explained.

The organic doctrine of society, rightly understood in all **its** bearings, is in itself a complete *theoretical* solution of the problem of the sphere of government; and it contains also the *practical* key to the thousand and one **forms** into which **that** problem splits itself in the world of politics. All hard and fast rules inconsistent with the fluidity or elasticity of an organic whole—all mechanical contrivances likely to crush or trammel **the** growing organs or to interrupt the **free** union of part with part—must be at once discarded.

In formulating, then, a few practical rules embodying the conclusions arrived at as to the proper province of government in actual politics, three guiding principles must be borne in mind : (a) the nature of the State itself as an organic brotherhood of men essentially connected with all other portions of humanity ; (b) the end of all government and legislation in the " good" of this community, looking to posterity as well as to the existing citizens ; and (c) the means of realizing this end in the unlimited sovereignty of the State over all its subjects.

In the light of these three broad principles a number of practical conclusions may be laid down.

(1) The righteous State must do everything in its power to further its own end. This is merely axiomatic, for the ultimate end or final cause of the State means that one great object to which all others are subordinate. If the State refuses to further its own highest development after the law of its nature, it will fight against destiny. In the language of Job it will "curse God and die." In scientific phrase it will violate the laws of nature and must pay the penalty.

(2) The means to this end must next be sought. As all abstract principles have failed, there seems to be no criterion left but that of *expediency*. This word by no means implies, however, the acceptance of an utilitarian philosophy on a hedonistic basis. Expediency indeed always involves the adaptation of means to ends ; but these ends are not necessarily ignoble ones, nor need they exclude the idea of "right" as an element—indeed the chief element—of the whole. The end of the State and of humanity is neither an empty universal nor an unrelated series of particulars. It is not an abstract right like the categorical imperative of Kant manifesting itself apart altogether from the positive well-being of individuals ; nor is it the sum of the joys and selfish interests of the citizens to which Bentham and Mill would reduce it, by making it dependent on the principle of contingency and the infinite vicissitudes of chance. Right, then, is included in "the end of the State" as one moment of that whole of which happiness is the other. An act or policy is useful because it is right. It is not right because it is useful. To say otherwise is deliberately to play with words, and to set up as an end what is by definition merely a means.

The goal must be determined on a principle quite different from mere expediency. Subject to this explanation, expediency is the guide of the statesman and legislator, and all abstract **principles** must be discarded.

This involves the truth that the State, **in** striving for its **great** ends, must **use** whatever instruments come to hand, and in the way best suited for the **purpose** held in view. In adjusting available means to effect **its high ends,** it must never lose sight of its **own true nature—embracing** the most despised of individuals and the remotest posterity as essential parts, and embodying social, moral, and spiritual interests as well as material ones. **It must recognize, too,** its obligations to other States, and to humanity as a whole.

(3) From this follows **the** corollary that the various organs of government must be invested with just so much legal power as will **best** forward this end. There is no presumption either **for or** against government intervention. Where it is proved **bad it must** be abandoned; where good, it must be adopted.

(4) It would be a gross breach of duty to allow to any class, **interest, or** individual an immunity in opposing such measures **as are** for the good of the whole. All so-called natural inalienable rights must be denied. At **the** same time every right, however alienable and relative, must be fully weighed and appreciated before it is annihilated, and must never be touched at all unless a more urgent right **or interest of** the community as a whole calls categorically for it; and the best compensation of which the circumstances of the case allow must always be given for all rights infringed. The philosophical justification of this rule is that all rights are relative and not absolute; and that no true right of **the** individual *can* be opposed to **the** rights **of a** moral **State.**

(5) The necessity of coercion must be clearly faced. As force **cannot** be eliminated from human life, it should be **placed** where it will do least harm. The supreme right of **coercion must rest with the** body or organ which expresses the **rational will of the** nation. This is to be found in the legislature, if it is constructed on a right model. There should **be no** dubiety in the mind of any one as to where the supreme power lies. The constitution must make this

2 E

clear beyond a doubt; and this is exactly what British constitutional law does in making the Queen in Parliament supreme.   Further, there should be adequate machinery provided for enforcing this coercive power of the national sovereign in every corner of the land.   No loophole of escape should be allowed anywhere—no barrier to the arm of the law.   To tolerate the possibility of effective opposition is to nourish seeds of anarchy and disintegration.

(6) Government must remember that persuasion is usually better than force. Thus, when a recalcitrant individual opposes his will to that of the State, coercion should be kept as a last resource.   It is best to allow a presumption in favour of liberty, just as a prisoner is treated as innocent until he is proved guilty.   Where there is no pressing emergency, coercion should only be used when all other plans have failed, and even then not more of it than is clearly necessary and proportionate to the end in view.   This is the substance of Sir J. F. Stephen's three well-known rules : " Compulsion is bad—

1. When the object aimed at is bad.
2. When the object aimed at is good, but the compulsion
     employed is not calculated to obtain it.
3. When the object aimed at is good, and the compulsion
     is calculated to obtain it, but at too great an
     expense."[1]

These principles seem to carry us beyond two of Sir James's own theories, viz. that the distinction between force and persuasion is at bottom illusory when analyzed, and that, *caeteris paribus*, coercion is just as good a thing as liberty.   Any idea made abstract and pushed to its extreme is meaningless and void, and therefore becomes the same as any other idea similarly caricatured.   The abstract ideas of liberty and coercion may ultimately meet, but undoubtedly a regime of practical liberty is to be preferred to a regime of coercion : else why should there be even a *presumption* one way or the other ?

(7) No limits can safely be placed to the law-making power of the sovereign body, and no competing legislative authority can be tolerated.

[1] *Liberty, Equality, Fraternity*, p. 49.

(8) As **far as** possible the same laws should **everywhere** rule within one State.[1]

(9) Municipal corporations and counties may **be** allowed powers of making bye-laws and local regulations, **so** long as **these** do not encroach on the proper province of the legislature, **nor** contradict the provisions of **any actual law, nor** infringe the rights of voluntary associations or individuals in such a way as Parliament considers unjust or disproportioned to the objects to be gained.

(10) Many of the executive **acts necessary** for the mere existence of the nation, **as well as for** its development towards the highest perfection it can attain, can **only** be performed by the central authority. Government action **should not** be *assumed* to be necessarily bad, any more **than** necessarily good. If there is a presumption against it, it is one that **can** be rebutted by evidence and argument in any particular case.

(11) There are, however, many things necessary **for progress** which can be much better performed by municipal and county authorities, conversant with **the varying needs of their** own districts, than by the **officials of** a central bureaucracy, living far from the seat of the varying local requirements, **and** not unnaturally more interested in their **own** affairs. Where this is the case, the central authority should simply authorize the local bodies to act; giving them reasonable immunities from the consequences of their own errors when acting *bona fide*, and also full powers of coercing recalcitrant individuals. The **number of** restraints on negative freedom increases with civilization; **but** with every restraint positive freedom makes a **new advance.** Thus a due measure **of** coercion must be allowed **to** local authorities.

[1] All branches of the law that affect either commerce or family rights in especial should be uniform in essentials throughout all the dominions of one State—if not throughout the world. The dangers of an opposite **system are** well illustrated by **the** experience **of** the United States. Professor Munroe Smith is of opinion that "Diversity of commercial rules in the several States impedes and annoys business, for American business pays little heed to State lines. Conflicting laws of marriage and divorce unsettle family relations, and undermine **the moral** basis of society." See article on "State, Statute, and Common **Law,"** in the *Political Science Quarterly* **for** March, 1888. Cf. also *supra*, p. 291.

(12) While the central government should give every encouragement and facility to the municipal and county and parochial authorities to manage their own affairs, it must never for a moment forego its own ultimate rights of sovereignty, or allow any measure which would render these difficult of enforcement.

Thus (*a*) it must preserve the right of defining what matters are local and what are imperial. (*b*) While it allows to localities the necessary powers of coercion over individuals, it must watch that these are not abused, or used unreasonably to crush out liberty.

(13) Some matters can be better performed through the agency of voluntary associations. Where this is the case, Parliament should refuse to allow either administrative departments of the central government or local authorities to interfere. Thus the existing fire-insurance companies perform their work efficiently and well on the whole. If a county council proposed a system of compulsory insurance of all property within its territory, Parliament ought undoubtedly to refuse its aid to such a scheme, not because compulsory insurance is necessarily a bad thing, but because the other is better. If a system of compulsory fire-insurance did commend itself to the nation, the least hurtful way of enforcing it would be to insist that every building should be insured in a sound respectable company, carrying on business on the principle of voluntary association. This might still involve an unwarrantable interference with the "right of private judgment," but would be free from the objection of burdening either the central or local authorities with a new task in addition to their already too extensive business of a more legitimate nature.

(14) Some things, however, are better left to the operation of the principle of "self-help" than of either the mutual help of voluntary association or the municipal help or State help of government authorities. In such cases Parliament should stand aside and put as few obstacles in the way as possible; but where it is quite clear that a little timely help from government is not opposed to the true principles of self-help, there is no reason why it should not render it. Such good

offices should, however, be performed by the government with the **greatest** reserve and care. Individualists assume, without **any attempt at** proof, that all State aid is opposed **to self-help.** It **is** true that if the State did everything for a **man,** self-help and individual responsibility **would** die. Stupid philanthropists do incalculable harm by ill-devised schemes **of** relief; but all disinterested kindness is not therefore bad, **or** it would be wrong for a **doctor to** dress a poor man's wound for nothing. To throw a life-buoy to a drowning man is surely not contrary to **the doctrine of self-help.** When you have replaced a fallen man on his legs, you ought probably to leave him to walk alone, if he is **able;** but your help may have **been** absolutely necessary **before** he could begin to help himself. **In** the same way, government aid is not necessarily opposed to self-aid. The government should leave every man free to conduct his own commercial **enterprises;** but there seems no reason why it should not **instruct its consuls** at foreign ports to collect statistics of trade **and finance,** or why it should refrain from instituting a system of national registration of titles to land, or of births, deaths, **and** marriages.

(15) As little arbitrary or discretionary power as possible should be entrusted to any executive official or administrative department, whether central, or municipal, or parochial. There is, of course, something arbitrary in all executive power, because such power must be vested in living finite beings **liable to** misconceptions, prejudices, and evil passions. This is the amount of truth contained in the individualistic indictment **of** existing society. All government coercion is bad so far as it is dependent on the caprice **of** one man or of a body of men. All Acts of Parliament are **bad which** directly vest such powers in officials. Increase of arbitrary executive power should be at all times looked on **with** the gravest suspicion. Though it can never be entirely eliminated, certain rules, such as the following, may be laid down with the view of keeping it within moderate bounds:—

(a) Every executive organ should be clearly subject **to the** legislature, and to the ordinary law of the land. The very keystone **of** the British Constitution on **its** legal side is the entire absence of any institution similar to the administrative courts of the continent, and any body of special laws conferring immunities on officialdom, such as the *droit administratif* in France.

(b) As far as possible the powers and immunities of the administrative departments should be accurately defined by law. This is not always possible or expedient, however, as a certain latitude is necessary to enable the humblest official —even the policeman or exciseman—to fulfil his duties. In the higher branches of statecraft, such as diplomacy, it is quite essential that a free hand should be given to the executive. Subject to such exceptions, however, all powers should be defined.

(c) Wherever the ends of justice can be equally well served by leaving the wronged individual to apply for redress through the channel of the law-courts, this course is to be preferred to the appointment of officials whose authorization is required before any specific course can be entered on.

(d) All functions performed by the executive should be so conducted as to interfere as little as possible with the self-respect of the individual, or the privacy of his family life. The intrusion of a stranger is the most common and perhaps the worst violation of privacy. Thus, unless in cases of extreme urgency, no medical health officer or sanitary inspector should be permitted to force his way into any citizen's house. It is not always easy to define wherein a violation of privacy consists, but " conduct which can be described as indecent is always in one way or another a violation of privacy."[1] Good examples are to be found in such arbitrary rights of government inspectors as those to which Mr. Spencer so vehemently objects, as, for example, laws recently enacted " giving sanitary officers powers to search certain premises for unfit food,"[2] compared by him to the law of Edward III., under which " innkeepers at seaports were sworn to search their guests to prevent the exportation of money or plate."

(16) As the State is essentially a moral being, it cannot shake itself free of responsibility for the moral welfare of

[1] Sir J. F. Stephen, *Liberty, Equality, Fraternity*, p. 160.
[2] *The Man versus the State*, p. 8.

its subjects. If by its direct interference it can advance its citizens in virtue, it is bound to do so. Experience, however, teaches that such direct interference has often defeated its own end. It has sometimes led not to morality but to hypocrisy, followed sooner or later by a frightful reaction to excesses of sensuality and sin. Indirectly, however, the government should do everything in its power to stimulate the moral worth of its subjects. Its institutions should be so modelled as to reduce temptations to fraud and corruption. It must in its international and constitutional relations observe a scrupulous uprightness of conduct. It must endeavour to fill its highest offices with men whose public if not private character is above reproach. It must secure for its citizens material and intellectual surroundings compatible with a virtuous life, and take care that greater facilities are not permitted for an immoral than a moral career.

(17) Lastly, indirect legislative control, when equally effective, is always less hurtful than government management.

The foregoing are a few of the practical conclusions directly deducible from the principles before laid down. Such rules are, of course, merely specimens, somewhat arbitrarily chosen from among many.

An obvious criticism suggests itself at this point, that these rules are merely truisms, patent to common-sense. Yet almost every one of them is directly opposed to the teaching either of Socialists or of Individualists. If any excuse is required for setting them forth in order here, and for endeavouring to ground them on some philosophic principle, it may surely be found in the fact that though adhered to by most of those "practical politicians" who are objects of ridicule to some philosophers, they have been deliberately condemned by many theoretical politicians who have written on the limits of the province of government. The conclusions here arrived at may be, and it is hoped they are, supported by common-sense ; but they are certainly not admitted either by Mr. Spencer and his disciples on the one hand, or by the members of the Fabian Society on the other.

These conclusions, while they emphasize the facts that the present basis of society is on the whole a sound one, and that humanity is progressing steadily if slowly towards its own amelioration, are still far from implying a wholesale eulogy of the *status quo*, or a cheap optimism that "whatever is, is best." A few examples have been incidentally mentioned of practical conclusions inconsistent with current tendencies and opinions; but the main intention has been throughout to set forth the fundamental principles upon which all politics rest, and not to construct one competing system of reform among others. A complete political creed or programme, applicable to the present position of parties and suitable for electioneering purposes, is not only uncalled for, but would tend to throw suspicion on the impartiality of the more important preliminary investigation into fundamental principles. A few concluding suggestions may, however, be given, if only to show that the results arrived at by no means involve a blind or servile adulation of the existing order of society and government.

Four suggestions in especial may be made. I. Individual freedom should be increased wherever feasible by (*a*) curtailing all arbitrary or discretionary powers vested in officials of every kind; (*b*) affording facilities of appeal from all local authorities and voluntary associations to the central government; (*c*) removing all unnecessary restraints on freedom of action, such as censorships of the press and undue restrictions on the transfer of land; and (*d*) reducing the expense of and obviating delay in obtaining access to justice through the courts of law.

II. Where it is necessary for the State to interfere with the actions and liberties of its citizens, it is always best to effect this with the minimum of executive interference sufficient for the purpose. The legislature in defining rights, and the law courts in redressing wrongs, can never carry their intervention to an undue extent; but administrative interference is always to be viewed with suspicion as an infringement of individual liberty and a possible deterrent to private enterprise. All extensions of regimentation and State initiation into new spheres must be jealously watched until the benefits conferred are clearly shown to compensate for the inherent dangers and demerits of the system. In this light much recent legislation seems to have been based on mistaken principles, and to have run unnecessary risks by resorting to government management where legislative control would have proved equally effective.

III. The State must never relieve individuals of the primary responsibility for their actions and possessions. While it must accept more and more an ultimate or joint responsibility, legal and moral, for all that its citizens do, it should contrive that the full weight of each man's misdeeds or culpable carelessness fall upon his own back in the first instance. It should define and rigorously enforce the legal duties that form the counterpart of every right it secures. The law must not, however, attempt to reduce all moral duties to legal obligations, for fear it should strangle all generosity and spontaneous morality in a network of legislative casuistry. It should aim at enforcing a minimum rather than a maximum of duty; but this minimum should progress with the advance of society. The only criterion for fixing it, according to the varying requirements of different times and countries, is the somewhat leaden rule of public opinion. The State must not aim at creating an official standard by which to dictate the line of advance. Its duty is rather to bring up the stragglers to the lowest standard tolerated by public opinion. In particular, the law must define and enforce (a) the duties of property, and (b) the duties of paternity. The ship-owner must not be allowed to skulk behind the fiat of a government official, and thus screen himself from blame. The owner of dwelling houses must see that they are fit for human habitation, or take the consequences in the form of liability to consequential damages or a criminal prosecution. "To my mind," Mr. Goschen declared in his Edinburgh Address,[1] "the argument is almost irresistible that it is as just to prevent, and, if necessary, to punish house owners who let out rooms unfit for human occupation, as tradesmen who offer putrid food for sale." The remedy for existing abuses is not the socialistic one of abolishing private property altogether, but simply the enforcement of such duties as equitably accompany it. A similar

[1] On *Laissez faire* and Government Interference.

criticism applies to the scheme advocated openly by some
Socialists, and forced more or less upon all by the unconscious
logic of their position, of breaking up the unity of the family
as at present constituted, and making the State primarily
responsible for the rearing and education of children in
place of the individual father. The State indeed may accept
a joint or ultimate responsibility, but ought in the first
place to enforce the burden where it naturally falls. This
is necessary, not only for preserving intact the natural
affections that bind the members of one family together,
but, what is of even more importance, for maintaining the
only check that keeps the increase of population within
manageable bounds. The State ought to enforce an increased
measure of responsibility on the parents of all children,
illegitimate as well as legitimate. In this light all schemes
of free education, as opposed to compulsory education provided by the parents, are of a retrogressive tendency. They
are condemned on moral grounds, since they encourage the
unworthy father to shirk his natural duties, and thus undermine the basis of the national character. They are condemned
on economic grounds, because they stimulate the root of all
industrial distress—over-population.

The same rules may be applied to the duties associated with
every other factor of human life. The State must never allow
individuals to throw off their responsibilities on to the broad
shoulders of the government. " Whatever action the State
may ultimately take," said Mr. Goschen in the address already
quoted, " it is to be hoped that while the duties of the community are enlarged on and pressed, the duties of individuals
and the propriety of enforcing them may not be neglected."
While all schemes of Socialism and regimentation tend to
discourage individual energy and invention, and so to relax
the moral fibre of the governed, a more thorough State
control, applied through the stringent definition of personal
duties, must have a healthy and bracing effect. Public
responsibility may be allowed to supplement private responsibility, but must never be made its substitute. In this
way a new integration of society may be effected, while
individual energy is stimulated rather than relaxed, thus

realizing in due combination the two requisites of a truly organic State.

IV. While the prime necessity is at all times to realize this organic unity, giving due prominence alike to the solidarity of the whole and the independence of the part, the more pressing problem of the present day is the reconstruction of society—especially on its industrial or economic side. A century of rampant Individualism, beginning in the redress of abuses and the removal of artificial restraints on progress, has ended in the partial disorganization of society ; the war of class against class; the material waste and moral deterioration of continual strikes; and the unlimited selfishness of industrial competition. The harmony of the organism has been disturbed. It is in this aspect that even the extreme theories of Socialists, dangerous as they are in themselves, may be not unfraught with good by counteracting the extreme evils of *laissez faire*, while they are powerless to overthrow the essentially individualistic basis of modern society. The most pressing task of the present age is to build up a system of government control comprehensive enough to include and reconcile the conflicting economic agents whose mutual struggles periodically convulse the entire social fabric, and powerful enough to regulate the industrial monopolies which reduce free competition to an empty name, and threaten to usurp the place and authority of government.

INDEX.

GLASGOW: PRINTED AT THE UNIVERSITY PRESS BY ROBERT MACLEHOSE AND CO.